ATTACKS ON THE *PRESS* IN 2006

On the cover are eight of the 55 journalists killed in the line of duty in 2006. Clockwise from top left: Ogulsapar Muradova, Turkmenistan; Jorge Aguirre, Venezuela; Martin Adler, Somalia; Anna Politkovskaya, Russia; Paul Douglas, Iraq; Atwar Bahjat, Iraq; Hayatullah Khan, Pakistan; Mohammed Taha Mohammed Ahmed, Sudan. *See page 2 for photo credits.*

The publication of Attacks on the Press in 2006 *is underwritten by a grant from Bloomberg.*

25th ANNIVERSARY
CPJ
1981 | 2006

THE COMMITTEE TO PROTECT JOURNALISTS
330 Seventh Avenue, 11th Fl., New York, NY 10001
t: (212) 465-1004   f: (212) 465-9568   info@cpj.org
visit us online for more information: **www.cpj.org**

Founded in 1981, the Committee to Protect Journalists responds to attacks on the press worldwide. CPJ documents hundreds of cases every year and takes action on behalf of journalists and news organizations without regard to political ideology. To maintain its independence, CPJ accepts no government funding. CPJ is funded entirely by private contributions from individuals, foundations, and corporations.

The Associated Press and Reuters provided news and photo services for *Attacks on the Press in 2006*.

Editorial Director: Bill Sweeney
Senior Editor: Robert Mahoney
Designer: Justin Goldberg
Copy Editors: Barbara Ross, Robin Lauzon
Maps: The Associated Press/Francois Duckett
Proofreader: Joe Sullivan

Photo credits for cover and page 1:
Radio Free Europe/Radio Liberty (Muradova); *El Mundo* (Aguirre); The Associated Press (Adler); *Novaya Gazeta* (Politkovskaya); CBS (Douglas); Al-Arabiya (Bahjat); European Pressphoto Agency (Khan); The Associated Press (Taha).

Attacks on the Press in 2006:
A Worldwide Survey by the Committee to Protect Journalists

ISSN: 1078-3334
ISBN: 978-0-944823-26-2

ATTACKS ON THE PRESS IN 2006
· · · · · · · · · · · · · · · · · TABLE OF CONTENTS · · · · · · · · · · · · · · · ·

PREFACE

• • • • • • • • • • • • • • • • • *by Anderson Cooper* • • • • • • • • • • • • • • • • • •

Silence. **When a journalist is killed, more often than not, there is silence.**
In Russia, someone followed Anna Politkovskaya home and quietly shot her to
death in her apartment building. The killer muffled the sound of the gun with a silencer.
Her murder made headlines around the world in October, but from the Kremlin there
was nothing. No statement. No condolences. Silence.

When Vladimir Putin was finally asked by reporters about the murder of one of
his nation's most prominent investigative journalists, he said Politkovskaya's influence in
Russia was "insignificant." Anna Politkovskaya was anything but insignificant. Her reporting on human rights abuses in Chechnya had upset many powerful people. Threats
against her life were nothing new. She was an award-winning writer for *Novaya Gazeta*
and had been named by CPJ as one of the most prominent defenders of press freedom in
its 25-year history. She deserved more than silence.

According to CPJ, Politkovskaya was the 13th journalist killed in Russia in a gangland-style hit since Putin became president in 2000. Guess how many of the people responsible have been brought to justice? None.

Silence. As CPJ documents in this important book, all too often, attacks on journalists go unsolved. Authorities either refuse to investigate, or refuse to acknowledge the
possible link to the reporter's work. When a bomb exploded outside Yelena Tregubova's
Moscow apartment in 2004, police said it was an act of hooliganism—nothing to do with
her reporting.

In Turkmenistan, there is silence surrounding the death of Ogulsapar Muradova,
a radio reporter arrested in June 2006. Branded a traitor by Turkmenistan's president,
she was imprisoned for more than two months and wasn't allowed contact with anyone.
Then she was put on trial. It lasted all of a few minutes. She was sentenced to six years
in prison, and three weeks later she was dead. Authorities refused to say what happened
when they handed her body to her family on September 14. They would not allow an
autopsy or an investigation. Silence.

In the United States, we worry about access, objectivity, and the legal consequences of protecting confidential sources; for most of us, however, security fears are not a
daily concern. Reading this book, you will be reminded just how lucky we are. This past
year, I've reported from Iraq, Afghanistan, Lebanon, Israel, and the Democratic Republic of Congo, and in each of these war-ravaged lands I've met local journalists who
encounter conditions every day that many of us in the West simply cannot imagine.
They face threats not only against their own lives but against the lives of their spouses,
their children.

In Iraq and Afghanistan, many Western reporters now travel with Kevlar vests and private security guards, or they embed with U.S. and British militaries. Few local journalists, however, have such protections. Afghan reporters face threats from Taliban insurgents, al-Qaeda operatives, warlords, corrupt officials, drug traffickers, nervous soldiers, and security services. All too often, their sacrifices go unnoticed.

In Pakistan, especially in the tribal areas along the Afghan border, journalists are under constant threat. While Pakistani authorities

Cooper reports from the Democratic Republic of Congo in October.

made arrests in the 2002 killing of *Wall Street Journal* reporter Daniel Pearl, investigators have produced nothing in the slayings of seven journalists since. Silence.

Iraq, of course, remains the most dangerous place for journalists, but as you will read in the following pages, there are many countries where editors and writers, correspondents and photographers risk their lives daily to report the truth. In Ethiopia, more than 20 journalists are in jail. Only China and Cuba imprison more members of the press.

In the Democratic Republic of Congo, massive corruption and a complete lack of judicial protection allow gunmen to operate with impunity. Tens of thousands of women have been raped, and rarely are the attackers arrested. Journalists are killed or threatened, and there is no investigation, no justice. Silence.

It would be easy to pretend that all these attacks on journalists do not have an impact, do not stop reporters from pursuing important stories. But, of course, they do. In the former Soviet Union, CPJ notes that attacks on the press have a "chilling effect on media coverage of the sensitive issues of corruption, organized crime, human rights violations, and abuse of power." In countries around the world, the effect is the same.

That is why this book and CPJ's work are so important. They serve as witness. They give voice to those who have been silenced. They speak. Too many others no longer can.

• • • • • • • • • • • • • • • • • • •

Anderson Cooper is a CNN correspondent and host of the primetime weeknight news show "Anderson Cooper 360°." A contributor to CBS News' "60 Minutes," he is also author of the 2006 best-seller *Dispatches from the Edge*, which recounts his coverage of the South Asia tsunami, Hurricane Katrina, and other major news events. (CNN Photo)

PRESS FREEDOM ALMANAC

CPJ'S 10 MOST CENSORED COUNTRIES

1 NORTH KOREA

Radio, television receivers are locked to government-set frequencies. News is supplied by the official Korean Central News Agency.

0: Number of independent journalists.

2 BURMA

The military junta owns all dailies and television channels. Citizens can be arrested for listening to the BBC in public.

2: Journalists jailed in 2006 for filming the new capital, Pyinmana.

3 TURKMENISTAN

The president approves front-page newspaper content. Newscasters pledge allegiance to the state during each broadcast.

2005: Year the government closed public libraries and banned foreign publications.

4 EQUATORIAL GUINEA

Private newspapers rarely publish due to political pressure. State radio warns citizens they'll be crushed if they criticize the regime.

1: Broadcast outlets not owned by the state. RTV-Asongo is owned instead by the president's son.

5 LIBYA

The state owns all print and broadcast media, and it blocks undesirable political Web sites. Criticism is not permitted.

0: Private news outlets.

6 ERITREA

The only country in sub-Saharan Africa without a private news outlet, Eritrea intensively monitors foreign reporters.

2001: Year the government shut down all private news outlets.

7 CUBA

News media are supervised by the Department of Revolutionary Orientation. Independent reporters are harassed and arrested.

24: Journalists imprisoned.

8 UZBEKISTAN

Three foreign news agencies forced to close bureaus. Reporters arrested, harassed, and pushed into exile.

12: Reporters working for foreign media who were forced to flee.

9 SYRIA

Publications must get licenses from the prime minister. Coverage is so bland that even a top official called it "unreadable."

2: Independent newspapers forced to close since 2003.

10 BELARUS

Authorities seize press runs and impose prison penalties for criticizing the president.

5: Newspapers printed outside the country and smuggled back in.

Most Censored Online:
www.cpj.org/censored

JOURNALISTS KILLED: 1992 - 2006

CPJ analyzed 15 years of records to produce the special report, "Deadly News," which details how, where, when, and why journalists are killed. Here are some main findings.

WHO*

Print reporters/writers: 32%
Broadcast reporters: 20.7%
Editors: 15.9%
Camera operators: 9.4%
Photographers: 7.4%
Columnists/commentators: 9.4%
Producers: 6.1%
Publishers/owners: 3.3%
Technicians: 2.2%

* *Total exceeds 100% because more than one category applies in some cases.*

Local: 85.2% / Foreign correspondents: 14.8%

Male: 93% / Female: 7%

Freelance: 11% / Staff: 89%

HOW

Murder: 72.6%
Crossfire/Combat related: 17.6%
During other dangerous assignment: 9.7%
Undetermined: 0.1%

WHEN

2006: 55	1998: 24
2005: 47	1997: 26
2004: 57	1996: 26
2003: 40	1995: 51
2002: 21	1994: 66
2001: 37	1993: 57
2000: 24	1992: 42
1999: 36	

WHERE

1. Iraq: 92
2. Algeria: 60
3. Russia: 44
4. Colombia: 39
5. Philippines: 32
6. India: 22
7. Bosnia: 19
8. Turkey: 18
9. Rwanda: 16
   Sierra Leone: 16
   Tajikistan: 16
12. Somalia: 14
    Brazil: 14
    Afghanistan: 14
15. Mexico: 13
16. Bangladesh: 12
    Pakistan: 12
18. Sri Lanka: 9
19. Angola: 8
    Yugoslavia: 8

WHY*

Beats covered by victims:

War: 44.6%
Politics: 34.5%
Corruption: 29.7%
Crime: 18.5%
Human rights: 18.9%
Sports/culture: 5.4%
Business: 2.2%

Deadly News Online:
www.cpj.org/deadly

SPOTLIGHT ON MURDER: 1992 - 2006

SUSPECTED PERPETRATORS

Political groups: 26.7%
(armed groups opposed to the government)

Government officials: 20.1%

Criminal groups: 12%

Paramilitaries: 8.4%
(armed groups allied with the government)

Military: 6.8%

Local residents: 1.5%

Mob: 1.1%

Unknown: 23.4%

IMPUNITY

Complete impunity: 85.7%

Partial justice 7.7%
(killers convicted but masterminds unpunished)

Full justice: 6.6%
(killers and masterminds convicted)

Threatened before murdered: 25.8%

Taken captive before murdered: 18.6%

JOURNALISTS IMPRISONED: 2006

TOP JAILERS OF JOURNALISTS *as of December 1, 2006*

1. China: 31   2. Cuba: 24   3. Eritrea: 23   4. Ethiopia: 18   5. Burma: 7

MOST COMMON CHARGES

1. Subversion, divulging state secrets, acting against the interests of the state: 63%

2. Held without any charge: 15%

3. Retaliatory charges such as regulatory violations, association with extremists: 10%

4. Spreading ethnic or religious hatred: 4%

5. Criminal defamation: 3%

6. Violation of censorship rules: 3%

IMPRISONED BY YEAR

2006: 134	2001: 118
2005: 125	2000: 81
2004: 122	1999: 87
2003: 138	1998: 118
2002: 139	1997: 129

BY MEDIUM

Print: 50%

Internet: 37%

Television: 6%

Radio: 6%

Film/documentary: 1%

IN THEIR WORDS

*"What concerns me is that they keep killing journalists.
This hurts me personally, and it hurts Colombia."*

—*Colombian President Álvaro Uribe to a CPJ delegation in March (page 70).*

*"I don't believe in killing people.
I believe in locking you up for the rest of your life."*

—*Gambian President Yahya Jammeh to local journalists in September
as he denied government involvement in an editor's assassination (page 30).*

*"Karzai has promised support, but it's not there for us. ... The authorities
don't want to come to the aid of journalists."*

—*Farida Nekzad, news director of Pajhwok Afghan News, to CPJ (page 102).*

*"A newspaper that belongs to the government
should not criticize the government."*

—*Kyrgyz government spokesman Jediger Saalaev to Radio Free Europe/Radio
Liberty in defending a January crackdown on a state newspaper (page 158).*

*"I don't want to be identified going in and out of the compound where
the Washington Post bureau is based. ... Paranoia has become my shield."*

—*Iraqi reporter Bassam Sebti in a CPJ report (page 191).*

*"My main intent and concern is for journalists not to upset the
conservative fabric. If children fight, you say go to your room. To the
writer, you say please do not write."*

—*Saleh Namlah, Saudi deputy information minister, to CPJ (page 208).*

*"She was our voice, our pen, and Russia's conscience. Left without her,
where do we go?"*

—*A letter to Novaya Gazeta, reacting to Anna Politkovskaya's slaying (page 160).*

INTRODUCTION

• *by Joel Simon* •

As Venezuelan elections approached in November, President Hugo Chávez accused news broadcasters of engaging in a "psychological war to divide, weaken, and destroy the nation." Their broadcast licenses, he said, could be pulled—no idle threat in a country where a vague 2004 media law allows the government to shut down stations for work deemed "contrary to the security of the nation."

In Russia, President Vladimir Putin signed a measure in July that equates critical journalism with terrorism, broadening the definition of extremism to include "public slander toward figures fulfilling state duties." Within months, a human rights publisher was shut down.

In Iraq, gunmen raced up to a group of journalists covering the February attack on the Shiite Askariya shrine, seized one the region's best-known reporters, Atwar Bahjat, and executed her and two members of her crew.

And as fighting raged in southern Lebanon in July, an Israeli missile killed photographer Layal Najib as she was traveling by taxi to cover fleeing civilians. Israel later announced that all vehicles traveling in southern Lebanon, including those carrying journalists, would be subject to attack.

These four scenes, taken from the pages of this book, illustrate two grave and emerging threats to the press. Events in Iraq and Lebanon reflect the erosion in war correspondents' traditional status as neutral observers. Presidents Chávez and Putin represent a generation of sophisticated, elected leaders who have created a legal framework to control, intimidate, and censor the news media.

The rise of "democratators"—popularly elected autocrats—is alarming because it represents a new model for government control of the press. These leaders stand for election and express rhetorical support for democratic institutions while using measures such as punitive tax audits, manipulation of government advertising, and sweeping content restrictions to control the news media. The democratators tolerate the façade of democracy—a free press, opposition political parties, an independent judiciary—while gutting it from within.

These leaders emerged as the authoritarian response to positive historical developments. The end of the Cold War and the collapse of the Soviet Union discredited a political system that not only necessitated state control of information but also justified it in moral terms. Human rights and press freedom groups such as CPJ, which celebrated its 25th anniversary in 2006, have also made it far more difficult for governments to engage in overt terror, such as the widespread "disappearances" of Latin American journalists in the 1970s.

Even repressive governments are now compelled to present themselves as democracies in order to gain international legitimacy. That's a big advancement for press freedom and human rights, but the democratators' new techniques cannot be underestimated.

Leaders who jail journalists sometimes argue that they are complying with international law and are respectful of due process. The Ethiopian government raised the specter of the slaughter in Rwanda when it arrested and jailed more than a dozen journalists on charges of attempted genocide. In a meeting with a CPJ delegation in March, Prime Minister Meles Zenawi insisted he was acting within the law to protect the state. But CPJ's review of the evidence found the charges entirely without merit.

Other nations take a revolving-door approach, imprisoning journalists and releasing them before an international outcry. Iran is the best example. Since 2000, Iranian courts have banned more than 100 publications and jailed dozens of journalists; most were freed after relatively short periods but with the official threat of re-arrest hanging over their heads. Journalists get the message. In August, Akbar Ganji, one of the few Iranian journalists to spend an extended period in prison, visited CPJ's office and argued that the debate over Iran's nuclear ambitions has obscured the government's efforts to destroy civil society and wipe out a once-vibrant independent media.

Other nations manipulate state advertising to reward supportive news outlets and to punish the critical ones. In countries where government agencies and national companies are economic engines, the practice can be devastating to media organizations that ask tough questions. In Argentina, President Néstor Kirchner's administration directs an advertising budget of 160 million pesos without clear safeguards against partisanship. An independent Argentine research group said the advertising practices have caused serious damage to press freedom.

Certainly, there are countries that still rely on brute force; Cuba and Eritrea, where dozens of journalists are imprisoned, are among them. But overt repression, more and more, has given way to other techniques.

Calculated indifference is one. In "Deadly News," a 2006 CPJ investigation, our researchers found that 85 percent of journalist murders in the last 15 years were committed with complete impunity. Even when some convictions were obtained, masterminds were brought to justice in just 7 percent of cases. This unsolved violence provokes massive self-censorship. And that suits many governments just fine.

Thirteen journalists in Russia, including investigative reporter Anna Politkovskaya, have been murdered since President Vladimir Putin took power in 2000. None of the killers have been brought to justice. This record causes reporters to ask fewer questions, to probe less deeply, to pass up risky stories. After all, one reporter told CPJ, to follow in Politkovskaya's path would be "taking on a suicide mission." Putin, while professing concern, benefits from this state of fear.

In Colombia, a long history of impunity has blunted critical reporting in provincial areas where violence remains rampant. President Álvaro Uribe Vélez had publicly denied the prevalence of self-censorship until he met with a CPJ delegation in March. After some prompting, Uribe acknowledged the problem and recognized that government officials who interfere with the press are "committing a crime against democracy."

The practice of journalism, in fact, is protected by international law. Article 19 of the Universal Declaration of Human Rights guarantees the right to seek, receive, and impart information; this right is reinforced in many regional human rights agreements. Journalists operating in war zones are also protected under the Geneva Conventions, which state that journalists are civilians who cannot be deliberately targeted.

But in an era in which even U.S. officials describe the Geneva Conventions as "quaint," these protections increasingly exist in name only. The breakdown of international norms is reflected in many ways. In southern Lebanon, Israel refused to make any provision to allow news coverage during the summer offensive, and, in several instances documented by CPJ, its forces actually targeted press vehicles.

In Iraq, the most dangerous conflict in CPJ's history, insurgents so routinely target reporters that more than two-thirds of media deaths are murders, not acts of war. Fourteen journalists have been killed by U.S. forces' fire; while CPJ has not found evidence that the killings were deliberate, none were adequately investigated by the military. U.S. forces have also detained at least nine Iraqi journalists for months at a time without charge or due process. The most recent was Pulitzer Prize-winning photographer Bilal Hussein of The Associated Press.

Journalists traditionally rely more on savvy than international law to stay alive in war zones, often promising insurgent and guerrilla groups an opportunity to get their message out to the world. But many insurgents today aren't interested in the bargain, preferring to speak via the Internet. Among these groups, journalists are dispensable.

The state of affairs is deeply disturbing because it means that the public knows little about vital issues—from the goals and leadership of the Iraqi insurgency to the implications of China's breakneck economic development. Even as China builds a modern and prosperous economy, it is depriving its citizens of basic information. More than 120 million people are online in China, but the government has erected massive firewalls and, at times, enlisted corporate cooperation to control the medium.

The flood of information that circulates in the Internet age can blind us to the fact that enemies of press freedom still succeed in keeping vital stories from the public eye. As these pages make clear, we are saturated with information but often deprived of essential news.

· · · · · · · · · · · · · · · · · · · ·

Joel Simon is executive director of the Committee to Protect Journalists.

African Union Fails to Defend Press Freedom 18

The African Union doesn't use its tools to promote press freedom, and it fails to speak out against abusers in the Gambia and Ethiopia. Can the AU shake off suspicions that it's a club of dictators?

by Julia Crawford

PHOTOS

Section break: Reuters/Thomas Mukoya — *Workers pick through rubble after Kenyan police stormed* The Standard *in March and set thousands of newspapers on fire.* Analysis (next): AP/George Osodi — *The media center for July's African Union summit features a huge poster of Gambian President Yahya Jammeh.*

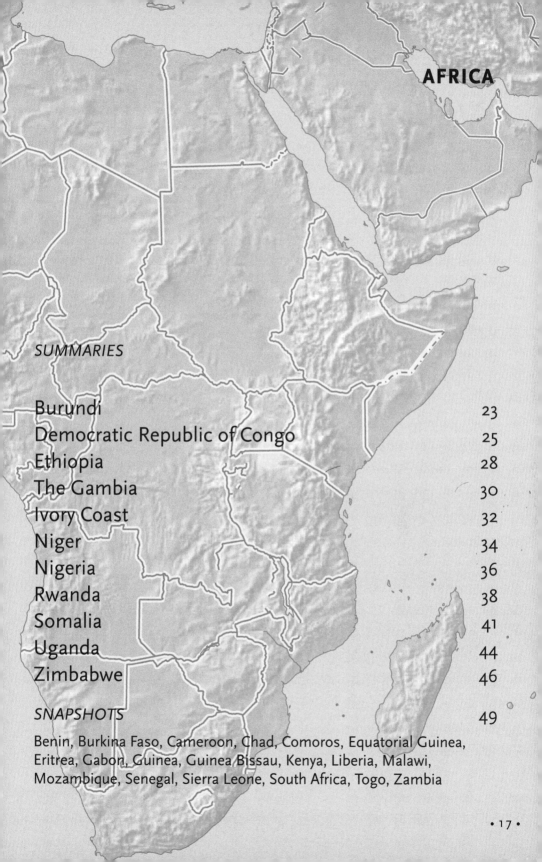

AFRICA

SUMMARIES

AFRICAN UNION FAILS TO DEFEND PRESS FREEDOM

by Julia Crawford

WHEN AFRICAN HEADS OF STATE GATHERED IN JULY IN THE GAMBIA'S sleepy seaside capital, Banjul, their host had just shut down a leading private newspaper, jailed journalists, and halted a planned freedom of expression forum on the fringes of the summit. At the summit, the African Union swore in judges for a future pan-African court of justice and human rights, but said nothing about human rights abuses in the Gambia or the lack of due process for its detainees. In a declaration marking the 25th anniversary of the African Charter on Human and Peoples' Rights, AU leaders vowed to rededicate themselves "to ensuring respect for human and peoples' rights" as a prerequisite to their common vision of "a united and prosperous Africa." The charter, binding on all AU members, includes freedom of expression as a fundamental human right. Yet the heads of state failed to comment on the Gambia's vicious repression of the independent press and its lackluster effort to solve the 2004 assassination of a leading editor.

The AU's failure to speak out against press freedom abuses while it maintains offices in the capitals of two of the continent's principal abusers—the Gambia and Ethiopia—casts doubt on its commitment to freedom of expression. The organization has a number of tools to defend freedom of the press, including the Banjul-based African Commission on Human and Peoples' Rights. In 2002, this human rights commission adopted a Declaration of Principles on Freedom of

Expression in Africa, which was hailed by rights activists. In 2004, it appointed a special rapporteur on freedom of expression in Africa, whose mandate includes the possibility of carrying out investigative missions. The AU's new African Peer Review Mechanism, a voluntary system under which member states are evaluated for good governance, is also a potential tool for the advancement of press freedom throughout Africa.

But progress is slow, and abuses continue on a massive scale in many member states. Ethiopia, where the AU has its headquarters, has at least 18 journalists behind bars, making it the world's fourth leading jailer of journalists. It is surpassed on the continent by Eritrea, with 23, most of whom have been held incommunicado and without charge for more than five years. (An Internet report considered credible by CPJ sources said three Eritrean journalists may have died in custody.) A CPJ survey found Eritrea, where the government shut down the entire private press in 2001, and Equatorial Guinea to be among the 10 Most Censored Countries in the world. Zimbabwe's litany of human rights abuses includes the use of repressive laws to persecute independent journalists and censor the private press. Many AU member states use outdated criminal laws to harass and imprison journalists, while impunity persists in the murders of journalists in countries such as the Gambia, Burkina Faso, the Democratic Republic of Congo, and Somalia. So why is the AU not doing more?

The AU maintains offices in the capitals of two abusers, the Gambia and Ethiopia.

The AU's special rapporteur on freedom of expression, South African attorney Faith Pansy Tlakula, told CPJ that the AU faces many challenges. "The question is, among all the challenges—democratization, peace and development, postwar reconstruction—whether, in the order of things, freedom of expression is going to be a priority," she said. "Of course it should be, as a precursor to the enjoyment of all the other rights."

Tlakula said her priorities were to monitor and report on freedom of expression, thereby raising awareness of the AU human rights commission's work in this field. She said she had not completed any investigative missions since her appointment in December 2005, although she was preparing a report on the Gambia. Tlakula said her office, like much of the AU, was hamstrung by limited staff and financial resources. "We're working on a part-time basis," she told CPJ. By all accounts, lack of resources is a significant problem for the human rights commission as a whole. "Some of the rapporteurs of the commission do a good job, but it's always a struggle because there is no money," said Darian Pavli, an attorney at the Open Society Justice Initiative in New York, which has brought cases before the commission.

Lack of political will is another issue. "The root of the problem is misguided solidarity at the top political level," Pavli told CPJ. "Most leaders are reluctant to say things that could come back and hit them."

Misguided solidarity at the top political level contributes to the problem.

At its December 2005 session in Banjul, the commission condemned human rights violations in Zimbabwe and Eritrea, and enjoined the leaders of those countries to respect their obligations under the charter. It called on Zimbabwe to support "the fundamental rights and freedoms of expression, association and assembly, by repealing or amending repressive legislation," and it issued a blunt appeal to Eritrea to "immediately free the former cabinet ministers, government officials, members of parliament, journalists, media practitioners, and other individuals who have been arrested and detained for many years without trial." The commission also asked the Ethiopian government to "release arbitrarily detained political prisoners, human rights defenders, and journalists," and urged it to "guarantee at all times freedom of opinion and expression."

Eritrea remains Africa's most repressive country following a September 2001 crackdown in which authorities suspended all private press operations, jailed political dissidents and journalists in secret locations, and forced many others into exile. In Zimbabwe, the government has waged a relentless war on critical voices since 2000, using repressive new laws to imprison and harass journalists and driving dozens into exile. The laws have also led to the closure of several newspapers, including the country's only private daily.

At a summit in Khartoum in January, AU heads of state adopted the human rights commission's decisions "except for those containing the resolutions on Eritrea, Ethiopia ... and Zimbabwe," admonishing the commission for not having enlisted responses from those member states. Six months later, the Banjul summit made no mention of human rights abuses in those countries.

In addition to its recent tough resolutions, the commission, which was inaugurated in 1987, has produced some jurisprudence on press freedom issues, although Pavli said not enough cases have been brought. Part of its mandate is to interpret the charter, Article 9 of which states, "Every individual shall have the right to receive information. Every individual shall have the right to express and disseminate his opinions within the law." Pavli described this as "the weakest of all free speech articles among the regional bills of rights," but noted that the commission has given "within the law" a broad interpretation by applying international standards.

Pavli said the human rights commission has also been gaining in moral authority. "The decisions are not strictly binding, but they have the potential to be embarrassing. In the beginning, states wouldn't even show up for a commission hearing, but in the last five to 10 years it has gained some authority," he said. "States, if they can avoid it, would rather not be found in violation of the charter." For example, Pavli helped bring a case against the government of Cameroon on behalf of award-winning journalist Pius Njawe, whose Freedom FM radio station was shut down as it attempted to launch in May 2003. Njawe, winner of a 1991 CPJ International Press Freedom Award, has shown continuing courage in the face of imprisonment, harassment, and censorship. Cameroonian officials, confronted with a potentially embarrassing complaint, signed an agreement to allow Freedom FM to launch, although they have dragged their feet thus far in honoring the pledge.

There is hope, too, that the future African court will give human rights decisions more teeth. "The court will strengthen our work," the AU's Tlakula told CPJ. "If we take cases to the court, it will issue enforceable orders, which will enhance the protection of human rights. A court order is much better than a recommendation." Pavli said the independence of the court nevertheless remains to be seen, as does the AU's willingness to enforce its decisions. "Ultimately, the test for enforcement will be political," he told CPJ. "It will be up to the organization as a whole to ensure compliance."

Many AU members use outdated criminal laws to harass and imprison journalists.

Peer pressure is the cornerstone of another AU tool, the voluntary African Peer Review Mechanism. The process involves a self-assessment by the country submitting to the review—one that is supposed to be inclusive of civil society—and an assessment by an outside team of AU experts; the team then draws up a report, including a "Program of Action" for improvements. Ghana and Rwanda were the first countries to complete the process; their reports were released in 2006. About half of the AU member states have now signed up for a review.

Still, activists complain that civil society is sidelined from the process, the reports are sanitized, and not enough attention is paid to critical issues—in par-

Action is needed if the AU wants to shake off suspicions that it is a 'club of dictators.'

ticular, freedom of expression and the media. The report on Rwanda, which has a pattern of violence and intimidation against journalists, contains only scant and inconclusive reference to press freedom. "The African Peer Review Mechanism is something of a sham, I think," said veteran South African journalist and press freedom activist Raymond Louw. He said the need for a free press was originally included in the self-assessment questionnaire, but it was removed from the final draft. Louw is among those leading an effort to have the heading reinserted, a battle he described as uphill.

The Peer Review Mechanism can certainly be improved. AU human rights tools are gaining ground, while the establishment of an African court of human rights will also be important. The AU, like its predecessor, the Organization of African Unity (OAU), nevertheless remains reluctant to point the finger at individual member states, let alone sanction them. If the African Union wants to finally shake off suspicions that it is still a "club of dictators," as critics once dubbed the OAU, then it must be prepared to take tough action against human rights abusers and give press freedom the importance it deserves in the development of democracy and human rights in Africa.

• • • • • • • • • •

Julia Crawford is CPJ's Africa program coordinator.

•••••••••••••••••••• BURUNDI ••••••••••••••••••••

AFRICA

Under fire for alleged corruption and human rights abuses, the government of former rebel leader Pierre Nkurunziza cracked down on a wide range of critical voices, including those in the press, during its first year in power. Authorities imprisoned a journalist for five months after he allegedly slandered the state in a private barroom conversation, and they launched a vicious campaign of harassment, threats, and intimidation against three independent radio stations, including Radio Publique Africaine (RPA). Government threats against RPA Director Alexis Sinduhije, who won a CPJ International Press Freedom Award in 2004, drove him into hiding. Journalists said the government used the existence of an alleged coup plot as a pretext to silence dissent, including critical reports by the independent media.

The government stepped up its campaign against the radio stations in November, jailing Editor Serge Nibizi and reporter Domitile Kiramvu of RPA and Director Matthias Manirakiza of Radio Isanganiro for stories about the alleged coup plot. The detentions made Burundi Africa's third leading jailer of journalists, after Eritrea and Ethiopia, when CPJ conducted its annual survey of journalists jailed for their work.

Nkurunziza's CNDD-FDD party, formerly the biggest Hutu rebel group battling a minority Tutsi dictatorship, came to power in a 2005 general election, raising hopes of lasting peace and democracy after more than a decade of brutal civil war. The election was the culmination of a lengthy transition backed by the United Nations and South Africa, which in 2000 had mediated a peace accord. In September 2006, the last remaining rebel group, known as the FNL, signed a cease-fire agreement with the government. However, a report by U.N. Secretary-General Kofi Annan in October noted heightened political tensions, "particularly following the government's allegations of a coup plot and the resignation of ... Second Vice President Alice Nzomukunda on September 5."

Nzomukunda had accused the administration of gross human rights abuses, and was particularly critical of the CNDD-FDD's president, Hussein Rajabu. The U.N. report also noted strained relations between the government and the media, and that "in a speech on September 3, the CNDD-FDD party president accused the Burundian media and journalists ... of 'divisiveness.'" Divisiveness is often political code in Burundi for stoking tension between Hutus and Tutsis.

••••••••••

Summaries in this chapter were reported and written by Africa Program Coordinator **Julia Crawford,** Research Associate **Mohamed Keita**, and freelance writer **Alexis Arieff**.

Announcing a foiled coup plot, the government in August jailed several leading opposition figures, including the previous transition president, Domitien Ndayizeye. Also in August, police raided the home of RPA head Sinduhije, forcing him into temporary hiding. Authorities said the raid was linked to investigations of the alleged coup plot, but Sinduhije said the allegations were being used as a pretext to curtail the press and the opposition. "They are trying to shut me up," he told CPJ in a telephone interview while in hiding. Citing the nonpayment of broadcast license fees, the government also suspended local broadcasts of RPA in the northern province of Ngozi. Several local sources told CPJ the move was in retaliation for RPA's critical reporting. The ban was lifted following local and international protests.

But RPA and two other independent stations, Radio Isanganiro and Radio Bonesha, remained in the government's line of fire, especially after they questioned the truth of the alleged coup plot. Pressure intensified after the stations broadcast an interview at the end of August with one of the political detainees, who stated that he had been coerced into confessing that he had taken part in the plot. Sinduhije went into hiding again in September, denouncing a campaign of threats and harassment against himself, his staff, and his radio station. CPJ sources in Bujumbura confirmed that RPA had been subjected to intimidation and harassment, and that government officials had accused the station of working for the opposition.

Worryingly, officials raised the specter of ethnic violence to justify their action. In an interview with CPJ in September, Communications Minister Karenga Ramadhani likened RPA to Radio Télévision Libre des Mille Collines, the station that incited genocide in neighboring Rwanda in 1994, saying that RPA had broadcast false allegations against him. RPA had become one of Burundi's most popular radio stations and had worked to heal the country's ethnic divisions, notably by recruiting staff from both ethnic groups.

Pro-government media, and particularly the Web site of the ruling CNDD-FDD party, ran articles smearing Sinduhije and Gabriel Nikundana, editor of Radio Isanganiro. Nikundana also complained of threats. The harassment continued in October, when the state prosecutor questioned reporters from RPA, Radio Isanganiro, and Radio Bonesha, along with their editors, about sources for another story broadcast in August. The story, carried by all three broadcasters, said that elements within the police had prepared fake attacks on the presidential palace and on Rajabu's residence to bolster the government's claims that it had foiled a coup plot. The information was attributed to police sources, according to the BBC's monitoring service.

The government's crackdown was not limited to the private press. In June, a correspondent for the state news agency Agence Burundaise de Presse, Aloys Kabura, was jailed in the northern province of Ngozi after he publicly criticized police for having beaten journalists in April.

His remarks were made during a barroom conversation with a state intelligence agent. The government alleged that Kabura's comments included a slur, which he denied, according to his lawyer. On September 18, after having already served more than three months in detention, Kabura was sentenced to five months in jail for slandering the state, according to media reports and his lawyer. He was released on October 30.

In April, police besieged and attacked journalists who refused to hand over recordings of a press conference held by ousted ruling party politician Mathias Basabose in a house in Bujumbura. Security forces surrounded the house immediately after the press conference concluded, preventing more than 30 reporters and human rights activists from leaving for more than seven hours. One female journalist was hospitalized, according to her colleagues.

·········· DEMOCRATIC REPUBLIC OF CONGO ··········

The murder of freelance journalist Bapuwa Mwamba in the weeks before historic national elections cast a deep chill over the media, whose members were already subject to frequent attacks and intimidation. Mwamba was the second journalist to be shot to death in his home in eight months. Attacks on the press rose sharply in the run-up to July 30 parliamentary and presidential polls; the presidential race, which went to a runoff in October, was particularly divisive. Journalists were subject to violence, censorship, and arbitrary imprisonment by government forces, political factions, and rogue elements. Authorities also expelled a foreign correspondent. The courts provided little protection against abuses in this war-ravaged, corruption-plagued country. Partisan and inflammatory reporting in some sections of the media contributed to the political tensions.

The elections were marked by violence. Conflicts between sections of the security forces loyal to President Joseph Kabila and his challenger, former rebel leader Jean-Pierre Bemba, killed at least 20 people in the capital, Kinshasa, at the end of August. On November 16, Kabila was announced the winner of the runoff. At least three journalists were arrested covering the aftermath, when Bemba contested the results and the Supreme Court was set ablaze during clashes between his supporters and police.

The election was the first since the country's independence from Belgium in 1960. The polls, boycotted by one of the main opposition parties, were overseen by the United Nations, which has a force of more than 17,000 peacekeepers in the country. Even before Mwamba's murder, U.N. Secretary-General Kofi Annan said in a June report that he was "concerned by reports of increasing intimidation of the media, which threatens to undermine the transparency of the elections."

Mwamba bled to death after being shot by men who burst into his Kinshasa home in the early hours of July 8. Local sources said his attackers took only a cell phone. The day before his death, he had published a commentary in the independent daily *Le Phare*, criticizing Congolese authorities and the international community for what he deemed the failure of DRC's political transition. The reason for his murder remained unclear, and CPJ continued to investigate the circumstances.

Journalists staged a silent march through the streets of Kinshasa to protest the killing, followed by a one-day news blackout. The marchers presented a memorandum to the United Nations calling for a U.N. investigation into killings, kidnappings, and threats to journalists, and urging it to pressure Congolese authorities to respect the rights of the press. At the end of August, Congolese police told the press they were holding a former soldier and two civilians in connection with Mwamba's murder, and investigators claimed that the motive was robbery.

It was not until July, just days after Mwamba's death, that three members of the military went on trial for the November 2005 murder of another journalist, Franck Ngycke Kangundu, and his wife, Hélène Mpaka. Police had presented the three suspects to the press on November 21, 2005. State media suggested in a report the same day that the motive was theft, according to the local press freedom group Journaliste en Danger (JED). However, an investigation by JED found that the killers were not motivated by money and that their actions may have been part of a wider conspiracy. Kangundu was a veteran political affairs writer for the Kinshasa independent daily *La Référence Plus*. Authorities promised to commission an independent investigation but did not immediately deliver. JED received anonymous threats in connection with its inquiry, forcing JED President Donat M'baya Tshimanga and Secretary-General Tshivis Tshivuadi into temporary hiding in February.

Local journalists faced the constant threat of imprisonment for their work under outdated criminal laws. Those reporting allegations of corruption and human rights abuses were most at risk. Several reporters, editors, and publishers were detained for weeks or months, sometimes without charge and often without trial. Patrice Booto, publisher of the Kinshasa papers *Le Journal* and *Pool Malebo*, spent nine months in jail for running stories alleging government corruption at the highest level. He was charged with reporting false information, offending the head of state, and insulting the government. In May, a court handed down a six-month jail term and a fine, ruling that he could go free on payment of the fine, since he had already served seven months in prison. Booto paid the fine, but the state prosecutor appealed, and the journalist remained in jail. He was not freed until August 3, just after the first round of voting in the presidential election.

Media outlets and journalists were subject to frequent violent attacks. In the lawless east, where the United Nations tried to disarm militias, rebels forced Radiotélévision La Colombe in Rutshuru off the air for two weeks in January by looting equipment and terrorizing journalists. In May, Dupont Ntererwa, a journalist in Bukavu with the Centre Lokole radio production studio, an initiative of the U.S.-based nongovernmental organization Search for Common Ground, was accosted by a group of youths who threatened him over his reporting on insecurity in the town. Ntererwa's attackers were believed to be linked to demobilized soldiers.

In April, soldiers from the Republican Guard, a military detachment that falls under the president's authority, attacked journalist Anselme Masua from Radio Okapi as he was trying to report on a military training program in the central city of Kisangani, according to a U.N. spokesman and JED. Radio Okapi is jointly run by the United Nations and the Switzerland-based nongovernmental organization Fondation Hirondelle. And in May, in the southeastern town of Lubumbashi, state-television reporter Ricky Nzuzi was kidnapped, beaten, and abandoned in the bush in an attack that local sources said was linked to his work. In Kinshasa, armed assailants smashed and looted equipment at broadcaster Radiotélévision Message de Vie (RTMV), forcing it off the air. Several sources told CPJ they believed the attackers, although dressed in civilian clothes, were state security agents. A report posted to the Web site of Radio Okapi said they were police. The attack came after a rally by evangelist pastor Fernando Kuthino, whose church owns RTMV and who was jailed after expressing political views at the rally.

Richard Mukendi Mukamba, a cameraman with Radiotélévision Debout Kasai, was beaten and stoned by unidentified attackers while covering a demonstration in the central town of Mbuji-Mayi in June. He was hospitalized with head wounds. The Association of Community Radios called on stations across the country to stage a "day of silence" on June 17 to protest attacks on its members.

In July, on the eve of elections, the government expelled Radio France Internationale (RFI) correspondent Ghislaine Dupont without any written explanation and despite the fact that she had a valid visa. Dupont said she was fingerprinted and photographed by police, who escorted her to the airport. JED called Dupont's expulsion a "shameful and scandalous end to a months-long standoff between RFI and the Congolese government, which indicates the desire of certain Congolese authorities to get rid of a journalist who irritates them because of her professionalism and independence." Several sources told CPJ in May that Information Minister Henri Mova Sakanyi had pressured RFI to withdraw Dupont, while offering to accredit other RFI correspondents. At that time, Mova told CPJ in a phone interview that Dupont's accreditation was withheld because of alleged violations of accreditation rules and not the content of her work. Mova confirmed, however, that he had met with RFI management in Paris to complain about her. Dupont is known for her well-informed and critical coverage of the DRC.

A U.N. official criticized reporting by some media outlets, many of which have links to political parties or local dignitaries. In August, the U.N. secretary-general's special representative in the DRC, William Lacy Swing, expressed concern about "hate messages" in the local media that he said were inciting Congolese to target and take revenge on "white people and foreigners." This came shortly after the High Authority on Media (HAM), an official watchdog body, slapped 24-hour bans on three Kinshasa television stations for allegedly inciting violence through what it called "emotionally charged" broadcasts. The stations included state-owned RTNC 1, the pro-Kabila RTAE, and CCTV, owned by presidential challenger Bemba. The stations were targeted for airing images of alleged atrocities by the other side as election results were awaited, according to news reports. The HAM had itself been attacked in July when Bemba supporters emerging from a political rally looted and burned down its offices.

•••••••••••••••••••••• **ETHIOPIA** ••••••••••••••••••••••

As it launched cross-border attacks in support of a shaky transitional government in Somalia, Addis Ababa maintained a repressive media climate at home by jailing some journalists, intimidating other reporters, and forcing still others into exile. CPJ's annual census found 18 journalists jailed for their work in Ethiopia, at least 15 of whom were on trial for antistate crimes that could carry the death penalty. Government actions led to the banning of at least eight newspapers that once published in the capital. Self-censorship was rife among those still publishing. The government expelled two foreign reporters, including a longtime Associated Press correspondent, and it moved to block critical Web sites.

The government's offensive against the independent press, which began in late 2005, prompted CPJ to send a delegation to Addis Ababa in March. In a meeting with CPJ, Prime Minister Meles Zenawi accused the jailed journalists of trying to stage a violent insurrection to overthrow the government in the wake of the controversial May 2005 elections. Jailed journalists whom CPJ was allowed to meet denied the charges, saying they were doing their jobs in questioning government actions.

The journalists were charged along with dozens of opposition leaders as part of an alleged antistate conspiracy. Their joint trial, which began in February, was expected to last many months or years. Charges against the journalists included "outrage against the constitution and the constitutional order." They were also charged with "genocide," a count later changed to "attempted genocide." The government alleged that their writing had harmed members of the ruling EPRDF party and the Tigrayan ethnic group that forms its base. Most of the accused did not offer a defense, saying the trial was politicized and the court biased against them.

CPJ questioned the government's case in a special report in April, "Poison, Politics, and the Press," in which it reviewed 12 of 20 articles cited by the government as evidence. While the editorials were antigovernment, some harshly so, none called for violence and none made reference to ethnic aggression. CPJ found no evidence to support the prosecution's contention that the pieces were intended to provoke acts of violence or genocide.

CPJ and human rights groups have raised concerns about the treatment of some of the prisoners, including journalists Eskinder Nega and Sisay Agena. The two were separated from the other prisoners during the August/September court recess and subjected to abuse, according to several CPJ sources. They were not told why they had been moved from Kality to Karchelle Prison, which is known for its harsh conditions, the sources said. CPJ wrote to Zenawi in August expressing deep concern. CPJ sources said the journalists' conditions had improved somewhat by the time their trial resumed in October.

Other journalists continued to be charged, harassed, and imprisoned under the country's repressive 1992 Press Law, often on allegations that dated back several years. The actions came despite Zenawi's assurances to CPJ that prosecution of years-old Press Law charges was against government policy and that his administration would review its handling of the cases. At least three journalists sentenced under the Press Law remained in jail when CPJ conducted its annual census of imprisoned journalists on December 1.

The Press Law lays down criminal penalties for offenses such as publishing what the government deems to be false information or news that "defames" state institutions. Press Law reform has been a longstanding point of contention between the government and the private press. Zenawi told CPJ in March that the Press Law would be reviewed by international advisers to ensure it met international standards. At the government's request, donors financed a comparative study of media laws in various countries, which was submitted to parliament for deliberation. Yet for all that, the future of the long-promised reform remained unclear.

CPJ expressed concern about another journalist, Goshu Moges, who was imprisoned in a February "antiterrorism" sweep along with a lawyer who had offered pro bono services to imprisoned journalists. CPJ sought details of the evidence against Moges, but the government did not respond. His arrest followed the first in a series of small explosions in Addis Ababa that the government blamed on Eritrea and antigovernment forces. No one claimed responsibility for the attacks. Border tensions persisted between Ethiopia and Eritrea, which fought a bitter war over their frontier from 1999 to 2001. In December, Addis Ababa cited national security concerns in launching an all-out offensive that pushed the Islamic Courts Union from power in neighboring Somalia and restored a U.N.-backed transitional government.

The government continued to target foreign radio services broadcasting into Ethiopia, including the U.S.-based Voice of America (VOA) and critical Web sites run by exiled Ethiopians. More than a dozen exiled journalists working for media outlets abroad were charged in absentia in a late 2005 crackdown; cases against five VOA journalists and one other U.S.-based reporter were later dropped. Ethiopian authorities denied press reports that they were responding to U.S. government pressure.

In January, the government expelled AP correspondent Anthony Mitchell and accused him of "tarnishing the image of the nation" and "disseminating information far from the truth about Ethiopia." Ethiopian authorities disclosed no supporting evidence for the accusations. Mitchell had reported in Ethiopia for AP and the United Nations news agency IRIN for several years, and he was widely respected for his independent journalism. His expulsion was seen as a major blow to the press corps.

With most private media outlets cowed or silenced, independent Ethiopian journalists turned increasingly to the Internet, according to CPJ sources. In May, sources confirmed that Web sites critical of the government were being blocked, although Information Minister Berhan Hailu denied that the government had taken such action. Sites run by members of the Ethiopian diaspora, including the well-known *Ethiopian Review*, were among those blocked. Elias Kifle, publisher of *Ethiopian Review*, was charged in absentia with treason in late 2005, and an Addis Ababa correspondent for the site was imprisoned for six weeks in early 2006 before being released without charge.

•••••••••••••••••••• THE GAMBIA ••••••••••••••••••••

The government's announcement in March that it had foiled a coup plot was followed by a wave of arrests and an unprecedented crackdown on the independent press in the run-up to presidential elections in September. President Yahya Jammeh was declared the winner with 67 percent of the vote, giving him a third term in office. But the government's brutal repression of the press and other independent voices made a mockery of democracy. Opposition leader Ousainou Darboe rejected the official results, saying there had been widespread intimidation by local chiefs, governors, and security agents.

Government forces shut down a leading independent newspaper, jailed journalists without due process, forced others into exile, and brought criminal charges against a reporter under a repressive media law. Just before the elections, a state television reporter, Dodou Sanneh, was jailed secretly for almost a week and interrogated about his coverage of Darboe's campaign. Self-censorship increased, and the authorities pressured management at the country's only private daily newspaper, the *Daily Observer*, to adopt a pro-Jammeh editorial line. The government retained a firm grip on the broadcast sector, despite the presence of some private commercial and community radio stations. With the December 2004 murder of newspaper editor Deyda Hydara still unsolved and a string of arson attacks on independent media outlets unpunished since 2000, the crackdown confirmed the Gambia as one of Africa's worst places to be a journalist.

At his first news conference after re-election, Jammeh signaled no letup in his repression of the independent press. "Let me tell you one thing," Jammeh told selected local and foreign journalists on September 23. "The whole world can go to hell. If I want to ban any newspaper, I will, with good reason." The BBC and Reuters also quoted him as saying: "If you write Yahya is a thief, you should be ready to prove it in a court of law. If that constitutes lack of press freedom, I don't care."

Jammeh denied that government security agents were involved in Hydara's assassination, telling journalists: "I don't believe in killing people. I believe in locking you up for the rest of your life. Then maybe at some point we say, 'Oh, he is too old to be fed by the state,' and we release him and let him become destitute. Then everyone will learn a lesson from him."

The Independent, one of the country's leading private newspapers, remained closed after security agents sealed its offices in the capital, Banjul, on March 28. Editor Musa Saidykhan and General Manager Madi Ceesay, who is also president of the Gambia

Press Union (GPU), were detained on the same day. Both were held at the government's National Intelligence Agency (NIA) for three weeks amid allegations of abuse, before being released without charge on April 20. Lamin Fatty, a reporter for *The Independent*, was also detained at the NIA for more than a month without access to legal counsel. He was subsequently put on trial for publishing "false news," a charge that could bring a jail sentence of at least one year. CPJ honored Ceesay in November with an International Press Freedom Award in recognition of his courage in defending press freedom in the Gambia.

In late May, at least four more journalists, including BBC correspondent Lamin Cham, were jailed in connection with a crackdown on the critical U.S.-based Web site *Freedom Newspaper*, although the NIA and other government authorities denied ever holding them. Cham, along with Pa Modou Faal of the state broadcasting service GRTS and Musa Sheriff of the private weekly *Gambia News & Report*, were released after several days; Malick Mboob, a former reporter for the pro-government *Daily Observer*, based in Banjul, remained in custody for nearly five months before being released without charge, according to CPJ sources. All except Cham figured on a list of purported contributors to *Freedom Newspaper*, which is run by exiled former GPU Secretary-General Pa Nderry Mbai. The list was published on the private *Gambia Post* Web site and reprinted in the *Daily Observer*, which claimed that Mbai had renounced the publication and was joining Jammeh's ruling APRC party. Mbai promptly issued a denial, saying that the disclosure of the list was the work of computer hackers.

The government seemed to observe a brief respite in its crackdown on the local press during an African Union summit in Banjul in early July, which went ahead despite pleas from human rights and press freedom groups that it be moved because of the Gambia's appalling record. Less than a week after the summit ended, *Daily Observer* journalist "Chief" Ebrima B. Manneh went missing. He was believed to be in NIA custody, although authorities said they had no knowledge of his whereabouts.

Toward the end of July, two Banjul-based Nigerian journalists were held for four days before being released without charge. Sam Obi, a veteran radio journalist, and Abdulgafar Oladimeji, a freelance journalist, were arrested by the NIA and held in a cell at the agency's headquarters in Banjul, Oladimeji told CPJ. They were arrested after Obi launched a new publication, the *Daily Express*, for which Oladimeji also worked. The inaugural issue of the *Daily Express*, published on July 1 to coincide with the African Union summit, reprinted a press release from a coalition of civil-society organizations protesting the government's decision to block a planned freedom of expression forum. On July 5, the *Daily Observer* printed a letter that accused the *Daily Express* of seeking to "tarnish the image of this country."

Although Obi and Oladimeji were released, Sulayman Makalo, who worked briefly for the *Daily Express* and was once assistant editor at *The Independent*, went into hiding after NIA officials said they were looking for him, local sources told CPJ. He joined a growing number of Gambian journalists in hiding or in exile because of government threats and fears for their security.

• • • • • • • • • • • • • • • • • IVORY COAST • • • • • • • • • • • • • • • • •

The news media were caught in the middle of political tensions that have split the country between a government-ruled south and a rebel-held north since 2002. In the south and west, militant groups harassed, intimidated, and attacked media outlets as a U.N.-backed power-sharing government installed at the end of 2005 failed to bring much progress on disarmament. Elections were postponed for the second time in two years, and the aftermath of a deadly toxic waste dumping scandal fueled a public row between interim Prime Minister Charles Konan Banny and President Laurent Gbagbo.

On January 18, hundreds of Young Patriots, the radical militia supporting President Laurent Gbagbo, seized control of the state television and radio broadcaster Radiodiffusion Télévision Ivoirienne (RTI), using it to broadcast calls for protests against the French and U.N. presence in the country. They had besieged RTI's offices in Abidjan, the commercial capital, for two days before gaining access without any apparent resistance from government security forces guarding the premises.

This came amid a wave of demonstrations after international mediators recommended the dissolution of parliament, whose mandate had expired. Gbagbo's party, Front Populaire Ivoirien (FPI), temporarily withdrew from the transitional government in protest and called for the departure of U.N. and French peacekeepers monitoring the country's fragile peace.

The Young Patriots broadcast messages over RTI directing protesters to specific targets for demonstrations, including the RTI offices, U.N. headquarters, and the French embassy in Abidjan. Large crowds formed at each site. RTI was not able to resume its normal operations until the following day, after Young Patriots leader Charles Blé-Goudé called off the demonstrations.

The Young Patriots also ransacked Radio Tchrato, a community radio station in the central town of Daloa, and forced it off the air after journalists at the station refused to broadcast the militia's messages.

Legal moves were also used to intimidate journalists. In June, an Abidjan court sentenced Editor Honoré Sépé and Publication Director Fatoumata Coulibaly of the opposition daily *Le Front* to three months in jail for publishing an allegedly false document; the court also ordered the paper to pay large fines for allegedly defaming both Blé-Goudé and Henri Amouzou, president of a cocoa and coffee producers association. Although the journalists remained free on appeal, the sentence appeared to contradict a December 2004 press law that was supposed to eliminate prison terms for press offenses.

The two journalists were sentenced in connection with a February 21 article in *Le Front* alleging that Blé-Goudé had received the equivalent of US$500,000 to stage a demonstration outside the French embassy in January. To back its claim, the newspaper published a copy of a purported letter from Amouzou to Blé-Goudé. A suit from Amouzou ensued.

In September, three journalists of a pro-opposition private daily were detained overnight in connection with an article alleging that First Lady Simone Gbagbo and two public officials hastily formed a front company to dump deadly toxic waste in Abidjan in mid-August. A week later, an Abidjan court fined Coulibaly Seydou, Edouard Gonto, and Frédéric Koffi of *Le Jour Plus* 15 million CFA francs (US$29,000) for "contempt of the head of state." At least 10 people died after inhaling fumes from the waste.

Fallout from the toxic waste scandal continued in November, when President Gbagbo fired management of RTI and the state-owned newspaper *Fraternité Matin*. RTI had aired a statement from the prime minister's office criticizing Gbagbo's decision to reinstate public officials implicated in the affair. *Fraternité Matin* was said to have "erroneously reported" a meeting between the president and prime minister. The sackings highlighted a growing rift between Gbagbo and Banny after the U.N. Security Council extended their mandates for an additional year.

There was continuing international concern about inflammatory reporting by some media outlets. In a report to the U.N. Security Council in April, Secretary-General Kofi Annan stated that "sections of the Ivoirian media actively participated in propagating calls to violence and stirring up hatred" against the United Nations, international mediators, France, and selected local groups during unrest in January. He did not cite any specific outlets.

The FPI daily *Notre Voie* continued to launch virulent attacks, particularly on the former colonial power France. On January 5, it ran an article claiming that France was preparing to create chaos in Ivory Coast, and it accused Radio France Internationale (RFI) of being a propaganda arm of the French government.

RFI's FM broadcasts were allowed back on the air in May, after a 10-month ban by the state-run National Council on Audiovisual Communication (CNCA), a media regulatory agency. The CNCA had banned RFI in July 2005, accusing it of biased and unethical reporting. An RFI source confirmed media reports that the broadcaster had agreed to pay 9 million CFA francs (US$17,200) to Ivoirian authorities, but the source denied that it was a fine and said that RFI stood by its reporting. RFI also agreed to recruit a local correspondent in Abidjan. The broadcaster's Abidjan bureau had been closed since its last correspondent, Jean Hélène, was killed by an Ivoirian police officer in October 2003.

Franco-Ivoirian relations remained tense over the French-led investigation into the April 2004 disappearance of French and Canadian freelance journalist Guy-André Kieffer. Kieffer was investigating corruption in the lucrative cocoa sector when he disappeared from an Abidjan parking lot.

In January, French authorities arrested a new suspect, former Ivoirian army officer Jean-Tony Oulaï, as he arrived in Paris. News reports said Oulaï was suspected of leading a commando unit that kidnapped and killed Kieffer, but Oulaï denied any involvement. He was released in February but remained under investigation in France.

Shortly after Kieffer's disappearance, Ivoirian authorities arrested Michel Legré, an in-law of First Lady Simone Gbagbo, and charged him as an accessory to kidnapping and murder. But authorities released Legré in October 2005 and have not responded to a request from French investigating magistrate Patrick Ramaël that he be allowed to question the suspect in France. Legré was the last person known to have seen Kieffer.

Ramaël reportedly compiled a list of 17 suspects after an August visit to Abidjan during which a number of Ivoirian informants came forward. Agence France-Presse quoted Bernard Kieffer, the missing journalist's brother, who accompanied Ramaël to Abidjan, as saying that five of the suspects were active members of the Ivoirian army but that Ramaël had not been allowed to question them. Judicial secrecy rules bar Ramaël from speaking to the press. Ivoirian authorities have denied any government involvement in Kieffer's disappearance.

• NIGER •

Authorities used a repressive press law to jail journalists despite President Mamadou Tandja's 2004 pledge to abolish prison terms for so-called press offenses. Three journalists spent months behind bars, prompting demonstrations and international outcry. In a country suffering from chronic food shortages, the private press frequently accused public figures of corruption and the mismanagement of public resources. In response, authorities banned an independent newspaper and censored a BBC report on hunger.

On August 4, police arrested Director Maman Abou and Editor Oumarou Keita of the private weekly *Le Républicain* in connection with a July 28 opinion piece that criticized Prime Minister Hama Amadou. After a one-day trial that defense lawyers called biased, a Niamey court sentenced both defendants to 18 months in prison for defaming the government and publishing false news. In its September 1 verdict, the court also fined each journalist more than 5 million CFA francs (US$10,000). The journalists were freed in November pending a hearing before the Supreme Court of Appeal.

The article suggested that the prime minister was redirecting Niger's foreign policy to favor Iran and Venezuela after the country came under criticism from Western donors for a lack of transparency in its disbursement of foreign aid. Abou said he believed the government wanted to punish *Le Républicain* for a series of articles beginning in April that alleged corruption in primary education financing. He said the charges led to a donor audit in June. Niger's ministers for health and education were fired on June 27, following allegations of corruption made by donors and development partners, according to international news agencies.

Salif Dago, a reporter for the private newspaper *L'Enquêteur*, was jailed for three months on charges of publishing false information in an August 14 story headlined, "Black Mass in Niamey Cemetery." The story recounted an alleged macabre ritual involving the killing of a baby by an unidentified man. Convicted and sentenced to six months in prison, Dago was freed in November when an appellate court tossed out the case.

All three journalists were released on November 27, a day after hundreds of people demonstrated on their behalf in the central town of Agadez, according to local media reports. CPJ and other press freedom groups had also called for the cases to be dropped.

The prosecutions ran counter to Tandja's electoral promise in 2004 to abolish prison penalties for libel and other press-related offenses. A commission appointed in March 2005 to study reform of the 1999 Press Law submitted a report to the government in early 2006 proposing that prison sentences be replaced with fines, according to a government spokesman. The spokesman said reforms may be submitted to Niger's parliamentary body in 2007, but local journalists remained skeptical.

A journalist had also been imprisoned earlier in the year. In February, Ibrahim Manzo, director of the newspaper *L'Autre Observateur*, spent 18 days in preventive detention before being given a one-month suspended sentence for allegedly defaming a local businessman in a December 2005 article. Another newspaper director, Salifou Soumaila Abdoulkarim, was placed in preventive detention for almost a month in a separate defamation case in November 2005. Abdoulkarim, the director of the private weekly *Le Visionnaire*, was released from prison in January after serving a two-month sentence for defaming the state treasurer in an article alleging embezzlement.

Authorities also used the state-controlled High Council on Communications, known by its French acronym, CSC, to censor the press. In June, the CSC banned the independent weekly *L'Opinion* indefinitely, accusing it of insulting the president and inciting "rebellion," according to international news reports and Abdourahmane Ousmane, president of the local group Journalists for Human Rights. The accusations stemmed from an article published in mid-June that compared Tandja's administration unfavorably to that of former military leader Seyni Kountché, who ruled Niger from 1974 to 1987, Agence France-Presse reported. The ruling came despite the CSC's failure to meet a legal requirement to change its membership to provide journalists greater representation. Eleven of its 12 members were government appointees.

An image-conscious government censored press coverage of hunger and malnutrition. In April, the government withdrew accreditation for a BBC television crew after it reported on the prevalence of hunger in the central region of Maradi. The BBC's South Africa-based crew said it found many people who faced food shortages. The government claimed the reports were biased, but it has since allowed the BBC to operate in the country, local journalists told CPJ. Officials were forbidden to talk to the media about the food situation in the country, CPJ sources said.

In 2005, authorities had sought to repress local coverage of a developing nationwide famine for fear that the news would tarnish the country's image, according to the Ghana-based Media Foundation for West Africa. In early August 2005, Tandja publicly denied the existence of famine in Niger, despite widespread media reports and a vast international aid campaign. In November of the same year, he accused the opposition and humanitarian organizations of "exaggerating the food crisis for political motivations."

• NIGERIA •

President Olusegun Obasanjo's attempt to amend the constitution so he could seek a third term in the April 2007 election galvanized opponents and stoked political tensions and violence. Media critical of the president's move found themselves the targets of harassment by security services. But the climate for all media worsened, and attacks on the press increased, according to local journalists. The media took a leading role in opposing Obasanjo's amendment bid, which was eventually blocked.

The arrest of two journalists on sedition charges in June raised local and international alarm. Some journalists saw this as part of a pattern of reprisal against the independent media for having thwarted Obasanjo's third-term ambitions. The president denied he was cracking down on the press, yet CPJ research shows that at least three journalists were imprisoned by the State Security Service (SSS), which reports directly to the president. "I believe that I am one of the most tolerant presidents in the world," Obasanjo

told The Associated Press in June. "I believe responsible journalism has an important role to play in democracy and in any civilized society." But he went on to criticize journalists who "fabricate," the AP reported, and said he would sue any who defamed him.

The upcoming general election is to choose a president and national assembly, as well as state governors and regional assemblies. It should usher in the first handover of presidential power since the end of military rule in 1999. But Obasanjo's attempt to hang on to office sharpened political rivalries, particularly between the president and his deputy, Vice President Atiku Abubakar, who opposed a term extension.

In March, the government's National Broadcasting Commission (NBC) slapped sanctions on Freedom Radio, an independent station in the northern city of Kano, for allegedly violating provisions of the country's broadcasting code. The NBC did not provide specific examples. Several local journalists said the government had targeted the station over a song it aired that protested a third term for the president. The sanctions, which included suspension of call-in shows and political programs, were widely criticized by local journalists and press freedom organizations. The restrictions were lifted after two weeks.

In May, plainclothes security agents told managers at the Abuja bureau of Africa Independent Television (AIT), the leading independent TV station, to stop broadcasting a privately produced 30-minute documentary about past failed efforts by Nigerian leaders to prolong their time in office. The agents also confiscated the master copy of the documentary, which had aired several times. Raymond Dokpasi, chairman of Daar Communications, which owns AIT, said the agents claimed to be acting on orders from the president. Dokpasi said he had also received telephone threats over AIT's decision to broadcast live the parliamentary debate on the amendment, which was defeated on May 16.

In mid-June, SSS agents detained overnight Mike Gbenga Aruleba, an AIT presenter, and demanded that his station turn over a tape of the previous day's "Focus Nigeria," hosted by Aruleba. The discussion program had picked up a newspaper report that questioned the age and cost of the presidential jet. This had sparked controversy, especially since Obasanjo came to power promising to fight corruption and unnecessary government expenditures.

Aruleba was rearrested later the same month, along with Rotimi Durojaiye, the senior Daily Independent correspondent who wrote the report. In his June 12 article, Durojaiye said research conducted by the newspaper showed that the government had bought a five-year-old aircraft from the German carrier Lufthansa and not, as it claimed, a new jet directly from Boeing. The two journalists were charged with six counts of sedition, including conspiring "to bring into hatred or contempt or excite disaffection against the person of the president or the government of the federation."

Aruleba and Durojaiye were jailed for several days before being released on bail. In October, an Abuja court dropped the charges against Aruleba and his news organization,

Daar Communications, after the prosecution said the defendants had shown "sufficient remorse." But prosecutors said the trial against Durojaiye and his news organization, Independent Newspapers Limited, would continue because they were not "remorseful."

The charges against Durojaiye were referred to the federal Court of Appeal, after the defense claimed they were unconstitutional.

Outdated criminal laws were also used to jail two journalists for more than two months in southeastern Ebonyi state in connection with an article criticizing the state governor. Director Imo Eze and Editor Oluwole Elenyinmi of the local bimonthly *Ebonyi Voice*, were charged with sedition over an article accusing Gov. Sam Ominyi Egwu of corruption and mismanagement, according to several sources. The two were freed on bail in late August after international and local pressure, including mediation by the Nigeria Union of Journalists, which said it hoped the case could be settled out of court.

In April, another journalist was briefly detained and charged with eight counts of "conducting himself in a manner likely to cause a breach of the peace" for an article detailing political tension between the governor of southern Bayelsa state and his deputy over who would run for governor in the 2007 election. The journalist, Alfred Egbegi, publisher of the weekly tabloid newspaper *Izon Link* in the state capital, Yenagoa, also reported receiving threats from anonymous callers and state government officials after the article appeared.

Journalists in many parts of the country operated in a climate of insecurity and sporadic violence that was often linked to ethnic and religious tensions. For example, Muslim protests in February against Danish cartoons of the Prophet Muhammad republished by European newspapers spiraled into violence that killed dozens of Christians and Muslims.

One of the most dangerous areas was the oil-rich Niger Delta, where militant groups have attacked government and oil company targets and kidnapped foreign oil workers.

In June, a veteran U.S. freelance photographer, Ed Kashi, and his Nigerian fixer, Elias Courson, were imprisoned for four days for allegedly filming an oil facility in Bayelsa state without permission, although local journalists said they were not aware of regulations requiring special permission to film oil installations. The two were initially held by the Nigerian Navy and then transferred to the custody of the SSS, before being released without charge. Kashi was on assignment for the U.S. magazine *National Geographic*.

• **RWANDA** •

The Rwandan media continued operating in an atmosphere of pervasive self-censorship periodically reinforced by government repression. In a January 24 speech broadcast on state radio, President Paul Kagame accused Rwandan journalists of unprofessional conduct, including corruption, and suggested that this justified limits on press freedom.

Authorities used allegations of unethical reporting and participation in the 1994 genocide to suppress critical reporting. Jean-Léonard Rugambage, a journalist with the private local-language newspaper *Umuco*, was freed in July after spending 11 months in jail on the orders of a "gacaca," or community, court. CPJ sources said they believed he had been imprisoned for his journalistic work. His imprisonment fueled concern that the gacaca courts were subject to abuse in some cases. The government established some 11,000 gacaca courts in 2002 to try tens of thousands of suspected participants in the genocide. Under this system, suspects are judged by their peers and have no recourse to a lawyer.

Rugambage's arrest came shortly after an August 2005 article in which he reported alleged corruption and false accusations in gacaca courts in one locality. One of those courts then ordered his preventive detention on a genocide charge. When Rugambage challenged the proceedings before a second gacaca court, he was sentenced to 12 months for contempt and intimidation; he was later placed in the highest category of genocide suspects, meaning he would be tried in a national court and face the death penalty. A gacaca appeals court overturned his contempt conviction in July but kept Rugambage in pretrial detention on the genocide charge. Two days later, he was suddenly released, apparently on orders from the national agency overseeing gacaca proceedings. The status of the genocide charge against him remained unclear; CPJ sources said the charge had been based on vague and contradictory testimony related to a murder.

At a government conference in January on press freedom, the minister of information and the head of the state information agency took turns criticizing Lucie Umukundwa, a correspondent for the Voice of America (VOA), and BBC correspondent Jean-Claude Mwambutsa for their coverage of critical reports issued by Amnesty International and Human Rights Watch. The police spokesman also stated that police would investigate their "ideology." CPJ sources said this was a clear reference to a 2004 parliamentary report's accusations that international radio stations were guilty of "genocidal ideology." In July, unidentified men assaulted Umukundwa's brother, telling him the attack was a response to her broadcasts on the VOA, according to CPJ sources. This came after another VOA correspondent, Gilbert Rwamatwara, fled the country in late 2005 in fear for his security. Rwamatwara complained of threats and harassment in the wake of interviews he conducted with opposition leaders. Both the VOA and  the BBC carry programs in the local Kinyarwanda language, as well as in French and English.

Foreign radio stations remained an important source of independent news, despite the spread of local private radio stations. By late 2006, Rwanda had 10 private radio stations—four commercial, four religious, and two community stations—in addition to the state-owned Radio Rwanda and three affiliated community stations. The commercial radio stations mostly shied away from investigative news and political commentary, according to CPJ sources. A notable exception came in late summer when some commercial stations aired talk shows criticizing authorities over a ban on motorcycle taxis in the capital, Kigali. Television broadcasting remained a state monopoly.

In June, immigration authorities ordered Sonia Rolley, the Rwanda correspondent for Radio France Internationale (RFI) since October 2004, to leave the country within 48 hours. Rolley had received her press accreditation from the Ministry of Information only a month earlier. The government provided no official explanation. RFI began broadcasting on FM in Rwanda in late 2005.

By November 27, RFI was off the air entirely as the government retaliated against the French. Rwandan authorities pulled the station from the FM frequency after a French judge formally accused Kagame, the Tutsi former rebel leader, of involvement in the death of his predecessor in 1994, according to international media reports. Kagame denied any involvement but severed diplomatic relations with France. The downing of Hutu President Juvénal Habyarimana's plane triggered the massacre of more than 800,000 Tutsis and moderate Hutus.

Several journalists also reported intimidation and harassment. *Umuco* Editor Bonaventure Bizumuremyi went into hiding in August to avoid a police summons, after the High Council of the Press found he had published "unethical" articles. The council is an official media regulatory body attached to the president's office. Bizumuremyi had also received threatening phone calls. In January, four armed men came to Bizumuremyi's home at night and broke the door, awakening neighbors, who intervened before the intruders could enter. The attempted break-in occurred after *Umuco* carried an article critical of the ruling RPF party, according to local sources.

Also in August, Jean Bosco Gasasira, editor of the new Kinyarwanda periodical *Umuvugizi*, claimed that he received threatening phone calls after publishing an article alleging that nepotism in the current government was comparable to that under the pregenocide regime of Juvénal Habyarimana. He also complained that he was under police surveillance.

Authorities have also used criminal laws against critical journalists. The High Court in August overturned the November 2004 conviction of Charles Kabonero, editor of the private newspapers *Umuseso* and *Rwanda Newsline*, for criminal libel, while affirming his one-year suspended sentence and a fine equivalent to US$2,000 for insulting a public figure. Kabonero had published an article in August 2004 stating that the vice president of parliament's lower house was challenging Kagame's leadership and engaging in corruption.

In the course of the year, the government drafted press legislation that would represent a modest improvement in the repressive 2002 Press Law. The bill limited criminal liability to journalists and media owners, thus eliminating liability for printers and vendors. It also deleted the requirement that judges impose maximum sentences on journalists convicted of certain criminal offenses. However, it retained many restrictive features of the existing law. Definitions of criminal offenses remained vague, ambiguous, and broad; the bill also kept libel as a criminal offense. A separate bill gives the High Council of the Press increased authority to regulate and sanction the private media. Both bills were before parliament in late year.

· **SOMALIA** ·

The killing of a Swedish photojournalist at a pro-government rally in Mogadishu underscored the dangers faced by journalists covering renewed political turmoil in Somalia, which has had no effective central administration since the fall of dictator Siad Barre in 1991.

Against a background of military conflict between the U.N.-backed transitional government and the Islamic Courts Union (ICU), journalists faced attacks, imprisonments, and censorship so pervasive that the National Union of Somali Journalists described 2006 as "the most dangerous year for press freedom for more than a decade." Many attacks on journalists went unreported for fear of reprisal, according to the union, also known as NUSOJ. Both sides in the conflict abused press freedom as tensions escalated,

driving the media to censor itself. The year was marked by dramatic shifts in the balance of power, with the ICU seizing the capital, Mogadishu, and a large swath of the south in early June only to be routed in late December when Ethiopia's powerful military launched an all-out offensive in support of the transitional government.

The government, established by a peace conference of warlords and political leaders to restore order to Somalia, had previously been unable to establish authority much beyond its seat in Baidoa, 155 miles (250 kilometers) northwest of the capital. One of the riskiest topics for journalists in Baidoa was the movement of Ethiopian troops; prior to its direct military intervention on December 20, Ethiopia had denied having any troops inside Somalia. Addis Ababa sought to justify its late-year intervention by saying that the ICU, which had threatened holy war, menaced Ethiopian security. At year's end, transitional government forces were in Mogadishu, still backed by Ethiopian troops, while the ICU had fled without a fight from its last stronghold in the southern city of Kismayo.

The ICU's brief hold on power was marked by attacks and harassment of the press. On June 23, less then three weeks after seizing Mogadishu, the ICU organized a rally in the center of the capital. Martin Adler, an award-winning Swedish freelance journalist and documentary filmmaker, was in the thick of the crowd filming when an unidentified gunman came up behind him and shot him in the back.

Adler, a long-time contributor to Britain's Channel 4 News and several newspapers, including the Swedish daily *Aftonbladet*, died instantly. The gunman escaped. Several reports said Adler, 47, was filming demonstrators burning U.S. and Ethiopian flags. Anti-foreigner sentiment had been stoked by reports that the widely despised warlords who had opposed the ICU had received financial backing from the CIA to capture al-Qaeda suspects in Somalia. International journalists had previously been stoned or heckled while reporting on demonstrations, The Associated Press said.

NUSOJ reported that Adler was working outside the heavily guarded area where many other journalists and Islamist leaders were standing. The ICU condemned the murder and promised to investigate, but no one was brought to justice immediately. The murders of two journalists the previous year also remained unpunished. Kate Peyton of the BBC, one of several foreign reporters who entered the country to cover the peace process in early 2005, was shot outside her hotel in Mogadishu, while local radio journalist Duniya Muhyadin Nur was shot six months later while covering a protest near the capital.

In August, unidentified gunmen ambushed NUSOJ leaders on the road from Baidoa to Mogadishu, fatally shooting their driver, Madey Garas, according to NUSOJ Secretary-General Omar Faruk Osman. Another NUSOJ official who was in the car, Fahad Mohammed Abukar, was injured. Osman told CPJ that he, Abukar, and Garas were traveling with two bodyguards to Mogadishu, where they hoped to hold talks with ICU officials on press freedom issues. The attack took place in no-man's-land, about 28 miles (45 kilometers) outside Baidoa. Osman said it was not clear what had motivated the attack. He said it had been well known that NUSOJ officials were traveling to Mogadishu.

The ICU showed increasing signs of intolerance to criticism. In July, authorities in Jowhar, an airport town 50 miles (80 kilometers) north of the capital, briefly detained Abdikarim Omar Moallim, a correspondent for the private, Mogadishu-based Radio Banadir, after he reported on clashes between militiamen and traders protesting new taxes. Although Moallim was released, ICU authorities banned him from continuing to work for Radio Banadir. In September, Islamist authorities jailed journalist Osman Adan Areys of the private station Radio Simba for two days in the western town of Beledweyne, then released him without charge. Local journalists said they believed the arrest was linked to interviews in which local residents criticized ICU-imposed restrictions. A CPJ source said the restrictions included a curfew in Beledweyne, which lies near the border with Ethiopia.

Also in September, the ICU closed the private station Radio Jowhar for two days, allowing it back on the air only after it agreed to tight restrictions on its musical content. The AP quoted an Islamic official, Sheik Mohamed Mohamoud Abdirahman, as saying that the station's programs were "un-Islamic" and that it was "useless to air music and love songs for the people."

Just over two weeks later, ICU militias closed a substation of HornAfrik Radio, a prominent private radio station, in the southern port town of Kismayo and detained three of its journalists for questioning about the station's critical reporting. Sheik Ibrahim Mohamed, a spokesman for the Islamic courts in Kismayo, was quoted by the AP as saying, "We have arrested them for conveying wrong messages to the people that are against the Islamic courts." A HornAfrik source told CPJ that the station had been covering demonstrations against the Islamists who took control of Kismayo on September 25. HornAfrik was allowed back on the air in Kismayo four days later. The broadcaster received a set of guidelines against playing love songs and airing reports critical of the ICU, Ahmed Abdisalam, one of HornAfrik's managing partners, told CPJ. He said the station had not agreed to these conditions and would maintain its editorial independence. However, other local sources said its content had changed, and that critical news coverage was much more limited.

Attacks on the press by forces loyal to the transitional government also increased. In June, Maryan Mohamud Qalanjo, a reporter for the private, Mogadishu-based station Radio Shabelle, was assaulted twice by militias loyal to the Rahanweyn Resistance Army (RRA) in Baidoa, according to NUSOJ and other CPJ sources. The RRA controls the southwestern regions of Bay, in which Baidoa lies, and Bakool. Government officials accused Radio Shabelle of spreading "disinformation" about government leaders, including corruption allegations against Sharif Hassan Sheik Adan, speaker of the transitional parliament, NUSOJ reported.

Also in June, government authorities shut down Radio Shabelle's local station in Baidoa after it broadcast a report saying that 300 Ethiopian soldiers had crossed into Somalia. Militiamen following orders from acting Interior Minister Col. Hassan Mohammed Nur entered the station and detained journalists Mohamed Adawe and Ali Mohamed Saed for about eight hours, according to the station's deputy director, Mohamed Amiin. The transitional government gave no explanation for its action. For much of the year, the transitional government and Ethiopia denied the presence of any Ethiopian troops in Somalia.

In October, security forces of the transitional government arrested three radio journalists near Baidoa, holding two of them for nearly 10 days before releasing them without charge. Fahad Mohammed Abukar of Baidoa-based Warsan Radio, Mohammed Adawe Adam of Radio Shabelle, and Muktar Mohammed Atosh of HornAfrik Radio were arrested as they were returning to Baidoa from Burhakaba, which had been the scene of fighting between forces of the transitional government and the ICU. Police Chief Aaden Biid said authorities arrested the journalists because they filmed Ethiopian troops and government forces outside Baidoa, the AP reported. The journalists said they had been questioned about their activities and the content of their recordings in Burhakaba.

In December, authorities in the semi-autonomous region of Puntland, which is an ally of the transitional government, detained Abdi Aziz Guled, a correspondent for Radio Simba in Mogadishu, for more than two weeks without charge, according to local journalists. Authorities had accused him of reporting false information in a story about plans for a pro-Islamist demonstration in the Puntland city of Bossasso, according to NUSOJ.

• UGANDA •

Uganda held multiparty presidential elections in February for the first time in President Yoweri Museveni's 20-year reign, with multiparty district council elections following in March. While Museveni easily won a new five-year term, according to official results, the election was marred by government harassment of the media and the leading presidential opponent, Kizza Besigye. Uganda generally boasts a diverse, sophisticated, and relatively free press, but during the campaign authorities set new restrictions on foreign journalists, expelled a prominent foreign correspondent, harassed radio stations airing opposition views, and pursued criminal charges against several journalists. Self-censorship was widespread, reporters said.

Throughout the campaign, government officials publicly criticized journalists and media outlets, particularly the leading independent newspaper, *The Monitor*, which they accused of favoring Besigye and his opposition Forum for Democratic Change (FDC) party. Besigye was jailed from mid-November 2005 until January 2 on treason, terrorism, and rape charges. Opposition supporters, international observers, and journalists denounced the charges as politically motivated. The charge of terrorism was dropped before the election, and Besigye was acquitted of rape two weeks after the vote. He still faced trial along with 22 co-defendants on treason charges.

Two journalists from the respected Kampala-based *Weekly Observer* faced charges of "promoting sectarianism" in connection with a 2005 article criticizing the government's prosecution of Besigye. The article reported FDC allegations that Museveni and a small group of army generals from the president's ethnic group had coordinated "an operation to keep Besigye in jail." Editor James Tumusiime and reporter Ssemujju Ibrahim Nganda stood by the story. The prosecution was put on hold in June when a constitutional challenge to the law, brought by Monitor Publications in 2005, came before the Supreme Court.

A new body known as the Media Centre was appointed by the government in early January to review foreign journalists' applications for accreditation during the election campaign. Information Minister James Nsaba Buturo said the step was taken because foreign journalists had become a "security threat," according to *The Monitor* and other local sources. Previously accredited journalists were told to re-register with the center.

The new head of the Media Centre, Robert Kabushenga, said that the accreditation of foreign journalists—previously an apolitical process—would be tied to an official evaluation of their work. Canadian freelance journalist Blake Lambert, who had reported from Uganda for more than two years, was denied re-accreditation and was deported on March 9. Lambert had worked for a variety of international media outlets, covering

donor nations' disenchantment with Museveni, the government's AIDS strategy, and the charges against Besigye. After Lambert was forced to leave, Information Minister Buturo said that "instead of developing the government, which is working in the interest of the people, he wrote stories to make people in other countries believe that Uganda is a bad country."

At least four times in February and March, security forces interrupted radio programs, detained journalists, and harassed staff. On February 21, police officers stormed the Catholic-owned station Radio Pacis FM in the northwestern town of Ediofe and halted a talk show featuring a high-ranking FDC official, Kassiano Wadri. The police accused the station of broadcasting "abusive language which could incite the public," a charge the talk show moderator denied. On March 20, police arrested two journalists from Open Gate FM in the eastern city of Mbale, accusing them of "destroying evidence" for failing to turn over a recording of a program in which an opposition member of parliament criticized the election of ruling party members. The journalists, who said that there was no recording because of a technical error, were released on bail.

Days before the March 3 district council elections, police raided the premises of the independent radio station Choice FM in the northern city of Gulu, confiscating audiotapes and detaining the station's programming manager overnight without charge. Police accused Choice FM of being a security threat because of a talk show in which opposition supporters criticized local military and civilian authorities. Ten days after the vote, police shut down Choice FM on orders from the Uganda Broadcasting Council, a government regulatory body. The council accused the station of operating without a license, which station officials denied. The station reopened in July after paying a fine of 4.95 million Ugandan shillings (US$2,700) and agreeing to personnel restrictions.

There were several reports during the election campaign that authorities had sought to block critical Web sites within the country. A week before the vote, the state-owned daily *New Vision* and other local media reported that a highly critical U.S.-based site, *Radio Katwe*, was blocked inside Uganda on the orders of the government-controlled Uganda Communications Commission. On the day of the vote, Monitor Publications said that its radio station, KFM, and the Web site of *The Monitor* were blocked because they were reporting an independent vote tally that showed Besigye polling closer to Museveni than official results reflected. Information Minister Buturo told CPJ that the government had not blocked *The Monitor* Web site, but he declined to comment on whether it had jammed KFM's broadcast.

In August, the elusive Lord's Resistance Army (LRA), a rebel group that has fought the Ugandan military in the north for more than 20 years and was responsible for massive human rights violations in the region, entered direct negotiations with the government for the first time in more than a decade, raising hopes that an end to the insurgency might be near. In the past, Ugandan officials have restricted journalists' access to regions affected by the LRA, and have accused local reporters who maintained contacts within the LRA of collaborating with the rebels. The negotiations stumbled, though, and there appeared to be no substantial change in journalists' ability to cover the region.

In October, the editor-in-chief and CEO of *New Vision*, William Pike, resigned from his position after more than 20 years at the paper. Though *New Vision* reported that Pike, a British national, left to "explore other business opportunities," Museveni had made it known that the newspaper had been "useless for a very long time." The news raised fears that *New Vision* would take a stronger pro-government slant.

ZIMBABWE

The state-owned daily *The Herald* marked President Robert Mugabe's 82nd birthday in February with a 16-page supplement of photos and "congratulatory messages from government departments." Such hagiographic and pro-government propaganda dominates the media landscape in Zimbabwe, where Mugabe's ZANU-PF party has waged a crackdown on the private press though a series of highly restrictive media laws. Having used these laws to close several of the country's private newspapers, the government turned its focus to the broadcast sector, jamming overseas radio signals and shutting a local news production company whose reports were transmitted into Zimbabwe via shortwave. They had been an important means of information in a country where radio and television stations are government-owned.

Voice of the People (VOP), a local company that produced news and commentary from an office in Harare, was shut down in a government raid in December 2005. According to local sources, authorities charged three staff members, the company's director, and six members of the board of directors under the Broadcasting Services Act, which prohibits the possession or use of broadcasting equipment without a license. VOP management said that the company did not own or operate such equipment; staffers produced programs that were then transmitted via shortwave from overseas.

In a victory for the press, a court in Harare threw out the VOP case in September, calling the prosecution a "circus" after a long series of government delays. In a number of press-related decisions over the past four years, Zimbabwean trial courts have demonstrated independence from the executive branch and turned back efforts to enforce some the country's most arbitrary media restrictions.

The Broadcasting Services Act requires that broadcast media obtain a license, but the government has not issued licenses to any private outlets since the law's inception in 2001. In January, the Ministry of Information announced it would amend the act to improve distribution of licenses to private broadcasters. Instead of doing so, however, the government sought to restrict the transmission of overseas news broadcasts into Zimbabwe via medium-wave and shortwave. A report in *The Herald* declared that broadcasters such as the U.S. government-funded broadcaster Voice of America (VOA) and the London-based SW Radio Africa had mounted "a one-sided campaign against Zimbabwe and ZANU-PF."

In June, the VOA said the medium-wave transmission of its popular Studio 7 service, which had been on the air in Zimbabwe for 90 minutes each weekday, was being blocked in Harare.

SW Radio Africa, a station run by exiled Zimbabwean journalists, also said its medium-wave broadcasts were blocked in Harare starting in June. The station added a medium-wave frequency in 2005 to counteract the jamming of its shortwave broadcasts, which began during the March 2005 parliamentary elections.

The government continued to tighten laws criminalizing free expression, increasing in March the fines under the Public Order and Security Act for "presidential insult" and "communicating falsehoods." In May, ZANU-PF introduced a bill in a parliamentary committee that would empower the government to intercept electronic communications on national security grounds. Local lawyers said the bill was so vaguely worded that it could be used broadly against journalists, political opponents, and human rights activists. Zimbabwe's deputy minister of information and publicity, Bright Matonga, told the United Nations news agency IRIN that the pending measure was "born out of realization that the Internet has been used to destroy the image of Zimbabwe and that this was made possible by the lack of regulation in cyber-communication."

The most notorious media law is the Access to Information and Protection of Privacy Act, known as AIPPA, which requires all journalists and media outlets to register with the government-controlled Media and Information Commission (MIC). The law has been used to silence several local publications, including the *Daily News*, the country's only independent daily, and the *Daily News on Sunday* in 2003. Zimbabwe's High Court ruled in February that the MIC must reconsider its July 2005 decision to deny registration to the banned papers. But by year's end, the MIC had yet to rule on the case.

In addition to official harassment, local journalists in Zimbabwe face the daily hardship of scraping together a living amid the country's economic collapse. Zimbabwe's inflation rate, the highest in the world, is threatening the financial survival of the country's remaining private papers, with soaring printing costs and a diminished spending capacity among the population.

The government regularly accuses unemployed journalists of working "illegally" for foreign news outlets, a charge carrying up to two years in prison under AIPPA. In January, police in the eastern town of Mutare detained a former *Daily News* journalist, Sidney Saize, for three days; he was accused of working illegally for the VOA and filing a "false" story alleging that ZANU-PF members had beaten local teachers. While Saize was released from custody without charges being filed in this case, he faced the same charge of violating AIPPA in connection with his work for the *Daily News*. Dozens of former journalists for the paper remained in a similar legal limbo.

Soon after Saize's arrest, State Security Minister Didymus Mutasa was quoted in the government-owned *Manica Post* as threatening journalists he said were "driven by the love for United States dollars and British pounds, which they are paid by foreign media houses to peddle lies." He added: "They should be warned that the net will soon close in on all those involved in these illegal activities."

AIPPA also makes it illegal for foreign correspondents to reside full-time in Zimbabwe, and it serves to restrict the entry of foreign journalists. In April, police in the southwestern border town of Plumtree arrested two journalists from BTV, the state broadcaster of neighboring Botswana. Reporter Beauty Mokoba and cameraman Koketso Seofela were accused of practicing journalism without a license and violating Zimbabwean immigration law. They had traveled to the region to report on an outbreak of foot-and-mouth disease in local livestock and the possible role of cross-border cattle rustling in driving the epidemic, according to BTV management. The journalists pleaded not guilty to the charges. On November 7, a Plumtree court convicted both journalists and fined each of them 5,000 Zimbabwean dollars (US$20).

BENIN

- Editor Fulric Richard Couao-Zotti and Managing Editor Virgile Linkpon of the private weekly *La Diaspora de Sabbat* were imprisoned for three days in September over a story about the president's family. The article claimed that President Yayi Boni's eldest son had a mental illness, according to Joseph Perzo Anago, head of the Benin media center, and local media reports. A presidential spokesman said the journalists had attacked Boni's family.

- In September, police detained overnight Cyril Saïzonou, director of the private daily *Djakpata*, and questioned him about a series of articles critical of the police and a top government official, according to CPJ sources. He was released without charge.

BURKINA FASO

- Security forces in April detained and questioned Antoine Bationo, a journalist with the private daily *Le Pays*, after he interviewed former soldiers accused of attempting a coup, according to local sources. The gendarmerie also summoned the paper's publication director, Boureima Jérémie Sigue, and questioned him for several hours. Both journalists were released without charge, but a seized recording device was not immediately returned.

- The examining magistrate investigating the 1998 murder of journalist Norbert Zongo dropped charges in July against the only indicted suspect, presidential guard member Marcel Kafando. The judge cited a lack of evidence. Press freedom and human rights activists expressed outrage at the decision and a lawyer for the victim's family said he would appeal. An independent commission of inquiry had concluded in May 1999 that Kafando was one of six "serious suspects" in the murder.

CAMEROON

- Arsonists set fire in January to the premises of the stillborn private radio station Freedom FM, founded by award-winning journalist Pius Njawe. The fire damaged the station's antenna. Police found a gasoline can at the scene and opened an investigation. The government had shuttered Freedom FM in May 2003, just as the station was about to launch. Its studios were unsealed in July 2005, but authorities did not honor their pledge, pursuant to a June 2005 agreement, to grant the station "provisional authorization" to operate, Njawe told CPJ.

- In March, at least one managing editor was sentenced to prison on a charge of criminal defamation after three private newspapers published lists of alleged "secret homosexuals." Jean-Pierre Amougou Belinga, director of *L'Anecdote*, was sentenced to four months in jail, fined 1 million CFA francs (US$2,000), and ordered to pay symbolic damages of 1 CFA franc (less than 1 U.S. cent) to Grégoire Owona, a cabinet minister. Owona filed a complaint against Belinga after his name appeared in one of the lists. Belinga filed an appeal and stood by his decision to publish the names, claiming to be a crusader against homosexuality in Cameroonian society.

- Agnès Taile, the host of a popular news talk show with the private radio station Sweet FM in Douala, was dragged at knifepoint from her home on November 6 by three unidentified assailants, who choked her, beat her, and left her in a ravine, according to local media reports and the Cameroon National Journalists Union. On the last show before the attack, she asked listeners to assess the record of President Paul Biya's party, in power for 24 years. Tailé had received several phone threats weeks before the attack, local journalists said.

CHAD

- Rebel fighters who briefly seized the central town of Mongo abducted journalist Eliakim Vanambyl, editor of the N'Djamena-based radio station FM Liberté, in April. Vanambyl had traveled to Mongo to report on a human rights conference. He was released six days later, and the reason for his capture remained unclear. Vanambyl was not mistreated while in captivity, local journalists said.

- Also in April, security forces in the capital, N'Djamena, detained and badly beat René Dillah Yombirim, a correspondent for the BBC and the state-owned Radio-diffusion Nationale Tchadienne, following an attempt by rebels to overthrow the government. It was unclear what motivated the attack. Security forces confiscated Yombirim's recording equipment and listened to recordings of his interviews, according to journalist and human rights activist Dobian Assingar.

- At the end of April, Iranian-born journalist and then-head of the Chadian Union of Private Radios Tchanguis Vatankah was jailed for three weeks after he signed a union press release calling for a postponement of the May presidential elections. Vatankah told CPJ that authorities had dropped a threat to deport him after he promised to keep out of politics and to step down as the head of the union. The threat dated from 2005, when Vatankah, founder of the community station Radio Brakos, had been jailed for two months.

- Evariste Ngaralbaye, a journalist for the private weekly *Notre Temps*, was jailed October 27 for four days without charge at the gendarmerie, the national police headquarters, in the capital, N'Djamena. Police pressed him to reveal his sources for an editorial critical of the government's conduct of its war against rebels in eastern Chad. The article alleged that the gendarmerie and the army widely conscripted underage youths. Ngaralbaye was released because of procedural irregularities, Justice Minister Abderamane Djasnabaye told CPJ.

- On November 13, authorities barred private newspapers and radio stations from reporting on issues "likely to threaten public order," according to a government statement. This was part of a state of emergency introduced in response to clashes between Arab and non-Arab communities in eastern Chad. The measures were taken initially for 12 days and then extended to six months. Newspapers in N'Djamena suspended publication for a week in protest, or published black strips to show where text had been censored, according to local journalists.

COMOROS

- Paramilitary police detained Aboubacar Mchangama, director of the independent weekly *L'Archipel*, for two days in March in the capital, Moroni, over an article detailing discontent among army officers. He was charged with "divulging military secrets," according to the pan-African news agency Panapress.

EQUATORIAL GUINEA

- On May 3, World Press Freedom Day, CPJ named Equatorial Guinea one of the 10 Most Censored Countries in the world, ranking it behind only North Korea, Burma, and Turkmenistan. Criticism of President Teodoro Obiang Nguema Mbasogo's brutal regime is not tolerated, the survey found. Broadcast media are state owned, except for one private station owned by the president's son. A handful of private newspapers officially exist but rarely publish due to financial and political pressures. Foreign correspondents have been denied visas or expelled without official explanation.

ERITREA

- CPJ named Eritrea one of the 10 Most Censored Countries in the world. It is the only country in sub-Saharan Africa without a single private media outlet, CPJ's survey found. The government's repressive policies have left the tiny Horn of Africa nation largely hidden from international scrutiny and with almost no local access to independent information. The handful of foreign correspondents in the capital, Asmara, are subject to intensive monitoring by authorities.

- Authorities required all foreigners in June to obtain permits to travel within the country, in addition to the usual visas needed to enter the country, Agence France-Presse reported and several CPJ sources confirmed. The new restrictions were at least partly aimed at curtailing foreign journalists from reporting outside the capital, the sources said.

- At least 23 Eritrean journalists were jailed or held against their will when CPJ conducted its annual census of imprisoned journalists on December 1. Fifteen had been held since a vicious 2001 crackdown shuttered the independent press. Another eight journalists, all working for state media, were detained in November.

GABON

- The government-controlled National Communication Council allowed the private newspaper *L'Autre Journal* to resume publishing in July, according to the state-owned daily *L'Union*. No official reason was given, a local journalist told CPJ. The decision came two and a half years after *L'Autre Journal* was banned for articles that might "disturb public order," amid a broad crackdown on the media. The newspaper appears intermittently and had published only two editions before it was forced to close.

- The state-controlled National Council on Communications banned the private weekly *Les Echos du Nord* for three months in September over an editorial that criticized the government's handling of a territorial dispute with Equatorial Guinea, according to local and international media. The article also suggested that there was fighting within the government in anticipation of the end of Gabonese President Omar Bongo's rule, and that the strife was indicative of a dying regime. The director of the paper, Désiré Ename, went on a hunger strike to protest the ruling.

- Norbert Mezui, editor of the private Libreville-based weekly *Nku'u Le Messager*, was jailed on October 18 and forced to serve a 21-day sentence for defamation. His sentence was suddenly implemented three years after it was handed down and despite a pending appeal. The defamation charges stemmed from a 2003 article alleging mismanagement of state treasury funds.

GUINEA

- In February, the National Communication Council, an official regulatory body known by its French acronym, CNC, suspended the private bimonthly newspaper *Les Echos* for two months and banned two of its journalists from working during that time. The council cited "the publication of false news and an attack on the honor and dignity" of a government minister, Kiridi Bangoura. Bangoura brought a complaint against the paper after it published an article accusing him of "becoming rich off the back of Guineans."

- The CNC suspended the semimonthly private newspaper *L'Enquêteur* for two months for publishing allegedly "tendentious and unfounded information" that could endanger national security. The offending article spoke of divisions among senior government leaders, corruption, and a lack of political dialogue, according to a CPJ source. The suspension was imposed in April.

- Guinea became the last country in the West African subregion to allow private broadcasting. The CNC allocated frequencies in August to the country's first two private radio stations, ending a 48-year-long state broadcasting monopoly. Legislation liberalizing the airwaves was passed in December 2005.

- Managing Director Ibrahima Sory Dieng and Editor-in-Chief Alhassane Souare of the state-owned newspaper *Horoya* were suspended indefinitely in October by Minister of Information Aboubacar Sylla for not publishing a photograph of President Lassana Conte. According to news reports, the photograph was supposed to have appeared alongside the president's speech in the Independence Day edition of the paper.

GUINEA BISSAU

- In June, police arrested Augusto Queba Barbosa, a reporter for the private radio station Bombolom FM in the southwestern town of Bolama, after he broadcast a report accusing a local police officer of violence against a woman, according to Panapress and a local source. Barbosa was accused of broadcasting "false news." He was beaten while in custody and detained for 24 hours before being released without charge, the local source told CPJ.

KENYA

- Police raided two alternative newspapers in February, detaining journalists as well as vendors. Local journalists linked the attack on the *Weekly Citizen* to a story alleging that President Mwai Kibaki was "senile" and no longer in control of the government. Reasons for the raid on *The Independent* were unclear. Ezekiel Mutua, secretary-general of the Kenya Union of Journalists, said the government, amid widespread accusations of corruption, was seeking excuses to intimidate journalists. The alternative press is known for reporting on sex and political scandals.

- In February, police detained three journalists with *The Standard*, Kenya's oldest daily newspaper, over a story alleging that Kibaki had held a secret meeting with a fired former minister to bring him back into the shaky government. The weekend edition's managing director, Chaacha Mwita, copy editor Dennis Onyango, and reporter Ayub Savula were charged two days later with publishing "alarming statements" and released on bail. Their trial began in August. In late September, local media reported that the state had dropped the case after two key witnesses failed to show up in court.

- Armed and masked police officers conducted a midnight raid at the offices of *The Standard* on March 2, harassing staff, vandalizing equipment, and setting fire to roughly 20,000 copies of the next day's edition. Internal Security Minister John Michuki told journalists that the raid was carried out to protect state security, while a police statement said the newspaper had accepted money to print "a series of fabricated articles aimed at achieving instability." A similar raid was made on the offices of the Kenya Television Network (KTN), which is owned by the Standard Group; several staffers were detained, and as many as 40 computer hard drives were confiscated.

- In May, Michuki warned journalists that he would use force against local media outlets that criticized the government, according to local and international news reports. Referring to the March raids on *The Standard* and KTN, Michuki said, "I have no apologies to make on the destruction that the government meted out." He said he would order "a repeat performance to any media house which is out to destroy the government."

LIBERIA

- Journalists Morris Gayboe of *The Informer* and Charles Yates of *The Inquirer* were assaulted by security forces in April while covering a police eviction of street vendors in the capital, Monrovia, according to media reports and the Press Union of Liberia.

- George Watkins, of the Catholic Church-owned Radio Veritas, was assaulted by Special Security Services (SSS) agents in May while reporting on the alleged enlistment of a former rebel commander by the SSS, according to the independent daily *The Analyst* and the Press Union of Liberia.

- SSS agents harassed and briefly detained four local journalists at the Executive Mansion in Monrovia in June. Alphonsus Zeon, secretary-general of the Press Union, told CPJ that the journalists were trying to report on the alleged dismissal of several senior SSS personnel.

MALAWI

- Three journalists for the private weekly *The Chronicle* were detained for one day in May and charged with criminal libel in connection with an article alleging that Malawi's then-attorney general was involved in the theft of a computer.

- General Manager Jika Nkolokosa and reporter Maxwell Ng'ambi of the private media group Blantyre Newspapers Limited were charged with criminal libel in May. The charge stemmed from a December 2005 article in Blantyre's weekly *Malawi News*, which alleged that the health minister at that time, Hetherwick Ntaba, was being audited for failing to account for public funds, according to the Media Institute of Southern Africa.

MOZAMBIQUE

- In January, a Maputo court convicted Anibal dos Santos Jr., known as Anibalzinho, for the second time in the 2000 murder of investigative journalist Carlos Cardoso. He was sentenced to almost 30 years in prison for recruiting Cardoso's killers. Anibalzinho, who twice escaped from custody, was convicted in absentia in 2003. The Supreme Court had granted him a retrial in December 2004.

- A prosecutor in the western district of Manica ordered three journalists from the community newspaper *Mabarwe* detained in May after a local businessman accused their paper of defaming him, according to local news reports. They were held for a week, then released without charge.

SENEGAL

- A high-profile criminal case against Madiambal Diagne, editor of the independent daily *Le Quotidien*, was dropped in May on a procedural issue. Diagne had been charged in connection with articles about alleged executive interference in the judiciary and corruption in the customs service.

- Also in May, attackers beat Pape Cheikh Fall, a correspondent for the private radio station RFM in the central city of Mbacke, with metal cables, causing head and back injuries. RFM's parent group, Futurs Médias, linked the attack to a report criticizing a local religious leader's foray into politics.

- Mustapha Sow, managing editor of the private newspaper *L'Office*, was imprisoned in June for two weeks following a conviction for defaming a local businessman. A court sentenced him to six months; Sow was granted bail after his lawyer filed an appeal.

SIERRA LEONE

- Attorney General Frederick Carew said in February he would not pursue manslaughter charges against Fatmata Hassan, a ruling party member of parliament, three of her children, and two others accused of assaulting journalist Harry Yansaneh in May 2005. A judicial inquest had found that the attack contributed to Yansaneh's death from kidney failure in July 2005, and ordered the six arrested for manslaughter. But Carew told CPJ there was insufficient evidence to prosecute. At the time of his death, Yansaneh was acting editor of the private daily newspaper *For Di People*.

- In August, authorities announced they would seek extradition of Hassan's three children from the United Kingdom on charges that they assaulted Yansaneh with intent to wound. This move followed local and international pressure, which peaked during the July anniversary of Yansaneh's death.

SOUTH AFRICA

- In February, the Johannesburg High Court banned Sunday newspapers from publishing cartoons depicting the Prophet Muhammad, ruling that they were an affront to the dignity of Muslims. A local Muslim group had sought the injunction after one of the cartoons appeared in the independent weekly *Mail & Guardian*. Ferial Hafferjee, the *Mail & Guardian's* editor, received threats after the cartoon appeared.

- The government approved a controversial bill in August that would bring print and broadcast media under the Film and Publications Board and subject them to potential censorship. Local press freedom groups said they would consider a constitutional challenge if parliament approved the bill. In October, the government announced it would delay the bill until 2007 to allow for more consultation, according to news reports.

TOGO

- In October, unidentified attackers savagely beat Dimas Dzikodo, managing editor of the critical independent weekly *Le Forum de la Semaine*, after knocking him from his motorcycle in the capital, Lomé, local sources told CPJ. They sprayed an unidentified liquid from an aerosol can into his face and forced him to drink another liquid, which he managed to spit out. Dzikodo was taken to a hospital. Dzikodo had been previously targeted for his journalistic work, notably in 2003, when he spent two weeks in jail.

ZAMBIA

- In February, a court dismissed a criminal case against Fred M'membe, editor of Zambia's leading daily, *The Post*, after the state decided not to prosecute. M'membe, a 1995 recipient of CPJ's International Press Freedom Award, was charged with insulting the president in November 2005. He was released on bail after six hours in police custody.

- Two journalists working for Radio Chikuni, a community station in the southern district of Monze, were arrested and charged in March with publishing "false news with intent to cause fear and alarm to the public." The journalists were detained overnight by police and released on bond, according to the Media Institute of Southern Africa. The charge stemmed from a broadcast about a young boy found dead after going missing. The body was said to be mutilated, and local residents suspected that the boy was the victim of a ritual killing.

Leftists Lean on the Latin American Media   60

Many of Latin America's new leaders are leftists, populists, and liberal progressives. But in their relations with the press they borrow heavily from the region's deep-rooted authoritarian culture.

by Carlos Lauría

PHOTOS

Section break: Reuters/Daniel Aguilar – *A Mexican police officer tries to seize a camera from AP photographer Eduardo Verdugo during May unrest in the village of San Salvador Atenco. Analysis (next): AP/Lucas Nunez – An image of Simón Bolívar over his shoulder, Hugo Chávez addresses Paraguayan university students in April.*

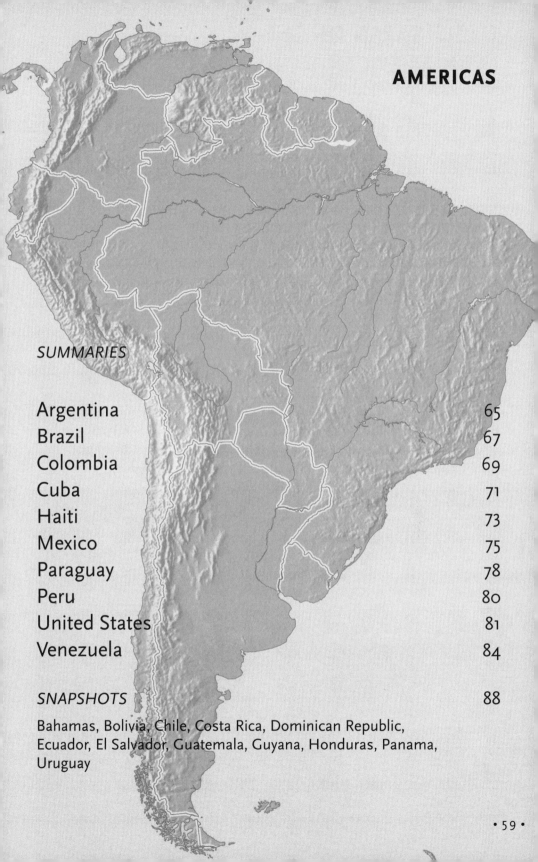

AMERICAS

LEFTISTS LEAN ON THE LATIN AMERICAN MEDIA

by Carlos Lauría

LATIN AMERICA'S NEW LEFTIST LEADERS MAY TRY TO PORTRAY THEMSELVES as good news for the press, using the rhetoric of liberal democracy. But political and media analysts say these recently installed left-wing administrations are deeply rooted in the region's longstanding culture of authoritarianism.

Independent journalists had hoped that the new breed of populist political leaders that emerged over the past six years would herald greater press freedom. Many ordinary people in Latin America had become disenchanted with traditional politics after the failure in the 1990s of free-market policies, promoted by the United States and the International Monetary Fund, to deliver improved living standards. In Venezuela, Brazil, Argentina, Uruguay, Bolivia, Nicaragua, and Ecuador, citizens elected reformist presidents who are redefining domestic and foreign policy.

The new leaders, some of whom are stridently anti-American, are a mixed bag of leftists, populists, social democrats, and liberal progressives. Yet they share one thing: intolerance of a critical press. Independent journalists have found themselves labeled enemies of the people in Venezuela, and they have been denied access to official news and events in Argentina. This has not prevented the media from unearthing facts that governments would prefer to keep buried, but it has made for a bruising relationship between presidents and the press.

"A number of leaders in Latin America consider the media to be powers

The new leaders are a mixed bag of leftists, populists, social democrats, and liberal progressives.

that are dangerous for democracy, but they forget that the press is a form of popular representation for citizens," said Fernando Ruiz, a professor of journalism and democracy at Austral University in Argentina.

For their part, leftist leaders point to the concentration of media ownership in the region and contend that transnational conglomerates skew coverage in favor of business or other special interest groups. In the past 15 years, in fact, some large corporations have consolidated control, particularly in broadcasting. These include Grupo Cisneros in Venezuela, Televisa in Mexico, Globo in Brazil, and Grupo Clarín in Argentina.

In other Latin American countries, media outlets are often controlled by a small number of family-owned companies, some of them tied to political parties or corporations. An example is the Bolivian television station Unitel, based in Santa Cruz, the center of Bolivia's conservative opposition. Unitel's owners also have interests in banking and agriculture, and they enjoy close ties with opposition political parties.

Bolivia and Venezuela provide the starkest examples of confrontation between leftists and the press. Presidents Hugo Chávez Frías in Venezuela and Evo Morales in Bolivia have railed against the private media, accusing them of aligning with antigovernment forces. Some media proprietors in Bolivia and Venezuela have indeed dropped the pretense of objectivity to assume the mantle of the opposition. The day after Morales took office, news shows on Unitel described inauguration celebrations in terms that Morales supporters found discriminatory. Remarks such as, "in Congress, Aymara is the only language," and "booze during the celebrations at Evo's house" were used on the air. By adopting opposition rhetoric, media outlets became easier targets for intolerant leaders.

"In some Latin American countries there is a highly negative situation," said Eduardo Ulibarri, a former Costa Rican newspaper editor who is the president of the press freedom group Instituto de Prensa y Libertad de Expresión. "Alleged independent media are putting narrow interests above basic professional and ethical standards, while supposed democratic governments are manipulating freedom of expression through all sorts of pressures, both open and subtle."

Chávez and Morales have taken the frontal approach. Having survived a coup attempt, crippling strikes, and a recall effort since taking office in 1998,

Chávez consolidated power with his re-election on December 3. He has introduced legislation to counter his opponents and silence his critics in the press. Changes in the penal code, introduced in 2005, and provisions of the Law of Social Responsibility in Radio and Television contain vaguely worded restrictions that severely limit freedom of expression. One provision of the social responsibility law, for example, forbids "graphic descriptions or images of real violence" on the air from 5 a.m. to 11 p.m., except when the broadcast is live and the content is either "indispensable" or emerges unexpectedly.

Morales, an Aymara Indian and former coca farmer, has borrowed from Chávez's script. "The number one enemies of Evo Morales are the majority of the media," he said in September, a day after his government published a list of Bolivia's most hostile media outlets. The list provided names and affiliations of hard-line opponents in television, radio, and newspapers. Morales claimed the media were biased against his administration and participated in an "anti-Evo campaign."

In Bolivia and Venezuela, some media outlets have dropped any pretense of objectivity.

Instead of demonizing the media Chávez-style as "coup plotters" and "fascists," Argentine President Néstor Kirchner and Uruguayan President Tabaré Ramón Vázquez Rosas refer to the press as the "unelected political opposition." Journalists in Argentina and Uruguay, in turn, accuse their governments of deliberately blurring the lines between opposition and critical press.

One Argentine analyst finds a basis in both views. "There is nothing wrong with a media outlet having a position of empathy or opposition toward a government, but it is wrong to adjust the reality of the information to a certain ideological profile. And that is what's happening today in Argentina," Nelson Castro, a renowned broadcast journalist and ombudsman for the weekly *Perfil*, said in an interview.

Government tolerance of criticism has worn thin. Kirchner's administration has orchestrated state advertising, a vital source of revenue for all of the country's media, in ways that punish critical news outlets and reward supportive ones. Argentine leaders who feel targeted by critical journalists block access to official sources and events; politicians angered by news stories make hostile calls to reporters and editors.

"Sometimes Chávez, Kirchner, and Morales want to eradicate critics," said Ruiz, the Argentine professor. "In order to build consensus, these leaders use strong state media at the service of their governments, and they control private media that support their policies by funneling official advertising. It is an attempt to strangle the critics. This represents a step backward in terms of democratic quality in the region."

In Brazil, scandals at all levels of government haunted President Luiz Inácio Lula da Silva, known popularly as Lula, and strained his relationship with the press. The print media in particular harshly criticized Lula's failure to respond to allegations of corruption. Lula declined to give any interviews, alleging that press reports were excessive and unproven. After Lula won re-election on October 29, some officials in his Workers' Party affirmed their commitment to press freedom in an attempt to ease tensions with the print media. But during victory celebrations in São Paulo, signs along the major artery Paulista Avenue read, "The people defeated the media." In Brasília, Workers' Party militants shoved and insulted journalists covering a victory party.

Kirchner has used state advertising to punish critical news outlets and reward supportive ones.

The landscape is not yet clear in Nicaragua and Ecuador—both of which elected left-leaning leaders in November—but some conflict emerged during the campaigns.

The press divided along party lines in Nicaragua's presidential race, won by Sandinista leader Daniel Ortega. Ortega enjoyed the support of a few media outlets, but the influential Managua-based daily *La Prensa* and other news outlets favored conservative challenger Eduardo Montealegre. The newspaper ran columns and commentaries by U.S. officials, including the U.S. ambassador to Nicaragua, Paul A. Trivelli, that criticized Ortega and the Sandinista party. Ecuadorian Rafael Correa, the self-described Christian leftist who won a presidential runoff, had a contentious relationship with the press during his campaign, asserting that reporters were uninformed and needed to be enlightened.

In polarized situations, some leftist leaders have used state-owned media to further their political agendas, journalists across the region said. This is often in violation of the law, many contend, since state media were created to serve the public, not the interests of a particular administration.

In Bolivia, Morales was blunt in saying that state radio and television were the weapons of his government in thwarting what he saw as private media distortions. In Argentina, officials cancelled two independent shows on public broadcast stations, then failed to respond to allegations of government censorship and editorial interference.

Critical journalists said that Chávez frequently relied on state media during the 2006 campaign; his simultaneous, nationwide radio and television broadcasts sought to overshadow private news coverage. The Venezuelan government owns three television stations: Telesur, Venezolana de Televisión (VTV), and ViVe. Launched in July 2005, Telesur is a 24-hour Spanish-language satellite station controlled by Venezuela (the state owns 51 percent) and financed by the governments of Argentina, Uruguay, Bolivia, and Cuba. Chávez promoted Telesur as an alternative

Critics say the publicly funded Telesur should be called 'TeleChávez.'

to U.S. networks such as CNN and Fox News; the station's president, Andrés Izarra, said that the Latin American network was "looking for greater diversity and deeper views on subjects." Telesur General Director Aram Aharonian went further, proclaiming in an interview, "It is the first time in Latin America that the state has returned to projects that serve the citizenry." But critics say Telesur should really be called "TeleChávez," as the government funnels public funds to finance a network that is bound to give leftist leaders supportive coverage.

Using resources from his nation's oil profits, Chávez is exerting regional influence as well. Venezuela will finance a network of dozens of community radio stations across Bolivia, Morales said in September. The Bolivian leader also revealed plans to launch in 2007 his own version of Chávez's weekly radio show, "Aló Presidente," during which the president answers listeners' questions.

Leftist leaders' intolerance of criticism in the media stems from a culture of authoritarianism that, whether masked or submerged, is still alive in many Latin American democracies that were ruled by military regimes not so long ago, analysts said. This helps explain why one of the only conservative leaders still popular in the region, Colombian President Álvaro Uribe Vélez, reacts in a similar way. Uribe, who won re-election by a landslide in March, has frequently attacked the independent media and, at times, treated critics as traitors. "Dishonest" and "harmful" to national interests Uribe labeled one recent report about his country's intelligence service. It's not so different, as it turns out, from the "enemies" that leftist leaders find in Bolivia and elsewhere.

• • • • • • • • •

Carlos Lauría is CPJ's Americas program coordinator.

ARGENTINA

President Néstor Kirchner's administration continued its practice of funneling government advertising to friendly news outlets and withholding it from critical media. Amid increased tension between Kirchner and the press, authorities were also accused of editorial interference in the abrupt cancellation of two independent shows on state-owned broadcast networks.

The national government's advertising budget increased from 127 million pesos (US$41 million) in 2005 to 160 million pesos (US$52 million) even as controls on spending remained loose. Asociación por los Derechos Civiles (ADC), a nonpartisan group that promotes constitutional rights, said that the allocation of state advertising in the "absence of clear rules" was causing serious damage to press freedom.

Editorial Perfil, the nation's largest magazine publisher, sought a court injunction against the executive branch in July, alleging that the government discriminated against the company in retaliation for its critical reporting. The company said its weeklies, *Noticias* and *Fortuna*, and its Sunday paper, *Perfil*, were denied government advertising and their journalists were barred access to official sources and events.

Perfil and ADC, which filed a supporting brief, argued that the government was manipulating the media in defiance of free expression guarantees contained in Articles 14 and 32 of the Argentine Constitution, and Article 13 of the American Convention on Human Rights. In its brief, ADC said that the legislature should adopt regulations and objective criteria for government advertising.

In September, Sen. Ricardo Gómez Diez of the provincial party Partido Renovador, introduced a bill aimed at ensuring objective distribution of state advertising. The bill would guarantee that 15 percent of state advertising be shared among all media, with the balance distributed according to circulation for publications and ratings for broadcasters.

Two independent shows on public broadcast systems were unexpectedly canceled. José "Pepe" Eliaschev said his radio show was pulled suddenly in January after his supervisor told him an order had come "from above." His show "Esto Que Pasa," on state-owned Radio Nacional, had been on the air since 1985. Eliaschev, who also writes a column for *Perfil*, is a harsh critic of the government.

The weekly television news show "Desayuno," hosted by Víctor Hugo Morales on state Channel 7, was canceled in July. Morales said an executive told him the station

Country summaries in this chapter were reported and written by Americas Program Coordinator **Carlos Lauría**, Research Associate **María Salazar**, Program Consultant **Sauro González Rodríguez**, and Washington Representative **Frank Smyth**. The Robert R. McCormick Tribune Foundation provided substantial support toward CPJ's work in the Americas in 2006.

AMERICAS

wanted to control the editorial stance of its programming. Morales covered issues sensitive to the government, including the conflict with Uruguay over construction of pulp paper mills and the removal of a deputy-elect accused of human rights abuses.

Both Channel 7 and Radio Nacional are part of the National System of Public Media (SNMP). According to the May 2001 presidential decree creating SNMP, the public media system is designed to "ensure the Argentine people the right to plural, impartial, and truthful information." On August 3, CPJ wrote a letter to Kirchnez expressing concern that authorities had not clarified the motives behind the abrupt cancellations and urging him to publicly explain the reasons. Kirchner did not respond, nor did the administration offer a public explanation.

The moves come amid Argentine officials' increasing intolerance of press criticism. In the summer, for instance, Kirchner and his wife, Sen. Cristina Fernández, sought to discredit journalists who criticized new laws allowing expenditure changes without congressional approval. The president labeled the press "perverse" and lacking "intellectual quality."

A media company owner and a prominent columnist, both outspoken critics of Kirchner's administration, received anonymous death threats in September. Joaquín Morales Solá, columnist for the daily *La Nación*, got two threatening telephone calls one day after Kirchner responded to criticism by reading aloud at a public event a 1978 article in which the columnist purportedly praised former dictator Jorge Videla. Morales Solá told CPJ he did not write the story attributed to him by the president. He said one caller warned him to stop his critical work "if you don't want to see the seed from below."

Jorge Fontevecchia, chief executive officer of Editorial Perfil, received intimidating e-mails and calls that same week, according to news reports. Referring to the executive's home, one e-mail message said, "Recoleta is a nice area to live, a nice area to explode a bomb. ... Stop bothering the president."

Some independent journalists said they received hostile phone calls from officials after critical stories, followed by subsequent denials of interviews and access to information or state facilities. Argentina's chief of cabinet, Alberto Fernández, said that the government is not attacking the press. "The press has an opinion, we have a different one. What we do is expose journalists' contradictions," he told the daily *La Nación*.

Of the eight people convicted in the 1997 murder of photographer José Luis Cabezas, only one remained in prison by late year. Two were freed on parole in 2006, and a third was moved into home confinement. The defendants took advantage of legal provisions that allowed each year they served to be computed as two years while their appeals were pending.

Cabezas, a photographer for *Noticias* magazine, was brutally murdered in one of Argentina's most exclusive beach resorts. Armed men abducted Cabezas while he was leaving a party where he had photographed powerful business tycoon Alfredo Yabrán, reputed boss of the Argentine mafia. The men shot Cabezas twice in the head, placed his body in his car, and ignited it. Yabrán committed suicide in 1998, after being subpoenaed to testify in the murder trial.

· **BRAZIL** ·

Although freedom of expression is enshrined in Brazil's 1988 constitution, journalists' ability to cover the news was impeded by judges whose legal interpretations effectively restricted the press. During the run-up to the October 1 general election, electoral courts banned media outlets from covering corruption allegations against political candidates.

Many journalists also worked in dangerous conditions. Even reporters in large government and business centers such as Brasília, São Paulo, and Rio de Janeiro court risk whenever they report on organized crime, drug trafficking, or political corruption. On August 12, TV Globo reporter Guilherme de Azevedo Portanova and technician Alexandre Coelho Calado were seized in São Paulo by members of the First Capital Command (PCC) criminal gang. Calado was freed later that day with a recorded message demanding improved prison conditions. The kidnappers warned that Portanova, who had covered a wave of PCC attacks in May, would be killed if TV Globo did not broadcast the message. After consulting international security agencies, TV Globo aired the three-minute tape on August 13, and Portanova was released unharmed the next day.

In the Northeast interior and in the region bordering Paraguay, journalism and politics often intertwine, a volatile situation that exposes journalists to threats, attacks, and murder. In rural areas, where radio is the primary source of news, commentators routinely campaign for political candidates, attack political adversaries, and use the airwaves as a springboard for their own political aspirations. In 2006, the general elections again saw journalists and radio hosts seeking and winning political office.

Outspoken and highly partisan, these radio commentators have become targets of violence. Five radio journalists have been killed in as many years in the Northeast alone, making that region one of the deadliest for journalists in the Americas. The slayings prompted CPJ to dispatch a mission to the Northeastern states of Ceará and Pernambuco in August.

In "Radio Rage," a special report released in October, CPJ documented widespread abuse of 1998 legislation intended to diversify radio broadcasting by allotting radio licenses to community-based nonprofits. Instead, CPJ and other researchers found, politicians have come to own and control hundreds of these "nonprofit" stations. Nearly nine out of every 10 community radio applicants presented for parliamentary approval in 2002, for example, were not legitimate nonprofits, said Israel Bayma, a University of

Brasília researcher whose work has been cited nationally. Despite explicit regulatory bans on political propaganda, these stations function as mouthpieces for politicians at nearly every level of government.

The misuse of the community broadcasting law has clogged the regulatory system and slowed the approval of legitimate applicants. Community organizations complained that ANATEL, the telecommunications regulatory agency, closed dozens of community radio stations operating without broadcasting licenses and confiscated their equipment. Several thousand community stations now on the air have formally requested licenses, but the approval process takes many years. Government officials blamed the delays on the difficulties in identifying legitimate community stations, as opposed to those controlled by politicians and businessmen.

Politicians also own many commercial broadcast outlets, concessions for which are auctioned by the federal government. The Institute for the Development of Journalism (PROJOR), a media ethics and press freedom organization, reported in 2005 that 51 out of the 513 deputies in the lower chamber of the Congress were partners or directors in radio and TV stations nationwide. PROJOR filed a complaint with the federal attorney general in October 2005, arguing that political ownership of broadcast outlets violated Article 54 of the Constitution, which says federal legislators cannot be affiliated "with a company that has obtained a concession for a public service." The attorney general's preliminary analysis found no unlawful activity.

Political control of all forms of radio has given rise to a stridently partisan, attack-oriented form of commentary. "Almost all radio stations belong to political groups, and these groups confront each other through the stations," said Aquiles Lopes, a reporter with the Recife-based daily *Diário de Pernambuco*. The confrontational commentary, in turn, has generated threats and attacks against journalists, he said.

Brazilian electoral law strictly regulates the distribution of political advertising in print and broadcast media during the run-up to an election. Newspapers are allowed to publish an opinion favorable to a candidate, political party, or coalition, provided that the article is not paid for by a political campaign. As for broadcast outlets, electoral legislation bans radio and TV stations from "broadcasting political propaganda or disseminating an opinion favorable or contrary to a candidate, political party, or coalition" in the three months prior to an election. A system of regional electoral courts is charged with ruling on complaints.

The electoral provisions, as well as others related to the honor and reputations of political candidates, are frequently abused by politicians who claim that any criticisms or allegations of corruption are designed to favor their rivals. They frequently succeed in their complaints. On September 30, for example, an electoral judge in Amazonas state shut down the Manaus-based channel TV A Crítica for 24 hours in response to a complaint filed by incumbent Gov. Eduardo Braga. During a September 27 debate that Braga did not attend, TV A Crítica introduced segments with reports about corruption allegations in the governor's administration. The judge ruled that the reports were electoral propaganda offensive to Braga's honor and dignity.

Other, harsh provisions restricting the work of the press remained on the books. Both the penal code and the infamous 1967 Press Law—the latter approved under a military regime—criminalize defamation and slander. The Press Law sets prison terms of six months to three years for slander, while the penal code calls for imprisonment of three months to a year for defamation. Defamation lawsuits against the media—mostly civil complaints—have numbered in the thousands over the last few years, according to local news reports. Businessmen, politicians, and public officials often file multiple lawsuits against news outlets and journalists in an effort to strain their financial resources and force them to halt their criticisms. Plaintiffs seek disproportionately large amounts of money for "moral and material damages."

In the name of protecting privacy and reputations, judges routinely issue injunctions banning media outlets from covering corruption allegations involving public officials, politicians, and businessmen. On May 8, for instance, a judge in Campo Grande, capital of Mato Grosso do Sul state, granted gubernatorial candidate André Puccinelli an injunction against the local daily *Correio do Estado*. Puccinelli sought to constrain the paper from reporting on a federal money-laundering probe first disclosed in the April 25 edition of the large São Paulo daily *O Estado de S.Paulo*. Following up on the report, *Correio do Estado* had sought comment from Puccinelli, who denied any wrongdoing. The judge granted Puccinelli's request and ordered *Correio do Estado* to meet the requirements of "objectivity of information," "verification of sources," and "impartiality and independence in news reporting" in its coverage of Puccinelli. If it failed to do so, it would be fined 500 reals (US$230) for each copy of any story that fell short of those criteria. The paper appealed the ruling.

The concentration of media ownership remained a concern, particularly in a broadcasting sector dominated by the Organizações Globo group, one of the world's largest media companies and the perennial national leader in advertising revenue. In some of the largest domestic markets, a dominant media group controls newspapers, network and cable TV channels, radio stations, and Internet portals, limiting the diversity of news offerings for Brazilians.

· **COLOMBIA** ·

Investigative reporting and in-depth coverage of the civil conflict again fell victim to fear in the country's most troubled areas, where threats and intimidation forced at least seven provincial journalists to flee their homes. The climate of intimidation is the legacy of years of murderous attacks on journalists. With 39 journalists killed since 1992, Colombia ranks as the fourth deadliest country in the world for the press, according to the CPJ analysis "Deadly News," published in September.

Two provincial reporters were murdered in retaliation for their work in 2006, and CPJ is investigating the circumstances surrounding a third slaying. The number of journalist murders has declined in the past three years, sparking a debate over whether government actions have slowed the killings or, as press organizations affirm, widespread self-censorship has taken hold instead.

Colombian reporters said self-censorship continued to be pervasive in vast areas of the country where state protection was minimal and the presence of illegal armed groups high. Recent reports by local and international organizations, including CPJ's 2005 account "Untold Stories," found that threats and attacks from all sides in the ongoing civil war had caused the press to seriously restrict coverage of armed conflict, human rights abuses, organized crime, drug trafficking, and corruption.

With coverage of important issues often limited, a CPJ delegation traveled to Colombia before the May 28 presidential election to meet with President Álvaro Uribe Vélez and outline its concerns. The delegation, led by CPJ's Joel Simon and Carlos Lauría, urged the president to make a statement about threats against the press.

Uribe, who was later re-elected in a landslide, told the delegation that he supported the work of provincial journalists and that any government official who impedes their reporting "is committing a crime against democracy." The Colombian president said that while his administration dislikes media outlets interviewing guerrilla and paramilitary fighters, it respects their right to do so. Provincial officials and military commanders have long denounced journalists who use non-official sources, often linking the reporters to the illegal armed groups. CPJ research shows that these "links" are sometimes followed by violent attacks.

Twice in 2006, shadowy organizations tried to connect prominent journalists to one side in Colombia's civil war. In March, a group issued a video that sought to tie independent television reporter Hollman Morris to the leftist guerrilla group FARC. In June, a separate group sent e-mails accusing the press freedom group Fundación para la Libertad de Prensa and other civil-society groups of having ties to guerrillas. The accusations were made by two previously unknown organizations, Frente Social por la Paz and Frente Democrático Colombia Libre.

In his meeting with CPJ, Uribe also expressed support for journalists who report on corruption, and said that violence against journalists remains a major concern of his administration. "What concerns me is that they keep killing journalists. This hurts me personally, and it hurts Colombia."

Colombian journalists considered Uribe's statement an important acknowledgment of the need to cover all sides of the conflict and said it could set the tone for a long and difficult battle against intimidation and self-censorship. "A statement by a president who has accumulated so much power like Uribe could serve as an umbrella to protect provincial journalists who work under threat, but the government has to do much more to ensure safety for the press," said Jineth Bedoya, a reporter who covers security issues for the national daily *El Tiempo*.

For its part, the government has touted the effectiveness of its press protection program. Over the past three years, more than 300 journalists have taken part in the program, which offers training in self-defense and provides armored cars, bulletproof vests, cellular phones, and bodyguards to threatened journalists. History shows that the protective measures are needed.

In "Deadly News," CPJ reported that murder goes virtually unpunished in conflict-ridden countries, where police and judicial systems are typically dysfunctional. Impunity reigns in Colombia, where none of the 39 journalist slayings since 1992 have been fully solved, CPJ found. In the few cases where some convictions were obtained, masterminds were not brought to justice.

Despite his statement in support of the press, Uribe reacted strongly to press criticism of his administration. In April, when the Bogotá newsweekly *Semana* reported allegations of paramilitary infiltration of the country's intelligence service, Uribe accused Director Alejandro Santos of being "dishonest" and said the magazine was "harming" Colombian democratic institutions.

But it is provincial journalists who face the gravest risk: At least seven local reporters left their homes in 2006 after being threatened with death. The case of Jenny Manrique, a reporter for the Bucaramanga-based daily *Vanguardia Liberal*, was particularly alarming. Manrique fled Bucaramanga after receiving anonymous telephone death threats stemming from her reports on abuses by right-wing paramilitary forces. In March, when the phone threats followed her to her parents' home in Bogotá, she fled the country.

• **CUBA** •

Facing intense international interest in President Fidel Castro's hospitalization and the transfer of power to his brother, the Cuban government severely restricted information about Castro's illness in the name of state security and selectively blocked foreign journalists' entry into the country.

In a July 31 proclamation aired on Cuban television without advance notice, Castro announced that he had undergone emergency surgery for intestinal bleeding and would temporarily hand over power to his brother, Raúl. A second message by Castro, released on August 1, dispelled any doubts as to how the Cuban government would handle news of his illness. Castro labeled his health condition "a state secret," and officials refused to disclose the severity of his illness, its cause, its prognosis, or even the hospital in which he was being treated.

From there on, the 80-year-old Castro's appearances were few and carefully managed. After 40 days in September and October in which no information at all was released, the government finally circulated images and a brief interview with Castro that sought to combat rumors about his failing health. Government statements said vaguely that he was recovering, but they offered no details; photos showed a gaunt and pale president. At one point, officials said he would return to office in December, but that timetable was postponed indefinitely in the fall. The information, scarce and imprecise as it was, fueled speculation that Castro might not return to power in full capacity.

Foreign journalists flocked to Cuba to report on one of the year's top stories, but many, including *Washington Post* columnist Eugene Robinson, were rebuffed, ostensibly because they did not have proper visas. CPJ documented at least 10 cases in which the government barred entry to foreign journalists carrying tourist visas. Under Cuban immigration law, foreign reporters must apply for specialized journalist visas through Cuban embassies abroad. CPJ research shows that Cuban officials have historically granted visas to foreign journalists selectively, excluding those from media outlets deemed unfriendly. Cuban law further specifies that foreign journalists who travel to the country on a tourist visa "should abstain from practicing journalism."

The government also canceled the visas of at least four foreign journalists who had received approval to travel to Havana, according to CPJ research. Several Reuters reporters who managed to get into the country on tourist visas were told to leave. And Ginger Thompson, a reporter for *The New York Times*, was tracked down and expelled after her paper published a non-byline story from Havana. *The Miami Herald* succeeded in getting some of its reporters into Cuba on tourist visas. They went undetected for several weeks, filing stories that surveyed Cubans about their thoughts on the transfer of power and the nation's future.

Contrary to some predictions that the regime would crumble in the absence of Castro, the episode showed that the ruling elite could retain a tight grip on power. A government headed by Raúl Castro, younger than his brother by five years, was expected to eventually institute some economic reforms but continue to suppress the press and political rights.

In a report marking World Press Freedom Day, May 3, CPJ named Cuba one of the world's 10 Most Censored Countries. CPJ's analysis noted that the Cuban Constitution grants the Communist Party the right to control the press, and it recognizes the rights of the press only "in accordance with the goals of the socialist society." The government owns and controls all media outlets and restricts Internet access. The three main newspapers represent the views of the Communist Party and other organizations controlled by the government.

The media operate under the supervision of the Communist Party's Department of Revolutionary Orientation, which develops and coordinates propaganda strategies. Those who try to work as independent reporters are harassed, detained, threatened with prosecution or jail, or barred from traveling. Their relatives are threatened with dismissal from their jobs. A small number of foreign correspondents report from Havana, but Cubans do not ever see their reports.

Independent Cuban journalists, who file stories for overseas news Web sites, continued to cover news that the official media ignored. During 2006, independent journalists reported extensively on outbreaks of dengue fever, a mosquito-borne viral disease, that were occurring throughout the island. Meanwhile, authorities and the official media refused to recognize the existence of dengue fever in Cuba for much of the year, focusing instead on government efforts to eradicate the mosquito that transmits the disease. Finally, in October, the Cuban Ministry of Health informed the Pan American Health Organization (PAHO) about dengue outbreaks in four Cuban provinces. Health officials claimed the number of cases had declined significantly—without providing PAHO with figures for the total number of documented cases.

Cuba continued to be one of the world's leading jailers of journalists, second only to China. During 2006, two imprisoned journalists were released, but two more were jailed. One of them—Guillermo Espinosa Rodríguez, who was sentenced to two years of home confinement—had covered an outbreak of dengue fever in Santiago de Cuba.

Of the 24 journalists who remained imprisoned, 22 were jailed in a massive March 2003 crackdown on the independent press. Their prison sentences on antistate charges ranged from 14 to 27 years. Many of them were jailed far from their homes, adding to the heavy burden on their families. Their families have described unsanitary prison conditions, inadequate medical care, and rotten food. Some imprisoned journalists were being denied religious guidance, and most shared cells with hardened criminals. Many were allowed family visits only once every three months and marital visits only once every four months—a schedule of visits far less frequent than those allowed most inmates. Relatives were harassed for talking to the foreign press and protesting the journalists' incarceration.

· HAITI ·

Attacks on Haiti's press dropped significantly, even as its streets were ravaged by violence—but journalists said the decline was attributable to widespread self-censorship. Haiti's media continued to operate in a polarized environment, which both skewed and limited coverage of the government and street gangs.

AMERICAS

René Préval, an agronomist who served as president of Haiti between 1996 and 2001, became the first democratically elected leader since Jean-Bertrand Aristide was ousted in February 2004. Despite Préval's appeals for peace, scores of people were kidnapped at gunpoint on the streets of Port-au-Prince. More than 100 abductions were reported in the first six months of the year alone, *The Miami Herald* reported.

The Haitian press has been divided between media outlets sympathetic to Aristide's Lavalas political party and those who supported his ouster. There were some small signs of improvement during the year. Press freedom advocate Guyler Delva, director of the local press group SOS Journalistes, and other journalists said some news outlets had begun pursuing a more neutral approach.

For the time being, though, local journalists said the polarization had affected their ability to gather the news, particularly in gang-controlled areas of the capital such as Bel Air, Cité Soleil, and Solino. Only journalists perceived as Lavalas supporters had safe access to such neighborhoods.

"Some media outlets refer to the people who live in the slums as bandits, and that is not true," said Georges Venel Remarais, director general of Radio Solidarité and the news agency Agence Haïtienne de Presse. "Not everyone living in the poor neighborhoods is a bandit; we give them a voice and they trust us."

Journalists viewed as anti-Lavalas stayed out of the neighborhoods in fear of retaliation. As a result, most media outlets relied on secondhand information while reporting on gang-related crime, said Richard Widmaier, director of the Port-au-Prince-based Radio Métropole.

The Haitian press rarely conducted in-depth reporting on other critical issues, such as the rampant drug trade. In a climate of violence and unrest, journalists were afraid of being recognized as members of the media and took precautions to ensure their safety. For instance, reporters avoided carrying tape recorders or press credentials in the streets of Port-au-Prince, said Radio Kiskeya's news director, Marvel Dandin.

Since taking office in May, Préval's administration maintained a good relationship with the press. Yet some media directors in Port-au-Prince said that government information was difficult to obtain, which meant little in-depth analysis of the administration's efforts to restore peace and functioning democratic institutions. "This is not a government set on harming the press," Dandin said. "However, it is not engaged in facilitating an open exchange of information."

The country's overburdened and dysfunctional judicial system failed to make progress in two high-profile slayings. On January 12, a Port-au-Prince judge dropped murder charges against Rev. Gérard Jean-Juste, who had been accused of involvement in the murder of Jacques Roche, cultural editor of the Port-au-

Prince daily *Le Matin*. Roche was kidnapped and tortured in July 2005; his bullet-ravaged body was later found in a Port-au-Prince shantytown. According to press reports, the kidnappers who seized Roche sold the journalist to a gang that wanted him dead for sympathizing with an anti-Aristide group. It's not clear whether the murder was connected to his work, and CPJ continued to investigate.

The April 2000 murder of Jean Léopold Dominique, owner of Radio Haïti-Inter and one of the country's most renowned journalists, also remained unsolved. Beset by problems at the onset, the investigation into Dominique's murder has stagnated entirely since 2002. In April, CPJ called on Préval to make the murder investigation a priority of his administration. Dominique's widow, journalist Michèle Montas, visited Haiti for the first time since threats forced her into exile three years ago. During her visit, the government expressed strong interest in expediting her husband's murder investigation, Montas said.

Like Montas, many of Haiti's veteran journalists were forced to flee during the last decade following physical attacks and death threats. As a result, many young journalists lack training and experience.

"There is an urgent need to restructure the journalistic profession," Delva said. Better training is desperately needed in the country's interior, where community-based radio stations are booming, Widmaier added. Provincial journalists, who often lack basic services such as electricity, are especially vulnerable to political and gang pressure that, in turn, causes self-censorship and the loss of neutrality.

AMERICAS

• MEXICO •

Gunmen stormed the offices of the Nuevo Laredo daily *El Mañana* in February, firing assault rifles, tossing a grenade—and setting the tone for another dangerous year for Mexican journalists. The shocking assault, which seriously injured reporter Jaime Orozco, spurred the federal government to appoint a special prosecutor to investigate crimes against the press. The 2006 blotter was long: U.S. documentary filmmaker Bradley Will was murdered during civil unrest in the southern state of Oaxaca in October; Veracruz crime reporter Roberto Marcos García was slain in November; and Monclova journalist Rafael Ortiz Martínez went missing in July after exposing widespread problems related to prostitution. CPJ is investigating five other journalist murders to determine whether they were work-related.

Along with this alarming physical toll was the rising toll taken on news coverage itself. In the northern states, frequent attacks inspired further self-censorship among journalists covering drug trafficking and organized crime. In the crime-ridden border city of Nuevo Laredo, the powerful drug cartels essentially silenced the press on sensitive issues, CPJ found in a special report, "Dread on the Border," published in February.

In a series of interviews with CPJ's Sauro González Rodríguez, journalists in Nuevo Laredo said that identifying drug traffickers by name was off-limits, and that editors combed through articles to ensure no name slipped by. Threats were routine, the journalists said, and the danger so immediate that many did not work after dark or in the early morning. The journalists described a climate of widespread corruption in which drug cartel members routinely offered bribes, and some colleagues worked outright for criminal groups.

At *El Mañana*, Editor Ramón Cantú said he would further curtail the paper's already meager coverage of organized crime. *El Mañana* began censoring its pages in March 2004, when Editor Roberto Javier Mora García was stabbed to death.

Violence and fear had a devastating overall affect on Nuevo Laredo, a city of 300,000. A turf battle between competing drug traffickers claimed more than 160 lives in the first 10 months of 2006 alone; abductions over the past three years were said to number in the hundreds, according to press reports. The numbers, though shocking, may be understated because of self-censorship. Gunfights in downtown streets sometimes go unreported, according to the *San Antonio Express-News*, and even state police and the attorney general's office stopped making public comments on drug-related crimes.

In a bitterly contested presidential election in July, conservative Felipe Calderón, who enjoyed strong support from incumbent Vicente Fox, narrowly defeated leftist candidate Andrés Manuel López Obrador, the former Mexico City mayor. López Obrador, who unsuccessfully sought a recount, had a contentious relationship with the media. He accused the press of ignoring his campaign, and he alleged that a coalition of business leaders had unlawfully funded negative campaign ads on national television.

Fox ended his six-year term with a mixed record. He was widely criticized for his failure to implement major societal reforms; violence against the press became a grave problem as drug trafficking and crime escalated, especially in the north. But Fox was also willing to confront the violence as a national problem by creating a special prosecutor's office and by speaking out himself. His press freedom legacy was also burnished by the enactment of a public information law that allowed access to vast amounts of once-secret government records.

The appointment of a special prosecutor had been long anticipated. Fox pledged in a September 2005 meeting with CPJ that he would seek to establish the position in response to a wave of violence against the press in the northern states. CPJ had lobbied vigorously for the appointment after finding that northern Mexico had become one of the most dangerous places for journalists in Latin America. CPJ research showed that six journalists had been murdered in direct reprisal for their work since Fox took office in 2000; CPJ was investigating the circumstances surrounding the slayings of 10 other journalists during that period.

David Vega Vera, a well-known lawyer and human rights advocate, was named special prosecutor in February 2006. His office immediately took over investigations into crimes against journalists in 32 states, assembling data on press attacks and providing legal assistance and counseling to journalists who were assaulted or threatened. Vega, who issued a report every three months, received 108 cases between February and November, including assaults, threats, kidnappings, criminal defamation suits, and abuse of authority complaints. Although the special prosecutor's office did not produce any breakthrough results, it remained active throughout the year.

Press cases involving drugs and organized crime were handled by José Luis Vasconcelos, deputy prosecutor with the attorney general's organized crime division. In an interview with CPJ, Vasconcelos said the federal government faced an enormous challenge in breaking "the cycle of impunity" in such cases.

Mexican journalists themselves said they were skeptical of the special prosecutor's ability to effectively pursue cases, given Mexico's dysfunctional and overburdened criminal justice system. Yet the appointment signaled that the federal government recognized that attacks on the press had become a national issue—and that national action was needed.

One encouraging sign came via international police action. Arturo Villarreal, one of two alleged masterminds in the June 2004 murder of Tijuana newspaper editor Francisco Ortiz Franco, was arrested on August 14 as part of a sweep by U.S. Drug Enforcement Administration agents. Villarreal, known as "El Nalgón," and the reputed Tijuana drug boss Francisco Javier Arellano Félix were apprehended on a fishing boat off Mexico's Baja California peninsula and later brought to San Diego. Mexican authorities sought Villarreal's extradition.

At home, the new prosecutor took action to protect a journalist facing legal harassment in a tangled case that sparked scandal and headlines. Lydia Cacho Ribeiro, a columnist and human rights activist arrested in December 2005, faced criminal charges of defaming Puebla-based clothing manufacturer José Camel Nacif Borge. In her 2005 book *Los Demonios del Edén* (The Demons of Eden), Cacho alleged that a child prostitution ring operated in Cancún with the complicity of local police and politicians. She accused Nacif of having ties to an accused pedophile, an allegation the businessman denied.

The case took an unusual turn in February, when news outlets reported the contents of taped telephone conversations between local businessmen and Puebla state officials, including Gov. Mario Marín. Based on those leaked tapes, the special prosecutor began investigating whether there was a conspiracy to attack or jail Cacho. A spokesman for Marín denied that the governor was involved in any plot against Cacho and said the recordings violated Mexico's privacy laws. The origin of the tapes, left anonymously for news organizations, was not clear.

The special prosecutor's office questioned several people, including Marín. In March, Mexico's Supreme Court of Justice named a commission to investigate allegations that Marín had violated Cacho's constitutional rights. And in October, a judge in the state of Quintana Roo moved the defamation case against Cacho to Mexico City. The venue change was important to Cacho's legal defense because defamation is no longer a criminal matter in the capital city.

In a major advancement for press freedom, the Mexico City assembly unanimously adopted a measure in April that eliminated "honor crimes" such as slander and libel from the municipal penal code and directed such cases to civil court. National legislation to decriminalize defamation stalled in the Senate, but Deputy Carlos Reyes Gámiz, who introduced the federal bill, said that the Mexico City law took precedence in the capital. In the same session, the Mexico City assembly unanimously adopted a measure allowing journalists to withhold information about confidential sources from law enforcement, judicial, and government authorities.

In the south, months of unrest nearly paralyzed Oaxaca, and members of the news media were trapped in the middle. Authorities used tear gas to break up a demonstration by striking teachers in June, which prompted leftist activists to take to the streets in a bid to oust Oaxacan Gov. Ulises Ruiz Ortiz. Government and private radio stations were seized by leftist protesters; the facilities of the daily *Noticias, Voz e Imagen de Oaxaca* were attacked by masked gunmen; shots were fired at a university radio station that backed efforts to oust Ruiz; and several journalists were beaten and harassed while covering the unrest.

The conflict peaked in October with the killing of Will, an independent documentary filmmaker and reporter for the news Web site *Indymedia*. Will was shot on October 27 while documenting clashes between activists and government agents. Will had been covering the conflict in Oaxaca for at least six weeks, shooting footage for a documentary. Two local officials were detained in connection with Will's killing, but they were released within weeks.

• • • • • • • • • • • • • • • • • • • PARAGUAY •

The death of former dictator Alfredo Stroessner in August triggered a wave of stories about the widespread human rights and press freedom abuses woven into the fabric of Paraguayan history. As today's journalists reflected on the institutionalized attacks of the past, they confronted different, yet grave dangers of their own. Reporters in isolated regions were at risk in covering drug trafficking and crime, and their colleagues in the capital, Asunción, faced legal harassment when they criticized officials and exposed corruption.

"Press freedom in Paraguay has greatly improved with democracy," said veteran *ABC Color* columnist Alcibíades González Delvalle, who was once jailed by Stroessner. "We are no longer repressed by a dictatorship—but by a drug trafficking mafia," said González, who also directs the Department of Culture for the city of Asunción.

Particularly dangerous was Paraguay's eastern border with Brazil, where smuggling of drugs, cigarettes, fuel, clothes, and electronics was widespread. The February 4 disappearance of radio reporter Enrique Galeano illustrated the dangers that local reporters faced while covering organized crime. Galeano, host of a morning news and music program on the Horqueta-based Radio Azotey, reported on drug trafficking and alleged government corruption in the northern town of Yby Yaú. Galeano's wife accused Congressman Magdaleno Silva of the ruling Colorado Party of threatening her husband in connection with his work. Silva repeatedly denied any involvement and offered a reward for any information in the case. Prosecutor Camila Rojas told CPJ she believes there is a link between Galeano's disappearance and his reporting. Rojas said she questioned Silva but did not take any action.

CPJ also documented violent reprisals against two provincial journalists who reported on drug trafficking in border towns. Augusto Roa, correspondent for the Asunción-based *ABC Color* in the southern city of Encarnación, was attacked after writing three investigative pieces that detailed marijuana production and trafficking in southern Paraguay. On February 27, two men aboard a motorcycle shot at Roa's moving car. Roa, who was unharmed, said he believed his assailants were trying to dissuade him from following up on the drug trafficking story. Luis Alcides Ruiz Díaz, reporter for the weekly *Hechos* in the city of Pedro Juan Caballero, was threatened with death in July after publishing the names of alleged traffickers in the border city.

Radio is the most popular medium in the country's remote and impoverished interior, but journalists said news coverage there is highly influenced by local politicians. Julio Benegas, secretary-general of the Paraguayan Journalists Union, said at least 80 percent of commercial radio stations in the country's interior were owned by members of the ruling Colorado Party. In 2006, programming was overtly skewed to support Colorado Party politicians and attack rivals, said Benjamín Fernández Bogado, president of the press freedom group Instituto Prensa y Libertad.

Manipulation of state advertising was another means of swaying news coverage, particularly in the country's interior, where the financial stability of small media outlets depended almost solely on government revenue. Local governments controlled the allocation of state advertising to reward supportive media and punish critical reporting, said Fernández Bogado. Paraguayan journalists said much state advertising comes from Itaipú Binacional, a hydroelectric company owned by the Brazilian and Paraguayan governments.

Criminal sanctions for defamation have caused wide self-censorship among Asunción journalists who cover government corruption, journalists based in the capital told CPJ. On January 6, the Supreme Court of Justice upheld the December 2005 criminal defamation conviction of Aldo Zuccolillo, *ABC Color*'s editorial director. The ruling marked the end of a legal battle that

AMERICAS

began in December 1998 when prosecutors took up the case of Colorado Sen. Juan Carlos Galaverna, who alleged that Zuccolillo had defamed him by publishing articles accusing him of corruption, embezzlement, and abuse of power. In July, criminal defamation charges were also filed against *ABC Color* reporter Carlos Cáceres. The suit, brought by two former government officials, stemmed from a series Cáceres wrote on corruption in the construction of rural roads. A ruling in the case was pending.

ABC Color, founded in 1967, was Paraguay's first national daily and one of its first independent newspapers. Shut down in 1984 by the Stroessner dictatorship, it reopened in 1989 and remains one of the nation's leading independent voices.

· **PERU** ·

A Supreme Court decision overturning a local mayor's conviction in the murder of a radio journalist alarmed the news media and punctuated a year in which provincial reporters faced threats and attacks from local officials and their supporters.

Citing a lack of evidence, the high court ordered the release of Yungay Mayor Amaro León León and two other defendants convicted in the February 2004 slaying of Antonio de la Torre Echeandía, a radio reporter who had criticized the local government. León, who immediately retook office, threatened legal action against de la Torre Echeandía's wife, Dina Ramírez, when she sought more information on the Supreme Court's decision and a new investigation into her husband's killing. After León's supporters threatened her and protested outside her home, Ramírez told CPJ, she moved her family to Lima.

In September, Ramírez and the local press freedom group Instituto Prensa y Sociedad (IPYS) submitted the case to the Washington, D.C.-based Inter-American Commission on Human Rights, arguing that the government of Peru had allowed the murder to go unpunished. The commission—the human rights monitoring arm of the Organization of American States—can urge Peruvian authorities to reopen the case.

Although journalists in Lima are rarely targeted with violence, CPJ research shows that threats and attacks nationwide have trended upward since 2004. In interviews, journalists and press freedom advocates described an increasingly hostile climate, especially in the country's interior, where an aggressive and attack-oriented press has clashed with corrupt and criminal elements. As of November, IPYS reported receiving 27 complaints of physical attacks and 17 complaints of threats. Journalists said intimidation was especially pervasive in Ánchash, a region north of Lima that has been identified by IPYS as the most dangerous area for journalists.

Recent history provides some context for the trends. The era of corruption that defined Alberto Fujimori's presidency from 1990 to 2000 was marked by dogged and widely praised investigative reporting. Lima-based dailies and national television stations contributed to exposing the regime's excesses, eventually forcing Fujimori and his top aides to resign. In the years since, analyses by the *Columbia Journalism Review* and others have found that the investigative press itself has been prone to excess, even tapping phone conversations at times. Journalists interviewed by CPJ agreed that some journalists have been overzealous in their techniques and consumed by scandal.

Six newspapers circulate nationally; two radio stations broadcast nationally, as do several television stations. In Peru's interior, however, most citizens get their news from local radio stations that focus heavily on local politics.

Journalists who reported on drug trafficking also faced grave dangers. Marilú Gambini Lostanau, host of the weekly television program "Confidencial" on Canal 31 in the northeastern city of Chimbote, received death threats in March after reporting on the influence of drug traffickers in the country's politics. On April 2, Gambini and her family left Chimbote and reported the threats to authorities in Lima.

On several occasions during the 2006 presidential campaign, journalists were harassed by political activists angered by press reports they perceived as biased. Alan García of the Peruvian Aprista Party defeated Ollanta Humala, the Peruvian Nationalist Party candidate, in a June 4 runoff. IPYS documented at least four campaign-related attacks, three said to be perpetrated by Humala supporters. The Humala campaign complained about unfair coverage.

Protests also generated attacks on the press. In June, journalists were threatened, shoved, kicked, and hit with sticks by protesters demonstrating in Lima against the Free Trade Agreement with the United States, according to the National Association of Peruvian Journalists. In August, four television reporters covering violent protests against Yanacocha, a mining company, were held hostage for several hours in northern Cajamarca province, the Peruvian press reported. The same month, students protesting against the mining company claimed that the media were biased and attacked two television reporters, according to IPYS.

Five men were convicted in February in the 2004 slaying of Alberto Rivera, a host on radio station Frecuencia Oriental. Pucallpa Mayor Luís Valdéz Villacorta and three others still faced charges of plotting the killing. News reports said that Rivera had accused Valdéz of having links to drug trafficking.

AMERICAS

• • • • • • • • • • • • • • • • • • UNITED STATES • • • • • • • • • • • • • • • •

After consuming the press freedom landscape for more than two years, an investigation into the leak of a CIA operative's name wound down with a whimper. News organizations reported in August that special prosecutor Patrick Fitzgerald apparently knew from the day his investigation began in December 2003 that then-Deputy

Secretary of State Richard Armitage was the person who identified a CIA operative to columnist Robert Novak. Novak was the first to publicly identify Valerie Plame, also known as Valerie Wilson, in a 2003 column that sparked the controversial investigation.

Despite knowing the source from the onset, the special prosecutor's $1.4 million probe continued in an apparent effort to determine whether the leak was part of a concerted White House effort to discredit the operative's husband, former ambassador Joseph Wilson, for writing an op-ed critical of the administration. But Fitzgerald did not charge anyone with intentionally revealing Plame's identity. Vice presidential aide I. Lewis "Scooter" Libby, the sole person charged, was indicted on allegations of lying to investigators about his conversations with reporters. Libby's case was pending throughout the year. The only person jailed in the case was then-*New York Times* reporter Judith Miller, who served 85 days in 2005 for refusing to disclose confidential sources. Many lawyers and press freedom advocates said they feared the Plame case would inspire prosecutors seeking the source of government leaks to pursue journalists more aggressively.

Such aggressive tactics against the press were on display in San Francisco, where two reporters for the *San Francisco Chronicle* were held in contempt in September for refusing to reveal who leaked secret grand jury testimony about alleged steroid use by top athletes. Reporters Lance Williams and Mark Fainaru-Wada obtained grand jury testimony given by baseball stars Barry Bonds, Jason Giambi, and other elite athletes during a criminal investigation into the alleged distribution of steroids by the Bay Area Laboratory Co-operative. The journalists wrote a series of articles as well as a book that quoted the leaked testimony.

The reporters' coverage of the steroid scandal drew national attention to the widespread use of performance-enhancing drugs among professional athletes, helping spawn Congressional hearings and significant changes in Major League Baseball's drug-testing policies. The *Chronicle* and its reporters have appealed the contempt ruling, which could result in the reporters' jailing. Bonds, meanwhile, closed in on baseball's all-time home run record.

Reports that U.S. intelligence agencies gained access to a Brussels-based storehouse of international financial transactions led U.S. officials to make some of their harshest remarks against the press in recent memory. *The New York Times*, the *Los Angeles Times*, and *The Wall Street Journal* reported in June that the Bush administration had gained access to the Society for Worldwide Interbank Financial Telecommunications, or SWIFT, in search of monetary transfers that might involve terrorist suspects.

President George W. Bush told White House correspondents that "the disclosure of this program is disgraceful," adding that it "makes it harder to win this war on terror." Members of Congress went further. Sen. Jim Bunning accused *The New York Times* of "treason" and Rep. Peter King urged Attorney General Alberto Gonzales to pursue "possible criminal prosecution" of the *Times*. "This isn't about freedom of the press; it's about what is prudent in a time of war," said Sen. Pat Roberts on PBS' "News Hour with Jim

Lehrer."

The editors of the *Los Angeles Times* and *The New York Times*, Dean Baquet and Bill Keller, made the rare decision to respond together in an op-ed that ran in both newspapers on the same day. "In recent years our papers have brought you a great deal of information the White House never intended for you to know—classified secrets about the questionable intelligence that led the country to war in Iraq, about the abuse of prisoners in Iraq and Afghanistan, about the transfer of suspects to countries that are not squeamish about using torture, about eavesdropping without warrants. ...We understand that honorable people may disagree with any of these choices—to publish or not to publish. But making those decisions is the responsibility that falls to editors, a corollary to the great gift of our independence. It is not a responsibility we take lightly. And it is not one we can surrender to the government."

This unusually tense debate came five months after Gonzales told the Senate Judiciary Committee that the attorney general's office was investigating the source of leaks for a 2005 *New York Times* story disclosing that the National Security Agency was eavesdropping on phone calls within the United States without first obtaining court warrants. The Justice Department has yet to file any criminal charges.

In a policy shift, U.S. military officials pledged prompt, high-level reviews whenever journalists were detained in Iraq. "We are aware that journalists, by the nature of their duties, often will be at the scene of attacks when they occur," Pentagon spokesman Bryan Whitman told CPJ in confirming the shift. The change followed months of advocacy by CPJ, which documented at least eight prior cases in which U.S. forces jailed Iraqi journalists for weeks or months without charge or due process. One was finally charged then cleared; the others were eventually freed without charge.

Yet at least one long-term detention in Iraq renewed questions about U.S. practices. In September, The Associated Press revealed that Pulitzer Prize-winning photographer Bilal Hussein was detained by the U.S. military on April 12 and held without charge. In a May 7 e-mail, Maj. Gen. John Gardner told the AP that "the information available establishes that he has close relationships with insurgents." AP President and CEO Thomas Curley called for Hussein to be charged or freed, and CPJ Chairman Paul Steiger urged the Pentagon to give the photographer due process. The Pentagon's Whitman said Hussein was given a chance to provide information in his defense at two military hearings, but an AP lawyer said Hussein got notice of only one such hearing—and that notice came after the hearing had taken place.

The U.S. military continued to hold Al-Jazeera cameraman Sami al-Haj in detention at Guantánamo Bay, Cuba. Al-Haj, first detained in Pakistan in December 2001, has not been charged or provided due process. His lawyer, Clive Stafford Smith, contended that U.S. military authorities were instead intent on extracting information about his employer, Al-Jazeera. U.S. officials contacted by CPJ declined to discuss the case. CPJ outlined the case and called for due process in a special report in October, "The Enemy?"

The journalist and author Ron Suskind reported in his book *The One Percent Doctrine*, released in June, that U.S. forces deliberately targeted Al-Jazeera's Kabul bureau, which was bombed in November 2001. "My sources are clear that it was done on purpose," Suskind told CNN's Wolf Blitzer after the book's release. U.S. military officials declined to respond to the allegation, except to reiterate a long-standing claim that the military believed the building that housed the Al-Jazeera offices, which had satellite dishes on its roof, was a "known al-Qaeda facility."

The U.S. Defense Department inspector general found in October that a U.S. military program to pay Iraqi journalists and newspapers to report stories favorable to U.S. efforts in Iraq was legal under the Pentagon's rules for psychological operations. "Psychological operations are a central part of information operations and contribute to achieving the ... commander's objectives," according to the unclassified executive summary as quoted by the AP. The planted news stories convey "selected, truthful information to foreign audiences to influence their emotions ... reasoning, and ultimately, the behavior of governments."

In California, freelance video blogger Joshua Wolf was ordered to jail for refusing to hand over a videotape, subpoenaed by a federal grand jury, of a June 2005 protest in San Francisco. Wolf's tape documented clashes between demonstrators and police during a rally protesting a Group of 8 economic conference. The grand jury was investigating possible criminal activity, including an alleged attempt by protesters to burn a police vehicle. Wolf sold footage of the protest to San Francisco television stations and posted it on his Web site, the AP reported. Investigators were seeking Wolf's testimony and portions of his videotape that were not made public.

· · · · · · · · · · · · · · · · · · VENEZUELA · · · · · · · · · · · · · · · · · · ·

President Hugo Chávez Frías, who has outlasted a coup and a recall, swept to victory in the December 3 presidential election amid tense relations with the press. Chávez threatened to withhold licenses from broadcast outlets critical of his administration, while the attorney general quashed coverage of a prosecutor's assassination amid press reports that exposed weaknesses in the government's probe. Journalists faced physical dangers as well, with one murdered in 2006.

Chávez suffered a setback on the international stage in October, when Venezuela could not secure two-thirds approval in the U.N. General Assembly to gain a seat on the Security Council. Most analysts attributed the setback to Chávez's fiery address to the assembly in which he called U.S. President George W. Bush "the devil." But at home, the architect of Venezuela's "Socialism of the 21st Century" has continued to tighten his grip on power by packing supporters onto an enlarged Supreme Court and by purging the armed forces and the state-owned oil company of personnel who were not supporters. In June, the National Assembly gave initial approval to a bill empowering the executive branch to regulate nongovernmental organizations, or NGOs, including press freedom and human rights groups. The bill would also require such groups to register with the government. A coalition of local NGOs opposed the measure, fearing punitive action from an administration that construes criticism as an attempt to destabilize the country. The bill awaited final approval in the National Assembly, after which Chávez was expected to sign it into law.

To counter the largely pro-opposition private press at home, the Chávez administration used state-owned media as a government megaphone, stacking its personnel ranks with government sympathizers and influencing content to ensure that Chávez received vast amounts of uncritical coverage. Authorities sought to marginalize the private press by blocking access to government-sponsored events, government buildings, and public institutions; by refusing to give statements to reporters working for private media; and by withholding access to public information.

In June, Chávez threatened to block the license renewals of privately owned television and radio stations. Without naming any specific broadcasters, Chávez said some outlets were waging "psychological war to divide, weaken, and destroy the nation" as part of an "imperialist plan" to overthrow his government. Days later, the minister of communication and information said the government was legally entitled to refuse license renewals for stations it deemed in violation of the law. Minister Willian Rafael Lara said broadcasters had demonstrated "a systematic tendency to violate" the Law of Social Responsibility in Radio and Television. The Caracas daily *El Universal* quoted Lara as saying there was a good possibility that some licenses would not be renewed in 2007.

The social responsibility law, passed in 2004, has been widely criticized for its broad and vaguely worded restrictions on free expression. Article 29, for example, bars television and radio stations from broadcasting messages that "promote, defend, or incite breaches of public order" or "are contrary to the security of the nation."

Many private media outlets have taken an openly partisan role, actively seeking Chávez's ouster, embracing the positions and language of his opponents, and giving away time for opposition advertising. But private media recently have shown some signs of moving away from a fiercely partisan approach, promoting greater balance on opinion pages and investing more in hard-news reporting. The Caracas daily *El Nacional*, for instance, opened its op-ed pages to pro-government columnists and writers considered nonpartisan.

Most notably, several news organizations published investigative reports that pointed to deep flaws in the government's probe of the November 2004 assassination of prosecutor Danilo Anderson. The reports questioned the credibility of the government's primary witness, Giovanny Vásquez de Armas, revealing that he was actually in a Colombian

AMERICAS

jail when he purportedly attended a 2003 meeting in Panama where Anderson's murder was allegedly planned.

Anderson had been investigating the alleged involvement of businessmen, politicians, and former government officials in the April 2002 coup that briefly deposed Chávez. When Anderson was killed in a car bombing in Caracas, government officials called it a "terrorist act" and eulogized the prosecutor as a hero who died while trying to bring coup plotters to justice. But the local press, citing witness statements, later reported that police found a large amount of money in Anderson's apartment and that investigators were examining his possible connection to an extortion ring of lawyers and prosecutors.

Although three men were convicted of killing Anderson, prosecutors long believed that others planned the assassination. In November 2005, Venezuelan authorities issued arrest warrants for five people accused of orchestrating the murder—including Patricia Poleo, a columnist and director of the Caracas daily *El Nuevo País*. Poleo, who has supported the opposition in her writing, denied any involvement in the murder and called the prosecution politically motivated. She fled to Miami but said she would return if her right to a defense was guaranteed.

Attorney General Isaías Rodríguez reacted aggressively to news reports that raised questions about the government's case. In January, he obtained a court order banning the media from reporting on broad aspects of the Anderson slaying. Judge Florencio Silano's order barred "publishing, spreading, or exposition" of information from the Anderson court file, and he forbade any reference to the private life of the primary witness, Vásquez. The attorney general had said he wanted to protect Vásquez from what he called a media campaign of harassment and psychological pressure.

The same month, Rodríguez asked the National Telecommunications Commission, known as Conatel, to open administrative proceedings against broadcast outlets to determine whether they had violated the social responsibility law in their coverage of the case. In particular, he asked whether they violated Articles 1 and 3 by failing to exercise freedom of expression "with responsibility" and by failing to "promote balance between the duties, rights, and interests of people and those of broadcasting outlets and related parties." The commission opened an investigation but took no immediate action.

At the time, Rodríguez accused unnamed news organizations of "intimidating witnesses and experts to persuade them to lie, modify their statements, or abstain from testifying," and said they would be investigated on suspicion of obstructing justice. Within days, his office said it would investigate the private TV channels Televén, Venevisión, RCTV, Globovisión, CMT, and the state-owned Venezolana de Televisión; and the Caracas dailies *El Universal*, *El Nacional*, *Últimas Noticias*, and *El Nuevo País*.

By August, though, the star witness had begun giving interviews to the local news media, prompting the judge to partially lift his gag order and allow the publication of references to Vásquez's private life. That month, the attorney general acknowledged in an interview with *El Nacional* that Vásquez's testimony was filled with inconsistencies and gaps, including those reported by the news media.

In December, the government's case in tatters, Rodríguez announced that he would not press charges against one supposed mastermind and that he would temporarily shelve the investigation into the others.

One journalist was murdered in connection with his work in 2006. Jorge Aguirre, a photographer with the Caracas daily *El Mundo*, was shot on April 5 as he approached an anticrime demonstration in a car provided by *El Mundo* and marked with its logo. As the car neared the protest, a man driving a motorcycle approached and demanded that the driver stop the car. When the driver asked why, the motorcyclist responded that he was with the authorities, but he did not show any identification. After the driver refused to stop and proceeded to the protest scene, the motorcyclist followed and shot Aguirre four times as he was getting out of the car with his camera. Aguirre managed to take a picture of the killer's back as he fled the scene on his motorcycle.

Boris Lenis Blanco, a former police officer, was arrested in the killing on April 13. Members of the national crime police apprehended Blanco when a former colleague identified him as the motorcyclist, *El Universal* reported. Investigators later searched Blanco's home and found evidence connecting him to the crime scene, the local press said. Blanco was charged with murder and impersonation of a public official. Trial proceedings began in Caracas in June.

CPJ continued to investigate the murder of a second journalist. Jesús Rafael Flores Rojas, a columnist and coordinator for the daily *Región* in the state of Anzoátegui, was shot in front of his house on August 23. As Flores and his daughter Nancy were parking their car, an armed man approached. The daughter said she implored the attacker to take their car and money, but the man told her that he wasn't there for either and shot Flores repeatedly.

Investigators reported a breakthrough in the 2004 murder of Mauro Marcano, a radio host and columnist who was killed in the city of Maturín, Monagas state. Marcano, who was also a municipal councilman, aggressively denounced drug trafficking and police corruption. In August 2006, two men accused of planning Marcano's murder—an alleged drug trafficker and his son—were detained in neighboring Trinidad and Tobago and were awaiting extradition. The alleged middleman and two hit men were considered fugitives.

AMERICAS

BAHAMAS

- Cameraman Lázaro Abreu and reporter Alberto Tavares, Miami-based journalists with the Telemundo network, and Osvaldo Duarte, a cameraman for Univisión's Channel 23 in Miami, were detained on February 7 by Nassau prison guards when they reported on a group of Cubans rescued by the U.S. Coast Guard from an uninhabited Bahamian island. The Cuban refugees, found on the tiny Elbow Cay after surviving a journey that killed six others, were held at the Carmichael Detention Center in Nassau. Channel 23 reporter Mario Vallejo was pushed and punched by a guard when he called the station to report the journalists' detentions, Emilio Marrero, the station's news director, told CPJ. The journalists were held for several hours and released without charge, Marrero said.

BOLIVIA

- Unidentified attackers flung homemade bombs at the offices of Canal 7, a state-owned television station in the eastern city of Santa Cruz, around 3 a.m. on September 8, according to press reports. No injuries were reported, but one explosive shattered a window, and the other caused a small fire to an exterior wall. Canal 7 regional director, Sandro Jaramillo, told Bolivian reporters that unidentified people had threatened the station before the attack. He said callers told Canal 7 that it would suffer consequences for not giving positive coverage to a general strike by a local right-wing militant group, the Unión Juvenil Cruceñista.

CHILE

- Local police punched, kicked, and struck with riot shields six journalists covering clashes between security forces and high school students during a massive May 30 demonstration demanding education reform. More than half a million students protested in Santiago, calling for a reduction in public transportation fares and in the inequities between rich and poor schools. Marcos Cabrera, a cameraman for RedTV, Fernando Fiedler, a photographer for the daily *Diario Financiero*, and Livio Saavedra, a cameraman for the Concepción-based Canal 9, were injured. Julio Oliva, editor of the Santiago weekly *El Siglo*, said he and reporters Iván Valdés and Marcos Díaz were briefly detained after attempting to help a protester struck by a car. Police punched the three journalists and shoved them into a truck, Oliva told CPJ. After President Michelle Bachelet ordered an investigation, the chief of special police forces was fired.

COSTA RICA

- CPJ urged President Oscar Arias to bring Costa Rica's defamation laws into compliance with international standards on freedom of expression. In a June 8 letter, CPJ expressed concern about a May 3 decision by the Costa Rican Constitutional Court to uphold a press law that makes defamation a crime. Article 7 of the 1902 statute imposes a prison sentence of up to 120 days for defamation in print media. CPJ also expressed alarm over a bill introduced in Congress seeking to establish press regulatory agencies and impose strict controls on journalism. In a July 14 letter to CPJ, Justice Minister Laura Chinchilla said that the government "will not help or support any legislative proposal that hinders press freedom in any way."

DOMINICAN REPUBLIC

- Roberto Sandoval, host of opinion programs on Radio Comercial and Telecable Nacional's Canal 10, was abducted by three unidentified people outside his Santo Domingo home on March 8, according to Dominican press reports. His abductors drove Sandoval 25 miles (40 kilometers) outside of the Dominican capital, where they threatened to kill him, the reports said. The journalist escaped by jumping from a moving vehicle, as his assailants fired gunshots at him, colleague Rudy Germán Pérez told CPJ. One of the assailants' shots grazed Sandoval's back, and he suffered minor injuries when he leapt from the vehicle. News reports said the assailants searched for Sandoval, but he hid in a wooded area until they were gone. Sandoval, who often reports on crime and is critical of Dominican law enforcement, temporarily left his home with his family following the attack, Germán Pérez said.

- Dominican police arrested Vladimir Pujols, one of two gang members accused of the September 2004 murder of journalist Juan Emilio Andújar Matos of Radio Azua and *Listín Diario*. Pujols, who was arrested on March 29, denied involvement in the murder. A second suspect, Luis Tejeda Filpo, was shot to death by police two days after Andújar was murdered. Andújar was ambushed and shot in the head after a broadcast in which he reported on a bloody crime wave that pitted gang members against police in Azua.

- A Santo Domingo judge convicted journalists Enrique Crespo, Ali David Demey, and Anaylis Cañizales of criminal defamation on July 27. The Association of Art Reporters accused the three hosts of the cable television show "Los Dueños el Circo" of defamation when they suggested that winners of the group's annual Casandra Awards had paid off the judges. The association, known as Acroarte, said the accusation was untrue. Crespo and Demey were fined 4 million pesos (US$118,000) each, and Cañizales was fined 2 million pesos (US$59,000). Crespo told CPJ that he and his colleagues would appeal.

ECUADOR

- The body of José Luis León Desiderio, host of the daily news program "Opinión" on local Radio Minutera, was found in the coastal city of Guayaquil on February 14. León had often denounced gang violence and police inaction in the city. León, who had not been robbed, received a text message on his cell phone threatening him with death only days before his murder.

EL SALVADOR

- At least 14 Salvadoran reporters and photographers were harassed and attacked with stones, sticks, and pepper spray during violent July 5-7 street protests against increases in electric and public transportation fees in San Salvador. Violence erupted after police used tear gas to disperse the crowd. Protesters wearing red shirts identifying them as FMLN supporters were seen attacking journalists in at least two instances, CPJ research shows. FMLN leaders condemned the violence but said the acts were committed by elements outside its party. Protesters told some of the journalists that they were being targeted as alleged supporters of the "right-wing" Salvadoran government.

GUATEMALA

- On February 1, Guatemala's Constitutionality Court struck down laws that criminalized expressions deemed offensive to public officials. The court ruled the *desacato*, or disrespect, provisions to be unconstitutional, declaring them "an attack on freedom of expression and the right to be informed." The decision by Guatemala's highest court voided Articles 411, 412, and 413 of the penal code, which called for prison terms of six months to three years for those who offend government or other public officials.

- Radio host Vinicio Aguilar Mancilla was shot by an unidentified assailant during his morning jog on August 23. Aguilar, host of a daily political show on Radio 10 in Guatemala City, was approached by two men while jogging in a residential neighborhood. He said one of the men grabbed him by the hair, put a gun in his mouth, and said, "This is to shut you up." His assailant then fired, wounding Aguilar in the mouth and, because the journalist made a defensive motion, in the hand. Aguilar was taken to a local hospital, where he underwent reconstructive surgery on his cheek, jaw, and right hand. The journalist said he believed the attack was related to his work.

- Early on the morning of September 10, radio reporter Eduardo Maas Bol was gunned down inside his car on the outskirts of the central city of Cobán in Alta Verapaz. Maas, Cobán correspondent for the Guatemala City-based Radio Punto, was on his way home after a party, his brother Félix Maas Bol told CPJ. He was shot four times, and robbery did not appear to have been a motive; his wallet and gold jewelry were found inside the car, local prosecutor Genaro Pacheco told CPJ. Maas also worked as a supervisor for the Ministry of Education, as a spokesman for the local journalists union, and as a human rights advocate, his brother said. Local authorities detained a suspect in September but did not close the investigation. In November, the Alta Verapaz human rights ombudsman, Hugo Pop, told CPJ that Maas' journalism was a possible motive in the murder.

GUYANA

- Just before midnight on August 8, at least 12 gunmen stormed the *Kaieteur News* printing plant in an industrial area on the outskirts of the capital, Georgetown, the newspaper's owner, Glen Lall, told CPJ. The assailants ordered a security guard to open the gates and then shot him. They then forced five printing plant employees onto the floor and shot them in the backs of their heads, according to Lall. The five employees died, and the security guard was seriously injured. Georgetown Police Commissioner Henry Green told CPJ that three gang members were arrested in the attack. Green said gang members had been looking for weapons in a murderous rampage that resulted in five other deaths that night.

HONDURAS

- Octavio Carvajal, host of the opinion program "Zonas de Debates" and the news show "Más que Noticias" for the Tegucigalpa-based radio station STC Noticias, said he was punched and threatened by an official of the government-owned telecommunications company Hondutel on May 8. The official denied attacking the reporter. Carvajal, who filed a police complaint, said he had criticized the government-owned company.

PANAMA

- A commission of lawyers and academics set up by President Martín Torrijos to examine penal code reform presented a draft bill in June that would double the prison term for defamation to three years. After more than 50 journalists demonstrated in Panama City against the proposals, the administration agreed to include journalists in a new commission examining the plan.

URUGUAY

- In a September 18 ruling, the Supreme Court of Justice reinstated the criminal defamation conviction of reporter Carlos Dogliani Staricco for a series of articles published in March 2004. The case stemmed from a complaint filed by Álvaro Lamas, mayor of the western city of Paysandú. Dogliani's stories in the local weekly *El Regional* accused Lamas of forgiving most of a landowner's property tax debt, according to press reports and CPJ interviews. A local judge convicted Dogliani in 2004 and sentenced the reporter to five months in prison, but an appellate court overturned the verdict the following year. In its new ruling, the Supreme Court found that the right to a person's honor limits the media's right to inform, and that criminal defamation laws are intended to restrict freedom of expression. The court also asserted that the factual basis of the coverage was not a relevant defense, and that even accurate reporting can constitute defamation. The Uruguayan Press Association said it would take the case to the Inter-American Commission on Human Rights.

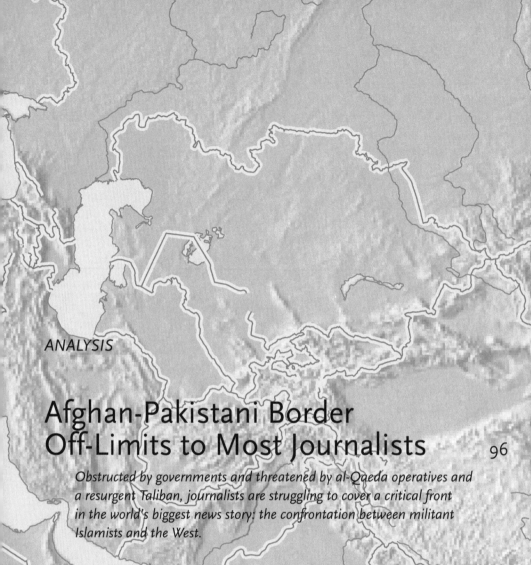

ANALYSIS

Afghan-Pakistani Border
Off-Limits to Most Journalists

96

*Obstructed by governments and threatened by al-Qaeda operatives and
a resurgent Taliban, journalists are struggling to cover a critical front
in the world's biggest news story: the confrontation between militant
Islamists and the West.*

by Bob Dietz

PHOTOS

Section break: AP/Rodrigo Abd — *As authorities burn seized narcotics in Kabul in
July, a radio reporter records the crackle and roar.* Analysis (next): Reuters/Saeed Ali
Achakzai — *A Pakistani soldier patrols the border near Chaman in October.*

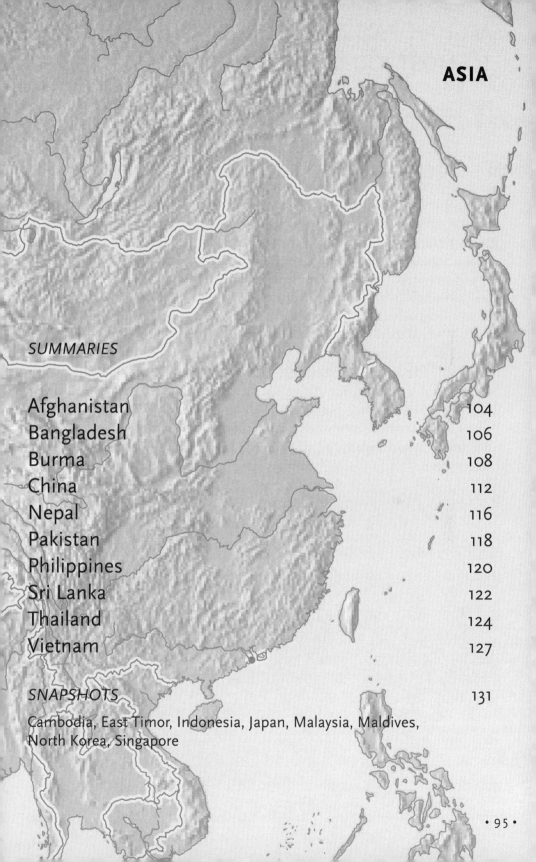

ASIA

AFGHAN-PAKISTANI BORDER OFF-LIMITS
TO MOST JOURNALISTS
by Bob Dietz

• •

THE AFGHANISTAN-PAKISTAN BORDER IS A CRITICAL FRONT in the most challenging news story in the world: the confrontation between U.S.-led Western countries and militant Islamists. Yet access to the border region has become increasingly restricted, and the Pakistani government continues to do everything in its power to dissuade outside journalists from entering. Few local journalists are left, most having fled or simply stopped working in what has become a high-risk profession, according to the Tribal Union of Journalists.

On the Afghan side, the country's post-Taliban press corps faces threats from all quarters. The government pressures them to stop interviewing political opponents or publicizing military and political setbacks. U.S. and NATO troops are wary of all local people, including those claiming to be journalists. Militants of every stripe are resentful of bad coverage. Faced with hostility from so many sides, Western journalists increasingly embed with the military to get to stories outside of Kabul, or they rely on local reporters willing to take the risk. Now, even the locals are saying the story is getting too hot to handle.

It is not surprising that the provinces straddling the countries' historically porous border—the disputed Durand Line, drawn by the British in 1893—have emerged as a prime theater of war. The Taliban, who withdrew from Kabul and northern Afghanistan after the U.S. invasion in 2001, have done more than just regroup in Afghanistan's southeastern provinces. They have also returned to safe

Western journalists increasingly embed with the military to get to stories outside Kabul.

havens on the other side of the line.

In Pakistan, they have deeply embedded themselves into Pakistan's Federally Administered Tribal Areas in the North West Frontier Province. They have also found a secure rear area in Baluchistan, which holds most of Pakistan's limited natural gas reserves. Baluchistan's capital, Quetta, has become a Taliban command post, tolerated and unbothered by the government of President Pervez Musharraf. Everything from food to weapons to drugs flows back and forth across the line, free of any government trade regulations.

Even though the Taliban have always portrayed themselves as a national movement, one committed to Islamic ideals, in South and North Waziristan they have formulated a potent ideological combination of Islam and Pashto nationalism. Pashtuns are the dominant ethnic group in Waziristan and the nearby Afghan provinces of Kandahar, Helmand, and Nangarhar. The 2001 American invasion may have driven them back into their Pashtun home territory, but the leadership still sees itself with a much broader base. "The Taliban has its roots not only among the Pashtuns, but all the ethnic groups of Afghanistan," Taliban spokesman Mohammad Hanif told the independent Pajhwok Afghan News agency. Their campaign to re-establish those roots through all of Afghanistan has accelerated as they have regrouped.

Anyone trying to govern either side of the border faces a diffuse enemy. Afghanistan expert Barnett R. Rubin, director of studies and senior fellow at the Center on International Cooperation at New York University describes it: "The Taliban are neither a purely Afghan phenomenon, as Pakistan claims, nor a group based solely in Pakistan, as the Afghan government claims. They are a phenomenon of the borderland, a joint Afghan-Pakistan network and organization, now increasingly integrated with the global networks of al-Qaeda."

Add to this region the flourishing narcotics industry and its supporting transport network, which reaches across Central Asia into Europe and the Mediterranean. The area overlapping the border is by far the world's largest supplier of opium, heroin, hashish, and other illegal drugs. The head of the U.N. Office on Drugs and Crime, Antonio Maria Costa, told a September 2 press conference in Kabul, "This year's harvest will be around 6,100 metric tons of opium, a staggering 92 percent of total world supply. It exceeds global consumption by 30 percent." Costa said the harvest had increased by 49 percent from the year before. The previous record, he said, was 4,600 metric tons in 1999.

After they invaded Afghanistan in 2001, the Americans quickly recognized the border problem, grasping early on that they could not fully count on their Pakistani allies to secure the area. U.S. forces regularly crossed the border into Pakistan targeting al-Qaeda groups.

The Americans recognized a border problem. They could not fully count on their Pakistani allies.

In early August 2006, NATO troops, mostly British and Canadian, replaced the larger U.S. force and immediately found themselves under intense fire. By September, they claimed they were stunned to find themselves facing more than ragtag guerrillas using hit-and-run tactics and called for 2,500 more troops as backup. "The Taliban's tenacity in the face of massive losses has been a surprise, absorbing more of our effort than we predicted it would," British Minister of Defense Des Brown told reporters. Yet he should not have been surprised; NATO had been warned.

Barry McCaffrey, the retired general who teaches international affairs at the U.S. Military Academy, had traveled to Afghanistan in May, and he reported in a widely distributed paper that "there is little question that the level of fighting has intensified rapidly in the past year. Three years ago, the Taliban operated in squad-sized units. Last year, they operated in company-sized units (100-plus men). This year, the Taliban are operating in battalion sized units (400-plus men). They now have excellent weapons, new IED [improvised explosive devices] technology, commercial communications gear, and new field equipment. They are employing suicide bombers who are clearly not just foreigners. In many cases, they appear to have received excellent tactical, camouflage, and marksmanship training. They are very aggressive and smart in their tactics. Their base areas in Pakistan are secure. Drug money and international financial support have energized their operations. Their IO [information operations] campaign is excellent."

Pakistan, conceding that it had little control in North Waziristan, signed a peace pact in September with the pro-Taliban tribal militants. The agreement was intended to end years of skirmishing and assassinations and to quiet the few pitched battles along the border.

Critics denounced it as a cave-in, saying the Musharraf government lacked resolve and had backed down from its role in the fight against worldwide militant Islamism. With the army gone from the Taliban's Pakistan rear bases, the number of conflicts in Afghanistan quickly increased, not only along the border but in Kabul and other areas.

TOLO TV HEADQUARTERS IN KABUL IS BUNKERED: SANDBAGS SURROUND locked gateways and windows, barbed wire loops along the tops of the walls separating the several rented houses that hold the privately owned station's ramshackle studios and newsrooms. Earthen mounds dot the neighborhood's narrow streets, creating zigzag passages that force cars to slow as they near the compound. As crews outside throw gear into cars, guards in civilian clothes with automatic weapons check visitors' identities before frisking them.

Inside the compound, Tolo News Director Sidiq Ahmadzada takes his job seriously, and he understands the threats his crews face. His camera operators and sound technicians are threatened, at times beaten, and often abused by police, members of the government, and thugs working for tribal leaders and the drug and smuggling mafias.

Tolo runs four crews outside of Kabul, in Kandahar, Mazar-i-Sharif, Herat, and Jalalabad. They are all one-man bands with, maybe, a driver. They work with no protection, are told to carry no weapons, and are expected to file stories twice a day. Ahmadzada relies on them to feed Tolo's two main evening news bulletins, which are broadcast in the official Afghan languages, Dari and Pashto.

It might be a grandiose claim coming from another news director, but when Ahmadzada says, "We are the front line for media freedom in Afghanistan," his flat assertion commands respect. "Tolo is not linked to the government and we will broadcast the reality to anyone." In the dimly lit operations room behind sandbagged windows, lines like that are not delivered lightly. Tolo TV has its critics, but few challenge its commitment to news reporting.

About 140 miles (225 kilometers) east of Kabul, across the border region into Pakistan, journalists at the Peshawar Press Club described similar threats in talks with a CPJ delegation in July. Peshawar is the dusty, crowded capital of Pakistan's North West Frontier Province (NWFP), which holds North and South Waziristan, where the Taliban have aligned themselves with the indigenous Pashtun population to generate a vigorous form of political Islam that finds a free press anathema. Couple that with a Pakistani government that increasingly pays no more than lip service to the concept of a free press, and you have a

> **When Ahmadzada says Tolo TV is on the front line for media freedom, his assertion commands respect.**

ASIA

deadly media atmosphere.

Just like Ahmadzada in Kabul, Behroz Khan, Peshawar correspondent for *The News*, sees himself and his colleagues in the Tribal Union of Journalists (TUJ) as being under the gun. "The government and the militants have a common cause—get rid of journalists," he says. "We're caught in a dangerous game. Journalists come in contact with everyone, including the militants, and we've become a target."

His colleague and competitor at the *Daily Times*, Iqbal Khattak, put it more bluntly: "You have to decide: Do I want this to be the last story of my life or do I want to write many more stories?" The two men were part of a group of about 15 tribal-area journalists who met several times with a three-person CPJ delegation in Peshawar.

One of the TUJ's most prominent members, Hayatullah Khan, was found dead in June. His body was dumped near the central market of Miran Shah, the tribal region's main town, not far from where he had been abducted in December 2005; he had been shot repeatedly. The day before he disappeared, Khan had photographed the remnants of a U.S.-made Hellfire missile that hit a house near Miran Shah in which senior al-Qaeda figure Abu Hamza Rabia was staying. Hellfires are typically fired from a drone or helicopter. The pictures—widely distributed by the European Pressphoto Agency—contradicted Pakistan's explanation that Rabia died in a blast caused by explosives within the house.

After Khan's body was found, Pakistani journalists called a strike, boycotting parliament. Under pressure, the government assigned the respected High Court Justice Mohammed Reza Khan (no relation) to investigate the journalist's

One Peshawar reporter asks: Do I want this to be the last story of my life?

disappearance and death. The Supreme Court weighed in and asked to be informed of Justice Khan's findings. NWFP and North Waziristan officials also investigated. It was a great show of official bravado, but by late year there was no public explanation from the government as to who had snatched and killed Hayatullah Khan.

In fact, of the eight journalists killed in Pakistan since 2002, only one case—that of *Wall Street Journal* reporter Daniel Pearl—has been investigated and publicly reported. Four of the eight were from the NWFP's tribal areas. Members of the TUJ say no legal efforts were made to discover the killers, and little or no aid was given to the victims' families.

"Except when we protest, there is no response from anyone," Behroz Khan told CPJ in Peshawar. "We are threatened. It has become part of the game. There is no law, no protection, no respect for freedom of expression. The state is not on our side."

Pakistani journalists are blunt in faulting the powerful Inter-Services Intelligence.

Who is responsible for such attacks in Pakistan? Without investigations there is no way to be sure, but the country's two most prominent journalist organizations are blunt in faulting the powerful Inter-Services Intelligence agency. In a joint statement issued August 9, the Pakistan Federal Union of Journalists and the All Pakistan Newspaper Employees Confederation said that they "put the blame squarely on the country's intelligence agencies for the attacks. The incidents of violence and threats to newsmen, particularly in the tribal areas of the NWFP, Baluchistan, and in the interior of Sindh, have created fear and panic among the journalists, which negate the government claim of freedom of the press."

While "fear and panic" may not be sweeping the entire country, Pakistan is growing more fragile as it tries to maintain a secular military regime in the face of a society rapidly politicizing along religious lines. The benefits of economic growth do not trickle down to most Pakistanis, and corruption is rife. The fairness of elections is viewed with great skepticism by Pakistanis and international experts alike, and there seems little room for political change. And while Pakistan may be stumbling, Afghanistan is tumbling into instability, never having recovered from the Soviet invasion or the years under the Taliban.

Khasif Hussein Waheed, a cameraman who worked for Associated Press Television News in Kabul during 2006, described the threats he faced when he ventured toward the border areas. It was not only the Taliban who worried him, he told CPJ in August. "Afghan forces are the toughest to deal with. During bombings and tense scenes, the police tend to get frantic. They say they are told to keep you away by the coalition forces. And the U.S. forces behave rougher than the NATO forces. The Americans humiliate you more readily and take the tough guy role. ... But they're good to you when you go on an embedded trip with them. Then there's no problem."

Simply being Afghan is of increasingly little help. "Really," Waheed said, "we're finding that even Afghan reporters who are not from the area are having a harder time getting cooperation from the local Afghan government militias."

Ruhullah Khapalwak, former Kandahar stringer for *The New York Times*, agreed that, for now, the Taliban aren't the greatest threat to Afghan reporters.

Ruhullah, now at Swarthmore College in the United States on a scholarship, says that he and his family were threatened, not because of his journalism but because he had been seen going in and out of the U.S. military base in Kandahar—guilt by association with Westerners.

In one recent CPJ assistance case, a Kabul-based fixer had to go into hiding when a group of armed men stormed his mother's house looking for him. He fled his neighborhood and stayed with friends around the city for days as he frantically contacted former clients asking for help. After two

Pakistan grows fragile as society divides along religious lines.

weeks on the run, CPJ was able to coordinate donations from some of the fixer's contacts in the United States and wire him enough money to leave the country. He suspected his pursuers were drug dealers angry about pictures he took several years ago of poppy fields, but he never knew for sure. What he did know as he moved from hiding place to hiding place was that he could not risk turning to the Afghan government for help out of fear that an informant would tell his pursuers where he was hiding.

As THE SITUATION DISINTEGRATES IN AFGHANISTAN, THE BLEAKNESS that those Pakistani tribal journalists in Peshawar expressed is growing in Kabul, too. Afghan journalists who fled during the Taliban years and returned after the U.S. invasion in 2001, and those who stayed and managed to survive in other roles (often working with international nongovernmental organizations), have moderated their hopes for a brighter future.

The offices of Pajhwok Afghan News lie down a short, dusty L-shaped lane across the street from the Ministry of the Interior in Kabul. Its chief editor and managing news director is Farida Nekzad, who went into exile in Pakistan in 1996, eventually returned to Afghanistan, and wound up running Pajhwok. Nekzad was frank in her meeting with CPJ's delegation: "[President Hamid] Karzai has promised support but it's not there for us. Gunmen and warlords are still in power and the authorities don't want to come to the aid of journalists. At our daily staff meetings we get reports of harassment or worse."

Were things improving for her 50 or so staff? Soon after the Taliban pulled back in 2001, she said, "it seemed like it was getting better. But we see it getting worse as the gunmen learn the power of the media. ... For now, Afghan journalists still feel empowered and entitled, but we know we have no guarantee of support from the government. If the government acted even once in our support it would have an effect." In a later message to CPJ, Nekzad added, "One thing I want to tell you: I will not leave Afghanistan for any reason, and I will fight to defend our rights as journalists as passionately as I can."

Another who has stayed is Barry Salam, who runs "Good Morning Afghanistan" and "Good Evening Afghanistan" on the official Radio Afghanistan. A well-known radio figure, Salam shares Nekzad's dismay. "I have heard no ambassadors or U.N. officials saying that things will be better in five years," he told CPJ. "These people indicate to me that the determination they have to improve the country exists in words only, not in practice."

Sounding weary beyond his 27 years, he continued. "I have grown so pessimistic over the past months. The U.S. lost focus on Afghanistan when it attacked Iraq. The war here will continue and grow until geopolitical change comes about. Despite what we had hoped, Afghanistan is still subject to those forces rather than being able to determine its own fate."

Since Salam made that statement in August, the attacks that were commonplace in the border areas have gotten worse. About a month after he spoke with CPJ, there was a spate of explosions, which grew into a steady string of car bombs, rocket attacks, and suicide attacks—five in September alone, with police claiming to have thwarted several others and American forces saying a suicide bomb cell was operating in the city. The target is usually, but not always, military, with civilians inevitably killed, too.

Afghan journalists have moderated their hopes for a brighter future.

Hekmat Karzai, President Karzai's nephew, heads the Center for Conflict and Peace Studies (CAPS), a think tank that focuses on terrorism and security. At last count, CAPS had documented 48 suicide attacks in 2006 alone, most of them in the provinces bordering Pakistan—and the year was not yet over.

With Afghanistan's stability precarious, it is not clear what comes next. Carlotta Gall, Kabul and Islamabad correspondent for *The New York Times*, has covered many conflicts over the years. Despite the resurgence of the Taliban, she was still weighing the situation. "The ruthlessness has increased over the year and has been specifically aimed at intimidating people. Will this become Chechnya, where journalists were attacked outright? I'm waiting to see."

· · · · · · · · · ·

Bob Dietz is CPJ's Asia program coordinator. He led a mission to Pakistan and Afghanistan in July and August.

···················· AFGHANISTAN ····················

The Taliban Islamist militia re-emerged in Afghanistan while the government of President Hamid Karzai wavered in its commitment to Western-style media. Despite the proliferation of media outlets since the fall of the Taliban government in 2001, reporters complained of little or no cooperation from officials, who were unwilling to meet with them or allow public offices to release information.

This antimedia approach was driven home on June 12 when the government summoned representatives from Tolo TV, *Kilid* magazine and Radio Kilid, *Kabul Weekly*, *Sibat*, the Pajhwok Afghan News agency, and other news organizations to a meeting with Hassan Fakhri, an official with the National Security Directorate. After lecturing them on the role of the media, Fakhri handed them a two-page document listing 17 recommendations on press conduct.

According to several of those who attended the meeting, the document was signed by Amrullah Saleh, head of the government's intelligence service. The group was told not to copy or distribute the document, which many of them immediately did. A similar document, unsigned and with minor changes to the text, was sent to more media groups in Kabul on June 18. Among the guidelines:

- Publication and broadcast of provocative statements of armed organizations and terrorist groups should be halted.

- Journalists should not report material that erodes people's morale and causes them disappointment.

- Criticism of the U.S.-led coalition or International Security Assistance Force troops should be prohibited.

- Interviewing "terrorist commanders" should be banned, along with videotaping and photographing them.

- News of antigovernment attacks or suicide bombings should not be a lead news story.

Karzai quickly distanced himself from the guidelines. At a press conference on June 22, Karzai told reporters, "If we want to be a democratic country with public accountability, we need a free press." Yet earlier statements issued by the office of the president's spokesman sought to justify the government's intervention in the work of the press,

· · · · · · · · · ·

Country summaries in this chapter were reported and written by Asia Program Coordinator **Bob Dietz**, Senior Research Associate **Kristin Jones**, and Program Consultant **Shawn W. Crispin**.

ıg the guidelines were needed to "refrain from glorifying terrorism r giving terrorists a platform." Regardless of Karzai's involvement, Kabul journalists said, the government had effectively sent a message that the press should temper its criticism.

After a brief postwar respite, Afghanistan grew increasingly violent in 2006, with a resurgent Taliban engaging coalition forces in the south and a rash of car bombings and political assassinations in Kabul and Kandahar.

Three journalists were killed. Aryana television cameraman Abdul Qodus died July 22 in a double suicide bombing in Kandahar. Qodus had just arrived at the scene of a suicide car bomb when a second attacker with explosives strapped to his body blew himself up. Qodus died of head injuries at a local hospital.

On October 7, Karen Fischer and Christian Struwe were fatally shot in a tent they had pitched along a road near Baghlan, about 95 miles (150 kilometers) northwest of Kabul. The two—journalists with German public broadcaster Deutsche Welle who were researching a documentary—had recently visited several United Nations Children's Fund projects in northern Afghanistan.

Journalists also faced widespread physical assault. Reporter Noorullah Rahmani and cameraman Qais Ahmad of the independent station Tolo TV were beaten on July 29. Gunmen attacked the crew at a demonstration against member of parliament Abdorrab Rasul Sayyaf in Paghman, Kabul province, according to the director of the station.

Low-powered radio stations and satellite TV are the most effective means of reaching audiences in outlying areas of Afghanistan, a country with a population of 27 million spread over 252,000 square miles (653,000 square kilometers) of inhospitable terrain; the illiteracy rate is roughly 65 percent. About 60 percent of Afghans had access to some sort of media in 2006, with six TV broadcasters and more than 60 independent radio stations providing content.

Print media were not regulated and new publications were easily launched. About 450 newspapers and magazines published in 2006, most tied to a political bloc or ethnic group. A number of business failures were reported in what had become a saturated market.

The Ministry of Information and Culture was generally supportive of broadcast media, particularly radio stations, although some of these outlets came under attack at the local level. Radio Istiqlal in Loghar, the province south of Kabul, was firebombed on August 11. It had not been threatened directly, but a "night letter"—an anonymous warning distributed by hand and posted on walls—had appeared in the town a few days before, condemning "corruption and decadence." Istiqlal broadcast a mix of news and entertainment, programming that often targeted women.

Journalism careers in Afghanistan continued to combine high risk with low pay, but members of the press played prominent roles at the village and community levels. Radio

ASIA

workers said stations run by women, or those where women could be heard on the air, were likely to anger local religious leaders in a country where, outside of a few urban areas, most women were expected to remain in the home as much as possible. The situation was aggravated when women called in to radio stations to voice their opinions. Most stations stood up to local pressure, but there was a growing fear that a conservative backlash could erase the government's support.

The pressures on women in the Afghan media are formidable, and the few female journalists working in the country have spoken of continual frustration. Aunohita Mojumdar, a freelance reporter from New Delhi who has found a way to survive in Kabul despite the high cost of housing and tight security, said she had seen incremental improvements in the rights of women since the Taliban left, but her ability to move around freely remained extremely limited. "Being a woman is the biggest problem, not the lack of security," Mojumdar said. "Being out in a public place makes me squirm as a woman. It's not the male physical threat. But the scrutiny is so intense, and men are trying to get close to you physically. To a lot of Afghans, an unescorted woman on the street is assumed to be a prostitute." She added, "I'm here to experience the country, but I've learned to put up a barrier to keep men at a distance. I don't want to do that, but I must do it to survive."

Added Farida Nekzad, head of the independent Pajhwok Afghan News: "I'm an editor, and I no longer like to go outside to report. And my female reporters complain that they are not respected when they assert themselves and take the microphone for questions at press conferences." But Nekzad added that Pajhwok, which had about 10 female reporters among its staff of roughly 50, was committed to bringing more women into the media, "even though there is still male resentment and discomfort."

· · · · · · · · · · · · · · · · · · · **BANGLADESH** ·

Rioting kicked off a three-month electoral season in October as the ruling Bangladesh National Party (BNP) was accused of bias in the installation of an interim government and election commissioner. Fears of physical attacks against a politically divided press corps deepened along with the political crisis, as leaders of the rival Awami League threatened to boycott the general election scheduled for January 2007. Journalists were tasked with covering a time of great uncertainty: President Iajuddin Ahmed, formerly a ceremonial head, installed himself as chief of a caretaker government and warned that the military could be brought in to quell violence.

Throughout the year, routine violence against journalists continued to inhibit coverage of corruption, poverty, and rising Islamic militancy. For the first time in three years, CPJ documented no cases of journalists killed for their work—but members of the press were threatened, intimidated, and physically attacked by party and student activists, police, criminal gangs, and fundamentalist groups. Journalists outside of the capital, Dhaka, were at particular risk.

A very active press in Bangladesh operated in relative freedom from direct government censorship. At the same time, public officials warned journalists against critical news reports in the name of protecting the image of Bangladesh. Addressing newly elected members of the Bangladesh Federal Union of Journalists in her office in April, Prime Minister Khaleda Zia called on the media to protect the country's interest and avoid harming the national economy through their reporting, according to local media reports.

Some high-level officials also took advantage of outdated criminal defamation laws to file cases against journalists whose critical reporting affected public perceptions. Public Works Minister Mirza Abbas filed a defamation case in February against the editor and publisher of the popular Dhaka-based Bengali-language daily *Prothom Alo*, saying that an article claiming a disagreement between the minister and police had tarnished the minister's image and status. Mahfuz Anam, publisher of *Prothom Alo* and editor of the English-language *Daily Star*, told CPJ that the case was one of three ongoing defamation cases against him.

In some instances, particularly in regions outside of Dhaka, official legal action against journalists was accompanied by physical threats and violence. Three journalists fled the western town of Kushtia in May fearing for their safety after local ruling party lawmaker Shahidul Islam filed extortion cases against them. Journalists from Dhaka and elsewhere traveled to the town to protest treatment of their colleagues only to be targeted themselves. At a rally in support of the press, men identified as BNP activists attacked the journalists with bricks, stones, and chairs, injuring as many as 25 without apparent police intervention. After vocal protests from Bangladeshi media organizations and international human rights organizations, including CPJ, the lawmaker apologized in July, dropping the cases against the journalists and allowing them to return to their homes.

Police continued a grim tradition of violence against the media in April, beating a sports photographer for using the wrong entrance at the opening of an Australia-Bangladesh cricket match in the southeastern city of Chittagong. The situation escalated when dozens of baton-wielding police officers brutally beat 20 journalists who were protesting the initial attack on their colleague. Several of the journalists were hospitalized, and a government committee later recommended monetary compensation for the injured reporters.

Little progress was made in solving a series of journalist murders. A disturbing pattern emerged in the cases of Shamsur Rahman, Manik Saha, Sheikh Belaluddin, and others killed for their work in recent years. Investigations

moved slowly, suspects were released, and trials repeatedly postponed—all of which served to ensure near total impunity in the killings. The failure of justice indicated a lack of either political will or ability on the part of the government.

"That's their strategy," Mainul Islam Khan, a press advocate for the Bangladesh Center for Development, Journalism, and Communication, told CPJ. "To delay as long as possible so the drive for justice becomes weaker and people will finally forget about the verdict."

In anticipation of the 2007 election between bitter rivals Zia, leader of the BNP, and former prime minister Sheikh Hasina of the Awami League, the issues of widespread corruption, violent crime, high rates of inflation, and poverty were brought to the forefront. Awami League leaders also blasted BNP's coalition with the conservative Islamic Jamaat-e-Islami party, accused of having close links to banned militant Islamist groups in the country.

The presence of an organized militant network—long reported by the media despite clear risks—was belatedly acknowledged by the government with the arrests of high-profile suspects in the coordinated nationwide bombings of August 2005. Journalists were denied access to captured militants Bangla Bhai (the alias of Siddiqul Islam) and Shaikh Abdur Rahman, prompting speculation that the leaders of the recently banned groups Jagrata Muslim Janata Bangladesh and Jamaat-ul-Mujahedeen would implicate others.

A sedition case proceeded against journalist Salah Uddin Shoaib Choudhury, editor of the Dhaka-based tabloid *Blitz*, who was released on bail in 2005 after spending 17 months in prison. Choudhury was arrested in November 2003 after trying to travel to Israel for a conference organized by the Hebrew Writers Association. Bangladesh has no formal relations with Israel, and the government has made it illegal for Bangladeshi citizens to travel there.

· **BURMA** ·

Military-run Burma, also known as Myanmar, remained one of the most repressive places for journalists, trailing only North Korea on CPJ's 10 Most Censored Countries list. The junta, which calls itself the State Peace and Development Council (SPDC), exerted Orwellian control over all media, harassing or jailing journalists who strayed from the official line in their reporting or who helped foreign correspondents with critical reporting. Two journalists were imprisoned for attempting to film outside the country's controversial new capital, Pyinmana, after the generals decided without warning to move the seat of government from Rangoon. The administration held at least seven journalists behind bars, earning Burma the rank of the world's fifth leading jailer of journalists.

International pressure grew from governments and bodies such as the United Nations and the Association of Southeast Asian Nations, calling for the release of the nation's 1,200 political prisoners. Ibrahim Gambari, U.N. undersecretary-general for political affairs, visited Burma in May and November seeking an easing of authoritarian control. But the SPDC maintained and in some cases even intensified restrictions on the media, which it censors through the Press Scrutiny and Registration Division (PSRD).

Reporting on detained opposition leader Aung San Suu Kyi and her National League for Democracy political party, debates about government policies, news that unfavorably reflected upon the junta—all were strictly prohibited. In February, the government stepped up its campaign to counter critical news about its leadership and human rights record by harassing journalists that provided information to foreign and exile-run media in countries such as neighboring India and Thailand. The Military Security Force, a government intelligence agency, acquired new surveillance technology to track people who spoke with international journalists. The junta interrogated businessmen, civil servants, and journalists on suspicion of providing information to foreign media, including live telephone interviews with the immensely popular Burmese-language broadcaster Radio Free Asia.

One victim of the intensified surveillance was Maung Maung Kyaw Win, a senior reporter and editor at the Burmese-language *Myanmar Dana* economics magazine. Military intelligence officials had threatened him with death in December 2005, accusing him of helping a U.S. journalist meet with a recently released political prisoner. Fearing for his safety, Maung Maung, along with his family, fled Burma for Thailand in early 2006. He was later granted refugee status in Cambodia by the U.N. High Commissioner for Refugees. It was not the first time Maung Maung had gone into exile in connection with his reporting activities. He left for a time in the early 1990s to help translate into Burmese the popular book *Outrage: Burma's Struggle for Democracy*, which chronicles the crackdown on the popular pro-democracy uprising in 1988.

On March 27, Thaung Sein (also known as Thar Cho), a photojournalist, and Ko Kyaw Thwin (also known as Moe Tun), a columnist at the Burmese-language magazine *Dhamah Yate*, were arrested for videotaping on the outskirts of Pyinmana. The following day, they were sentenced to three years in prison under the draconian 1996 Television and Video Act, which bars the distribution of video material without official approval. The junta had ordered the military to detain anyone taking pictures near the city, 250 miles (400 kilometers) north of Rangoon, to which the government had abruptly moved in November 2005. An appeals court upheld the guilty verdict against both journalists on June 21, without allowing defense witnesses to testify.

ASIA

The journalist in detention the longest was U Win Tin, who had served more than 17 years on various antistate charges. The 76-year-old's health had deteriorated in recent years, according to the Assistance Association for Political Prisoners in Burma (AAP-PB), an advocacy group based in Thailand. According to Amnesty International, U Win Tin was eligible for early release with time off for good behavior in July 2006, but he was still imprisoned when CPJ conducted its annual census of imprisoned journalists on December 1.

Journalists Maung Maung Lay Ngwe, Aung Htun, Thaung Tun, and Ne Min were also in prison on December 1. Maung Maung Lay Ngwe was first imprisoned in 1990 for publishing information that "makes people lose respect for the government." CPJ is investigating his whereabouts and legal status.

Aung Htun, a writer and activist, was imprisoned in February 1998 for writing and publishing a seven-volume book that documents the history of Burma's politically active student movement, which crucially led the pro-democracy uprisings of 1988. Sentenced to a total of 17 years, his health had deteriorated in recent years, according to the AAPPB.

Thaung Tun, an editor, filmmaker, and poet, was arrested in 1999 and subsequently sentenced to eight years in prison for his role in producing unauthorized films that exposed government mismanagement and human rights abuses. He was a member of the opposition NLD party and spent three years in prison for his political activities in the late 1970s. He is currently detained at Moulmein Prison in southern Burma, far from his family in Mandalay, according to the AAPPB.

Ne Min, a lawyer and former stringer for the BBC, was sentenced to 15 years in prison on May 7, 2004, on charges that he had illegally passed information to "antigovernment" organizations based outside the country.

Censorship and harassment of the local media were pervasive in 2006. The 1962 Printers and Publishers Registration Act requires that all editorial and advertising material be approved by the PSRD, a time-consuming process that requires most Burmese periodicals to publish as weeklies or monthlies. The PSRD has often required publications to carry articles drafted by the government, especially government propaganda recycled from *New Light of Myanmar*, the official daily newspaper.

On January 3, the junta ordered the sacking of popular *Yangon Times* columnist Major Wunna, who wrote under the pseudonym Mar J, after the periodical published two articles by him that government censors had rejected. The satirical pieces lampooned the government's relocation to Pyinmana and the ongoing National Convention to draft a new constitution.

The immensely popular *Weekly Eleven Journal* was forced by the censorship board to remove the names of four of the 15 people it had identified for its year-end edition as the country's leading personalities, including writer Ludu Daw Amar, journalist Ludu Sein Win, businessman U Tay Za, and artist Maung Than Sein.

In February, the PSRD issued a directive prohibiting all media from reporting on the reaction of Burma's minority Muslim community to the controversial Danish cartoons of the Prophet Muhammad. At least one publication had two articles it had drafted on the subject banned by censors, and no Burmese media covered the cartoon story, according to CPJ sources.

The PSRD in June ordered all local journals and magazines to stop publishing articles by Ludu Sein Win, who had been jailed by a previous military government. The order came soon after the 65-year-old journalist, who relies on an oxygen mask to breathe, wrote an op-ed piece for the *International Herald Tribune* that criticized the SPDC's policy toward the political opposition and called on the international community to pressure the junta. In another case of overt censorship, the monthly magazine *New Spectator*, which launched in May, was forced to cancel its July edition after government censors banned four of its top stories.

Despite this, the Ministry of Information claimed to be implementing a more open policy toward the local media. Information Minister Brig. Gen. Kyaw Hsan and top-ranking censor Maj. Tint Swe repeatedly vowed to adopt more flexible censorship policies and allow local publications more editorial independence. Favored publications were allowed to report for the first time on natural disasters, poverty, and certain public health issues, including the country's growing HIV/AIDS problem.

Brig. Gen. Kyaw Hsan led press conferences that, for the first time, allowed open question-and-answer sessions and, in May, participated in a government-run journalist training course. Not surprisingly, his lectures stressed journalism that serves "the interest of the state and the people," according to news reports.

The SPDC upgraded its Internet filtering and surveillance technologies, which it has procured from U.S. technology company Fortinet since 2004, according to information compiled by the OpenNet Initiative, a collaborative of several universities that focuses on Internet censorship issues.

The government has a monopoly on all 40 or so domestic Internet service providers, and it has attempted to force local e-mail users onto the government-run Mail4U service by periodically blocking access to internationally hosted services Yahoo and MSN Hotmail.

Government censors also sought to block Google's Gmail and online voice service GTalk. Users complained in mid-June that when they attempted to log on they received an "access denied" message and that service was only sporadically available in the months that followed.

Exiled journalists and press freedom advocates in Thailand and India told CPJ that the blockage was most likely part of the Ministry of Information's August 2005 "media to fight media" policy, a crude effort to block the flow of information critical of the government to foreign media organizations and exiled opposition groups.

ASIA

••••••••••••••••••••• **CHINA** •••••••••••••••••••••

In President Hu Jintao's fourth year in power, his administration effectively silenced some of the best journalists in China by sidelining independent-minded editors, jailing online critics, and moving to restrict coverage of breaking news. The government drew international criticism for its actions against foreign news agencies and their employees—including convictions of Zhao Yan, a *New York Times* researcher, and Ching Cheong, a correspondent for the Singapore-based *Straits Times*—along with new rules appointing the official Xinhua News Agency as sole distributor of foreign news services in the country.

The year saw some of the country's most steadfastly progressive working journalists demoted or fired, continuing a trend of dismantling prior advancements in the commercial press. Journalists were not universally cowed, however. In January, when the Central Propaganda Department shut down the thoughtful news supplement *Bing Dian* (Freezing Point), attached to the national newspaper *China Youth Daily*, Editor Li Datong openly lodged a complaint with the Communist Party's internal affairs watchdog. *Bing Dian* reopened but was forced to run an apology for an essay criticizing textbooks' nationalist treatment of 19th-century events. And editors Li and Lu Yuegang were removed from their posts and demoted to the News Research Institute, a separate department of the *China Youth Daily*.

"It's a place for children and the elderly," Li told CPJ in describing his new position.

Li became a vocal critic of government control over the media. "I wanted to be a role model to the media for challenging the Central Propaganda Department, to show people that it's OK to do this," he explained in a March meeting with CPJ in Beijing. "I think there will be more and more [challenges], and they will force the government to start reforming the media. The way the system operates now is unconstitutional and a total abuse of power."

Outside of major media centers in Guangzhou and Beijing, journalists were subject not only to the policies of the central government, but also to the whim of local authorities, who sometimes responded to embarrassing news stories with brutal vengeance. In February, *Taizhou Ribao* editor Wu Xianghu died from injuries sustained months earlier when traffic police stormed his newspaper's office in the eastern coastal city of Taizhou and severely beat him in retribution for a report alleging corruption. It was the first known killing of a journalist in China since 2001, though physical attacks on journalists have been on the rise, according to CPJ research. Local media were ordered not to mention his death, and no criminal charges were reported.

Other journalists were imprisoned after offending local officials. Yang Xiaoqing, a reporter for *China Industrial Economy News* in central China's Sichuan province, was jailed in January after spending months in hiding. He was accused of blackmail and extortion and sentenced to a year in jail after reporting on alleged corruption by officials in his home county of Longhui. Through the online advocacy of his wife Gong Jie and Internet journalist Li Xinde, the case gained the attention of Chinese citizens, who believed Yang was unfairly targeted. He was released after serving seven months in prison. In the southern province of Fujian, *Fuzhou Ribao* Deputy News Editor Li Changqing was not as lucky. Jailed after writing about a whistleblower's denouncement of corruption among local Communist Party officials, he was sentenced in January to three years in prison on charges of "spreading false and alarmist information" for reporting a dengue fever outbreak on the U.S.-based online news service *Boxun News*.

Just as local public pressure appeared to play a part in the early release of the Longhui reporter Yang, international criticism had an apparent—though limited—effect in the case of *New York Times* researcher Zhao Yan, jailed since 2004. Acquittals are extremely unusual in Chinese criminal cases, but Zhao was exonerated on a charge of leaking state secrets through his work for the Beijing bureau of *The New York Times*. He was not freed, however; the Beijing court sentenced him to three years in jail on a separate fraud charge, which his supporters believed was a pretext for continuing to hold him. Denied an open trial because of state secrets concerns, which were later discredited, Zhao was also denied an open appeal hearing on the fraud conviction.

Likewise, *Straits Times* correspondent Ching Cheong was denied an open appeal hearing after he was convicted of espionage and sentenced to five years in prison. Ching, a resident of Hong Kong and a veteran reporter, was jailed in 2005 while trying to obtain sensitive transcripts of interviews with ousted former leader Zhao Ziyang; he was charged with using his journalistic contacts to gather information for an academic organization in Taiwan that China said was a front for the Taiwanese intelligence agency. The Hong Kong Journalists Association condemned the verdict, saying it seriously jeopardized press freedom. Ching's jailing was seen as a shot across the bow for Hong Kong journalists reporting in China. His appeal was rejected in November.

A CPJ reporting mission to China in March focused on the government's efforts to suppress news coverage of tens of thousands of protests around the country, many of them related to the confiscation of farmers' land for development without adequate compensation. Concerned that reports of local protests would lead to instability at the national level, the government undertook one of the worst crackdowns on the media since the aftermath of demonstrations at Tiananmen Square in 1989, journalists told CPJ. Reporting on sensitive issues such as protests has been taken up by activists who use the Internet to spread news, commentary, and calls for action, CPJ's Kristin Jones found in a special report, "China's Hidden Unrest."

A lawyer known for his defense of activists was himself arrested and charged with "inciting subversion." Months before his arrest, Gao Zhisheng organized a hunger strike in protest of the official harassment of people like Guo Feixiong (Yang Maodong), a writer and activist who has drawn attention to the plight of farmers seeking redress from local officials. Several online writers were arrested in a crackdown apparently instigated by the hunger strike, including blogger and documentary filmmaker Wu Hao. Wu, who was working on a documentary about underground Christian churches, was detained after meeting with Gao and held without charge for more than four months, drawing protests from bloggers and friends around the world.

Writers Guo Qizhen and Zhang Jianhong were arrested for their online political commentary. Guo was sentenced to four years in prison for his criticism of Communist Party rule and widespread poverty and corruption. Zhang was imprisoned and accused of "inciting subversion" two days after posting an essay criticizing China's human rights record in the run-up to the 2008 Olympics. They joined the list of 31 journalists imprisoned in China, including pro-democracy writer Yang Tongyan (known by his pen name Yang Tianshui), who was sentenced to 12 years in prison in May on subversion charges.

The imprisonment of Zhang—who linked China's human rights failures to the Games and called it "Olympicgate"—was ironic given Beijing's promise in its 2001 Olympic bid that "there will be no restrictions on media reporting and movement of journalists up to and including the Olympic Games." But in the countdown to the Games, official policy has not followed official promises; instead, Beijing has tightened controls on the press. In November, a CPJ delegation met with Olympic Games Executive Director Gilbert Felli and Communications Director Giselle Davies at the headquarters of the International Olympic Committee (IOC) in Lausanne, Switzerland, to raise alarm about the erosion of press freedom in China.

In particular, CPJ expressed concern that Chinese journalists and sources would be at risk of official retribution once the Games ended if they reported anything deemed unfavorable. The IOC leaders did not address the safety of Chinese journalists or trenchant government control of the press, but they pointed out steps taken to ease restrictions on movements and access for foreign journalists during the Games. In December, the government lifted requirements that foreign journalists obtain official approval for travel and interviews. The change, effective through mid-October 2008, extends to Hong Kong, Macau, and Taiwan reporters, but it does not apply to mainland citizens.

China's tightening grip was evidenced in July, when central authorities made an effort to bolster their control over the media with a proposal to fine news agencies for reporting "sudden events" without official authorization. News organizations could be fined up to the equivalent of US$12,500 for their reporting, part of a regulation that seemed intended to forestall coverage of riots, natural disasters, and other unforeseen incidents before propaganda authorities could issue orders on how the events should be reported. An official of the Ministry of Foreign Affairs said that the regulations would apply to international news agencies as well as the domestic media. The proposal provoked open derision among working Chinese journalists, and it was unclear how the regulation would be implemented.

At the international level, much more attention was paid to a surprise announcement by the official Xinhua News Agency in September that all foreign news would be distributed solely through a Xinhua agent with authority to censor content. The regulations departed from conditions in effect since 1997 that allowed financial news agencies such as Reuters, Dow Jones, and Bloomberg to provide economic news and information directly to Chinese banks and media outlets. Concerned news agencies met with Xinhua and took a strong stand against their implementation, sources involved in negotiations said. Japanese, European Union, and U.S. officials were also quick to express concern about the measures, which appeared to violate norms set forth by the World Trade Organization. At year's end, the new rules had not gone into effect, and it appeared China might back away from them.

The stance of the international news services, one supported by foreign officials, was in contrast to the position of technology companies—many of them American—that China's strict rules restricting expression are nonnegotiable and that companies have no choice but to obey. Members of the U.S. Congress in March berated Microsoft, Google, Yahoo, and Cisco Systems over their complicity in Chinese government efforts to restrict free expression and to jail Internet users for criticizing the government. A particular target of criticism was Google's launch of a self-censoring search engine, Google.cn, in January. (The new version proved unpopular in China.) The companies' policies did more than just restrict searches or censor information. Journalist Shi Tao remained in a high-security prison, serving a 10-year term imposed in 2005 for "leaking state secrets" on his Yahoo e-mail account; evidence brought against him included account-holder information provided by the U.S. company.

In the fall, CPJ took part in discussions with U.S. and international Internet and communications companies, investor groups, human rights organizations, and leading U.S. academics to develop business principles that would safeguard free expression and privacy worldwide. The participants worked to establish voluntary guidelines for companies that would be modeled after the Sullivan Principles, which were adopted by U.S. businesses in response to apartheid. Discussions were expected to continue in 2007.

Liu Zhengrong, deputy director of the Internet Affairs Bureau of the State Council Information Office, told reporters in February that China blocks just a "tiny fraction" of Web sites available worldwide, and defended the country's massive and sophisticated firewall as being in line with international norms. He denied that any journalist was imprisoned for expressing views online. In October, Yang Xiaokun, a diplomat from the Chinese mission to the United Nations in Geneva, went further and denied that any Web sites were blocked in China. "We don't have restrictions at all," he said in response to a question posed at a conference in Athens on Internet governance. "How can I elaborate on it if we don't have any restrictions?"

Such assertions disregarded the facts.

ASIA

At least 19 journalists were jailed in China in 2006 for online news and commentary, according CPJ research. In court documents, Chinese prosecutors themselves repeatedly cited online articles as evidence of "inciting subversion." In March, authorities publicly defended the shutdown of a popular literary and news Web site known as *Aegean Sea*, one in a long line of Web sites censored by the government.

· **NEPAL** ·

Journalists played a lead role in resisting and ultimately reversing an audacious 14-month power grab by King Gyanendra Bir Bikram Shah Dev. Hundreds took to the streets in the capital, Kathmandu, and elsewhere to protest measures by the king to suspend radio news broadcasts and deploy the country's security forces and civil authorities to harass and censor the press. Journalists' refusal to bend to these restrictions contributed to a popular shift in favor of democracy. In April, political party leaders, civil-society activists, and journalists joined in mass demonstrations held in defiance of the government's shoot-on-sight curfew orders. Nineteen people were killed in a crackdown on the protests, but the violent response backfired on the king. By April 24, his support eroding, Gyanendra pledged to return power to Parliament.

The king's ostensible reason for seizing direct control of the country in February 2005 was to force an end to the 10-year conflict between the government and Maoist rebels fighting to overthrow Nepal's constitutional monarchy. In the end, it was Gyanendra's downfall that brought this goal within tenuous reach. After wresting control of the Royal Nepalese Army from the king, the Seven Party Alliance headed by newly appointed Prime Minister G.P. Koirala entered into peace talks with Maoists under rebel leader Prachanda. The two sides bridged differences over rebel disarmament and the future of the monarchy to forge a peace deal in November declaring a formal end to the war. The accord cleared the way for the 2007 election of a constituent assembly expected to decide the ultimate fate of the monarchy and rewrite the country's constitution.

Serious problems remained. The country had been torn apart by conflict, and reports of extortion, abduction, and the recruitment of children to the Maoists' People's Liberation Army marred hopes for an immediate recovery. Journalists, who had long been targeted by both the government and the rebels, received assurances from Koirala and Prachanda that press freedom would be respected; improvements in media conditions after the king relinquished control were indisputable. Outside of Kathmandu, though, members of the press faced continued threats and harassment by local government officials, criminal groups, and, particularly, Maoist cadres.

Hundreds of journalists were detained throughout 2005 and in early 2006 for participating in or covering protests, but most were held only briefly. A greater threat was neutralized in July, when the interim government announced that no new cases would

be filed under the repressive Terrorist and Disruptive Activities Ordinance (TADO), and that all prisoners held under TADO would be freed. The ordinance had been used to imprison accused Maoists, including journalists allegedly sympathetic to their cause, for long periods without charge or trial. Among those released in July was former *Yojana* newspaper editor Tej Narayan Sapkota, who was held in a series of army barracks and detention centers after his arrest at a printing facility in 2003. No journalist remained behind bars in Nepal when CPJ conducted its annual census of imprisoned journalists on December 1.

The war left a record of routine abuse and torture by security personnel, who were largely given free rein under legislation like TADO. Journalist and lawyer Jitman Basnet, who was imprisoned under the antiterrorism ordinance in 2004 under suspicion of supporting the Maoists, filed a petition before the Supreme Court in October calling for action against security forces involved in torturing detainees. Basnet said that while detained, he had been held under water, underfed, and forced to urinate on an electric heater.

The Seven Party Alliance government scrapped antimedia ordinances and policies promulgated after the king's coup, including a practice of purchasing advertising from loyal news outlets only. The alliance also solicited advice on promoting press freedom from a 13-member media commission composed of prominent independent journalists and media executives. The commission presented its report in September with recommendations on simplifying the procedures for obtaining a license to run an FM radio station, detaching public media from government control, and allowing greater foreign investment in the media.

The panel also recommended that drafts for a new constitution should note the role of the press in restoring democracy in the country and ensure press freedom and the right of information. Media advocates pointed out that an interim draft constitution proposed in November differed only slightly from the country's 1990 constitution in regard to press freedom—and included restrictions on the rights to seek information and report matters of public interest. Political leaders pledged the need for wider media protections in the drafting of a permanent constitution, which is expected after the 2007 constituent assembly elections.

Private FM radio news, a primary source of information for the large, illiterate population in Nepal and a particular target of Gyanendra, continued a recovery that began in 2005 with legal challenges to the king's ban on private radio news programming. As many as 2,000 radio journalists who had lost their jobs went back to work broadcasting news. Requirements for registering radio stations were eased, raising hopes for a revival exceeding pre-2005 conditions.

ASIA

Despite these improvements, journalists continued to face threats and harassment in outlying rural areas. Intimidation by Maoist cadres posed a threat to independent reporting on obstacles to the peace process in regions under Maoist control. In October, the Federation of Nepalese Journalists (FNJ) released a report detailing attacks on journalists after the democratic uprising, including an attempt by Maoists in Nawalparasi to force two print correspondents to become members of their party; an incident in which a group of people padlocked the offices of a newspaper in the district of Morang after it reported an alleged sexual assault of a minor by a Maoist; and the three-hour detention of journalists who had traveled to the district of Bara to report on the construction of a dam. On October 16, a local Maoist leader in the eastern district of Udaypur warned journalists that only Maoists could write about Maoists.

· **PAKISTAN** ·

The military-backed government of President Pervez Musharraf, now in its eighth year, said in 2006 that it was fostering a free press, but the details belied the claim, and journalists continued to be targeted from many sides.

While the government has allowed the expansion of broadcast media, a three-person CPJ delegation that met with dozens of journalists in Islamabad and Peshawar in July heard a lengthy string of complaints of government abuse and neglect, as well as concerns about pending legislation that could allow monopolization of the country's burgeoning media. The CPJ delegation had gone to Pakistan to meet with government officials after the high-profile slaying of Hayatullah Khan in June. Khan was the seventh journalist to be killed in Pakistan since the murder of *Wall Street Journal* reporter Daniel Pearl in 2002, according to CPJ research. Only Pearl's case was investigated to any degree of competency and publicly reported. The CPJ delegation contended that Pakistani journalists deserved the same level of attention from the authorities.

Though Interior Minister Aftab Khan Sherpao and Secretary of Interior Syed Kamal Shah promised CPJ timely reports on the information it had gathered on the eight deaths, none were immediately released. In the Khan case, an investigation was carried out by High Court Justice Mohammed Reza Khan (no relation), but the government refused to release the judge's findings. Khan's case captured international interest after he was abducted near his home in Mir Ali in North Waziristan on December 5, 2005. He had taken photographs the day before suggesting that a U.S.-made Hellfire missile had struck a house and killed al-Qaeda leader Abu Hamza Rabia. Khan's photographs seemed to contradict official accounts that explosives within the house had caused the deadly blast. Khan, who was abducted by five men, turned up dead on June 16, 2006.

During his absence, government officials appeared to mislead his family about his where-abouts and imminent safe return home.

Khan's case heightened awareness of the threat against journalists, which might have helped motivate authorities in responding to the September 14 shooting death of report-er Maqbool Hussain Sail. After a national and international outcry, local police investi-gated the killing. Sail, a correspondent for the Online-International News Network, was shot by two masked gunmen on a motorcycle as he was on his way to interview a leader of the Pakistan People's Party Parliamentarians at the Press Club in Dera Ismail Khan, southwest of Islamabad. The motive for the killing remained unclear, and it may have been related to sectarian violence rather than Sail's journalism. Despite the investigation, there was no official explanation of the incident.

Incidents of violence and threats against journalists occurred nationwide, but the Federally Administered Tribal Areas in northwest Pakistan were a particular focal point. On August 30, Taimor Khan, the 16-year-old brother of Dilawar Khan, a reporter for the BBC Urdu-language news service, was found murdered in Wana, South Waziristan. Unknown assailants seized Dilawar Khan in November, holding him for a day against his will and interrogating him about his sources.

At least three journalists were detained under questionable circumstances. Members of a reporting team with the privately owned satellite broadcaster Geo TV—including correspondent Mukesh Rupeta and freelance cameraman Sanjay Kumar—were taken by authorities on March 6, when they were reportedly taking pictures of an air base near Jacobabad near the Sindh-Baluchistan border. Rupeta and Kumar were held for more than three months without charge before being released on bail; they were later charged with violations of the Official Secrets Act.

On July 2, authorities detained Mehruddin Mari, a correspondent for the Sindhi-language newspaper *The Daily Kawish* in Golarchi. Mari was taken by police on the road between Golarchi and the town of Jati, southeast of Karachi. He was not released until October 24, and police refused to comment on the case either during or after his deten-tion. Mari told the BBC Urdu-language service that he was interrogated, beaten, and subjected to electric shocks and other forms of torture in an attempt to make him confess to ties with the Baluch nationalist movement.

Another journalist was abducted. Saeed Sarbazi of the *Business Recorder* was dragged from his car by unknown kidnappers on September 20 in Karachi. When he was re-leased three days later, Sarbazi told colleagues at the Karachi Press Club that he "was interrogated about my personal and professional details, my family members, and my connection with the so-called Baluch Liberation Army." Sarbazi said he was kept awake, beaten, and tortured. There was no official explanation of the incident or any apparent police investigation.

The string of cases—almost all of them uninvestigated and unexplained—contrib-uted to a feeling of isolation among Pakistani journalists, and a fear that they were easy

ASIA

targets for thugs, gunmen, and government agents. Members of the Pakistan Federal Union of Journalists told a CPJ delegation in Islamabad that they felt they had little backing from their employers or their government. While a small group working for mainline media is relatively well paid, most Pakistani journalists are not. Pay increases enacted by the Wage Board in October 2001 still had not been implemented.

Journalists said they were also concerned that their employers were being drawn into a comfortable agreement with the government that would allow media owners to hold companies across print and broadcast platforms. Critics of the Pakistan Electronic Media Regulatory Authority Bill (PEMRA), which was making its way through the legislature, said the bill would give media owners power to control the press through cross-ownership and potentially unrestricted monopolistic practices. Pakistani journalists told CPJ they feared that once owners of newspapers—which are not regulated—got involved in the regulated broadcast sectors, editors would inevitably be restricted in their coverage.

$\bullet \bullet \bullet \bullet \bullet \bullet \bullet \bullet \bullet \bullet \bullet \bullet \bullet \bullet \bullet \bullet \bullet \bullet$ **PHILIPPINES** $\bullet \bullet \bullet \bullet \bullet \bullet \bullet \bullet \bullet \bullet \bullet \bullet \bullet \bullet \bullet \bullet$

The Philippines remained one of the world's most dangerous countries for journalists, but it also became one of the more litigious as numerous criminal defamation lawsuits were filed by President Gloria Macapagal Arroyo's husband and other political figures. A deteriorating political situation and increased security concerns in February led Arroyo to declare a state of emergency and prompted her government to take a series of repressive actions against the press.

The administration billed the state of emergency as a way to preempt a coup by dissident soldiers, communist groups, and political opponents. It quickly issued broad guidelines that barred reporting considered destabilizing, and it positioned troops around the Manila headquarters of the country's two largest television broadcasters, ABS-CBN and GMA-7.

Without a warrant, national police raided the facilities of *The Daily Tribune* in Manila, seizing editorial materials and padlocking its printing presses for one night. The paper, which was known for its critical news coverage of Arroyo's administration, had run a series of articles earlier in February that predicted and analyzed the government's possible motives for imposing a state of emergency.

After lifting martial law on March 3, the government filed sedition charges against the paper's publisher, Ninez Cacho-Olivares, and columnists Ike Seneres and Herman Tiu-Laurel. Cacho-Olivares told CPJ that the indictment did not specify the offending *Daily Tribune* articles or columns, and she later won a Supreme Court appeal on grounds that the constitution protected press freedom during times of national crisis.

Still, government officials and their close associates continued to harass the press, filing a string of criminal libel cases against several journalists at a time. On October 2,

a court in the city of Barangay Santa Fe issued arrest warrants for Publisher Rudy Apolo and 10 staff members of the *Asian Star Journal* and *Asia Star Balita* based on a criminal defamation complaint filed by provincial Gov. Irineo Maliksi. The governor took issue with the papers' reporting on alleged corruption in a government rice purchase.

On October 16, the Manila Regional Trial Court issued arrest warrants for nine editorial staff members of the English-language daily *Malaya* in relation to a criminal libel suit filed by Jose Miguel Arroyo, the president's husband. The suit stemmed from a May 19, 2004, report alleging that Arroyo was involved in attempted vote-rigging in favor of his wife during the 2004 presidential election—charges he strongly denied.

Arroyo filed at least 10 different criminal libel lawsuits against 43 different journalists seeking damages totaling 70 million pesos (US$1.4 million). Penalties for criminal libel convictions in the Philippines also include imprisonment of six months to six years. In response to politicians' use of criminal libel suits, a coalition of more than 600 journalists and 30 local and foreign international media freedom organizations issued a joint petition calling for the decriminalization of libel.

At least three Philippine journalists were killed in retaliation for their reporting, bringing to 32 the total number of reporters killed for their work over the past 15 years, CPJ research shows.

President Arroyo, who has repeatedly vowed to better protect the press, established a national police unit in 2004 to track down journalists' killers. The unit has made some inroads, but government spokesmen have overstated its progress. In response to inquiries made by U.S. Sen. Richard Lugar, spokesman Ignacio Buyne issued a public statement in May claiming that roughly half of Philippine journalist murders had been solved. But by the government's definition, a case is considered "solved" merely when a suspect is identified and some type of court case filed—regardless of whether the case results in a conviction. Research by CPJ, which considers a case solved when killers and masterminds are convicted, shows that the impunity rate in the Philippines is well over 90 percent.

Progress was made in one high-profile case. On October 6, a judge in Cebu convicted three suspects in the March 2005 murder of investigative reporter Marlene Garcia-Esperat, sentencing each to 30 to 40 years in prison. The three gunmen—Estanislao Bismanos, Gerry Cabayag, and Randy Grecia—pleaded guilty and testified that they had been hired to assassinate Garcia-Esperat in retaliation for her stories about corruption in Mindanao's Department of Agriculture.

As the verdict was announced, Justice Secretary Raul Gonzales ordered the reinstatement of murder charges against the two agriculture officials suspected of masterminding the murder, finance officer Osmeña Montañer and accountant Estrella Sabay. Charges against the two officials had been dropped the previous year, but Gonzales said evidence

ASIA

presented in the case supported their reinstatement, The Associated Press reported.

Yet with other investigations progressing slowly, the culture of impunity remained firmly in place. In May, two gunmen on motorcycles shot radio commentator Fernando Batul six times as he drove to work at DZRH in Puerto Princesa on Palawan Island. His murder came a week after two hand grenades and a threatening letter were left at his home.

Police officer Aaron Madamay Golifardo was later arrested and charged with Batul's murder. In a May 11 broadcast, Batul had criticized Golifardo for allegedly showing a weapon during a disagreement with a waitress in a karaoke bar, according to news reports. Hearings in Golifardo's trial began in September. The other person on the motorcycle was not immediately identified. Batul, a former vice mayor, was also highly critical of city government, and his reporting often touched on alleged government corruption and nepotism.

The next month brought another pair of murders on another island—under strikingly similar circumstances. Two unidentified gunmen on a motorcycle shot and killed radio broadcasters George and Maricel Vigo on the island of Mindanao while the couple were walking home from a public market. George Vigo was a contributor to the Bangkok-based, church news agency Union of Catholic Asian News. His wife, Maricel, hosted a radio program on local station DXND. The couple had earlier founded a tabloid called *The Headliner*, which sought to expose police and government corruption. That newspaper's office was mysteriously burned down in 2001.

Police painted the two journalists' deaths as a retaliatory act by the New People's Army (NPA), a militant Communist group. The couple, previously active in left-wing student groups, had cultivated contacts within the NPA as part of their reporting, according to colleagues. In 2003, George Vigo reported on the NPA for a BBC documentary titled "One Day of War," according to journalist Orlando Guzman, a friend who did reporting for the documentary.

CPJ continued to investigate the circumstances surrounding the July murder of radio broadcaster Armando Pace, who was killed while riding home from Radyo Ukay DXDS in Digos City on the island of Mindanao. Digos City Police Director Caesar Cabuhat said that Pace's killing could have been "a personal or work-related crime," according to news reports. One suspect was charged.

SRI LANKA

Hopes that the Sri Lankan government and Tamil rebels would be able to salvage their crumbling cease-fire were dashed in 2006. By September, the military and the Liberation Tigers of Tamil Eelam (LTTE) were again locked in combat in the north and east of the country. While the conflict looked similar to that of past years, the government did permit a freer flow of information about the separatist fighting and did not impose the censorship that had prevailed in earlier years. But impunity continued to be the rule for those who attacked journalists and media facilities, despite international pressure from press freedom and human rights groups on both sides of the conflict.

The LTTE had launched its rebellion in 1983 seeking to establish a separate state for the country's 3.2 million Tamils. Before the government and rebels signed a cease-fire in 2002, some 65,000 people died. The situation grew more complicated in March 2004, when the LTTE split into two factions after a rebel leader known as Colonel Karuna formed his own rival army in eastern Sri Lanka. The LTTE accused the Sri Lankan army of supporting Karuna's rebellion.

Tamil journalists have been particular targets of hit squads and bombings, account-ing for all seven of the journalist murders in Sri Lanka between 2000 and 2005. The source of these targeted attacks is not always the government or groups linked to the Sinhalese ethnic majority. Some of the attacks are tit-for-tat killings, the result of rivalries among the various armed Tamil groups.

Subramaniyam Sugitharajah, a reporter for the Tamil-language daily *Sudar Oli*, was shot and killed on his way to work in January—just a few weeks after his published photographs contradicted an official military account. The photos showed that five men said to have been killed by their own hand grenades during an attack on the military had actually been shot.

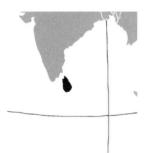

CPJ sent a letter on February 22 to President Mahinda Rajapaksa and LTTE leader Anton Balasingham, calling on all parties in the conflict to recognize that journalists are not valid targets for arrest or abuse. "We urge all sides to make a commit-ment to ensure that journalists are able to carry out their duties without fear of intimidation or reprisal," CPJ said.

Tamil media facilities were also attacked during the year. On October 16, Sri Lankan Air Force planes destroyed the broadcasting towers of the Voice of Tigers (VOT), the LTTE radio station in the northern guerrilla-held town of Killinochchi. The LTTE said that two workers, whom it did not identify, were injured in the strike. The government's Media Centre for National Security said the VOT radio tower was not directly targeted but could have been damaged during air strikes on other LTTE targets in the area.

One Tamil newspaper was targeted repeatedly, but the source of the violence was not clear. On May 2, five masked gunmen killed two employees and wounded at least two others, one seriously, when they sprayed the offices of the Jaffna-based Tamil newspaper *Uthayan* with automatic weapon fire. On August 19, warehouses containing the paper's printing equipment were burned down. Four days earlier, an *Uthayan* driver was killed in Jaffna.

For *Uthayan*, the situation had become so dire that E. Saravanapavan, the paper's managing director, contacted CPJ on September 7 to make a public plea: "Please tell everyone that I have repeatedly asked the government for protection for my staff, and I have appealed to all of the high commissions and to everyone I can think of in civil-society organizations to help us. The government has removed all protection from my staff, despite our repeated pleas for assistance." Saravanapavan made the call from Colombo, where he had moved because he was afraid he would be attacked if he continued to live and work in Jaffna. He said some *Uthayan* staffers, fearing for their lives, rarely ventured onto the streets, living instead in the paper's offices. CPJ has documented a series of attacks on *Uthayan* dating back to 1999. Despite the newest threats and the flaccid government response, the paper has continued to appear regularly.

The northern Jaffna peninsula was the site of most military conflicts between government and Tamil forces, but other regions were not immune. On July 31, the Tamil-language dailies *Thinakkural* in Amparai district and *Sudar Oli* (a sister publication of *Uthayan*) in Batticaloa district stopped distributing after receiving threatening phone calls. Both newspapers eventually resumed production, but the circulation of *Sudar Oli* dropped by a third, the paper's management said. On October 23, about 20,000 copies of the Tamil daily *Virakesari* were seized from the paper's distributor and burned. In a press statement made in Colombo, the paper's owners said they thought the Karuna faction of the LTTE was responsible for the attack.

The media situation is complicated by the fact that many journalists are openly partisan, favoring a particular side or faction within the conflict. Despite their overt political positions, in its February 22 letter CPJ called "on all parties to recognize that even journalists who choose political sides are not valid targets for arrest or abuse." Yet such partisanship, coupled with the government's unwillingness to assert its authority and pursue assailants, adds to the ongoing threats facing all Sri Lankan journalists—partisan or not.

• THAILAND •

A year of political turmoil climaxed in a military coup that accelerated the deterioration of Thailand's press freedom climate. Royalist generals seized power on September 19 while Prime Minister Thaksin Shinawatra was in New York attending the U.N. General Assembly. The coup was condemned abroad, but the new leadership was endorsed by King Bhumibol Adulyadej, who is widely revered by Thais. It was the country's first coup in 15 years but its 18th since it became a constitutional monarchy in 1932.

Army commander Gen. Sonthi Boonyaratklin ordered tanks placed outside Thailand's six main television stations, and national radio and television programming was interrupted. Broadcasters aired pictures of the monarchy while the coup was under way. Soldiers entered newsrooms to bar the broadcast of news footage of Thaksin. During the coup and its immediate aftermath, the military blacked out international broadcasters CNN and BBC whenever they aired news reports on Thaksin.

Thai television Channel 9, which is managed by the prime minister's office, aired part of a statement by Thaksin, who attempted to declare a state of emergency and order the removal of Gen. Sonthi. The statement was cut off midway, and Thaksin's loyalists in the armed forces were quickly neutralized. The station's managing director, Mingkwan Sangsuwan, was taken into army custody for questioning and later removed from his position.

The coup leaders, who after a number of name changes called themselves the Council for Democratic Reform (CDR), and ultimately the Council for National Security, promptly scrapped the 1997 constitution, which had broadly protected press freedom. It was replaced with an interim charter that omitted the media provisions outlined in the old constitution. On September 21, the CDR called a meeting with senior media representatives, ordering all radio stations to cancel phone-in news programs and instructing television broadcasters to stop displaying text messages sent in by viewers.

By military decree, the junta closed about 400 community radio stations in Thaksin's political strongholds in the north and northeast of the country. The move brought into question the legality of more than 2,000 other community radio stations operating across the country—not just those loyal to Thaksin. Immediately after the coup, the CDR empowered the Ministry of Information and Communications Technology to censor any news that undermined the junta's authority, according to local media reports. There were no reported cases of direct censorship of the print media, but the ministry ordered the closure of the activist-run *19sep* Web site, which had posted comments critical of the coup.

On September 23, junta spokesman Maj. Gen. Thaweep Netniyan threatened to take action against unnamed foreign correspondents and news organizations that allegedly insulted the monarchy during their coverage of the coup and its aftermath. He ordered the Ministry of Foreign Affairs to follow up on the charges, which could carry penalties of up to 15 years in prison. No action was taken on the threat, but many foreign correspondents who spoke with CPJ expressed concerns that they might encounter difficulty extending their work visas and press cards. The move was seen as an indicator of the junta's hostility toward the media.

In an October 5 letter to CDR-appointed Prime Minister Surayud Chulanont, a former army commander and close adviser to the palace, CPJ protested the military crackdown on the media and called on his government to restore the press freedom provisions of the old constitution. A few

weeks after the coup, print media, including the English-language daily *The Nation* and the Thai-language *Matichon*, began to test the new limits by running critical news and commentaries about the coup leaders and the civilian-led interim administration they had appointed.

At a November 7 function sponsored by the Foreign Correspondents Club of Thailand, Surayud promised to take a more liberal approach toward the media than the previous government, and he referred to Thaksin's attempt in 2002 to expel two foreign journalists with the *Far Eastern Economic Review* newsmagazine. "We may not always agree with how you report what you see, but any disagreement with this interim government will be addressed by transparent, rational debate, not emotion, and certainly not the stick," he said.

The media had come under intense government harassment during Thaksin's five years in power. As street protests against his government intensified during the year, Thaksin responded by filing a string of criminal and financially crippling civil lawsuits against critical news publications. Criminal defamation charges in Thailand carry possible two-year jail terms and fines of 200,000 baht (US$5,500); there is no limit on damages in civil suits.

In March, Thaksin's lawyer filed criminal complaints against the Thai-language dailies *Manager Daily*, *Krungthep Tooragit*, *Post Today*, and *Thai Post* over their coverage of antigovernment rallies. The complaints centered on the publication of speeches by protesters who accused the government of corruption and illegally selling national assets to foreigners. In June, Thaksin targeted three additional Thai-language dailies—*Matichon*, *Khao Sod*, and the *Daily News*—for publishing opposition comments that accused him of unjustly clinging to power after democratic elections were annulled. In the three civil defamation suits, Thaksin sought the combined equivalent of US$21 million in damages.

Media firebrand Sondhi Limthongkul, a founder of the Manager Media Group, a conglomerate of print, radio, and broadcast media, led many of the antigovernment rallies. In March, when the Thai-language daily *Kom Chad Luek* published remarks Sondhi made in an apparent critical reference to the monarchy, 3,000 protesters staged noisy demonstrations in front of the publication's offices and physically harassed its reporters. More than 200 police were summoned to maintain order, but the protesters refused to leave the premises until *Kom Chad Luek* executives agreed to fire the editor and suspend publication for five days.

By June, Sondhi told CPJ, government officials, police, and private individuals had filed more than 50 criminal lawsuits against him, involving both criminal defamation and violations of *lèse-majesté* laws, for comments he made and his media reported during antigovernment rallies. However, the status of the various charges Thaksin filed against the media was uncertain, given his retreat into exile following the coup.

Despite these setbacks, journalists did score one legal victory during the year. On

March 15, media activist Supinya Klangnarong and four journalists from the *Thai Post* were acquitted of criminal defamation charges brought by telecommunications giant Shin Corp. The court ruled that public companies that hold government concessions, like public figures, should be open to criticism in the public interest. Shin, which had been owned by Thaksin family members, had filed a criminal complaint against Supinya and the *Thai Post* journalists in October 2003. The defendants had faced possible two-year jail terms and fines of 200,000 baht (US$5,500). The company later filed a related civil suit seeking 400 million baht (US$10.9 million) in damages.

· **VIETNAM** ·

As Vietnam continued a period of impressive economic growth, two milestones marked its increased presence on the world stage. In November, Hanoi hosted its most important international event, the Asia-Pacific Economic Cooperation (APEC) summit, which brought together U.S. President George W. Bush, Russian President Vladimir Putin, Japanese Prime Minister Shinzo Abe, and other major world leaders. That same month, the World Trade Organization (WTO) formally invited Vietnam to become its 150th member, bringing to fruition Hanoi's 11-year effort to join the group.

Government efforts to allay international concerns over the country's human rights record ahead of these events gave national media and dissident writers a rare opportunity to test official control over news and opinions. State-controlled media appeared to push the limits of the censorship apparatus, and the samizdat opposition press grew louder despite lingering risks.

A bolder and increasingly competitive Vietnamese media took on a major corruption scandal that embroiled top officials early in the year. State-controlled domestic newspapers and Internet publications were uncharacteristically aggressive in their coverage of the investigation, beginning with allegations in January that the director of the Transport Ministry's Project Management Unit 18 (PMU18) had spent millions of U.S. dollars betting on international soccer matches. Demanding accountability and a response to the public's outrage, the media played a major role in prompting the resignation of Transport Minister Dao Dinh Binh and in spurring criminal investigations against a coterie of government officials.

Several journalists were physically attacked in an apparent attempt to inhibit their coverage of the scandal, local media reported. "It feels like journalists covering this case are in great danger," a *Doi Song va Phap Luat* newspaper reporter told the Ho Chi Minh City-based *Thanh Nien* after being assaulted. A man photographed attacking a *Thanh Nien* photojournalist was later revealed to be a police captain—who was reprimanded for failing to wear his uniform but not charged, according to the newspaper.

While a top official from the Ministry of Public Security promised to prosecute those who attacked and obstructed journalists, outgoing Prime Minister Phan Van Khai sent a very different message in May when he called for prosecution of news agencies he accused of "going too far" in their reporting on PMU18 and other cases, according to state media.

"Several state news agencies have committed legal violations by posting misleading information, infringing citizens' privacy, and raising public concerns," Khai charged in an official document sent to the Ministry of Culture and Information, government news agencies reported. The prime minister urged the ministry to take assertive action against offending news agencies instead of levying fines or extracting corrections; in the same document, Khai encouraged private citizens to file civil lawsuits against the press if they felt wronged by media misinformation.

The government's efforts to rein in the press went further in July, when it put in place a new system of fines of as much as 30 million dong (around US$1,900) for "violators of culture and information regulations." The decision listed a catchall of media crimes, including "denying revolutionary achievements; defaming the nation, great persons, and national heroes; slandering and wounding the prestige of agencies and organizations; publishing more than the registered number of 1,000 copies; and importing color photocopy machines without a license," according to state media. The rules supplemented existing criminal laws that restricted press freedom in the guise of protecting national security.

In October, the government temporarily suspended two newspapers for their reporting on corruption and printing problems with the country's new nonpaper banknotes. Eight other publications were fined for their reports on the notes. Some news agencies had published allegations that the son of a high-level banking official had profited from the printing contract. Another newspaper, *The Gioi*, was suspended indefinitely in November after publishing readers' letters criticizing government corruption.

Corruption scandals formed the backdrop of the government's 10th Party Congress, a five-year gathering in April that mandated a transition in leadership. But the new administration—President Nguyen Minh Triet and Prime Minister Nguyen Tan Dung, whose appointments were confirmed in June—was not expected to diverge from the path of its predecessor. The government continued to focus on the country's economic integration into the world market and the Communist Party's monopoly on power within Vietnam.

Ahead of its accession to the WTO and its hosting of APEC, the government took steps to ease diplomatic concerns over its human rights practices, including its detention of several dissidents who were U.S. citizens. Nguyen Van Dai, a lawyer who helped launch an online publication promoting democracy, noted that conditions for dissidents appeared to have improved in recent years. Though the government questioned him extensively about the publication, he told CPJ in a telephone interview that, "three years ago, you wouldn't be talking to me right now because I would be in jail." In a late-year concession to U.S. pressure, the government announced that Vietnamese-American political prisoners would be deported.

Several other high-profile prisoners were freed in amnesties declared during the year, including two Internet writers. Nguyen Khac Toan was released in January after serving more than four years of a 12-year sentence imposed in connection with his reporting on demonstrations outside the National Assembly in December 2001 and January 2002; and Pham Hong Son was released in August after serving four years on "antistate" charges arising from his translation and online posting of an essay headlined "What Is Democracy?" that initially appeared on a U.S. State Department Web site. Both continue to face years of political and travel restrictions. Journalist Nguyen Vu Binh, jailed in 2002 after criticizing border agreements between Vietnam and China, was the sole member of the press who remained in prison because of his work. He was serving a seven-year jail term on espionage charges.

But the amnesties did not indicate official tolerance for opposition to the Communist Party. Independent writers who dared to be vocal in their calls for multiparty democracy were frequently detained, harassed, followed, and interrogated. As one example, for months authorities cut off all telephone lines of formerly imprisoned writer Nguyen Thanh Giang, isolating him, his wife, and his ailing father from contact with the outside world.

Actions against dissidents came to a head in the run-up to Independence Day on September 2. Among those targeted were signatories to a petition circulated in April outlining calls for democracy and expanded freedom. Authorities attempted to thwart the efforts of five people, including freed writer Nguyen Khac Toan, to launch an online newspaper called *Tu Do Dan Chu* (Freedom and Democracy), which was to be downloaded and distributed in print on September 2. Toan and fellow writer Hoang Tien were among those repeatedly detained and interrogated.

An official Voice of Vietnam radio report slammed CPJ's criticism of their harassment: "CPJ claimed that they have been acting to protect dissidents in Vietnam who are not allowed to publish private newspapers. This is just a pretext to conceal their biased and unjust views on Vietnam." The report called independent publishers "opportunists who are dissatisfied with the regime and want to run and use private newspapers as a tool to disseminate slanderous allegations against the people's peaceful life and the country's renovation process."

The writers succeeded in posting *Tu Do Dan Chu* online, but it was quickly blocked by Vietnam's Internet filtering system. The Internet censorship research organization OpenNet Initiative reported that the government, with a focus on silencing political criticism, had stepped up its efforts to filter and monitor content for the more than 10 million

Vietnamese citizens thought to be online.

In September, the family of U.S. citizen and Vietnamese opposition party member Cong Thanh Do revealed that he had been imprisoned. He was known to CPJ as a writer whose online articles on imprisoned dissident cases were posted under the name Tran Nam. After three weeks, he was released and deported to California, but other members of the party arrested in the same sweep remained in jail. During the APEC summit, police and security forces kept dissidents under heavy surveillance and held recently freed writer Pham Hong Son under virtual house arrest.

Foreign journalists continued to need explicit government permission to travel outside of Hanoi, where all of them are required to live. Some told CPJ that they assumed that authorities were monitoring their activities and communication, especially any contact with dissidents or banned religious leaders. Correspondents feared that if they angered the government while doing their jobs, their visas would not be renewed.

SNAPSHOTS: **ASIA**
Attacks & developments throughout the region

CAMBODIA

+ Military police arrested Hem Choun, a reporter with the Khmer-language newspaper *Samrek Yutethor*, as he reported June 7 on the government's eviction of squatters in the village of Sombok Chab, 11 miles (18 kilometers) outside Phnom Penh. The Cambodian Center for Human Rights said authorities refused to recognize Choun as a journalist. A Phnom Penh judge charged Choun with wrongful damage of property and denied bail.

+ Legislation eliminating prison terms for defamation was passed into law on June 23. Terms had ranged up to one year. Criminal defamation laws remained in effect, punishable by fines of 1 million to 10 million riels (US$255 to US$2,550).

+ On July 14, the government filed a criminal defamation case against Dam Sithek, publisher of the Khmer-language *Moneakseka* newspaper, for allegedly publishing false information. The case stemmed from a June 13 article that accused the government of corruption and described a power struggle within the ruling Cambodian People's Party, according to the Alliance for Freedom of Expression in Cambodia.

+ Despite Prime Minister Hun Sen's announcement that charges would be dropped, a Phnom Penh court left criminal defamation cases intact against three journalists: Mom Sonando, head of Sambok Khmum (Beehive Radio); Kem Sokha, a radio commentator and president of the Cambodian Center for Human Rights; and Pa Guon Tieng, a journalist and activist. Each had been jailed for criticizing a new border treaty with Vietnam. They were released on bail on January 18 amid international pressure, but the cases were pending throughout the year.

EAST TIMOR

• Members of an Australian peacekeeping force manhandled and detained for four hours Jose Belo, a freelance cameraman working for The Associated Press in Dili. The AP said the Australian troops treated Belo in a "violent and disrespectful" manner during the June 10 incident. Belo was released only after non-Timorese AP reporters intervened. Belo told the AP that Australian forces handcuffed him, refused to let him film, and seized his camera, mobile phone, and other equipment.

INDONESIA

• The South Jakarta District Court dismissed charges against Teguh Santosa for publishing a cartoon of the Prophet Muhammad in February. Judges ruled in September that the case was too weak to bring to trial. Santosa, editor of *Rakyat Merdeka's* online edition, faced up to five years in prison on charges of defaming Islam. Santosa removed the drawing from the Web site and issued a public apology after local Muslim groups protested.

- Herliyanto, a freelance reporter with the *Radar Surabaya*, and *Jimber News Visioner* newspapers, was found dead with numerous stab wounds on April 29 in a wooded area near the town of Banyuanyar in East Java province. The Alliance of Independent Journalists said Herliyanto was investigating corruption allegations involving school construction funds in the village of Tulupari. CPJ confirmed that Herliyanto, who, like many Indonesians, used only one name, was killed because of his work as a journalist. On September 26, Probolinggo police arrested three men suspected of involvement in the murder and identified four additional suspects.

- In February, the Indonesian Supreme Court overturned the 2004 criminal libel conviction of *Tempo* magazine's top editor, Bambang Harymurti. The three-judge panel ruled unanimously that civil, and not criminal, laws should apply. Lower courts had applied criminal statutes to convict and sentence Harymurti to a one-year prison term in September 2004. The charges stemmed from a March 2003 *Tempo* article alleging that prominent businessman Tomy Winata stood to profit from a fire at a Jakarta textile market. Winata, who denied any connection to the fire, subsequently launched several civil and criminal actions against the magazine.

JAPAN

- An unidentified man hurled a Molotov cocktail at the headquarters of Japan's largest business daily, *Nihon Keizai Shimbun*. No one was hurt in the July 21 attack. Police investigated the possibility that the attack was motivated by the newspaper's exclusive story about the late Emperor Hirohito's refusal to visit the Yasukuni Shrine after it began honoring 14 convicted war criminals in 1978.

MALAYSIA

- Three newspapers in Malaysia faced penalties related to the publication of controversial cartoons depicting the Prophet Muhammad. In February, the government ordered the indefinite suspension of the publishing license of the English-language *Sarawak Tribune* and began a criminal investigation of its staff. The Chinese-language *Berita Petang Sarawak* and *Guangming Ribao* were each suspended for two weeks.

- The Malaysian Ministry of Information in June ordered the Chinese-language radio program "The Mic Is On, With Love, Without Obstacles" to restructure its format and stop live broadcasts after it aired listeners' views about a controversial government order affecting Chinese-language schools.

MALDIVES

- Internet journalist Ahmed Didi was released from house arrest and pardoned in February, four years after receiving a life sentence because of his work. Didi, a founder of the Dhivehi-language Internet publication *Sandhaanu*, was arrested in February 2002 and held for several months in solitary confinement before being sentenced on charges of defamation, incitement to violence, and treason. Didi was charged with "insulting" Maldivian President Maumoon Abdul Gayoom, calling for the overthrow of the government, causing hatred against the government, and spreading false news.

- A reporter with the opposition newspaper *Minivan Daily* was sentenced to life imprisonment in April on drug charges. Colleagues believe that Abdullah Saeed, known as Fahala, was framed and unfairly tried by a judiciary that is largely controlled by President Gayoom, who has ruled since 1978. Under international pressure, the Maldivian government made gestures toward democratic reform by allowing nongovernmental publications to operate on a limited basis in the country, but continued to harass, detain, and prosecute journalists sympathetic to the opposition Maldivian Democracy Party.

- Authorities detained and expelled Phillip Wellman, an American reporter working for the online newspaper *Minivannews*, and Graham Quick, a British freelance photographer working for London's *Observer*. The Minivan publishing group is closely associated with the opposition Maldivian Democratic Party. "They were asked to leave because their activities were not in line [with what] could be attributed to journalism," Foreign Minister Ahmed Saeed said after the November 3 action. The two journalists, traveling together, were covering the arrests of Maldivian Democratic Party activists on the southern Gaaf Dhall atoll, Wellman reported.

NORTH KOREA

- On May 3, World Press Freedom Day, CPJ named North Korea the world's Most Censored Country. All domestic radio, television, and newspapers are controlled by the government. Radio and television receivers are locked to government-specified frequencies. Content is supplied almost entirely by the official Korean Central News Agency, which serves up a daily diet of fawning coverage of "Dear Leader" Kim Jong-il and his official engagements. The country's grinding poverty is never mentioned. Only small numbers of foreign journalists are allowed limited access each year, and

ASIA

they must be accompanied by "minders" wherever they go.

SINGAPORE

- Prime Minister Lee Hsien Loong and his father, Lee Kuan Yew, filed criminal defamation charges in May against politicians responsible for the production of an opposition-run newspaper, *The New Democrat*. The Lees' lawyers also threatened to file defamation charges against Melodies Press Co., which prints the paper. The government in Singapore uses criminal and civil defamation charges to stifle criticism and independent reporting.

- The state-owned tabloid *Today* canceled in July the column of Lee Kin Mun, who writes under the name Mr. Brown. Lee, a well-known blogger in Singapore, wrote a satirical column in June headlined, "S'poreans Are Fed Up with Progress!" that criticized the government for announcing hikes in transportation and electricity costs only after May's general elections.

- On September 28, the government revoked the *Far Eastern Economic Review*'s right to distribute in the city-state. The Ministry of Information, Communications, and Arts said the Hong Kong-based monthly failed to appoint a legal representative and post a 200,000 Singapore dollar (US$129,000) security bond, as required by new regulations covering foreign publications. The action came a month after the prime minister and his father filed a civil lawsuit against the *Far Eastern Economic Review* alleging that they were defamed in a July story about opposition politician Chee Soon Juan. Damages would be set by a judge. In similar cases, Singapore's leaders have won hundreds of thousands of dollars in compensation from political opponents and news publications.

EUROPE AND CENTRAL ASIA

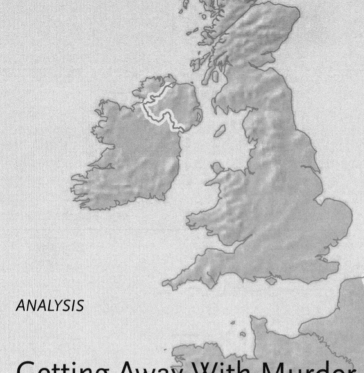

Getting Away With Murder
in the Former Soviet States

Impunity in journalist murders has dealt a severe blow to press freedom in the former Soviet states. As the region's political and moral force, Russia sets an example. Sadly, it is one of stonewalling and inertia.

by Nina Ognianova

PHOTOS

Section break: AP/Sergei Grits – *Two days before the Belarusian presidential election in March, police in Minsk seize a truck carrying thousands of opposition newspapers.* Analysis (next): Reuters/Gleb Garanich – *Mourners hold photos of the slain reporter Anna Politkovskaya at a vigil outside the Russian embassy in Kyiv, Ukraine.*

EUROPE AND CENTRAL ASIA

GETTING AWAY WITH MURDER
IN THE FORMER SOVIET STATES   *by Nina Ognianova*

· ·

THE ASSASSIN IN A BASEBALL CAP WHO GUNNED DOWN ANNA
Politkovskaya outside her Moscow apartment used a silencer. But reverberations from the contract-style slaying of Russia's icon of investigative journalism were felt around the world.

The October 7 killing drew international attention to impunity, the scourge of journalists in the authoritarian nations of the former Soviet Union.

From Ukraine to Turkmenistan, 46 journalists have been murdered in the former Soviet states over the past 15 years, with 90 percent of the cases unsolved, according to CPJ research. The message from the authorities has been clear: When it comes to journalists, you can get away with murder. This has had the intended chilling effect on media coverage of sensitive issues of corruption, organized crime, human rights violations, and abuse of power in countries such as Russia, Belarus, Ukraine, Azerbaijan, and Turkmenistan, CPJ research shows.

Shielded by institutional secrecy, authorities make little effort to track down the killers. CPJ has documented case after case in Europe and Central Asia where investigators ignore journalism as a motive. Instead, they classify the killings as common crimes and label professional assassins "hooligans." Prosecutors open and suspend investigations, rarely informing victims' relatives and colleagues, who have to scramble for information or do their own forensic investigation.

Detectives sometimes fail to study the dead journalist's notebooks, computers, and tape recorders. They fail to interview all witnesses, then ignore the testimony of those they do interview. Investigations are closed "for lack of suspects" despite glaring evidence to the contrary.

Russia has the worst record of impunity among countries in the region. It is also the third deadliest country for journalists worldwide, according to "Deadly News," a CPJ analysis of deaths over the past 15 years. Only Iraq, and Algeria when it was riven by civil war, outrank it.

Politkovskaya was the 13th journalist to be killed in a gangland-style hit since President Vladimir Putin entered the Kremlin in 2000. None of the masterminds behind those slayings have been prosecuted.

Across the former Soviet states, 46 journalists have been slain in 15 years.

Politkovskaya was a thorn in Putin's side, particularly for her dogged coverage of the Second Chechen War—a conflict underreported by mainstream Russian media and nearly forgotten by a public numbed by Kremlin-controlled national television. For seven years, she was threatened, imprisoned, forced into exile, and once even poisoned for her work. Yet she refused to stop or tone down her reporting on human rights abuses committed by federal troops, security forces, and Chechen militias in the southern republic of Chechnya.

Despite global media coverage, the Russian government said nothing for three days after the shooting of the award-winning reporter for *Novaya Gazeta*. Putin, pressed by reporters while on a visit to Germany, eventually broke the official silence with a verbal sideswipe. "I must say that her domestic political influence ... was insignificant," he said of Politkovskaya, a woman named by CPJ as one of the most prominent defenders of press freedom in the last 25 years.

Putin then effectively told prosecutors to rule out politicians and officials as suspects in any murder inquiry. "For current authorities in general and Chechen authorities in particular, Politkovskaya's murder did more damage than her articles," Putin said. "I cannot imagine that anybody currently in office could come to the idea of organizing such a brutal crime." He said the murder was ordered by overseas conspirators "to create a wave of anti-Russian sentiment internationally," the news agency Interfax reported.

Yelena Tregubova, a former Kremlin correspondent and author of a bestselling book critical of the government's attempts to muzzle the press, said anyone seeking to step into Politkovskaya's shoes "will be taking on a suicide mission." Tregubova, expelled from the Kremlin press corps in 2001 for refusing to follow government directives on coverage, had a bomb explode outside her Moscow apartment in 2004. Police classified the explosion as an act of hooliganism.

Even where those suspected of killing a journalist were brought to trial, court proceedings were secretive and riddled with abuses. The trial of two men accused of the July 2004 assassination of American Paul Klebnikov in Moscow was just such an instance. The accused were tried behind closed doors and ac-

Russia remains the region's political and moral force. Its stonewalling and inertia are widely emulated.

quitted in May of killing Klebnikov, the editor of *Forbes Russia*. The prosecution complained of procedural violations, jury intimidation, and misconduct by court officials who stalled an appeal by withholding the transcript of the closed hearings. In November, the Supreme Court overturned the acquittal and ordered a retrial.

Russia remains the political and moral force in much of the region, so its official hostility to independent media, sloppy police work in the investigation of journalists' deaths, official stonewalling, and judicial inertia are widely emulated.

In Azerbaijan, President Ilham Aliyev called the March 2005 assassination of journalist Elmar Huseynov a "provocation against the Azerbaijani state" and an "act of terrorism."

Strong words, but local journalists believe authorities have treated the case as a political tool and have no intention of identifying the real killers. Huseynov, founder and editor of the opposition newsweekly *Monitor*, was gunned down in a professional-style hit in his apartment building in the capital, Baku. A harsh critic of the president and his administration, Huseynov had endured scores of politicized lawsuits, tax inspections, and suspensions during the weekly's six-year existence.

Accusations have flown about with little substance or follow-up. A month after the killing, investigators identified two Georgian citizens as suspects but never provided enough evidence to persuade officials in Georgia to extradite them. The trail soon grew cold. Then, in July, a former Azerbaijani Interior Ministry officer, on trial on unrelated charges, professed that he helped plot Huseynov's assassination.

Huseynov's colleagues are skeptical about this latest allegation. Shahla Ismailova of the Baku-based Human Rights House told CPJ: "If they want to make someone 'confess' to a wrongdoing, they will succeed. Detainees in Azerbaijani prisons are subjected to torture. And under such pressure, anyone can confess to anything." Ismailova doubted the authorities wanted to solve the crime. "All of Elmar's work was [about] exposing the corrupt regime in Azerbaijan, and this is why an objective investigation cannot be expected from our current authorities."

Turan news agency Director Mehman Aliyev, who has been following the Huseynov case closely, told CPJ that Azerbaijani journalists do not expect the current inquiry to lead to prosecution. "According to police statistics, authorities have high rates of solved street crimes, but when it comes to attacks against journalists, none of them are solved," Aliyev said. "This shows that authorities are simply not interested in finding the killers or attackers of journalists. This is their unwritten policy." In such conditions, Aliyev added, editors of independent and opposition publications are sometimes forced to instruct reporters to tone down their coverage for safety reasons.

Aleksandr Starikevich, editor of the opposition newspaper *Solidarnost* in the Belarusian capital, Minsk, is also skeptical of the official probe into the October 2004 murder of co-worker Veronika Cherkasova. Colleagues of Cherkasova launched their own investigation into her death, saying officials treated the killing as a common crime and ignored forensic evidence pointing to a professional slaying. CPJ continues to investigate the case.

In an Azerbaijan case, accusations fly with little substance or follow-up.

"The investigation went in a wrong direction from the start, and then got stuck on the 'common crime' version," Starikevich said in an interview in the independent daily *Komsomolskaya Pravda v Belorussii* (Komsomol's Truth in Belarus). "I believe Veronika was killed for her work."

Two years after Cherkasova was found in her Minsk apartment with multiple stab wounds, prosecutors said they had suspended the investigation for lack of suspects. A Minsk investigator said the killing did not appear premeditated and continued to refer to it as a common crime, allegedly the result of a domestic quarrel, according to Belarusian press reports.

Authorities ignored her articles on surveillance by the Belarusian state security service (KGB) and her investigation of alleged arms sales by Belarus to former Iraqi President Saddam Hussein. Instead, the official investigation focused on the journalist's teenage son as a suspect and pressured him to confess to killing his mother.

Close to the second anniversary of Cherkasova's death, the Agency for Journalistic Investigations, an association of Belarusian reporters, released the findings of its own probe. Contrary to the official version, the association said the murder appeared to have been carried out by a professional who made it look like a crime of passion. The assassin, the report said, covered his tracks skillfully. Although stabbed repeatedly, Cherkasova had died from a single wound. Investigators have ignored the findings of the agency's investigation.

For Myroslava Gongadze, international support was crucial.

In Turkmenistan, even after a journalist died in official custody, authorities refused to investigate. Ogulsapar Muradova, 58, a correspondent for the Turkmen service of the U.S.-funded Radio Free Europe/Radio Liberty (RFE/RL), was arrested on June 18 and held incommunicado for more than two months in an Ashgabat jail. A day after her arrest, President Saparmurat Niyazov called her a traitor to the motherland on national television. In August, she was convicted on a bogus charge of possessing ammunition and sentenced to six years in jail after a closed-door trial that lasted only minutes. Three weeks later, authorities released Muradova's body to her family, refusing to give the time and cause of death and denying requests for an autopsy.

Muradova's relatives said the body bore a large head wound and multiple neck bruises. To this day, Turkmenistan has ignored international calls for an independent inquiry into Muradova's death, while media and human rights advocates are convinced that she was murdered in prison because of her work for RFE/RL—a broadcaster that Niyazov, who died in December, considered an enemy. Journalists affiliated with the Turkmen service, CPJ research shows, have endured years of harassment—from threats and surveillance to torture and imprisonment. Some have been forced into exile.

One glimmer of hope in the fight against impunity in the region has emerged in Ukraine. Myroslava Gongadze, widow of slain Internet journalist Georgy Gongadze, has made some headway in bringing his killers to justice.

Georgy Gongadze, the 31-year-old editor of the independent online newspaper *Ukrainska Pravda*, which criticized former President Leonid Kuchma, disappeared on September 16, 2000. Several weeks later, his headless body was discovered in a forest outside Kyiv.

"After months and years of fruitless struggle with Ukraine's prosecutor general's office, I realized that my husband's disappearance would not be fully investigated as long as President Kuchma remained in power," Myroslava Gongadze told CPJ. "I decided to use any available international mechanism to fight Ukrainian authorities."

Gongadze launched an international campaign for an investigation into her husband's death. The European Court of Human Rights agreed in March 2005 to hear her case and ruled in her favor eight months later. The court sent a strong message, finding that Ukrainian authorities failed in their duty to protect the editor's life, failed to thoroughly investigate his death, and treated the Gongadze family in a degrading manner. Gongadze was awarded 100,000 euros (US$132,700) in damages.

Her campaign also helped propel the 2004 Orange Revolution, which overthrew Kuchma. "The new president of Ukraine, Viktor Yushchenko, came to power with my husband's name on his flags," Gongadze said. "He promised that those responsible for Georgy's murder would be brought to justice in two months."

Justice did not come as quickly as she had hoped. "I have to admit that all this pressure brought some progress," Gongadze said, noting that three former police officers were on trial for the murder. "But I'm afraid that I do not see a political will in Ukraine today to bring the officials accused of ordering this crime to justice."

Still, she said, "My struggle is not over and I've promised to do everything I can, and I will, even if sometimes it feels as if it is hopeless."

Gongadze is convinced that mobilizing the international community was key to her success. "It is important to establish a precedent because every unsolved journalist killing triggers new killings."

Setting a precedent is the goal of Moscow lawyer Karen Nersisian, who represents the families of several slain Russian journalists, including that of *Novaya Gazeta* journalist Igor Domnikov, a colleague of Politkovskaya. Domnikov was shot, contract style, in Moscow in 2000 after he wrote articles critical of a regional governor. Three suspects in Domnikov's killing are currently on trial in Kazan, the capital of the Russian republic of Tatarstan. "We are doing everything possible to get the masterminds. We know who they are and I believe we can get them," Nersisian told CPJ. "If we succeed, this will be an important victory, not only for Rus-

The perception that murderers go free perpetuates the cycle of violence against reporters.

sia but for the entire region." Nersisian took part in a CPJ conference in Moscow in July 2005 that brought together the relatives and colleagues of journalists assassinated in Russia since 2000.

Oleg Panfilov, head of the Moscow-based press freedom group Center for Journalism in Extreme Situations, said that in their struggle for justice, regional journalists needed the support of organizations such as CPJ. "International advocacy must continue," Panfilov told CPJ. "Local authorities do not listen to our declarations. They do not pay attention to our protests. They only react to international statements and criticisms, and those should continue. There is just no other alternative."

Impunity for the killers of journalists has dealt a severe blow to already fragile press freedoms in Russia and the other nations of the former Soviet Union. The perception that murderers go free has perpetuated the cycle of violence against reporters who cover sensitive subjects and pushed even courageous journalists toward self-censorship. The public has suffered as a result, having been kept in the dark about human rights abuses, corruption, high-level crime, and, in the case of Chechnya, an ongoing war.

• • • • • • • • • •

Nina Ognianova is coordinator of CPJ's Europe and Central Asia program. She helped organize CPJ's 2005 Moscow conference on journalist murders.

• • • • • • • • • • • • • • • • • • • AZERBAIJAN •

Two prominent journalists were viciously assaulted in unsolved attacks,
and the 2005 murder of another top reporter was wrapped in questions. President Ilham
Aliyev and his allies used the courts as a hammer against the independent media, filing
criminal defamation lawsuits, lodging spurious drug charges, and imprisoning critical
journalists. Interior Minister Ramil Usubov, the second most powerful government official, filed five separate criminal defamation lawsuits against journalists with the Baku-
based *Milli Yol*, *24 Saat*, and *Azadlyg* newspapers.

The investigation into the May 2005 murder of Elmar Huseynov, founder and editor of the opposition newsmagazine *Monitor*, produced a surprising accusation—along
with continued skepticism about the government's probe. Haji Mammadov, a former Interior Ministry official being prosecuted on unrelated charges, stunned Azerbaijanis in
August by proclaiming in court that he had planned Huseynov's murder on the orders of
former Economic Development Minister Farkhad Aliyev. Mammadov was being tried on
charges of leading a criminal gang that carried out a series of murders and kidnappings
over 11 years. Farkhad Aliyev, already jailed on unrelated charges of planning a coup,
denied the accusation, according to local press reports. Neither Mammadov nor Aliyev
were immediately charged.

Journalists in Azerbaijan reacted skeptically to the news, saying there was little evidence to support Mammadov's courtroom revelation. They also noted that Huseynov
had written critical but often favorable articles about the former economic minister's
work. The new confession contradicted the government's initial theory in the case. In
2005, investigators accused two Georgian citizens of shooting Huseynov in the stairwell
of his apartment building, but authorities in Georgia cited a lack of evidence and refused
to extradite the pair, according to CPJ research.

The twisting but unresolved Huseynov investigation set the backdrop for a violent
year that saw savage attacks on two journalists: Fikret Huseinli, an investigative reporter
for the Baku-based opposition daily *Azadlyg* (Liberty), and Bakhaddin Khaziyev, editor-
in-chief of the Baku-based opposition daily *Bizim Yol*.

Huseinli, who was investigating alleged government corruption, was kidnapped on
March 5 and his throat slashed by unidentified assailants in the Patamdar area, a southwestern suburb of Baku, according to news reports. The journalist had received several
prior death threats by phone, warning him to discontinue his reporting. Huseinli survived the attack and returned to work. On May 19, five men abducted Khaziyev on the

• • • • • • • • • •

Country summaries in this chapter were reported and written by Europe and Central Asia
Program Coordinator **Nina Ognianova**, Research Associate **Tara Ornstein**, and freelance
writer **Chrystyna Lapychak**.

EUROPE AND CENTRAL ASIA

outskirts of Baku, beat him over several hours, and drove over his legs with a car, according to news reports. Khaziyev survived but suffered serious leg injuries.

No charges were filed in either case, prompting protests from journalists and from Miklos Haraszti, media freedom representative for the Organization for Security and Cooperation in Europe. The Azerbaijan Press Council pointed to an underlying problem. "The main reason these kinds of incidents repeat themselves, in the most violent forms possible, is that their perpetrators, as a rule, remain unpunished," the council said in a letter to Prosecutor General Zakir Qaralov.

In October, the National TV and Radio Broadcasting Council told private radio executives that they must discontinue programming from the BBC and two U.S. government-funded outlets, Radio Free Europe/Radio Liberty and the Voice of America. Council head Nushiravan Maharramli said his agency had determined that domestic radio licenses barred the broadcast of foreign-prepared content, the New York-based news Web site *EurasiaNet* reported. Regulators said they would set aside other frequencies for foreign broadcasts, but details were scarce.

After threatening the independent television station ANS for more than a year, the government shut the broadcaster for two weeks in late 2006. Authorities sealed off ANS facilities and confiscated its equipment on November 26, saying that the station had violated media laws and failed to pay fines.

Since President Aliyev and his Yeni Azerbaijan Party swept to victory in a November 2004 vote—which international observers said was neither free nor fair—top government officials have used the legal system to quash investigative reporting. Led by Interior Minister Usubov, public officials filed at least a dozen politicized lawsuits against critical journalists, according to local press reports.

Shakhin Agabeili, editor-in-chief of *Milli Yol*, was targeted in rapid-fire fashion in August. He was arrested on August 9 after Usubov complained that a *Milli Yol* story wrongly accused the minister of having ties to the disgraced Mammadov. The next morning, Agabeili was sentenced to a year in prison in a separate defamation lawsuit filed by Parliamentary Vice Speaker Arif Ragimzade. Usubov eventually withdrew his own complaint when Agabeili apologized following days of interrogation, according to local press reports. Agabeili was freed on a presidential amnesty declared on October 23, but the editor told CPJ that he was not allowed to leave the country.

Usubov also filed a criminal libel lawsuit against Eynulla Fatullayev, editor-in-chief of Azerbaijan's highest circulation independent weekly *Realny Azerbaijan*, in response to articles in July and August that alleged ties between Usubov and Mammadov. On September 26, Fatullayev was convicted and sentenced to a two-year suspended prison term, ordered to publish a retraction, and directed to pay 10,000 manats in damages to

Usubov. Fatullayev closed *Realny Azerbaijan* on October 3 without explanation, according to international press reports.

In August, Usubov filed criminal defamation charges against the Baku-based opposition weekly *24 Saat* and its editor-in-chief, Fikret Faramazoglu, in response to July articles that alleged the interior minister knew about Mammadov's crimes. At his hearing, Faramazoglu stood by his story. "It is impossible that the minister knew nothing about the criminal group that operated in the ministry for 10 years," the independent Turan news agency quoted him as saying. Faramazoglu was convicted on both charges and sentenced to a one-year suspended prison term.

The Mammadov case generated many legal complaints, but a story that touched on sensitive ethnic issues also inspired a prominent lawsuit. Samir Adygozalov, editor-in-chief of the opposition newspaper *Boyuk Millat*, was convicted of criminal libel in February and sentenced to a year in prison for a 2005 article that claimed Abel Magarramov, Baku State University rector and a parliament member, was an ethnic Armenian and had used university funds to support the Armenian diaspora. Ascribing Armenian heritage to someone is considered a slur in Azerbaijan, where relations with neighboring Armenia are very poor due to the decade-long Armenian occupation of the western province of Nagorno-Karabakh. Adygozalov was released in the October 23 amnesty, according to CPJ sources.

Authorities were also accused of setting up a prominent reporter on drug charges. On June 23, police arrested Sakit Zakhidov, a satirist for the Baku-based opposition daily *Azadlyg*, and charged him with carrying 10 grams of heroin. Zakhidov was sentenced on October 4 to three years in prison for drug possession.

Zakhidov denied the charge and said that the drugs were planted by police during his arrest. Journalists in Azerbaijan condemned the prosecution, noting Zakhidov's arrest came only three days after Executive Secretary Ali Akhmedov of the ruling Yeni Azerbaijan Party publicly called for "an end" to Zakhidov's work. Akhmedov said at a June 20 media freedom panel, "No government official or member of parliament has avoided his slanders. Someone should put an end to it," *EurasiaNet* reported.

In November, a Baku court said the State Property Committee could evict the opposition newspaper *Azadlyg* from its premises. The Turan news agency, *Bizim Yol* newspaper, and the Institute for Reporters Freedom and Safety, which had sublet space, were also targeted with eviction.

· · · · · · · · · · · · · · · · · · · **BELARUS** ·

Determined to forestall the kind of democratic uprising that toppled the government in neighboring Ukraine, authoritarian leader Aleksandr Lukashenko and his government crushed dissent in the run-up to the March presidential election—and

EUROPE AND CENTRAL ASIA

well beyond. Official results showed that Lukashenko collected 83 percent of the vote to gain a third term, but international observers said the election fell far short of democratic standards.

Authorities arrested dozens of domestic and foreign journalists who tried to report on the campaign and subsequent demonstrations in the capital, Minsk, over voting irregularities. In the months surrounding the election, the Lukashenko administration made it nearly impossible for independent and opposition media to deliver news and opinion to their audiences. The state postal service refused to deliver newspapers critical of the government; the state distribution agency banned sales of such papers on newsstands; printing houses refused to print them under government pressure; and border police confiscated entire press runs of publications that managed to find alternative printers abroad. Under such dismal conditions, papers set up distribution systems reminiscent of the underground press in Soviet times, selling copies from their newsrooms and dispatching volunteers to deliver them door-to-door to subscribers. Even then, some volunteers were arrested, CPJ research shows.

Despite all these difficulties, print media were freer and more diverse than their broadcast counterparts. With no independent radio or television, mainstream news programming was replete with pro-government and anti-West propaganda, CPJ found in a 2006 mission to Belarus. On May 3, World Press Freedom Day, CPJ named Belarus one of the world's 10 Most Censored Countries.

Attacks started in the first days of the year, when border police in the northeastern Vitebsk region confiscated two issues of the largest opposition newspaper, *Narodnaya Volya*. The January 3 and 9 issues—about 30,000 copies each—carried coverage of opposition presidential candidates and criticism of government efforts to suppress their campaigns, said Svetlana Kalinkina, deputy editor of *Narodnaya Volya* and a 2004 recipient of CPJ's International Press Freedom Award. *Narodnaya Volya* was banned from newsstands and denied postal distribution; banks refused to accept deposits into the paper's account from would-be readers trying to purchase a subscription. Authorities in the town of Soligorsk, Minsk region, harassed local residents who signed a petition asking that *Narodnaya Volya* be allowed to return to newsstands and be distributed through the mail. Police started visiting the 180 Soligorsk petitioners on January 6, according to press reports, asking them to explain their support of the newspaper.

On January 31, police in Zhlobin confiscated several hundred copies of *Tovarishch*, the official newspaper of the Belarusian Communist Party, from a distributor transporting copies out of town. The seized copies included coverage of candidate Aleksandr Milinkevich, Lukashenko's main rival. The national postal service, Belpochta, excluded *Tovarishch* from its 2006 subscription catalogue, effectively barring it from being mailed, the press freedom group Belarusian Association of Journalists (BAJ) reported. *Tovarishch* was one of several opposition titles forced to print in Smolensk, Russia, because printing houses in Belarus refused to take on the sensitive job. The state-owned distribution agency, Belsoyuzpechat, had announced in late 2005 that it would stop selling 19 opposition and independent newspapers, including *Narodnaya Volya* and *Tovarishch*, on newsstands, according to press reports and CPJ sources.

To assess press conditions in the run-up to the presidential vote, CPJ traveled to Belarus in February and documented authorities' aggressive campaign to suppress critical reporting and block alternatives to government-sanctioned news. In a subsequent press conference, CPJ called on the Russian Federation, the European Union, and the United States to renounce the March 19 election if the government continued its widespread suppression of campaign news and opinion. CPJ's news conference was held in Moscow because of Belarusian government press restrictions.

In February, Minsk prosecutors exploited an international controversy to obstruct and ultimately shutter the independent Minsk weekly *Zgoda*, one of the few news outlets to cover opposition candidate Aleksandr Kozulin. Belarusian state security service (KGB) agents confiscated the paper's computers, computer disks, and other electronic equipment after *Zgoda* reprinted in its February 17 edition several controversial Danish cartoons depicting the Prophet Muhammad. The drawings ran alongside an article headlined "Political Creation" that chronicled the uproar caused by the cartoons. The Higher Economic Court in Minsk closed the 5,000-circulation paper on March 17, two days before the presidential election, according to the Moscow-based Center for Journalism in Extreme Situations. *Zgoda* Deputy Editor Aleksandr Sdvizhkov, who authorized publication of the cartoon, fled Belarus in fear of criminal prosecution, local sources told CPJ.

Foreign journalists who tried to cover the campaign were also harassed. In late January, Belarusian police stopped a Ukrainian television crew at a border checkpoint and confiscated video footage they said was "antistate." The crew, from the independent Inter network, was returning to Ukraine's capital, Kyiv, from an assignment in the Belarusian region of Gomel when a border patrol seized videotapes of interviews with local residents, some of whom complained that the coming vote was not a presidential election "but a Lukashenko election," Inter journalist Aleksei Ivanov told the daily *Kommersant-Ukraine*. Belarusian authorities did not return the footage.

In late February, authorities expelled Polish journalist Waclaw Radziwinowicz, a reporter with Poland's largest daily, *Gazeta Wyborcza*, who had traveled on a valid visa and press accreditation to report on the elections. Border guards detained Radziwinowicz at a train station in the western city of Grodno and ordered him to return to Poland because his name was on an unspecified government list of people barred from entering the country, according to international press reports.

As the vote neared, authorities became more overtly aggressive in quashing dissent.

When Kozulin tried to enter a March 2 meeting where Lukashenko was to speak, plain-clothes agents assaulted the candidate and took him to a police station, according to press reports. As journalists tried to document the confrontation, officers turned on them. Oleg Ulevich, a reporter for the daily *Komsomolskaya Pravda Belorussii*, suffered a concussion and a broken nose; an unidentified Reuters cameraman was beaten as well.

Days before the election, four independent and opposition newspapers were forced to halt publication. The independent newspaper *Belorusskaya Delovaya Gazeta* and the opposition papers *Tovarishch* and *Narodnaya Volya* suspended publication on March 13 after their printing house in Smolensk said it was canceling their contracts for "economic and political reasons," according to the news agency Belapan. The titles had been printed in Smolensk since 2004, when Belarusian printers refused to accept the jobs. Workers for *Narodnaya Volya*, which found another printer in Smolensk, were stopped by border police when they tried to transport copies of the March 14 edition back to Belarus. Police in the city of Vitebsk confiscated the press run, the U.S. government-funded Radio Free Europe/Radio Liberty said.

The final days of the campaign also saw authorities in Grodno, Vitebsk, Pinsk, and Minsk arresting at least eight reporters, photographers, editors, and camera operators for offenses such as "hooliganism," "swearing in public," and "insulting officials," and handing them sentences of five, 10, and 15 days in jail.

Belarusian officials, wary of the sort of public uprising that toppled Ukraine's government in the 2004 Orange Revolution, moved aggressively to counter public demonstrations and news coverage of them. On election eve, KGB head Stepan Sukhorenko told a news conference that opposition supporters who took to the streets to "destabilize the situation" would be charged with terrorism, according to Agence France-Presse. The same day, Interior Minister Vladimir Naumov told journalists at a Minsk press conference that the ministry could not "guarantee their safety" if they sought to cover public demonstrations, the news agency BelTA reported.

During election weekend, independent news Web sites reported ongoing technical difficulties; police jailed three Belarusian editors without explanation; authorities barred at least four Russian journalists from covering the vote; and a border patrol seized a Ukrainian television crew's news footage from a Minsk opposition rally.

As Lukashenko emerged with a victory, he received important backing from Russian President Vladmir Putin. The Russian leader sent a congratulatory message to Lukashenko, saying that the results "demonstrate the confidence of the electorate in your policies." The Moscow-led Commonwealth of Independent States, a group of a dozen former Soviet republics, chimed in to declare the vote free and fair.

Other election observers disagreed. The Vienna-based Organization for Security and Cooperation in Europe called the vote "severely flawed," citing a pattern of government intimidation, suppression of independent voices, and vote-counting irregularities.

About 7,000 people gathered in Minsk's October Square on March 20, the day after the vote, to protest election flaws. Two hundred remained in the square several days later, forming an encampment in freezing temperatures. Early on March 24, riot police stormed the encampment, detained journalists, and barred others from filming or taking pictures of the crackdown. In all, the press freedom group BAJ documented the arrests of 26 Belarusian and foreign journalists, many of them on charges of "hooliganism," in the week following the election. Among those detained were a Canadian freelance reporter, two journalists with a Georgian television station, a Russian information agency correspondent, a Ukrainian newspaper reporter, and a Polish radio journalist.

The European Union and the United States denounced the postelection crackdown, imposing financial and travel sanctions against Lukashenko and a number of government officials. Only Russia's foreign minister, Sergei Lavrov, defended Lukashenko, saying the protests were unauthorized and the government's response appropriate. By September, a court in Minsk had sent one-time presidential contender Kozulin to jail for five and a half years for organizing an unsanctioned rally.

Local authorities also sought to retaliate. In April, the Ideological Department of the Minsk City Executive Committee, a municipal government body, told the independent weekly *Nasha Niva* that it was not welcome to operate in Minsk any longer. The April 10 letter to *Nasha Niva* cited Editor-in-Chief Andrei Dynko's presence and arrest at the October Square demonstrations. Despite the directive, *Nasha Niva* continued to publish, celebrating its centennial in November.

Authorities cracked down on other rallies and on the journalists who tried to cover them. A day before demonstrators gathered in Minsk on April 26 to commemorate the 20th anniversary of the Chernobyl nuclear disaster in neighboring Ukraine, police in the eastern city of Bobruisk detained journalists Nikita Bytsenko and Yuri Svetlakov, of the independent newspaper *Bobruisky Kuryer*, as they prepared to travel to the rally, BAJ said. Police stopped them in the street, checked their documents, and detained them without explanation. Both were held overnight and released after the rally was over. Border police also denied entry to two crews from the Polish public television channel Telewizja Polska that sought to cover the Chernobyl anniversary. The April 1986 disaster at the Chernobyl nuclear power plant in the now-abandoned northern Ukrainian town of Priyat led to considerable contamination in Belarus.

Authorities reported no progress in investigations into the July 2000 disappearance of Dmitry Zavadsky, a cameraman for the Russian television channel ORT who is presumed dead, and the October 2004 slaying of Veronika Cherkasova, a reporter for the Minsk opposition weekly *Solidarnost*. Prosecutors said they had no suspects and were thus suspending their investigation into the murder of Cherkasova, who was found in her apartment with multiple stab wounds. Cherkasova had written about KGB surveillance and alleged arms sales to former Iraqi president Saddam Hussein.

GEORGIA

Television news, which had rallied support for Georgia's pro-democracy revolution three years earlier, suffered serious blows from government harassment, business takeovers, and, as many saw it, self-inflicted scandal.

President Mikhail Saakashvili's administration took an aggressive approach in managing television coverage by pressuring and harassing critical TV reporters. Georgia's largest television company, with holdings that included the influential Rustavi-2 station, changed hands in November amid considerable intrigue. And the hard-hitting independent station 202 went off the air in the fall after getting caught up in an extortion scandal.

Television is the main source of news in Georgia, where newspaper readership is limited and only a small handful of papers are distributed nationally. Kibar Khalvashi, a Tbilisi businessman who spent three years building television holdings that came to include Rustavi-2 and Mze, suddenly sold his majority shares to a virtually unknown entity called Geotrans LLC. On the air, Rustavi-2 denied speculation that the sale was a politically inspired takeover. The statement offered few details except to call Geotrans "the biggest player" in Georgian television, and to say that the company might sell some of its newly acquired shares to attract capital. The sale became public November 19 amid a shakeup in Saakashvili's administration. Defense Minister Irakli Okruashvili, who counted Khalvashi among his close allies, resigned November 17 after being shunted to the Economic Development Ministry. Rustavi-2's tough, independent reporting had earned it near-legendary status in Georgia before and during the Rose Revolution, which brought down the corrupt regime of Eduard Shevardnadze. Under Khalvashi, the station was widely seen as having lost its critical edge; with its new ownership unknown, Rustavi-2's news department faced an uncertain future.

The government's efforts to manage television coverage were laid bare on July 6, when Eka Khoperia, the anchor of Rustavi-2's popular political talk show "Tavisupali Tema" (Free Topic), resigned on the air. The program was to focus on the January murder of Tbilisi bank official Sandro Girgvliani, whose death was linked to Interior Ministry employees, according to news reports. Khoperia claimed on the air that authorities had sought to dictate her choice of guests and the circumstances in which they would appear, according to those reports. "Such conditions are absolutely unacceptable for me, so this is my last program and I quit this television channel," the BBC quoted Khoperia as saying as she announced a commercial break. The show never returned from the break. At a press conference the next day, Khoperia said unnamed authorities sought in phone conversations to orchestrate the appearance of an Interior Ministry official by limiting comments and questions.

Rustavi-2 also made major personnel changes, sacking station director Nickoloz Tabatadze and news chief Tamar Rukhadze in August. According to the independent daily *Rezonansi*, Tabatadze had resisted presidential aide Giorgi Arveladze's attempts to set the editorial policy of the "Kurieri" news program. Tabatadze was replaced by Koba Davarashvili, a close friend of Arveladze who had no television experience, *Rezonansi* reported. Several Rustavi-2 journalists resigned in protest, saying the dismissals compromised their independence. International press reports quoted opposition leaders as saying they would no longer appear on Rustavi-2.

The private national station Imedi TV became known as the most independent television news source and as an outlet for opposition leaders. Badri Patarkatsishvili, Imedi TV's owner, said that the government launched politically motivated investigations into his business taxes in February, after the channel aired several reports critical of the Girgvliani murder investigation, according to local and international press reports. Patarkatsishvili told the New York-based news Web site *EurasiaNet* that regulators were "actively examining my companies in order to induce me to put pressure on Imedi TV journalists and encourage more favorable coverage of authorities."

Four junior Interior Ministry officials were arrested in the Girgvliani case. The night before the banker's body was found, witnesses said, he was seen in a Tbilisi bar arguing with officials who were accompanying Interior Minister Vano Merabishvili, according to international news reports. Imedi's reports went further, alleging that several top-level Interior Ministry officials were linked to the murder. In parliamentary hearings, Merabishvili denied any involvement.

The independent channel 202, which broadcast from Tbilisi, was mired in scandal. Shalva Ramishvili, co-owner of the station and former anchor of the tough political talk show "Debatebi" (Debates), was sentenced in March to four years in prison for attempted extortion, and David Kokheridze, the channel's general director, was sentenced to three years on similar charges. The two had been arrested in 2005 after police videotaped them receiving US$30,000 from a member of parliament. The member, Koba Bekauri, said the two extorted the money in exchange for not airing an investigative report that would have been critical of him. Ramishvili and Kokheridze denied the accusation, claiming that they took the money as part of an undercover investigation.

Although some journalists questioned the government's motives in the case, others told CPJ that the video spoke for itself and that the verdict was justified. Regardless, the case cut into 202's popularity and revenue, causing it to suspend broadcasting in October.

Despite behind-the-scenes pressure and government harassment, Georgian law affords some broad protections to the news media. A landmark measure passed in 2004 decriminalized defamation, made it subject to civil action, and placed the burden of proof on the plaintiff. The law also established the right to public debate and defined the notion of a public figure who can be subject to public criticism.

While reporters worked safely in the capital, those in the outlying regions reported

EUROPE AND CENTRAL ASIA

getting threats after covering sensitive topics such as corruption and border smuggling of cigarettes, agricultural products, and oil. Journalists in Shida Kartli, a region close to the self-proclaimed republic of South Ossetia, complained of particularly repressive restrictions, according to Nino Gvedashvili of the Tbilisi-based Georgian Human Rights Information and Documentation Center. The journalists accused the Shida Kartli administration of obstructing access to public information and forbidding the publication of local officials' photographs.

Fearing increased Russian influence in the breakaway regions of South Ossetia and Abkhazia, Saakashvili deployed troops to the Kodori Gorge and expelled several Russian military officers on spying charges. Moscow responded by imposing economic sanctions, severing transportation links, and deporting hundreds of Georgians living in Russia, according to press reports.

Media coverage in the breakaway areas was limited throughout the year. The only Russian-language channel targeting South Ossetian audiences was the Tbilisi-based, government-funded channel Alania. The channel's limited news content was critical of South Ossetian separatists. Perceptions of one-sided coverage led South Ossetian authorities to interrupt Alania's broadcasts in January, shortly after the station aired a report criticizing separatist leader Eduard Kokoity, *EurasiaNet* reported.

Local authorities in Abkhazia also obstructed the work of journalists. On March 7, local police detained freelance journalists Tea Sharia, Georgii Sokhadze, and Teimuraza Eliava on charges of espionage and illegally entering the self-declared republic. The three were sentenced to three months in prison but were released in late March. They had traveled to Abkhazia to make a documentary film about local churches and monasteries in cooperation with the Georgian Orthodox Church, according to local and international press reports.

•••••••••••••••••• KAZAKHSTAN ••••••••••••••••••

President Nursultan Nazarbayev strengthened his government's control of the news media amid a political crisis driven by the February assassination of prominent opposition politician Altynbek Sarsenbayev. Ten low-level government officials and security agents were soon charged and convicted in the killing, but members of the opposition Naghyz Ak Zhol party said government involvement reached much higher. As questions swirled, the administration signaled plans to limit Internet access, and authorities arrested a critical online journalist who covered the case. The government also consolidated national television ownership and imposed new regulations on print media.

Information Minister Yermukhamet Yertysbayev told the opposition weekly *Vremya* in July that his ministry would draft a bill to systematically block access to politically objectionable Web sites, calling it one of "the main priorities of state policy." Though the administration began drafting systemwide regulations, the details were not immediately disclosed, according to international and local press reports. Such a measure would broaden and codify the government's existing efforts, which now involve the targeted blocking of Web sites in the name of national security. The Almaty-based media foundation Adil Soz quoted Yertysbayev as saying that "online journalism threatens state security and uses defamation and lies of the lowest sort."

On August 28, Almaty police put the government's words into practice by charging Internet journalist Kaziz Toguzbayev with insulting the honor and dignity of the president, a criminal offense. Toguzbayev wrote two articles in May and April for the news Web site *Kub* alleging that only high-level government officials could have carried out the Sarsenbayev killing. Toguzbayev faced up to three years in prison in the case, said Yevgeny Zhovtis, a human rights lawyer.

In May, Yertysbayev announced the government would assume management of the Khabar television station, which it jointly owned with private shareholders that included the president's eldest daughter, Dariga, according to international press reports. No timetable was set for the move, which would make Khabar the third government-controlled national station, along with Kazakhstan and Yel Arna. "The state should dominate domestic TV broadcasting," Interfax Kazakhstan quoted Yertysbayev as saying. The move came amid a rift between Nazarbayev and his daughter, who had been accumulating media holdings and occasionally breaking with official government positions.

One division arose over the popular comedic character Borat, the "Kazakh reporter" who lampooned society in a movie and other performances. Nazarbayev famously condemned the caricature, threatened to sue, and blocked video clips of the performances, while his daughter said the aggressive stance merely drew attention to the character. The government softened its position after the film's U.S. release in November. Roman Vassilenko, a spokesman for the Kazakh embassy in Washington, said the Cultural Ministry would not interfere if private movie distribution companies wanted to show the film in Kazakhstan, the U.S. government-funded Radio Free Europe/Radio Liberty reported.

Most citizens get their news from television, but newspapers and other publications have traditionally been a source of information that is more critical of the government. In the summer, parliament passed and Nazarbayev signed into law a measure giving the state broad power to close independent and opposition media outlets on the merest of technical violations.

The measure broadens the grounds on which the government can deny registration to news outlets, and it requires re-registration for news outlets that make even slight administrative changes, such as the addition of a staffer or the alteration of a mailing address. The government's record over several years shows that such requirements are used as a pretext to deny registration to independent and opposition media outlets, to harass

EUROPE AND CENTRAL ASIA

them, and to close them. The measure was heavily criticized by local and international press and human rights organizations, including CPJ.

The new law also stipulated that no media outlet can be registered if it uses the same name, in full or in part, of a media outlet previously closed by a court, and it bars editors of previously shuttered media outlets from working in similar positions for other publications. The restrictions are significant because Nazarbayev's government has a long record of using politicized lawsuits, tax inspections, and criminal investigations to close critical news media. The opposition newspaper known most recently as *Aina Plyus*, for example, has been suspended several times by authorities for alleged technical violations, forcing it to publish under several different names, Adil Soz reported.

Nazarbayev and his allies also used behind-the-scenes techniques to obstruct print media. The country's biggest printing company, which is run by Nazarbayev's sister-in-law, Svetlana Nazarbayeva, refused in January to print seven Almaty-based opposition newspapers. Local press freedom groups said that the company, Dauir, told the editors of the weeklies *Svoboda Slova*, *Epokha*, *Apta.kz*, *Soz*, *Pravda Kazakhstana*, *Pravo.Ekonomika. Politika.Kultura*, and *Azat* that it would not renew their contracts, which expired on January 1, 2006, because it was changing equipment. Adil Soz President Tamara Kaleyeva said Dauir resumed printing the papers after an interruption of a few weeks.

In September, CPJ urged U.S. President George W. Bush to raise concerns about Kazakhstan's deteriorating press freedom record when he met with Nazarbayev in Washington. White House spokesman Tony Snow called oil-rich Kazakhstan "an important strategic partner in Central Asia" and said that the two leaders had a productive discussion that focused on energy trade and regional security. In a joint statement, the U.S. and Kazakh leaders said that they "reaffirm the importance of democratic development, and are committed to accelerating Kazakhstan's efforts to strengthen representative institutions that further invest its citizens in the political process, such as an independent media, local self-government, and elections deemed free and fair by international standards."

Nazarbayev has ruled Kazakhstan for 17 years. He gained a third term in a December 2005 vote that international observers said was marred by media and vote manipulation.

Two prominent journalists were attacked in 2006. On April 23, Kenzhegali Aitbakiyev of *Aina Plyus* was assaulted as he was walking along a street in Almaty. Aitbakiyev, who suffered a broken jaw and nose, a concussion, and heavy bruising, had been assaulted just a month earlier, according to international press reports. *Aina Plyus* Editor Ermurat Bapi said he believed the attack was connected to Aitbakiyev's work, Adil Soz reported. *Aina Plyus* was one of the few local publications that covered the so-called "Kazakhgate" affair, which entailed allegations of bribe taking by Kazakh officials from U.S. oil companies.

On April 13, Yaroslav Golyshkin, editor of the independent newspaper *Versiya*, was attacked on the porch of his home in the northeastern city of Pavlodar by two unidentified men, who severely beat him. *Versiya* is well-known for its investigative reporting on crime. Both Golyshkin and his father, Vasily Golyshkin, founder of the paper and a well-known journalist, said they believed the attack was in retaliation for an article about the kidnapping of a financial police officer who investigated organized crime, Adil Soz reported. Nothing was stolen from the victims in either of the attacks. No charges have been filed in either case.

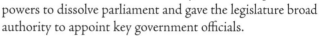

KYRGYZSTAN

Months of discontent over President Kurmanbek Bakiyev's failure to enact reforms to combat crime, corruption, and economic woes boiled over in November when thousands of protesters gathered for a week of demonstrations in the central square of the capital, Bishkek. Bakiyev, ushered into office in a popular uprising just 19 months earlier, averted a crisis when he agreed to a new constitution sharply restricting his own powers. The new constitution, which was hailed internationally, limited the president's powers to dissolve parliament and gave the legislature broad authority to appoint key government officials.

Tensions were high during the standoff as up to 10,000 demonstrators gathered outside the government seat. On the second day of protests, authorities blocked plans for opposition leaders to appear live on state television; on day six, a live radio broadcast of an emergency session of parliament was interrupted for three hours. The November 9 constitutional agreement, which Bakiyev called "the result of good sense and wisdom," avoided a violent showdown and allowed the embattled president, whose term runs until 2010, to remain in office.

Yet conflict loomed in late year. The For Reforms movement, a coalition of opposition groups, urged Bakiyev to make good on his pledges to transform the state broadcaster into an independent public channel. Bakiyev, who had vetoed one such plan in September, said through a spokesman in mid-November that the National Television & Radio Broadcast Corporation (KTR) would remain state owned and controlled, The Associated Press reported. Bakiyev decreed that the channel would be managed by a new council of legislators, presidential appointees, and station managers.

The 2005 Tulip Revolution that toppled Askar Akayev's repressive government had raised hopes that a free press would flourish under a new president seen as more tolerant of independent media. But hobbled by political instability, organized crime, contract killings, and high unemployment, Bakiyev instead displayed an authoritarian hand in exerting tight control over public institutions and the media through much of the year. His justice minister, Marat Kaipov, twice advanced plans to regulate nongovernmental organizations under the guise of protecting national security.

On January 27, KTR journalists protested what they saw as government interference

EUROPE AND CENTRAL ASIA

after Bayama Sutenova, a close Bakiyev ally, was appointed deputy director of the agency. The government called Sutenova's appointment part of a KTR reorganization, according to local press reports. The government also discontinued its transmissions of the independent Kyrgyz New TV Net (NTS) in the Osh, Balykchy, Batken, and Talas regions, replacing it with a second state channel, El TV. NTS, which was reliant on government transmissions to reach those regions, said the government was retaliating for the station's critical reporting. The Production Association of Television and Radio Relay Lines, the government's regulator, said it was implementing a presidential decree to spread El TV's signal throughout Kyrgyzstan, according to international news reports.

Regional governments tried to emulate the national administration's hard-nosed approach. Local officials in the southern city of Osh directed the private television stations OshTV, Mezon TV, Almaz, and Pyramid, along with the newspaper *Vecherny Osh*, to regularly cover government efforts to prevent crime and drug use and to combat HIV/AIDS. Local media defied the order, saying government stipulations compromised their independence. "We have the right to decide what to cover and what not to cover; we will report on those issues that are in the interest of our viewers, not the authorities," the Bishkek-based Public Association of Journalists (PAJ) said.

Government authorities also exercised control over state print media. In January, Bakyt Orunbekov was fired as editor-in-chief of the state-owned *Kyrgyz Tuusu* (Kyrgyzstan's Flag). Jediger Saalaev, press officer for the Kyrgyz government, was blunt in saying that Orunbekov was fired for the critical nature of his work. "A newspaper that belongs to the government should not criticize the government," Radio Free Europe/Radio Liberty (RFE/RL) quoted him as saying.

Despite Bakiyev's efforts to impose order, criminal groups flourished. The Olympic wrestler Raatbek Sanatbaev was murdered in January amid a spree of contract-style killings. Journalists who reported on crime were vulnerable as well. On January 30, the office of *Vecherny Bishkek* was set on fire after it published several articles on an alleged crime boss. Police declared it arson, but no arrests were made or charges filed, according to international press reports.

Criminal groups were believed to have menaced independent television stations as well. In April, an unidentified man telephoned Yelena Chernyavskaya, director of the Bishkek-based Pyramid, to say, "Shut up or get ready for death," and someone sent her a text message with the same threat. After she filed a complaint, the Interior Ministry provided her with a bodyguard and sent officers to guard the station's office.

Pyramid was targeted twice more in late year. On September 28, unidentified vandals torched its transmission facilities outside Bishkek, causing 7,794,800 som (US$200,000) in damage and disrupting broadcasts for a month. The men also attacked a guard and two technicians, RFE/RL reported. And on November 7, five men attacked Pyramid's chief editor, Turat Bektenov, on his way home in Bishkek. The journalist suffered multiple bruises and abrasions, PAJ reported.

· RUSSIA ·

As Russia assumed a world leadership role, chairing the Group of Eight leading industrialized nations and the Council of Europe's powerful committee of ministers, the Kremlin cracked down on dissent and shrugged off astounding attacks on critics and journalists. In a grim year for the press, parliament passed a measure to hush media criticism by calling it "extremism," and an assassin silenced Anna Politkovskaya, the internationally known reporter who exposed government abuses in Chechnya.

On the eve of the G8 summit in St. Petersburg in July, parliament passed a bill broadening the definition of extremism to include media criticism of public officials. President Vladimir Putin soon signed the measure over the objections of media and human rights groups. CPJ likened the measure—which said extremist activity includes "public slander directed toward figures fulfilling the state duties of the Russian Federation"—to the catchall laws used in Soviet times to prosecute critics. The crackdown on dissent had begun in January when Putin signed a measure restricting the activities of nongovernmental organizations (NGOs). The law gave the Justice Ministry vast authority to shutter organizations for engaging in activities that run counter to the "political independence of the Russian Federation." Ten months later, authorities used the broadly worded law to close the Russian-Chechen Friendship Society, a human rights center and publisher.

Politkovskaya, 48, had survived dozens of assignments in conflict-ravaged Chechnya, but she did not survive a trip to a Moscow grocery store. She was killed in her apartment building on October 7, the 13th journalist to be slain, contract style, in Putin's Russia. All of the cases remained unsolved, a record of impunity that helped make Russia the third deadliest country in the world for journalists, CPJ found in a 2006 special report, "Deadly News."

Politkovskaya, special correspondent for Moscow's independent *Novaya Gazeta*, was regarded as one of the most knowledgeable experts on the war in Chechnya—a conflict greatly underreported in Russian media. For seven years, Politkovskaya endured threats, imprisonment, forced exile, and poisoning to chronicle the plight of Chechen civilians at the hands of federal troops, rebel forces, and the Kremlin-backed Chechen militia. In her reporting, Politkovskaya exposed human rights abuses, disappearances, corruption, torture, and murder. She sharply criticized Kremlin-backed Chechen Prime Minister Ramzan Kadyrov in her writing and in numerous interviews with international media.

Security cameras at Politkovskaya's apartment building and market caught a blurred image of her killer, a man in a dark baseball cap. At around 4 p.m., according to news reports and CPJ interviews, he followed her home and watched her unload several bags of groceries from her sedan. As she emerged from her elevator to retrieve the rest, the assassin shot her in the chest and head with a 9mm handgun fitted with a silencer. He dropped the pistol, its serial number erased, next to her body and strolled away. A neighbor discovered the body about a half hour later; investigators retrieved four bullets.

Within days, *Novaya Gazeta* received hundreds of letters from Politkovskaya's readers, sources, colleagues, and supporters. "She was our voice, our pen, and Russia's conscience. Left without her, where do we go?" asked one reader from Chechnya.

Politkovskaya's last report, unpublished at the time of her death, said Chechen law enforcement officials had tortured young Chechen men into confessing to crimes they never committed. "When prosecutors and courts work not to punish the guilty but on political commission and with the only goal of pleasing the Kremlin with accounts of combating terrorism, criminal cases are popping like cakes from an oven," Politkovskaya wrote.

At a press conference in Germany three days after the assassination, Putin downplayed the killing by saying that Politkovskaya had "insignificant" impact in Russia. He brushed off the possibility of any official involvement in the killing, suggesting instead that it was the product of an overseas conspiracy designed to undermine the Kremlin. He cited "solid evidence" that these unnamed conspirators planned to "sacrifice someone to create a wave of anti-Russian sentiment internationally."

Conspiracy theories abounded a month later when former Russian spy Aleksandr Litvinenko died in London, a victim of an extraordinary case of radiation poisoning. Litvinenko had been investigating Politkovskaya's murder when he was somehow poisoned by a rare substance known as polonium 210. From his own deathbed, Litvinenko's family said, he dictated a statement that accused the Kremlin of ordering the poisoning. Meeting with European Union leaders in Helsinki, Putin called the ex-spy's death a tragedy but lamented that it was being used for "political provocation."

Politkovskaya was herself poisoned en route to the 2004 Beslan school hostage crisis, putting her in the hospital and preventing her from covering the deadly siege.

Under Putin, the Kremlin has restricted domestic and international reporting from Chechnya, imposing travel and content restrictions and harassing reporters. From the onset of the war in 1999, the Media Ministry banned Russian television networks from broadcasting interviews with Chechen rebel leaders. Journalists such as Yuri Bagrov, a correspondent for Radio Free Europe/Radio Liberty, have been stripped of press credentials in retaliation for their reporting. A 2005 CPJ special report, "Rebels and Reporters," cited more than 60 instances of government harassment, obstruction, and legal action against journalists in Chechnya.

The government's aggressive tactics continued in 2006. A court in Nizhny Novgorod convicted Stanislav Dmitriyevsky, director of the Russian-Chechen Friendship Society and editor of its newspaper, *Pravo-Zashchita* (Rights Protection), on charges of "inciting ethnic hatred by using the mass media." The February conviction stemmed from publication of two statements by Chechen rebel leaders calling for peace talks, which appeared in the March and April 2004 editions of *Pravo-Zashchita*. Dmitriyevsky was sentenced to probation, but authorities used the conviction and the new NGO law as basis for closing the society in October.

Chechnya remained an extraordinarily dangerous place. In August, the Russian human rights group Memorial reported 125 abductions in just seven months. That month, masked men seized Elina Ersenoyeva, correspondent for the independent weekly *Chechenskoye Obshchestvo*, in Chechnya's capital, Grozny. Ersenoyeva reported on social issues, refugees, and, most recently, conditions in Grozny prisons, her editor, Timur Aliyev, told CPJ. Following the kidnapping, reports emerged that Ersenoyeva had been secretly, and some said forcibly, married to the notorious Chechen rebel leader Shamil Basayev. The separatist leader, who had claimed responsibility for hostage crises in Moscow and Beslan in which hundreds died, had been killed in an explosion in the republic of Ingushetia in July. Ersenoyeva's status was not clear in late year.

Authorities reported no headway in solving the July 2003 abduction of Agence France-Presse correspondent Ali Astamirov in Ingushetia. Astamirov had endured months of police and security service harassment in retaliation for his reporting in Chechnya.

Deadly violence, investigative ineptitude, and judicial indifference remained sad hallmarks in Russian press cases; a second reporter was also killed in retaliation for his work. Vagif Kochetkov, 31, a reporter in the city of Tula, 125 miles (200 kilometers) south of Moscow, died at a local hospital on January 8 from head injuries suffered in an attack two weeks earlier. Kochetkov, a correspondent for the Moscow daily *Trud* and columnist for the local newspaper *Tulsky Molodoi Kommunar*, had written about drug trafficking and aggressive practices in the pharmaceutical industry. Colleagues said he received telephone threats prior to the attack, the Web site *Newsinfo* reported.

CPJ sources said a bag believed to contain Kochetkov's passport, press card, credit card, and work-related documents were taken in the assault; his money and fur coat were not. Yet authorities did not focus on Kochetkov's work, labeling the case a street robbery and bringing a local man, Yan Stakhanov, to trial on manslaughter charges. The trial was pending in late year.

CPJ continued to investigate the murders of two other journalists to determine whether the killings were work related. Ilya Zimin, correspondent for the national NTV network, was found beaten to death in his Moscow apartment on February 27. Yevgeny Gerasimenko, reporter for the weekly *Saratovsky Rasklad*, was found dead on July 26 in his apartment in the southeastern city of Saratov, a plastic bag over his head and multiple bruises on his body.

Prosecutors reported no developments in the disappearance of Maksim Maksimov, a 41-year-old investigative reporter for the St. Petersburg weekly *Gorod*, who was last seen on June 29, 2004, when he went to meet with a source in the city's downtown district. Maksimov's mother, Rimma Maksimova, told CPJ she was losing hope of learning what happened to her son.

Maksimov had reported on corruption in the St. Petersburg branch of the Interior Ministry and had investigated the killings of several prominent businessmen and politicians, including Galina Starovoitova, a parliamentary deputy shot in her apartment building in 1998, according to press reports and CPJ sources.

Even in high-profile cases such as the 2004 assassination of Paul Klebnikov, the American editor of *Forbes Russia*, the Russian justice system produced no immediate results. Two ethnic Chechens were tried in secret but acquitted in May amid allegations of jury intimidation and procedural violations. Court officials said the introduction of classified evidence required closing the trial to the public, rebuffing pleas by Klebnikov's family and CPJ to close only those portions in which confidential information was to be reviewed. For four months following the verdict, Moscow City Court officials impeded the Klebnikov family's appeal by failing to provide them with a trial transcript.

But in November, the Russian Supreme Court tossed out the acquittals and ordered that Kazbek Dukuzov and Musa Vakhayev be retried. CPJ called on authorities to open the new trial to the public. In a statement, the Klebnikovs called the ruling a "hopeful sign" and reiterated their desire that authorities fully investigate those who ordered the killing.

The prosecutor general's office said the killing was ordered by Chechen separatist leader Khozh Akhmed Nukhayev, the subject of a critical 2003 book by Klebnikov, but it has not provided any evidence to support that assertion. Nukhayev's whereabouts were unknown, although some Chechen experts said he died in the mountains of Dagestan in the months before Klebnikov's murder.

Another unsolved case hit a roadblock. The European Court of Human Rights ruled in October that it could not take up an appeal filed by the parents of reporter Dmitry Kholodov, who was blown up by a booby-trapped briefcase in his office on October 17, 1994. The Strasbourg court said it did not have jurisdiction in the case because Russia did not ratify the European Convention on Human Rights until four years after Kholodov's murder.

The ruling was a blow to Zoya and Yuri Kholodov's 12-year effort to gain justice in their son's killing. Kholodov, 27, a reporter for *Moskovsky Komsomolets*, had exposed high-level corruption in the Russian military. Six defendants, four of them military intelligence officers, were acquitted by Russian military courts in 2002 and 2004 of organizing and carrying out the assassination.

In addition to physical attacks, critical journalists throughout Russia endured legal and bureaucratic harassment in retaliation for their work. Vladimir Rakhmankov, editor of the Web site *Kursiv* in the central city of Ivanovo, was convicted of insulting the president in a May article headlined "Putin as Russia's Phallic Symbol." The story satirized Putin's goal to boost the country's birth rate, making a tongue-in-cheek reference to an increase in births among some species at the local zoo. Rakhmankov declared that the animals "immediately responded to the president's appeal." Authorities were not amused;

investigators raided *Kursiv*'s newsroom, seized the paper's computers, sealed the premises, searched Rakhmankov's apartment, and confiscated his personal computer. Rakhmankov was fined 20,000 rubles (US$760), and his Web site went dark.

In August, a court in the western city of Kaliningrad ordered the opposition weekly *Novye Kolyosa* closed at the request of the federal media regulator Rosokhrankultura. The regulator claimed that the paper had disclosed secrets of a criminal investigation in a May 2005 series about the murder of a local businessman. Prosecutors also opened 16 criminal cases against *Novye Kolyosa*'s founder, Igor Rudnikov, and journalists Oleg Berezovsky, Aleksandr Berezovsky, and Dina Yakshina in response to the weekly's critical reporting.

Authorities in Perm launched an intensive campaign of harassment against *Permsky Obozrevatel*, the city's only independent newspaper. The business weekly regularly featured critical coverage of the local administration and analytical articles on corruption, privatization, and the redistribution of municipal property. Police raided the paper twice, once in May and again in August, confiscating servers, computers, disks, flash memory cards, staff records, and photographs. In August, all eight staffers were placed under criminal investigation for "insult," "violating the right to private life," and "disclosing state secrets." In September, police arrested photographer Vladimir Korolyov on suspicion of disclosing state secrets. Authorities did not elaborate on the accusation.

Over the past five years, companies with close ties to the Kremlin have purchased several prominent independent broadcast and print outlets. The trend continued in September when the metals magnate Alisher Usmanov, a Kremlin ally, purchased *Kommersant*. The business daily had earned a reputation for analytical journalism often critical of the Kremlin. Usmanov told *Kommersant* journalists he would not interfere with editorial policy. But such acquisitions, along with the Kremlin's tight control of national television, were widely seen as an effort to steer media coverage in advance of the 2008 presidential election.

The Central Election Commission in September rejected a call for a constitutional referendum that would have allowed Putin to run for a third term. The next month, Putin told a televised news conference that he would indeed not seek another term, but that he would remain involved in politics.

• TAJIKISTAN •

President Imomali Rakhmonov buried independent and international media under a blizzard of arbitrary licensing regulations, content restrictions, and fees. Though Rakhmonov faced no strong opposition in the November presidential election, his administration limited critical news coverage in the run-up to his victory over four little-known opponents. Regulatory agencies—wary, too, of the sort of news coverage that

EUROPE AND CENTRAL ASIA

helped fuel the 2005 uprising in neighboring Kyrgyzstan—moved aggressively to block international media from the public airwaves and to impose onerous controls on independent domestic media.

No daily newspapers circulated in Tajikistan; independent weeklies were suppressed; foreign television and radio stations were barred from the airwaves; and critical Internet news sites were blocked. Rakhmonov and his ruling People's 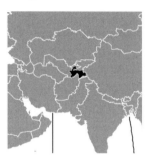 Democratic Party of Tajikistan appeared firmly ensconced politically; the constitution allows him to seek re-election through 2020. Opposition leader Said Abdullo Nuri, once seen as Rakhmonov's strongest opponent, died of cancer in August, and his Islamic Renaissance Party did not participate in the presidential race. Article 137 of the criminal code forbids public criticism of the president and sets a penalty of up to five years in prison; other sections of the code make it a crime to insult one's dignity.

During the year, parliament passed more than 40 new amendments to its media laws, including one that required all nonstate media outlets to obtain licenses from the Ministry of Culture, the independent news agency Asia Plus reported. The new regulations hardly seemed necessary for a government already adept at using existing regulatory tools. Foreign television stations have been available by satellite only since 2005, when government regulators removed the Russian television networks Channel One and RTV from the airwaves, according to the National Association of Independent Media of Tajikistan (NANSMIT).

In January, government regulators suspended FM broadcasts of the BBC, saying the network had not complied with new requirements to register with the Ministry of Justice and obtain a license from the Committee on Television and Radio Broadcasting of Tajikistan. The BBC said it was given 20-day notice of the new regulatory process—which required six months to complete. By July, the government had rejected the BBC's application outright, saying that it also needed a reciprocal broadcast licensing agreement between Tajikistan and Britain. The Tajik government did allow the BBC to open a news bureau in the capital, Dushanbe.

Broadcast news is the dominant source of information for citizens. In a country where the average monthly salary is just over US$27, few have access to satellite television or the Internet, according to data from the World Bank and the United Nations Economic Commission for Europe. Broadcast television is dominated by three national state-run stations: Tajik, Soghd, and Khatlon.

Regulators and courts were active in stifling independent domestic broadcasters. In June, the Ministry of Communications barred eight independent television and radio companies from sharing news and entertainment video, saying the exchange would violate licensing laws, the Khujand-based Tajik news agency Varorud reported.

Somonien, which was the last independent television station operating in Dushanbe, lost a court appeal in January that sought to overturn a 2005 State Licensing Commission decision to close the station and seize its equipment because of unpaid fees. Somonien staff said the Ministry of Communications had imposed higher fees in retaliation for the station's broadcasting of opposition views during the 2005 parliamentary election, the London-based Institute for War and Peace Reporting (IWPR) said.

Three independent provincial television stations—Isfara in the city of Isfara, Simo in the city of Panjakent, and Usturushana in the city of Istaravshan—settled a Ministry of Communications lawsuit in January over broadcast fees, the independent news agency Avesta reported. The ministry had raised fees to levels that the stations were unable to pay. As part of the settlement, the stations agreed to carry the state-produced program "Minbari Hukumat" (Government Tribune), according to Internews, a U.S.-based media training and advocacy organization.

The government increased funding to state television and radio stations by 25 percent, bringing the overall budget to the equivalent of US$1.25 million, IWPR reported. Independent stations typically have their own studios and broadcast equipment but depend on government-owned transmission equipment to get their signals into people's homes. The government interrupts transmission of these independent broadcasts to carry Rakhmonov's speeches, the BBC reported.

The once-popular independent weeklies *Nerui Sukhan*, *Ruzi Nav*, and *Odamu Olan* remained out of circulation in 2006. The three newspapers were forced out of print in 2004 as a result of politicized tax and regulatory inspections. CPJ sources said editors and publishers involved in the newspapers sought permission to resume publication, to no avail.

There are no daily newspapers, independent or state-run, functioning in the country. On October 4, the Ministry of Culture sent a letter to the private Dushanbe printing company Shafei, instructing it to stop printing the opposition weekly *Adolat*, according to international press reports. The ministry said it did not recognize the Democratic Party's leadership; *Adolat* staff protested the decision and continued to produce its newspaper using office copy machines. The paper had just resumed publication in September after regaining a license the government had pulled in 2004, according to NANSMIT.

Government officials moved to limit access to Internet publications, among the few remaining sources for independent news. On October 7, authorities blocked local access to five Web sites carrying Tajik and Central Asian news published from abroad, NANSMIT head Nuriddin Karshiboyev said. The sites—*Centrasia*, *Ferghana*, *Arianastorm*, *Charogiruz*, and *Tajikistantimes*—often cover human right abuses and restrictive government policies in Tajikistan and other Central Asian countries. Anvar Mamadzhanov, a senior official at the Ministry of Communications, instructed Tajik Internet providers to filter Web sites for security reasons and to block access to those that carry reports that "undermine state media policy," the independent Russian-language weekly *Business and*

Politics reported. The ministry later revised its position to say that the sites were closed for maintenance purposes, according to the BBC.

The government broadened its restrictive policies toward independent media to include nongovernmental organizations (NGOs), especially those receiving grants from abroad. In March, the government approved substantial revisions to the Law on Public Associations, requiring NGOs to register annually, according to IWPR. Critics said that the new law, which was to take effect in 2007, would be used arbitrarily to deny registration to NGOs, including those supporting the independent media.

A decade after the 1992-97 civil conflict, the wartime murders of 29 journalists remained unsolved. According to CPJ research, 17 journalists were killed because of their professional activities in that period, while another 12 died in unclear circumstances.

··················· TURKMENISTAN ···················

The December 21 death of Saparmurat Niyazov, the self-proclaimed president-for-life, ended a two-decade rule that plunged Turkmenistan into a dark abyss in which the state maintained absolute control over information. His sudden death from heart failure at age 66 left the nation with an indelible legacy of repression. Niyazov's eccentric personality probably won't be matched by his successor, but his press policies seem likely to survive. The national assembly named Deputy Prime Minister Gurbanguly Berdymuhammedov, a Niyazov loyalist, as acting head of state and scheduled elections for early 2007. Berdymuhammedov vowed to follow in the late president's path.

Turkmenistan's isolated, authoritarian government had earned the nation a place on CPJ's 10 Most Censored Countries list in 2006. Niyazov, who had led Turkmenistan since 1985, when it was still a Soviet republic, went much further than most autocrats by banning libraries, foreign publications, opera, ballet, and circuses. The state owns all domestic media, appoints editors, approves news content prior to publication, and orders television anchors to swear allegiance to the president during broadcasts. The U.S. government-funded Radio Free Europe/Radio Liberty (RFE/RL), which has maintained an informal network of correspondents, has been the nation's only alternative source of news and information.

Niyazov had built an extraordinary cult of personality, calling himself the "father of all Turkmen" renaming the month of January after himself, and installing thousands of portraits and statues nationwide in his own honor. The state-controlled media provided hagiographic coverage of the president, his speeches, his meetings with state ministers, and his family—all while ignoring drug abuse, the spread of HIV/AIDS, rampant unemployment, poor health care and education systems, budget deficits, pension cuts, and widespread corruption.

The climate of isolation turned vicious in 2006. The state of press freedom in Turkmenistan was encapsulated by the September death in prison of an RFE/RL reporter, who was arrested on a bogus charge, denied a lawyer and due process, and then killed while in the government's custody. Ogulsapar Muradova, Ashgabat correspondent for RFE/RL, suffered head and neck injuries while in prison, according to a Turkmen human rights group, which had spoken with relatives. CPJ and other international organizations called for an independent inquiry into the death, but a Turkmen government accustomed to being above accountability did not respond.

Authorities in the capital, Ashgabat, handed over the body on September 14 only after Western diplomats accompanied Muradova's children to the morgue, RFE/RL Turkmen Service Director Aleksandr Narodetsky told CPJ. CPJ sources and RFE/RL said authorities rejected the family's request for an autopsy and would not disclose the cause or date of death. Security forces then surrounded the Muradova home and prevented people from seeing the body or contacting Muradova's relatives, those sources said. The family's telephone lines were cut.

Muradova, 58, had been detained June 18 on a spurious charge of possessing ammunition, held incommunicado, and denied legal counsel. She was convicted and sentenced to six years' imprisonment on August 25 after a closed-door trial that lasted all of a few minutes, then placed in a women's prison in the northern city of Dashoguz that is notorious for abuse, according to CPJ sources and RFE/RL.

Muradova's body had a large head wound and bruises around the neck, according to the Bulgaria-based Turkmenistan Helsinki Foundation for Human Rights, which spoke with the journalist's adult children before the phone lines were cut. RFE/RL's Narodetsky also said the children reported that their mother had a head wound.

The foundation, relying on witness accounts, said a dazed and incoherent Muradova had already been forced to confess to taking part in a foreign conspiracy to smear the country. In addition to her work for RFE/RL, Muradova had monitored human rights for the foundation. The health and status of two human rights activists, tried along with her and convicted on similar ammunition charges, were unknown in late year. Annakurban Amanklychev and Sapardurdy Khadzhiyev had been sentenced to seven years each in the same closed trial.

Correspondents for RFE/RL were singled out for punishment throughout the year. Because authorities routinely persecute journalists, their friends, and family for being affiliated with RFE/RL, most journalists use pseudonyms to avoid government retribution. Over the years that retribution has ranged from threats and surveillance to torture and imprisonment.

The crackdown on RFE/RL intensified in February and escalated further in midyear. In late February, the Ministry of National Security (MNB) detained Balkansk correspondent Shamurad Akoyliyev and warned him that his affiliation with the broadcaster was "unacceptable." Akoyliyev reported on sports and did not cover sensitive subjects, RFE/RL's Narodetsky said. Following the interrogation, authorities cut off his telephone and placed him under 24-hour surveillance, the Turkmenistan Helsinki Foundation told CPJ. Relatives were pressured to halt communication with Akoyliyev, the group said.

In March, police arrested RFE/RL correspondents Meret Khommadov and Dzhumadurdy Ovezov, who reported from the southeastern city of Mary. Authorities charged Khommadov and Ovezov with "hooliganism" and accused them of interrupting a town hall meeting. They were sentenced to 15 days in a lice- and cockroach-infested jail without beds, mattresses, or sheets. To gain early release, they were forced to sign written statements, confessing to being traitors and instigators of religious hatred. Police officials threatened to harm their families if they continued to report for RFE/RL, according to an interview the two gave to the news agency after their release.

Muradova's arrest was preceded by an escalating series of terror-inducing attacks. She told colleagues that MNB agents were following her and were threatening to imprison her and her children. In April, her mobile and land phone lines were turned off. The day before her arrest, arsonists set her elderly mother's home on fire. Muradova's three adult children—Maral, Berdy, and Sona—were themselves arrested on June 19 and held for two weeks, RFE/RL reported.

Niyazov had routinely disregarded international criticism of his regime's abysmal human rights record, but his isolationism turned adversarial in June. He accused French diplomats and the Organization for Security and Cooperation in Europe (OSCE) of conspiring with Turkmen journalists and human rights advocates to film a documentary that would tarnish the nation's image and destabilize the country. Both the OSCE and the French Embassy denied the charges. On June 19, National Security Minister Geldymukhammed Ashirmukhammedov accused Tadzhigul Begmedova, chairwoman of the Turkmenistan Helsinki Foundation, of being involved in the same plot. Begmedova said the accusations were nonsensical.

$\bullet$ **UKRAINE** $\bullet\bullet\bullet\bullet\bullet\bullet\bullet\bullet\bullet\bullet\bullet\bullet\bullet\bullet\bullet\bullet\bullet\bullet\bullet$

Press freedom advances spawned by the Orange Revolution eroded in 2006 as political power struggles yielded the return of repressive tactics and attitudes toward the media. In October, the Kyiv-based Institute for Mass Information (IMI) said the number of beatings and threats against journalists had reached 32, double the number reported in all of 2005. There were no reported journalist murders or imprisonments, but limited progress in prosecuting past killings, and the failure to pursue the masterminds behind the crimes, contributed to an overall climate of impunity.

The March 29 parliamentary election was the first major test of the democratic changes promised by Ukraine's new leadership. Although international observers largely praised the conduct of the vote as the freest and fairest ever held in Ukraine, CPJ documented seven cases of journalists working for regional media who suffered threats, legal obstruction, or violent assaults in retaliation for their campaign coverage. In several cases, CPJ found, local police and prosecutors were reluctant to pursue those responsible. Police in the western city of Lviv waited 10 days before opening an investigation into a February 17 arson attack that destroyed the offices of the independent online newspaper *Vgolos*. The paper had recently criticized local politicians, and had also run a story about environmental problems at a regional industrial plant.

Provisions in a 2005 law regulating media coverage of election campaigns led to the temporary closure of local television stations in the Crimean city of Simferopol and the eastern industrial city of Dnepropetrovsk in February and March. The legislation gave courts the authority to suspend broadcast licenses or halt publications for up to four months preceding an election in response to candidate complaints. Media outlets could be muzzled for engaging in vaguely defined "political agitation" or for violating a rigid set of rules governing debates. The law also prohibited outlets from revealing the results of public opinion polls during that four-month period.

The tense political struggle leading up to the election grew fierce in its aftermath. The stakes in the election were high, as it heralded the country's transition from a presidential to a parliamentary system based on constitutional reforms negotiated in December 2004. Although the president retained key foreign, defense, and security portfolios, parliament was given control of finances and granted the power to dismiss ministers.

The poor third-place showing of President Viktor Yushchenko's Our Ukraine coalition revealed popular disillusionment with his unfulfilled pledge to prosecute corrupt members of the prior regime. The results led Yushchenko to engage in prolonged coalition talks with his former Orange allies—Yulia Timoshenko, whose party came in second, and the Socialists, who placed fourth. A new coalition agreement signed in June disintegrated the following month, when Socialist Party chief Aleksandr Moroz defected to a coalition led by former Orange foe Viktor Yanukovych and his Party of Regions. On August 3, Yushchenko agreed to nominate Yanukovych as prime minister after the former enemies signed a so-called Declaration of National Unity aimed at creating a grand coalition of their parties and promising to continue along a pro-Western path. Before the ink on their accord was dry, Yanukovych moved to consolidate his power, appointing numerous authoritarian figures from the prior regime and taking steps toward restoring opaque, post-Soviet norms of governance. Among the appointments was Mykola Azarov as first deputy premier. Azarov in turn replaced the chairman and five regional heads of the State Tax Administration, raising fears that the once notorious agency would resume chronic tax audits as a means of harassing opposition media.

The IMI documented 27 overt attempts at journalist censorship and denial of access by public officials, 16 cases of covert pressure and intimidation, and 22 civil defamation lawsuits filed by government officials as of October.

Much of the tension played out at the regional level. Regional councils in Crimea and Donetsk barred journalists from observing their selection of new speakers and other leaders. Ivano-Frankivsk city council deputies voted on May 18 to give the mayor's press secretary unilateral authority to strip any journalist of his or her credentials. That decision was later overturned, but local journalists continued to complain about official harassment.

Similar tactics soon spread to the capital. On July 12, Oleh Kalashnikov, a deputy from the Party of Regions, and several of his aides grabbed a two-member STB TV crew stationed in front of the parliament building in Kyiv and seized a videotape. The journalists had refused Kalashnikov's order to hand over footage they had just shot of a rally. Uniformed police nearby failed to respond to the crew's cries for help. On August 10, a crew from the independent 5 Kanal television station was denied access to a Yanukovych press conference in Kyiv. When the station demanded an explanation, the new premier's press secretary said that, effective immediately, state-run channel UT-1 held exclusive rights to live feeds of Yanukovych's news conferences. Journalists who attended said they were required to submit their questions in advance. The next day, the Kyiv mayor's office informed the media that new restrictions would bar journalists from contacting city hall officials directly for comments or information, limiting their access to the mayor's press office and official news conferences.

In early September, deputies from the Party of Regions submitted a new bill aimed at making libel a criminal offense. The legislation would penalize journalists for "spreading knowingly false fabrications that defame another individual" with fines, 200 hours of community service, or a year of hard labor. Ukraine eliminated its criminal libel statutes in 2001, when the legislature adopted a new criminal code to meet the standards set for its membership in the Strasbourg-based Council of Europe, the 46-member political organization that promotes human rights and the rule of law in Europe.

The pattern of abuse prompted a group of prominent journalists and advocates in Kyiv to launch a new public awareness campaign under the slogan "Hands off my freedom!" On September 15, the eve of the sixth anniversary of the gruesome murder of investigative journalist Georgy Gongadze, the group announced a plan to issue a list of "Enemies of the Press" each January to shed light on the top press freedom offenders in the country.

The watershed trial of three police officers accused of carrying out Gongadze's 2000 abduction and murder began on January 9 in a Kyiv court. Like the investigation that preceded it, the conduct of the trial inspired criticism from family members, colleagues, and press freedom advocates, including CPJ. The appellate panel trying the case, headed by Judge Irina Grigoryeva, closed significant portions of the trial to the press, and witnesses have claimed harassment.

Without describing a motive, Prosecutor General Aleksandr Medvedko claimed Gongadze's murder was organized by Gen. Aleksei Pukach, who fled the country in 2004, and was committed by the three men now on trial. All four belonged to a secret unit of the Interior Ministry. But critics, including former Justice Minister Serhiy Holovaty, said the prosecutor general's lengthy investigation shielded the top officials who plotted the journalist's murder. Holovaty called the trial a farce.

Prosecutors failed to persuade the court to accept as evidence audiotapes—made secretly by a former presidential bodyguard—in which former President Leonid Kuchma was heard instructing Interior Minister Yuri Kravchenko to "drive out" Gongadze and "give him to the Chechens." Kravchenko was found dead on the day he was to be interrogated about the murder in March 2005. His death was swiftly ruled a suicide, though doubts have lingered as to how Kravchenko was able to shoot himself twice in the head. Public pressure amid the release of new evidence forced prosecutors to reopen the Kravchenko investigation in the fall.

· · · · · · · · · · · · · · · · · · UZBEKISTAN · · · · · · · · · · · · · · · · · · ·

President Islam Karimov continued his crackdown on the independent press, political opponents, and civil-society groups. As his foreign policy shifted away from the West, Karimov's regime expelled dozens of foreign-funded nongovernmental organizations, including those supporting local media. The few remaining independent journalists were forced to choose whether to sever ties to foreign-funded media or face harassment, legal action, and imprisonment. A restrictive new law regulating the work of journalists for international media made it illegal for local reporters to contribute to foreign media outlets not accredited by the Ministry of Foreign Affairs.

Emboldened by the support of new regional allies Russia and Kazakhstan, Karimov turned aside international calls for an independent investigation into the May 2005 killing of hundreds of civilians by government troops in the eastern city of Andijan. He accused the West of waging an "information war" on Uzbekistan, and his government continued to use trumped-up charges of terrorism and extremism to jail media critics, political opponents, and human rights advocates.

Activist Saidjahon Zainabiddinov, head of the Andijan-based human rights group Appelyatsiya and a witness to the May 2005 killings, was sentenced in January to seven years in prison for talking to foreign reporters about the crackdown. Zainabiddinov was found guilty of spreading "false information" about Andijan, according to international press reports and human rights groups. He was tried in near secrecy; only the activist's elderly mother was allowed to attend.

On January 13, the U.S.-based nongovernmental group Freedom House announced that a Tashkent civil court had suspended its operations for "allowing human-rights defenders free access to the Internet" and for noncompliance with an unspecified Uzbek cabinet decree. Freedom House had supported efforts to combat and document human rights abuses. Throughout the year, the government closed or expelled a number of international groups; these included the U.S.-based Eurasia Foundation, an NGO that promoted free media and democracy, on a charge of failing to properly register with the Ministry of Justice.

Russian President Vladimir Putin publicly supported Karimov's response to Andijan. During his annual press conference on January 31, the Russian leader warned against the exportation of Western values. "We don't need a second Afghanistan in Central Asia," Putin told a U.S. reporter. "We know the situation there better than you know it."

Bolstered by Putin's support, Karimov reacted defiantly to the World Bank's February decision to stop lending money to Uzbekistan. The president claimed the World Bank's decision had been based on incorrect information, and he warned Western nations to stop interfering in Uzbekistan's internal affairs, Interfax and The Associated Press reported. In March, Karimov hosted his Kazakh counterpart, Nursultan Nazarbayev, at a summit in Tashkent. Uzbekistan and Kazakhstan have been traditional rivals in the region, but Karimov's foreign policy shift toward Russia helped spawn a partnership with Nazarbayev in the areas of security, trade, and economic cooperation.

To solidify its grip on Uzbekistan's battered independent media, the government tightened restrictions on local and international journalists working for foreign-funded media. The cabinet approved regulations in February that gave the Ministry of Foreign Affairs wide discretion to issue formal warnings to foreign correspondents, revoke their accreditation and visas, and expel them. Under Article 21 of the regulations, foreign correspondents are "forbidden to call for the forceful change of the current constitutional order, violate the territorial integrity of the Republic of Uzbekistan, propagate war and violence, cruelty, [and] national, race, and religious hatred." They are also barred from "interfering in the internal affairs of the Republic of Uzbekistan, harming the honor and dignity of citizens of the Republic of Uzbekistan, interfering in their private lives, and committing other actions that provide for legal accountability." The broad language does not define what constitutes interference in Uzbekistan's affairs or in the private lives of citizens, nor does it specify "other actions" that are prohibited.

Putting the new regulations to immediate use, the ministry issued reprimands in March to three local correspondents for the German public broadcaster Deutsche Welle, the Central Asia news Web site *Ferghana* reported. Obid Shabanov, rebuked for filing "inaccurate" news reports, had reported on a January incident in which 30 people froze to death when their bus broke down in the desert. Yuri Chernogayev, charged with working with nonaccredited journalists, had confirmed the accuracy of that report to an allegedly nonaccredited Reuters correspondent. And Salikh Yakhyev had allegedly reported without accreditation.

In a rare positive development, CPJ welcomed the release from prison on April 3 of journalist Sobirdjon Yakubov. A reporter for the state-run weekly *Hurriyat*, Yakubov had spent a year in jail on vague subversion charges based on unspecified allegations of religious extremism. A Tashkent court released him for lack of evidence, *Ferghana* reported. Yakubov's colleague, Gairat Mekhliboyev, remained in prison after being convicted of anticonstitutional activities in connection with a *Hurriyat* article that questioned the compatibility of Islam and democracy.

On May 3, World Press Freedom Day, CPJ named Uzbekistan one of the 10 Most Censored Countries in the world. U.S. lawmakers, including Sen. John McCain, called for the suspension of U.S. funding to Uzbekistan until the country showed progress on human rights and allowed an international investigation into the Andijan killings.

On May 13, the anniversary of the Andijan killings, the U.S. Department of State and the European Union issued statements condemning the crackdown and renewing calls for an independent probe. The state-controlled Uzbek press reacted by condemning the West's "information aggression" toward Uzbekistan, the U.S. government-funded Radio Free Europe/Radio Liberty said.

In September, Dzhamshid Karimov, a former correspondent for the London-based Institute for War and Peace Reporting (IWPR) who wrote critically about local and federal officials, was forced into psychiatric confinement in the central city of Samarkand. Karimov, the president's nephew, had been under close government surveillance for months; in August, authorities cut his long-distance and international phone connections and seized his passport. Ulugbek Khaidarov, who had reported for IWPR and the U.S.-based Internews Network, was arrested in September on trumped-up charges of extortion and bribery after writing several articles critical of local authorities. An appellate judge threw out the case in November and ordered Khaidarov released.

No form of dissent was immune from official harassment. On September 8, a Tashkent court sentenced poet and singer Dadakhon Khasanov to a suspended three-year sentence after a closed-door trial in which the defendant had no lawyer. Khasanov was charged with undermining the constitutional order of Uzbekistan, endangering the president of Uzbekistan, and producing and distributing materials that threaten public safety, according to the Moscow-based human rights news agency Prima. The charges stemmed from a song Khasanov wrote and recorded in commemoration of Andijan. The AP reported that the lyrics read in part: "Don't say you haven't seen how Andijan was drowned in blood .... The victims fell like mulberries, the children's bloodied bodies were like tulips."

ARMENIA

- On May 25, authorities denied independent television station A1+ a broadcasting license for the 12th time. According to press reports, the National Commission on Television and Radio justified the rejection by saying that competitors submitted stronger bids. A1+ said the refusal was politically motivated and appealed to the European Court of Human Rights. The court could urge Armenia to reconsider.

- Arman Babadzhanian, editor-in-chief of the opposition daily *Zhamanak Yerevan*, was arrested on June 26, days after publishing an article that questioned the independence of the Yerevan prosecutor's office, according to CPJ sources. Babadzhanian was charged with forging documents to escape military service; the journalist did not dispute the allegation but said the charge was pressed in retaliation for his work. On September 8, a district court in Yerevan sentenced Babadzhanian to four years in prison, according to the U.S. government-funded Radio Free Europe/Radio Liberty. The defense filed an appeal in September.

BOSNIA

- Mubarak Asani, correspondent for the Sarajevo-based public television broadcaster BHT 1, received telephone death threats in November after reporting the alleged involvement of local politicians in a prostitution ring, according to press reports. The politicians were not named in the report, which aired on the weekly political program "Javna Tajna" (Public Secret). Asani filed a complaint with police, who opened an investigation, the Association of Journalists of Bosnia-Herzegovina reported.

BULGARIA

- A bomb exploded April 6 outside the Sofia apartment of Vasil Ivanov, a Nova Television investigative reporter who had recently uncovered abuse of inmates in the Sofia Central Prison. No one was injured, but the explosion caused extensive damage, according to CPJ research.

CROATIA

- In early 2006, the Croatian parliament enacted penal code changes to decriminalize libel and direct such complaints to civil courts, according to Dragutin Lucic Luce, president of the Croatian Journalists Association. The European Union had encouraged Balkan governments to amend laws that restrict press freedom.

- The International Criminal Tribunal for the Former Yugoslavia at The Hague decided not to prosecute Marijan Krizic, editor-in-chief of the Zagreb-based weekly *Hrvatsko Slovo*; Stjepan Seselj, the paper's publisher; and Domagoj Margetic, a former editor with the newsweekly. The journalists had been charged in August 2005 with defying the tribunal's gag orders by publishing the identity of a protected witness. Chief Prosecutor Carla del Ponte withdrew the indictments in mid-June, saying her office was limiting the scope of its prosecutions, Agence France-Presse reported. The court convicted Josip Jovic, former editor-in-chief of the Split daily *Slobodna Dalmacija*, on a charge of publishing the name and testimony of a protected witness and fined him 20,000 euros (US$26,650) on August 30.

- Ladislav Tomicic, a correspondent for the national daily *Novi List*, received an anonymous letter threatening to kill him and his family. The letter came in July, shortly after he wrote articles about the involvement of former intelligence agents in organized crime, according to the Organization for Security and Cooperation in Europe. Tomicic reported the threat to police, who are investigating.

CYPRUS

- Turkey's attorney general, who has jurisdiction in North Cyprus, opened a case against Serhat Incirli, correspondent for the daily *Afrika*, on allegations of insulting Turkey in articles that criticized the Turkish presence in Cyprus and ascribed racist elements to the Turkish national anthem and history books, according to CPJ sources and local press reports. Incirli, who is based in London, said the April announcement led to persistent police harassment.

DENMARK

- The Viby-based daily *Jyllands-Posten* sparked worldwide protests in early 2006 with a series of cartoons depicting the Prophet Muhammad. The cartoons were published in September 2005 but drew wide international attention when they were later reproduced in other European publications. CPJ documented attacks on the press in 13 countries in Europe, Africa, Asia, and the Middle East, most stemming from decisions by newspapers to reprint versions of one or more of the cartoons. Government reprisals ranged from issuing censorship orders and jailing editors on criminal charges, to suspending and closing newspapers, according to CPJ research. Danish embassies were attacked and set on fire by angry protesters in Damascus, Beirut, and Tehran; dozens were said to have died in worldwide protests.

- On April 27, the state prosecutor charged Michael Bjerre and Jesper Larsen of the conservative Copenhagen daily *Berlingske Tidende* with revealing state secrets in 2004 news reports that questioned the existence of Iraqi weapons of mass destruction and Prime Minister Anders Fogh Rasmussen's decision to support the U.S.-led invasion of Iraq, according to international press reports. A Copenhagen judge acquitted the journalists on December 4.

GERMANY/POLAND

- On June 26, the national German daily *Die Tageszeitung* published a story headlined "Young Polish Potatoes" that criticized Polish President Lech Kacynski and his brother, Prime Minister Jaroslaw Kacynski, for their conservative policies. President Kacynski demanded an apology from the German government for the article, but German officials refused. Prime Minister Kacynski warned that relations between the countries would be damaged, according to international press reports.

ITALY

- Authorities in the central Italian city of Perugia jailed veteran crime reporter Mario Spezi on April 7, just days before the publication of a book he co-authored with U.S. writer Douglas Preston about the 1968-85 "Monster of Florence" murders in the province of Tuscany. Authorities did not show a warrant when they arrested Spezi, and they did not explain why or where they were taking him. He was placed under criminal investigation for allegedly defaming Perugia prosecutors, attempting to sidetrack an official murder probe by planning to plant evidence, and allegedly taking part himself in a 1985 murder. Spezi was detained for 22 days. After CPJ advocacy sparked international attention, a three-judge appellate panel on April 29 voided the order to detain Spezi and ordered his release.

LITHUANIA

- State security agents in September seized all 15,000 copies of the Vilnius-based semimonthly *Laisvas Laikrastis* (Free Newspaper) and briefly detained Editor-in-Chief Aurimas Drizius. The seized edition's lead story cited telephone conversations between politicians and a local casino operator as evidence of corruption. The 2004 conversations had been recorded by state security agents. Transcripts were obtained by *Laisvas Laikrastis* through sources the paper would not disclose, according to CPJ research. Ardivas Pocius, director of the State Security Department, or VSD, said the copies were confiscated because they contained secret investigative information, the news agency ITAR-TASS reported. Agents also searched the paper's newsroom and Drizius' home, confiscating the hard drives of all six newsroom computers and the editor's home computer. Drizius was released the next day on orders of Lithuania's prosecutor general, but the seized copies and computers were not returned, the editor told CPJ. Drizius filed a civil lawsuit against the VSD, saying the arrest had tarnished his reputation.

MACEDONIA

- Parliament amended the criminal code in May to abolish prison penalties for defamation. Prison terms had ranged up to three years. Macedonia is a candidate for membership in the European Union, which has urged the revision of laws restricting press freedom. Defamation is still subject to monetary penalties.

MOLDOVA

- Interior Ministry officials searched the independent television station Pro-TV Chisinau and arrested the station's sales director, Ghenadie Braghis, on bribery charges on September 7, the Chisinau-based Independent Journalism Center said. The actions came after the station aired broadcasts highly critical of Interior Minister Gheorghe Papuc, the center said. The criminal case was pending.

NETHERLANDS

- Reporters Bart Mos and Joost de Haas were jailed for three days in November for refusing to reveal their confidential sources. Mos and de Haas, of the Amsterdam-based daily *De Telegraaf*, had been called as witnesses in the trial of a former secret agent charged with leaking information about an organized crime gang. The reporters had written a series of articles beginning in January that detailed the local mafia's alleged access to classified information. In jailing the reporters, Judge J.A. van Steen said knowing how the two got information for their stories could bolster or undercut the case against the agent, *The New York Times* reported. After an international outcry, however, van Steen said there was insufficient evidence to hold the reporters.

POLAND

- Andrzej Marek, editor-in-chief of the weekly *Wiesci Polickie* in the town of Police, was sentenced on January 12 to three months in prison on a charge of libeling a city council spokesman. The case stemmed from articles written in 2004 suggesting that the spokesman had used his position to promote his private advertising business, according to CPJ research. The Constitutional Tribunal, Poland's highest court, suspended the sentence the same month after a public outcry, according to international press reports.

PORTUGAL

- Lisbon police raided the daily *24 Horas*, seizing journalists' computers and office files, after the newspaper published several articles on a child sex abuse scandal, according to Agence France-Presse and other news organizations. According to those reports, authorities conducted the February 15 search in an effort to identify the paper's sources. On April 26, the Lisbon Appeals Court rejected the newspaper's bid to bar police from examining the journalists' seized computers, according to Sindicato dos Journalistas, a Lisbon-based press organization.

ROMANIA

- On February 16, a Bucharest judge sentenced Marian Garleanu, correspondent for the opposition daily *Romania Libera*, to 10 days in jail on a charge of possessing classified military documents about coalition troops in Afghanistan and Iraq. Garleanu, who did not publish the information, received the documents from former Romanian soldier Ionel Popa, who was arrested for leaking classified information to radio stations and newspapers. On February 18, the Supreme Court overturned the ruling and ordered Garleanu's release. *Romania Libera* correspondents Ovidiu Ohanesian and Petre Mihai Bacanu were also investigated but not charged.

- Sebastian Oancea, Focsani correspondent for the national daily *Ziua*, was charged on February 22 with possession and distribution of state secrets related to military operations in Afghanistan and Iraq. Oancea faced seven years in prison if convicted, The Associated Press reported. Three other *Ziua* journalists—Bogdan Comaroni, Doru Dragomir, and Victor Roncea—were also investigated for possession of state secrets. Comaroni, Dragomir, and Roncea turned over the classified documents to police in early 2006. *Ziua* did not publish the contents of the documents or write a story about them. The *Bucharest Daily News* said the documents included encoding information for military radio transmissions, passwords and secret signals, and maps of military facilities.

SERBIA

- On July 19, parliament revised the country's broadcasting law to enable government regulators to revoke licenses unilaterally and without avenue for appeal. The broadly written bill could allow the state Republican Broadcasting Agency to act selectively, according to a report by the Organization for Security and Cooperation in Europe and the Belgrade-based Association of Independent Electronic Media.

SWITZERLAND

- The military opened an investigation in January into editor Christoph Grenacher and reporters Sandro Brotz and Beat Jost of the Zurich weekly *SonntagsBlick* after the paper published the contents of a fax about a purported CIA prison in Romania. The fax from Egyptian Foreign Minister Ahmed Aboul Gheit was sent to the Egyptian Embassy in London. Swiss military authorities were investigating allegations of military secrets having been published, but the journalists were not immediately charged.

THE MIDDLE EAST AND NORTH AFRICA

As Democracy Falters, Arab Press Still Pushes for Freedom

The Bush administration once vowed to spread democracy across a region of princes and potentates. While those heady days are now mere memory, independent journalists are still pushing the boundaries of press freedom.

by Joel Campagna

PHOTOS

Section break: AP/Nasser Nasser — *An Egyptian journalist, her hands in symbolic chains, protests a bill stiffening prison penalties for the press.* Analysis (next): Reuters/ Ahmed Jadallah — *A Bahraini man casts his vote at a polling station in Manama in November.*

THE MIDDLE EAST AND NORTH AFRICA

AS DEMOCRACY FALTERS, ARAB PRESS
STILL PUSHES FOR FREEDOM *by Joel Campagna*

• •

ACROSS THE MIDDLE EAST, POLITICAL REFORM GAINED MOMENTUM in the aftermath of the September 11, 2001, attacks on the United States and the U.S.-led invasion of Iraq in March 2003. Egyptians and Lebanese clamored for democracy; elections in Iraq, Palestine, Yemen, and Saudi Arabia offered a more pluralistic future. In a number of Arab countries, the media seized the moment. Newspapers in Egypt and Yemen smashed long-held taboos by openly criticizing political leaders, while in Iraq the toppling of Saddam Hussein opened the way for a vibrant news media. Autocrats known for smothering dissent suddenly touted the virtues of democracy, a system of government that U.S. President George W. Bush, buoyed by initial military success in Iraq, vowed to spread across a region of princes and potentates.

Those heady days seem a distant memory. The Bush democratization plan barely got off the ground. Washington's prodding of several regional allies proved fleeting. Middle East autocrats thwarted significant reform altogether or implemented mere cosmetic changes. "[Bush] promised the sky and obviously could not deliver," said Marina Ottaway, director of the Middle East program at the Carnegie Endowment for International Peace. "U.S. strategies do not do anything about the central problem in the Middle East: How do you diminish the power of omnipotent executives?"

The implications are clear. Change, if it comes at all, will take many years.

Bush promised the sky and could not deliver, says one analyst.

And while international pressure is important, sustained effort from within is essential.

Political reformers and press freedom advocates whose expectations may have been raised by the Bush administration ran into regional realities: entrenched, authoritarian elites in countries such as Egypt, Saudi Arabia, and Morocco; and what became murderous chaos in Iraq. Of the 34 journalists killed in the Middle East and North Africa in 2006, 32 died in Iraq, most at the hands of assassins. Outside Iraq, scores of journalists who challenged the political order were threatened by government agents, hauled before the courts, thrown in prison, or censored in media crackdowns that stretched from Algeria to Yemen.

The Bush administration was able to engineer elections in Iraq, which it touted as a democratic model for the Middle East. But the carnage did not stop, and journalists found themselves in the middle. Not only were they targeted by murderers, they also came under political fire from government officials angered by their reporting. A growing list of Iraqi journalists endured harassment, censorship, or criminal prosecution under crude laws revived from Saddam Hussein's regime. Others were detained and harassed by the security forces. The government continued to arbitrarily ban satellite broadcasters, as it did in September when it shuttered the Baghdad bureau of the Dubai-based satellite channel Al-Arabiya for a month on vague charges of fomenting "sectarian violence and war in Iraq."

With few checks on their powers, governments across the region preyed on critical journalists, using draconian press laws or outright intimidation. When U.S. pressure was at its peak after the 2003 Iraq invasion, Egyptian President Hosni Mubarak promised reforms that included the repeal of prison penalties for so-called press offenses. But by 2006, criminal penalties remained on the books, and a slew of Egyptian journalists faced the prospect of jail time for their critical writing. Egyptian journalists still spoke out but were confronted by arrests, lawsuits, and state-sponsored assaults. The government, like others in the region, maintained its tight hold on media ownership. "The broadcast media is still in the hands of the government, and [so is] 90 percent of the print press," remarked independent newspaper publisher Hisham Qassem, lamenting how the government has stalled the democratic reform movement. "You need credible media for civilians to address public opinion."

Half measures were the norm elsewhere in the region. Saudi Arabia, un-

THE MIDDLE EAST AND NORTH AFRICA

der enormous international pressure to open up its closed society following the 9/11 attacks, which were carried out mainly by Saudi nationals, initially loosened the shackles on its heavily censored press. Newspapers launched an unprecedented debate about the role of the country's powerful religious

The situation begs the question: Can autocrats reform themselves?

establishment in promoting extremism. But those once-promising media advances were followed by a government crackdown that included serial dismissals of outspoken writers and threats to others. That trend carried through to 2006, when, in April, journalist Rabah al-Quwai' was jailed for 13 days in retaliation for his writing about religious extremism. While Saudi media are freer than they have been in recent history, the government still bars them from covering central issues such as government corruption and the activities of the royal family.

Jordan's King Abdullah II has burnished an image of a reforming monarch, often telling journalists that the "sky is the limit" for press freedom. But reporters continue to chafe under an all-powerful security apparatus that has infiltrated much of the media and engendered widespread self-censorship. In May, security agents interrogated editor Fahd al-Rimawi for more than six hours over an article that cast a critical eye on an official announcement that the government had uncovered a Hamas arms cache. A month later, agents abruptly halted a live Al-Jazeera interview with the brother-in-law of the deceased Iraqi insurgent Abu Musab al-Zarqawi, briefly detaining interviewer Yasser Abu Hilala and his crew.

Press freedom in Libya, Tunisia, Oman, and the United Arab Emirates is either nonexistent or heavily constrained. And Syria pursues a relentless crackdown on dissidents that includes arrests of Internet journalists and bloggers.

The situation seems to beg the question of whether autocrats can be asked to reform themselves. In his 2005 inaugural address, President Bush pledged to "encourage reform in other governments by making clear that success in our relations will require the decent treatment of their own people." But the unraveling of the Bush strategy in Iraq has consumed Washington's attention and made the United States less bullish in advocating real change throughout the region.

In February, then-Defense Secretary Donald Rumsfeld held security talks with leaders in Algeria and Tunisia, both of which have abysmal press freedom records. That very month, the government of Algerian President Abdelaziz Bouteflika effectively decreed that the media could not investigate human rights abuses that occurred during the 1990s civil war, including the murders of at least

58 journalists. And editor Mohamed Benchicou was still languishing in prison, completing a two-year sentence for his criticism of Bouteflika's presidency. In Tunisia, human rights lawyer Mohamed Abbou was behind bars for having published an Internet article that compared torture in Tunisia's prisons to conditions in Iraq's infamous Abu Ghraib; other journalists and rights defenders remained under relentless pressure from the state security operation.

Yet for all the discouraging trends, there is hope.

If authoritarian regimes are firmly entrenched, a new political dynamism is evident. Attacks against the press are on the rise in many countries precisely because journalists are becoming more outspoken in their criticism. Writers in Egypt, Morocco, and Yemen have aggressively seized on political openings to publish daring news and commentary that would have been unprintable just a few years ago. In the press, a small pack of independent journalists has pushed the boundaries of what is tolerated in print by exposing corruption and government misdeeds. The wall of fear that once prevented citizens from freely expressing themselves has eroded, even in the most repressive countries.

Attacks are on the rise precisely because journalists are more outspoken.

Most dramatically, the state's monopoly on information has been broken in recent years by the preponderance of satellite television and the Internet. "The days when states ran public debate are over," noted Amr Hamzawy, a senior analyst at the Carnegie Endowment for International Peace. If calls for political reform have yielded few concrete results, they have produced unprecedented debate about democracy and pluralism, Hamzawy said. Popular channels such as Al-Jazeera have created a public expectation that the truth can be uncovered and the powerful held to account.

The prospects for achieving greater press freedom vary by country, but journalists in nations such as Egypt, Morocco, and Yemen express hope. "I am optimistic, not because the regime is allowing freedom of expression, but because I reckon that the internal forces in society are moving toward openness and liberalization," said Moroccan publisher Aboubakr Jamaï, who has weathered repeated government attempts to shut down his fiercely independent weekly *Le Journal Hebdomadaire*. "Having a free press is a demand of our society. The problem is that it isn't coming as rapidly as society would like, or demands." One indication is that papers such as *Le Journal* are more popular than ever despite severe pressure from officials.

In Egypt, democracy activists and independent journalists incur the wrath of authorities, but they continue to promote a robust political debate in the press and online. Even in the most politically closed states, like Syria, intellectuals and bloggers strike up debates that would have been impossible not so many years ago.

The struggle for an effective free press is destined to be long, arduous, and buffeted by wider political forces. In many nations, the continuing absence of independent political institutions and the pervasive presence of state security services hinder the ability of the press to grow and to exert influence.

"I've come to the conclusion that I will never live in a Westminster-style democracy in Egypt," publisher Qassem said. "I will be part of the transition. Basically, there is no infrastructure here, and that is the problem." Infrastructure, for Qassem, includes not only judicial independence and effective political parties but also unfettered, commercially viable, and broad-based media.

A publisher gives up hope for a 'Westminster-style' democracy.

Ultimately, political and media reforms are two sides of the same coin. "You need to have both processes happening at the same time," said Morocco's Jamaï. "They go hand in hand." Change, where it occurs, will be incremental, and journalists will be required to battle to preserve and expand the small pockets of independence they have carved out, especially in the all-important electronic media. In doing so, they lay the foundation for a true Fourth Estate.

• • • • • • • • •

Joel Campagna is senior program coordinator responsible for the Middle East and North Africa. He led CPJ missions to Yemen and Saudi Arabia in 2006.

· EGYPT ·

The Egyptian Journalists Syndicate mounted a widespread campaign to pressure President Hosni Mubarak to fulfill a February 2004 promise to decriminalize press offenses. More than 20 newspapers went on strike for a day in July as part of the campaign, which many journalists credit with the last-minute deletion of a controversial amendment to the penal code. Mubarak removed a provision that would have stipulated prison sentences of up to three years for journalists who defamed public officials by alleging corruption. The provision was aimed at silencing independent and opposition newspapers that had increasingly carried reports on corruption scandals and influence peddling that allegedly involved high-ranking state officials and Mubarak's son and heir apparent, Gamal Mubarak.

Other amendments lifted some minor restrictions on the media but left intact prison penalties for journalists convicted of insulting the president and foreign heads of state. The National Assembly, controlled by Mubarak's National Democratic Party, passed the package of amendments, which also provided imprisonment for publishing "false" information and insulting state institutions such as the judiciary and armed forces. Prison sentences run as high as five years.

In a move that triggered concerns that the government was attempting to financially cripple outspoken newspapers, the amendment package doubled fines for writers and editors convicted of defamation and a range of vaguely worded offenses. Fines now reach as high as 40,000 Egyptian pounds (US$7,000).

Other restrictive legislation, such as the Law on the Protection of National Unity, the Law on the Security of the Nation and the Citizen, the Law on Political Rights, and the Emergency Law in force since President Mubarak came to power in 1981, may still be used to imprison journalists.

An upsurge in the number of journalists sentenced to jail by the courts, the detention of reporters for weeks without trial, and assaults on journalists by Cairo plainclothes police have prompted many in the local press corps to conclude that Mubarak will never honor his pledge. Many independent journalists said the reform process itself is flawed, leaving Egyptian law far short of international standards for free expression.

The Egyptian Organization for Human Rights documented 85 cases brought against journalists from February 2004 to July 2006, when newspapers staged the one-day strike. Most of those prosecuted had written about official corruption.

Prominent columnists and intellectuals writing in the beleaguered independent and

· · · · · · · · · ·

Country summaries in this chapter were reported and written by Senior Program Coordinator **Joel Campagna**, Research Associate **Ivan Karakashian**, and Program Consultant **Kamel Eddine Labidi**.

THE MIDDLE EAST AND NORTH AFRICA

opposition newspapers questioned the potential for the media to make a significant move toward freedom under a constitution that gives the president sweeping powers, unlimited terms of office, and the ability to silence his critics.

"The media and the judiciary are increasingly targeted and the circle of press freedom is narrowing. We will face the same plight as Tunisian journalists if we fail to take action," warned Al-Jazeera's Cairo bureau chief, Hussein Abdel Ghani, who was arrested in April for allegedly propagating false news. He was speaking on May 3, World Press Freedom Day, when for the first time in Cairo, journalists and human rights advocates from Egypt, Algeria, and Tunisia, backed by CPJ and the International Freedom of Expression Exchange, a clearinghouse for press freedom monitors, joined to urge Arab rulers to adopt international standards of freedom of expression.

The call came as journalists Saher al-Gad of *Al-Geel* and Ibrahim Sahari of *Al-Alam al-Youm* were behind bars for their opposition to Mubarak's rule. They were arrested in April while covering protests in Cairo against the trial of two prominent judges who publicly denounced the rigging of the 2005 legislative elections.

On February 23, a Cairo criminal appeals court upheld the 2005 conviction and one-year prison sentence against Abdel Nasser al-Zuheiry, a reporter for the independent daily *Al-Masry al-Youm*, for libeling a former minister of housing. Al-Zuheiry remained free pending further appeal.

Less than two weeks later, following an eight-minute hearing, a Cairo court sentenced in absentia Amira Malash of the independent weekly *Al-Fajr* to one year in prison for defaming Judge Attia Mohammad Awad in a July 2005 article alleging that he had accepted bribes. She was not immediately jailed.

The sentencing by a Cairo court in June of Ibrahim Eissa, editor-in-chief of the independent weeklies *Al-Dustour* and *Sawt al-Umma*, and Sahar Zaki, a reporter for *Al-Dustour*, to a year in prison apiece for publishing a report critical of Mubarak had an unusually chilling effect on the local press. Eissa, one of the most outspoken and intrepid Egyptian journalists, and Zaki were free on bail of 10,000 Egyptian pounds (US$1,750) pending appeal.

The case against Eissa stemmed from an April 2005 news item that reported efforts by an Egyptian lawyer to take Mubarak and his family to court on allegations of corruption, including the alleged misuse of foreign aid. The lawyer, Said Abdullah, was also sentenced to a year in jail.

In September, the government banned editions of three European papers that carried pieces about Pope Benedict's controversial comments on Islam: the French daily *Le Figaro*, the German daily *Frankfurter Allgemeine Zeitung*, and the weekly international edition of Britain's *The Guardian*. In a September 12 lecture at the University of Regensburg in Germany, Benedict cited centuries-old quotations asserting that Islam was spread by the sword. Use of the quotations, which the pope said did not reflect his own opinions, provoked widespread anger in Muslim countries.

· IRAN ·

With world attention focused on Iran's nuclear ambitions, the hard-line government of President Mahmoud Ahmadinejad turned the screws on press freedom and intimidated critical journalists into silence or self-censorship.

Ahmadinejad, who has pursued the conservative parliament's policy of relentlessly stifling independent journalism since his election in August 2005, used the nuclear debate to deflect criticism of his human rights record both internally and externally, according to Iranian journalists. He exploited a standoff with the United States over the acquisition of nuclear technology to rally domestic public opinion and insist that Iran had an "inalienable right" to enrich uranium for peaceful purposes. He accused Washington of double standards in seeking to deny Iran a nuclear industry while it backed the nuclear ambitions of other countries in the Middle East and Asia.

Freed Iranian journalist Akbar Ganji lamented Western countries' preoccupation with the nuclear issue at the expense of attention to Tehran's poor human rights and press freedom record. Ganji spent six years in prison for investigative articles that implicated top officials in a series of murders. Released in March and allowed to leave Iran, Ganji toured the United States and Europe in an attempt to put Iran's oppression of independent journalists and political dissidents back into the public arena.

Meeting with CPJ at its New York offices on August 17, Ganji said that the threat of imprisonment had kept most journalists from writing on sensitive topics, and that self-censorship had become the norm in Iran. He noted that authorities kept Iran low on the list of countries that jail journalists by sentencing reporters to lengthy prison terms but not actually putting them behind bars for long periods. The constant threat of incarceration has been enough to keep journalists at heel.

Since 2000, Iranian courts have banned more than 100 publications critical of the regime, forcing reformist journalists to abandon the profession or switch to blogs, which soared in popularity until the October 2004 arrest of more than 20 bloggers. All but one were eventually released. The exception was Arash Sigarchi, a blogger and former editor of the daily *Gilan-e-Emrouz* in northern Iran, who is serving a three-year prison sentence.

In January, an appeals court upheld Sigarchi's conviction on charges of espionage, engaging in propaganda against the system, undermining national security, and insulting supreme leader Ayatollah Ali Khamenei. The charges followed interviews he gave to BBC World Service radio and the U.S. government-funded Radio Farda. He was also vocal

THE MIDDLE EAST AND NORTH AFRICA

through his now-defunct blog, *Panhjareh Eltehab* (The Window of Anguish), in which he often criticized the government and protested the detention and mistreatment of other Iranian bloggers.

Even reporting the arrests of bloggers has drawn government persecution. Mojtaba Saminejad, a journalism student and blogger, spent nearly 20 months in jail after he reported that charges had been brought against three other bloggers. Authorities granted him home leave in June 2006 and he was officially freed in September.

On January 29, seven journalists including Mohsen Dorostkar, editor-in-chief of *Tammadon-e Hormozgan*, and Elham Afroutan, a journalist for the weekly, were jailed after publishing a satirical article by an Iranian blogger in Germany that likened Iran's 1979 revolution and Ayatollah Ruhollah Khomeini's subsequent reign to the AIDS virus. While five of the journalists were briefly detained, Dorostkar and Afroutan spent more than four months in jail and were released in early June after posting bail of 300 million rials (US$33,900). A court convicted Afroutan of propagating offensive material; Dorostkar was acquitted. In September, the Appeals Court in Tehran upheld Afroutan's conviction, but reduced her one-year prison sentence to the 91 days already served.

In battling Web discourse, the government augmented law enforcement with technology. The Ministry of Communications and Information Technology launched a filtering system that recognized Web sites containing "illicit" words. In January, the BBC reported that its Farsi Web site, the most popular of its non-English-language sites with 30 million page views a month, was blocked. The semiofficial Iranian Labor News Agency quoted officials as saying that the BBC had "crossed red lines." Journalists said it was increasingly difficult to know where those lines were drawn, but insulting Khamenei was certainly one. During the year, negative reporting on the nuclear issue became another. Beginning March 21, the National Supreme Security Council warned editors against publishing political analyses that deviated from official policy, according to the online daily *Rooz*.

Some of those who crossed red lines were sentenced to prison but not jailed. On August 19, Saghi Baghernia, publisher of the daily economic newspaper *Asia*, received a six-month jail sentence from a Tehran court for "insulting the regime," according to CPJ sources. She was not jailed but may be summoned at any time to serve her sentence, the sources said. On July 5, 2003, Baghernia published a photograph of Paris-based Iranian opposition leader Maryam Rajavi smiling after her release from a French prison, where she had been held on terrorism charges. Rajavi is the wife of Massoud Rajavi, leader of Mujahedeen Khalq, a group that the United States considers a terrorist organization, and which is dedicated to the overthrow of the government in Tehran. Baghernia was convicted as the license holder of *Asia*.

Issa Saharkhiz, managing editor of the now-defunct critical monthly *Aftab*, received a four-year prison sentence and a five-year ban on practicing journalism from a court of first instance in Tehran on August 28, according to the Iran Student News Agency. The court revoked the monthly's publishing license, which had already been suspended. Saharkhiz was convicted of disseminating false information in articles he published several years ago that criticized Iran's human rights record, particularly prison conditions. Saharkhiz was free pending appeal.

The government banned at least 12 pro-reformist publications during the year, according to Mashallah Shamsolvaezin, spokesman for the Iranian Committee for the Defense of Freedom of the Press. On September 11, authorities indefinitely shuttered the most prominent critical daily, *Shargh*, saying it had not replaced as ordered Managing Director Mohammad Rahmanian, who was accused of publishing blasphemous articles and insulting officials.

Iran's Press Supervisory Board criticized *Shargh* for publishing a cartoon of a donkey with a halo of light around its head. Some opposition Web sites had quoted Ahmadinejad as saying that he was protected by a divine halo during his U.N. General Assembly speech in New York in 2005, Reuters reported. The president's office denied he had made the comment. *Shargh's* criticism of the Supreme National Security Council, which was in charge of nuclear negotiations with the West, angered authorities, who viewed the cartoon as an attempt to undermine the council, Shamsolvaezin told CPJ.

· IRAQ ·

For the fourth consecutive year, Iraq was the most dangerous reporting assignment in the world, exacting a frightening toll on local and foreign journalists. Thirty-two journalists and 15 media support staffers were killed during the year, bringing to 129 the number of media personnel killed in action since the U.S.-led invasion in March 2003. Those numbers easily made Iraq the deadliest conflict for the press in CPJ's 25-year history. For the first time, murder overtook crossfire as the leading cause of journalist deaths in Iraq, with insurgent groups ruthlessly targeting journalists for political, sectarian, and Western affiliations.

Setting Iraq apart from earlier conflicts was the scale and ubiquity of the danger. For journalists as well as ordinary Iraqis, just stepping out the front door was risky. Suicide bombers, car bombs, murders, and abduction were among the dangers facing reporters, hindering their ability to travel and gather the news. "I don't drive a car to work because I don't want to be identified going in and out of the compound where *The Washington Post* bureau is based. I hail taxis instead, examining each driver's face in hopes that I can somehow discern whether he is a threat. ... Paranoia has become my shield," *Post* reporter Bassam Sebti wrote in a first-person account in CPJ's magazine, *Dangerous Assignments*, published in May.

Highly visible foreign journalists were obvious targets and increasingly unable to report on the street. The cost of security and insurance to maintain a foreign correspondent in Baghdad was so high that only major outlets could afford to do so. Iraqis took over the primary newsgathering role, and, whether working for a Western media company or one of the new Iraqi outlets that flourished after the fall of Saddam Hussein, they bore the brunt of the appalling violence. All but two of the journalists and media workers killed in 2006 were Iraqis; since 2003, more than 80 percent of all media fatalities were locals. Of the seven journalists kidnapped in 2006, six were Iraqis. At least three were still missing in late year.

The plight of Iraqi journalists became apparent in February, when gunmen murdered one of Arab television's best-known war correspondents. Atwar Bahjat, a reporter for Dubai-based Al-Arabiya who had gained renown reporting on post-conflict Iraq for Al-Jazeera in 2003, was gunned down along with her cameraman and engineer near Samarra. The crew had been on the outskirts of the city covering the bombing of the Shiite Askariya shrine. The gunmen drove up and demanded to know the whereabouts of "the presenter." CPJ honored Bahjat posthumously with its International Press Freedom Award in November.

The killings of Iraqi journalists peaked in October with an attack on the Baghdad offices of the fledgling satellite TV channel Al-Shaabiya. Masked gunmen stormed the station, which had not even begun broadcasting, and killed 11 employees. It was the deadliest assault on the press in Iraq since the U.S.-led invasion in March 2003. Al-Shaabiya was owned by the secular National Justice and Progress Party, which had failed to win any seats in the preceding election.

Western journalists who ventured out on assignment were also targets. Gunmen seized freelance U.S. reporter Jill Carroll, who was on assignment for *The Christian Science Monitor*, on January 7 as she left the office of a prominent Sunni politician in the Adil neighborhood of western Baghdad. The kidnappers murdered her interpreter, Alan Enwiyah. Carroll's abduction triggered sympathy and a storm of international protest from journalists, politicians, and religious figures from around the world. She was freed unharmed on March 30.

Similarly, the January bombing that gravely wounded embedded ABC News anchor Bob Woodruff and cameraman Doug Vogt, along with the May attack that killed CBS News cameraman Paul Douglas and soundman James Brolan and wounded reporter Kimberly Dozier, brought home to the American public the risks journalists faced in telling the Iraq story.

While violence by insurgents posed the greatest threat to reporters, Iraqi journalists said that the U.S. military continued to endanger them and inhibit their work. At least 14 journalists have died from U.S. forces' fire since the war began, and CPJ is investigating a 2006 death that also may have stemmed from U.S. actions. The U.S. military has failed to fully investigate or properly account for the killings of journalists by its forces in Iraq, CPJ research shows. Nor has it implemented its own recommendations to improve media safety, particularly at U.S. checkpoints. In October, a British inquest into the March 2003 death of ITN journalist Terry Lloyd concluded that Lloyd was unlawfully killed by U.S. troops in southern Iraq three years ago. The Pentagon said an investigation in May 2003 found that U.S. forces had acted in accordance with their rules of engagement. The findings of the U.S. inquiry, however, were not made public.

In October, CPJ filed an appeal under the Freedom of Information Act after the Pentagon refused to release information about the 2003 U.S. bombing of Al-Jazeera television's Baghdad bureau, which killed reporter Tareq Ayyoub. The appeal followed the revelation by Britain's Channel 4 that former British Home Secretary David Blunkett had suggested around the time of the March 2003 invasion of Iraq that bombing Al-Jazeera's Baghdad transmitters might be justified.

Iraqi journalists also faced harassment and detention at the hands of U.S. troops. PBS *Frontline* producer and former *New York Times* reporter and photographer Warzer Jaff told CPJ that U.S. troops detained him in early November as he attempted to film the aftermath of a car bombing in Baghdad's Al-Bataween neighborhood. Soldiers verbally abused him for an hour, cursing his work as a journalist, and confiscated his tape, which was later returned, he said. A U.S. soldier later recorded an obscene gesture on Jaff's cell phone camera before handing it back to him.

More troubling was the open-ended detention of reporters in the field by U.S. troops. Since March 2003, dozens of journalists—mostly Iraqis—have been held. While most were quickly released, CPJ has documented at least eight cases in which Iraqi journalists were detained for weeks or months before being freed without charges ever being substantiated. One of those was Abdul Ameer Younis Hussein, a freelance cameraman working for CBS, who was detained after being wounded by U.S. forces' fire as he filmed clashes in Mosul in northern Iraq on April 5, 2005. U.S. military officials said footage in his camera led them to suspect Hussein had prior knowledge of attacks on coalition forces, but it took them nearly a year to bring any charges. In April 2006, a year after his arrest, Hussein was freed after an Iraqi criminal court, citing a lack of evidence, acquitted him of collaborating with insurgents.

As Hussein's ordeal ended, that of another Iraqi journalist began. Associated Press freelance photographer Bilal Hussein was taken by U.S. forces on April 12 in Ramadi and held for "imperative reasons of security." Yet he was not tried or charged with a crime, and the military disclosed no evidence of criminal wrongdoing. U.S. officials put forward vague accusations against Hussein, such as his alleged close ties to Iraqi insurgents. According to the AP, one of the most specific allegations cited by U.S. officials—that Hussein was involved in the kidnapping of two Arab journalists in Ramadi by Iraqi insurgents—was discredited after the AP investigated the claim. The two abducted journalists had not implicated Hussein in the kidnapping; they had instead singled him out for praise for his assistance when they were released. The military's only evidence supporting its claim appeared to be images of the released journalists that were found in Hussein's camera, the AP said.

Only a month before Hussein's arrest, U.S. Maj. Gen. John Gardner announced a new process to ensure high-level, 36-hour reviews of all journalist detentions. U.S. troops across Iraq, he said, were ordered to report the arrest of anyone claiming to be a journalist to Gardner personally; he said news organizations would be given the chance to vouch for their journalists. "Once a journalist is detained," Gardner told Reuters, "it comes to me." The change, he added, was designed to ensure that "we don't hold someone for six or eight months." But the new policy applied only to journalists whom the military did not label "security threats," and it set no apparent standards of due process. Hussein's detention showed that Iraqi journalists remained vulnerable to long-term detentions without charge.

The Iraqi government was no better in its treatment of journalists. Although media have enjoyed unprecedented freedom since Saddam's ouster, Iraqi officials harassed, censored, and dragged journalists to court in reprisal for their work.

Iraqi journalists continued to complain about the behavior of Iraqi security forces that threatened or detained reporters or confiscated their equipment. In September, Iraqi authorities detained Tikrit-based *Al-Hayat* correspondent Kalshan al-Bayati and held her without charge for 26 days. Officials said they suspected her of having ties to insurgents. The journalist had gone to security forces headquarters in Tikrit to retrieve a personal computer confiscated during a raid on her home weeks earlier, when she was also detained. Al-Bayati was working on an article for the Saudi-owned newspaper about insurgents in Saleheddin province, and her prior reporting had been critical of security forces in Tikrit.

The government of Prime Minister Nouri al-Maliki continued a disturbing trend of his predecessors by closing down broadcast outlets on vague charges that they were engaged in "incitement." On September 7, the government closed the Baghdad bureau of Al-Arabiya for one month. Al-Arabiya Executive Editor Nabil Khatib said the government accused the station of fomenting "sectarian violence and war in Iraq" but did not provide evidence. It was the second time Al-Arabiya had been closed by the government in three years. In November 2003, the Iraqi Governing Council, the provisional government appointed by the United States, banned the station from broadcasting in Iraq. Authorities accused it of incitement after it aired an audiotape in which Saddam purportedly urged Iraqis to resist the U.S.-led occupation.

The government continued to enforce the closure of the Baghdad bureau of Qatar-based satellite channel Al-Jazeera. It was closed in July 2004 after former Iraqi Prime Minister Iyad Allawi accused the station of incitement to violence and hatred. Iraqi officials alleged that Al-Jazeera's reporting on kidnappings had encouraged Iraqi militants; a government statement also accused the station of being a mouthpiece for terrorist groups. Al-Jazeera operated openly in the Kurdish-ruled area in northern Iraq and still managed to cover news from other parts of the country through local sources and a network of contacts.

A number of Iraqi journalists faced prosecution for their work under restrictive laws. Editor-in-Chief Ayad Mahmoud al-Tamimi and Managing Editor Ahmed Mutair Abbas of *Sada Wasit*, a now-defunct daily in the southern city of Kut, faced more than 10 years in prison and heavy fines on defamation charges filed under a law revived from Saddam's penal code. The case, which drew international attention, languished in the courts throughout the year.

Before a court hearing in September, Abbas was mysteriously abducted by unknown gunmen and held for several days.

A surge in criminal prosecutions and draconian penalties against journalists working in Kurdistan signaled an alarming deterioration in press freedom in that region. In January, Kurdish-Austrian writer Kamal Karim was sentenced to 30 years in prison for articles he wrote on *Kurdistanpost*, an independent Kurdish news Web site, criticizing the Kurdistan Democratic Party and its leader, Massoud Barzani, whom he accused of corruption and abuse of power. Karim was eventually pardoned and released.

Elsewhere in the north, Hawez Hawezi, a high school teacher who wrote for the weekly *Hawlati*, was summoned by security forces in Sulaymaniyah and arrested. This followed an article criticizing his treatment by security forces when he was held March 17-19 in connection with a separate report critical of the region's two main political parties. Hawezi had accused the Patriotic Union of Kurdistan and the Kurdistan Democratic Party of governing the region badly, referring to them as pharaohs.

Also in May, a criminal court in Sulaymaniyah sentenced Twana Osman, editor-in-chief of *Hawlati*, and Asos Hardi, the paper's former editor, to six-month suspended jail terms and fines of 75,000 dinars each (US$50) for having published an article alleging that Prime Minister Omer Fatah of the Kurdish regional government ordered the dismissal of two telephone company employees after they cut his phone line for failing to pay a bill.

· ISRAEL AND THE OCCUPIED PALESTINIAN TERRITORY ·

Israeli troops and armor re-entered the Gaza Strip in late June to stop Palestinians from firing crudely made rockets from the north into Israeli towns along the border. Nearly 370 Palestinians, half of them civilians, were killed in the ensuing six-month Israeli offensive, which intensified after the seizure of an Israeli soldier. Palestinian journalists covering the military operations alleged that they were targeted by Israeli forces in several instances. The allegation was supported in one case by the Foreign Press Association (FPA) in Israel. The Israel Defense Forces (IDF) denied that it targeted journalists but said it would investigate the complaints.

THE MIDDLE EAST AND NORTH AFRICA

Reporters also complained of intimidation and harassment by Palestinian authorities, political factions, and militia. Rivalry between the Hamas-led government elected in January and the Fatah movement of the Palestine Liberation Organization (PLO) meant Palestinian journalists came under pressure to align themselves with particular groups. Political infighting prompted some groups to kidnap foreign journalists as a means of pressuring the authorities to accede to their demands.

In July, Israel launched an offensive in south Lebanon after a cross-border raid by the Lebanese Shiite group Hezbollah. Journalists covering the four-week conflict said Israeli airpower prevented them from traveling in south Lebanon.

On June 24, Israel launched its first search-and-capture raid in Gaza since its August 2005 withdrawal from the Strip, seizing suspected Hamas militants Osama Muamar and Mustafa Muamar. The following day, armed Palestinians crossed Gaza's southern border into Israel via an underground tunnel and attacked an Israeli army post, killing two Israeli soldiers, wounding four, and capturing Cpl. Gilad Shalit. On June 28, Israel launched Operation Summer Rain in an attempt to recover the corporal, destroy weapons-smuggling tunnels, and halt the launching into Israel of Qassam rockets, rudimentary steel tubes packed with explosives.

One month into the operation, an Israeli tank shell seriously wounded Palestine Television cameraman Ibrahim al-Atla during a lull in shooting between Palestinian militants and Israeli forces in the densely populated Shijaiyah neighborhood of Gaza City. The head of Palestine Television, Mohammed al-Dahoudi, alleged that the tank fired deliberately at al-Atla and other journalists with him. "The tank undoubtedly targeted us," witness Anas Rehan, a cameraman for the Cairo-based Ramattan News Agency, told CPJ. Al-Atla was wearing a vest clearly indicating that he was press.

In late August, an Israeli missile struck a Reuters armored car in the Shijaiyah neighborhood, seriously wounding Fadel Shana, a freelance cameraman for Reuters, and Sabbah Hmaida, a cameraman with a private Palestinian TV facilities house, Media Group. Reuters said the missile struck the letter *P* of the bright red "Press" sign on the car's roof. Shana lost consciousness for several hours and both cameramen suffered serious shrapnel wounds. Shana had rushed out to film a suspected Israeli air strike. He was about 1,300 yards (1,190 meters) from the nearest Israeli soldiers when the vehicle was struck, Reuters reported.

The FPA called the attack an "outrageous targeting" and demanded a full investigation, adding, "There is a serious risk that relations between the FPA and the IDF will be significantly damaged."

In the West Bank city of Nablus, members of two Arab television crews were wounded by rubber bullets during an Israeli army operation on July 19. Wael Tanous, a satellite technician with the Qatar-based channel Al-Jazeera, was hit in the left leg while standing near his uplink vehicle, Al-Jazeera reporter Guevara al-Budeiri told CPJ. Walid al-Omary, Jerusalem-based bureau chief for Al-Jazeera, told CPJ, "It was clear when they shot him that they knew he was press." Al-Budeiri said that before the shooting, an Israeli army jeep had sped toward her and stopped only inches from her leg as she was preparing to broadcast live.

Later that day, Faten Elwan, a correspondent for the U.S.-funded Arabic television station Al-Hurra, was hit in the torso and left hand by rubber bullets, according to al-Budeiri, who witnessed the incident. She said Elwan was standing at what she considered a safe distance from the fighting. Elwan was treated at a local hospital and returned to work.

The IDF denied targeting journalists. "Israel doesn't have a habit of hitting people not engaged in fighting," an IDF spokesman told CPJ. In all these cases, the Israeli army said it would conduct thorough investigations, but no tangible results were produced. Israeli forces' fire has killed several journalists and injured dozens since the upsurge in the Israeli-Palestinian conflict began in September 2000.

In April, a London coroner's court found an Israeli officer guilty of murdering a British cameraman in the Gaza Strip three years ago. James Miller, an award-winning filmmaker, was filming an HBO documentary about Palestinian children when he was hit by a single shot in the neck. Crew members said they were wearing jackets and helmets marked "TV," and they held a white flag illuminated by a flashlight. An investigation by the private British security company Chiron Resources Limited, commissioned by Miller's colleagues and family, found that IDF soldiers had "consciously and deliberately targeted" Miller and his crew. In April 2005, the army cleared an officer, identified only as Lieutenant H, of wrongdoing in Miller's death, drawing an official protest from the British government.

Palestinian journalists believe that the Israeli army's failure to investigate and prosecute soldiers for attacks on the press leaves them vulnerable throughout the Palestinian territories. In the West Bank, soldiers fired at a group of cameramen and photographers covering an Israeli army raid on a house in the Old City of Nablus on April 17. Nasser Ishtayeh and Abdal Ruhman Khabeisa of The Associated Press, Jaffar Ishtayeh of Agence France-Presse, and Abdel Rahim Qusini and Hassan Titi of Reuters said they were filming the raid and clashes between soldiers and stone-throwing youths from a distance of more than 1,500 feet (460 meters), beside an AP vehicle that was clearly marked "Press." Titi placed a video camera on a stand three feet (one meter) from the car. Israeli soldiers fired at the camera, forcing the journalists back into the vehicle, which also came under fire.

Reuters cameraman Ashraf Abu Shaweesh was hit twice, in the leg and chest, by rubber bullets while filming clashes between Palestinian protesters and the Israeli army in Nablus on April 22. Abu Shaweesh, who was wearing a vest that identified him as a journalist, had earlier argued with an Israeli soldier. On April 25, AP's Ishtayeh told CPJ that an Israeli army jeep nearly struck him and other Palestinian journalists who were trying to cover the eviction of families from a building during a military raid in Nablus'

THE MIDDLE EAST AND NORTH AFRICA

Al-Makhfiyeh neighborhood.

In the southern West Bank city of Hebron, cameramen Hossam Abu Allan of the official Palestinian News Agency (WAFA), Nayef al-Hashlamoun of Reuters, and freelancer Najeh al-Hashlamoun were beaten by soldiers on September 5 while covering an Israeli military raid on a house, Abu Allan told CPJ. The three men entered the house to film the soldiers, who were allegedly beating the residents. The Israeli soldiers kicked the cameramen in the stomach and back, and ordered them to leave.

The West Bank village of Bilein, west of Ramallah, continued to be fraught with risk for journalists covering weekly demonstrations against Israel's border security barrier. Israeli forces used rubber bullets and tear gas to disperse hundreds of Palestinians peacefully demonstrating in Bilein, injuring civilians and journalists. AP cameraman Iyad Hamad told CPJ that he and other journalists were regularly beaten by soldiers, adding that his camera was destroyed by soldiers earlier this year.

On several occasions, Israeli forces singled out and prevented TV crews of the pan-Arab satellite channels Al-Arabiya and Al-Jazeera from covering rocket attacks on northern Israel from Lebanon by the Shiite militia Hezballah. Walid al-Omary, Jerusalem-based bureau chief for Al-Jazeera, told CPJ that he was detained by Israeli police three times in two days for his reporting on the location of rocket attacks and held for several hours each time. On July 17, al-Omary was held for six hours and accused of assisting Hezballah by reporting on rocket hits in the Galilee village of Kfar Yassif. "We have been covering the situation along with 10 to 12 other crews, foreign and Israeli," al-Omary told CPJ. "We have not received any warnings from the Israeli military censor." Israel has a system of military censorship for all media, and censors can intervene if they consider military security breached.

The IDF often banned Israeli citizens from entering the West Bank and Gaza, but journalists were allowed to cross the border if they signed waivers. The IDF announced on June 26 that Israeli passport holders and dual nationals would be prohibited from entering Gaza following an attack the previous day by Palestinian militants on an Israeli military post. "Due to the current security assessments, journalists with Israeli citizenship or those holding a dual citizenship cannot enter the Gaza Strip at the present time," the statement said. The travel ban was lifted later that day after protests from foreign journalists and the FPA in Israel.

In the occupied Palestinian territories, journalists came under pressure from the Palestinian authorities and various political factions and militias. The Islamic Resistance Movement (Hamas) dominated the Palestinian legislative elections in January, winning 74 seats in the 132-member legislative council and ousting the government of the PLO faction, Fatah. This led to a power struggle between Palestinian President and Fatah leader Mahmoud Abbas and Hamas Prime Minister Ismail Haniyeh. A by-product was factionalism in the Palestinian media. Journalists endured consistent harassment, threats, and beatings by Palestinian security forces and the various factions in retaliation for their coverage of Palestinian politics.

Masked gunmen believed to be from Fatah destroyed the offices of the private Bethlehem television station Al-Roa on March 23. The station was forced off the air. It reopened at the end of May after receiving equipment donated by a TV station in Jericho. Two days before the attack, the station ran stories criticizing the Palestinian Authority, including former Fatah interior minister Nasser Yusef.

In Ramallah, masked arsonists burned three cars belonging to Al-Jazeera on May 20. According to AP, both Hamas and Fatah accused Al-Jazeera of bias. Fatah supporters were angry that the station did not cover an anti-Hamas demonstration in Ramallah earlier that day, news reports said.

In April, several Palestinian journalists received death threats for their critical coverage of Hamas, Reuters reported. Among them was Muwafaq Matar, a reporter for the pro-Fatah Al-Hurriya radio station in Gaza, who received several threats via cell phone and e-mail. Several other station employees were also threatened. Reuters reported that the Palestinian Journalists Union received complaints of threats from seven journalists in the Gaza Strip.

On June 5, nearly 50 armed militants stormed a studio of Fatah-affiliated Palestine Television in Khan Younis, in the southern Gaza Strip. The attackers, who wore Hamas headbands, ordered staff to leave and beat several cameramen and technicians, according to Palestine Television's Mohammed al-Dahoudi. They fired automatic weapons at the equipment and in the direction of employees, al-Dahoudi told CPJ. Damage to broadcasting equipment, archives, computers, and furniture totaled more than US$1 million, making the studio unusable.

Palestine Television, along with WAFA, Wafa Radio, and Voice of Palestine radio, is part of the Palestinian Broadcast Cooperation, which is under the control of President Abbas. The Hamas-led government accused the broadcasters of bias toward Fatah.

Several militants believed to be from Fatah attacked the Ramallah offices of Hamas' *Manbar al-Islah* newspaper on June 12, according to the Palestinian Journalist Block, a journalist-run committee. The gunmen assaulted editor Yazid Khader and designer Wajdi al-Aroury, threatened to set the offices on fire, and destroyed computers, equipment, and furnishings, the group said.

Western sanctions aimed at forcing Hamas to renounce violence and recognize Israel's right to exist have bankrupted the Palestinian government, rendering it unable to pay the wages of 165,000 public-sector employees. Government workers, the majority of whom are affiliated with Fatah, went on strike on September 2—a move seen by Hamas as undermining its rule. On September 19, Hamas thugs burned a tent set up by the striking workers in Gaza City, CPJ sources said. Several journalists covering the incident—including AP reporter Diaa Hadid, Palestine Television cameraman Khaled Boulboul, and Matar on assignment for the daily *Al-Hayat al-Jadida*—were chased and attacked by the militants, journalists told CPJ.

The weakening of the Palestinian Authority, the interim administrative body nominally governing the West Bank and Gaza, resulted in the complete destabilization of internal Palestinian security. Amid the chaos, small armed groups consisting of militants from the various factions proliferated. Often formed with personal goals in mind, such as the release of imprisoned relatives or the securing of government jobs, these groups increasingly resorted to abducting foreigners, including journalists, for use as bargaining chips. Since 2004, 13 journalists have been abducted, in addition to two failed attempts, CPJ research shows. All were released unharmed.

A wave of violence erupted in Gaza and elsewhere in the West Bank on March 14, after Israeli forces stormed a prison in the West Bank town of Jericho to arrest militants from the Popular Front for the Liberation of Palestine (PFLP) believed responsible for the 2001 assassination of an Israeli minister. British and U.S. monitors who had supervised the detention pulled out of the prison just before the Israeli raid. In retaliation, PFLP members abducted several foreigners. Caroline Laurent, a reporter for the French women's weekly *Elle*; Alfred Yaghobzadeh, a photographer from the photo agency SIPA; and Yong Tae-young, a correspondent for South Korea's public broadcaster, KBS, were abducted by gunmen from their hotel in Gaza. All three were released unharmed 22 hours later.

Fox News Channel correspondent Steve Centanni, a U.S. citizen, and freelance cameraman Olaf Wiig, a New Zealand citizen, were kidnapped in Gaza City on August 14 by a previously unknown group called the Holy Jihad Brigades. The group demanded the release of Muslim prisoners held by the United States. According to CPJ sources, the journalists were released unharmed on August 27 after efforts were made on their behalf by the Palestinian security services. Emilio Morenatti, a Spanish photojournalist for the AP, was abducted October 24 in Gaza City by gunmen who released him unharmed 16 hours later. Many Palestinians condemned the kidnappings. Hamas called them morally reprehensible. Despite this, the abductions have had a chilling effect on foreign journalists covering the conflict in Gaza.

• • • • • • • • • • • • • • • • • • • LEBANON • • • • • • • • • • • • • • • • • • •

Israel's summer offensive in Lebanon was filled with danger for hundreds of journalists who braved bombs and bullets to cover fighting between Israeli forces and Hezbollah guerrillas. The offensive began after guerrillas abducted two Israeli soldiers and killed eight near the Lebanese-Israeli border. During the 34-day conflict, one journalist and a media worker were killed, media facilities were bombed, and several reporters suffered injuries from Israel Defense Forces' (IDF) fire.

The media's first casualty was Hezbollah's Al-Manar TV. Just days into the fighting, Israeli missiles leveled the station's headquarters in the southern Beirut suburb of Haret Hreik and separately struck two Al-Manar TV transmitters, one near Baalbek, northeast of Beirut, and another in Maroun al-Ras in southern Lebanon. Station officials had long expected such an attack in the event of hostilities with Israel.

Israel acknowledged targeting the broadcaster, accusing it of propaganda and incitement. Al-Manar never appeared to have served any discernible military function that would have made it a legitimate target under the laws of war. Despite the bombings, Al-Manar managed to broadcast largely uninterrupted, according to international news media.

Critics have attacked the station for airing anti-Semitic content and propaganda videos that glorify violence. After the fighting began, Al-Manar dropped its sports and entertainment shows, limiting its programming to a mixture of news and talk shows, Quranic recitations, and propaganda.

During the offensive, Israeli forces singled out other media infrastructure for targeting, sometimes with lethal consequences. On July 22, Suleiman al-Chidiac, a technician for the Lebanese Broadcasting Corporation (LBC), was killed during Israeli air attacks that destroyed television transmitters and telephone towers in Fatqa, north of Beirut and well away from the fighting in the south. On the same day, Israeli warplanes struck towers in Terbol, near Tripoli in northern Lebanon, belonging to Al-Manar TV, the state-run channel Tele-Liban, and Future TV, as well as cellular telephone network towers. In al-Qura, also in the north, Tele-Liban technician Khaled Eid was seriously injured in an attack on a telecommunications tower belonging to the station. The stations' terrestrial transmission was interrupted, but they continued to broadcast via satellite.

Journalists covering the fighting, which was heavily concentrated in the country's south, were vulnerable to Israeli air strikes. Several international broadcasters and news organizations had made the Mediterranean port of Tyre their base in the south, and many reported IDF targeting of vehicles on the roads. Journalists in the city, which is 55 miles (90 kilometers) south of Beirut, said any vehicles, including TV vehicles, traveling between towns and villages were targeted by Israeli planes if spotted on the road. One journalist who ventured into the area was Layal Najib, 23, a freelance photographer for the Lebanese magazine *Al-Jaras* and Agence France-Presse. She was killed July 23 by an Israeli missile while traveling in a taxi to cover Lebanese civilians fleeing north. She was hit by shrapnel from a missile on the road between the villages of Sadiqeen and Qana, local media reported. She died at the scene.

Other journalists narrowly averted serious injury or death from what they alleged was deliberate Israeli fire. On July 22, a convoy of Al-Jazeera, Al-Arabiya, and Al-Manar vehicles was chased by Israeli fighter aircraft, which fired missiles on the road behind them as they approached an already bombed-out bridge near the southern village of

Hasbaya. The journalists said they managed to get away on back roads, but the planes followed and again trapped their vehicles by firing missiles at the road ahead of them and behind them. "Their cars were clearly marked 'Press' and 'TV,'" said Nabil Khatib, Al-Arabiya executive editor. The journalists alleged that Israeli aircraft fired missiles in order to prevent them from covering the effects of Israel's bombardment of the area around the town of Khiam, in the eastern sector of the Israel-Lebanon border. The IDF denied that Israel was targeting journalists and said it was instead "targeting the roads because Hezbollah uses those roads."

In early August, the Israeli military dropped leaflets warning that all vehicles traveling on roads south of the Litani River would be attacked—a move that heavily circumscribed the movements of journalists reporting from the south and complicated the efforts of TV crews to get footage out of the area. A subsequent statement from the IDF warned, "This is a combat zone from which terrorists operate, and as such, we cannot guarantee the safety of journalists in the area." At around the same time, Scott Anderson of *The New York Times Magazine*, Magnum photographer Paolo Pellegrin, and their driver were wounded when they attempted to cover the immediate aftermath of an apparent attack by an unmanned drone aircraft on an individual on a main road in Tyre. The three men, who, like the other journalists, were traveling in cars clearly marked as press vehicles, suffered concussions and shrapnel wounds.

Pro-Israel forces broadcast anti-Hezbollah propaganda and intimidated local reporters through the radio station Al-Mashraqiyeh, which Lebanese journalists believe broadcasts out of Israel and is affiliated with exiled members of the South Lebanon Army, Israel's military ally during its occupation of southern Lebanon in the 1980s and 1990s. The radio station singled out Al-Jazeera correspondents Katia Nasser and Abbas Nasser, accusing them of aiding Hezbollah and said, "The noble Lebanese will hold those who supported Hezbollah in destroying Lebanon to account."

Israeli forces were not the only source of concern for reporters. Some journalists reported attempts by Hezbollah guerrillas to control their movements and intimidate them. Freelance reporter Christopher Allbritton reported on his Web site that Hezbollah officials kept copies of individual journalist passports as a possible way to leverage positive coverage, and that they had harassed and threatened reporters in some instances. Hezbollah operatives denied some reporters access to areas controlled by the movement and shepherded others on carefully orchestrated media tours where they were barred from filming certain neighborhoods. At least one journalist said guerrillas threatened to kill him if his crew filmed Katyusha rocket launches by Hezbollah fighters.

Although the Israel-Hezbollah conflict dominated headlines, it was not the only press freedom story that concerned Lebanese journalists. A year after Lebanese journalist Samir Qassir was murdered in a Beirut car bombing, the perpetrators remained at large. So, too, did those responsible for the maiming of LBC's May Chidiac and the murder of *Al-Nahar*'s Gebran Tueni, both of whom were victims of car bomb attacks in 2005. The three incidents occurred amid a series of assassination attempts and attacks on journalists and political figures in Lebanon following the assassination of former Prime Minister Rafiq al-Hariri in February 2005.

In December 2005, the U.N. Security Council passed a resolution authorizing the International Independent Investigation Commission probing the al-Hariri killing to "ex-tend its technical assistance" to Lebanese authorities for their investigations into attacks on journalists and other political figures over the previous year. It also called on U.N. Secretary-General Kofi Annan to "present recommendations to expand the mandate of the commission to include investigations of those other attacks."

Lebanon's heavily politicized media are a reflection of the country's sectarian-based political system. Major political figures and groups own or control major media that often reflect their views. But taken together, they make up a diverse media landscape that, by regional standards, is among the most vibrant. Still, self-censorship persists for journalists, who face any number of legal and bureaucratic hurdles.

One such barrier is the courts, which enforce tough press laws that stipulate jail time and heavy fines for libel and other press offenses. In March, a state prosecutor brought criminal charges of defaming President Emile Lahoud against the pro-Hariri daily *Al-Mustaqbal*; its editor-in-chief, Tawfiq Khattab; and writer/talk show host Fares Khashan. The charges were brought four days after *Al-Mustaqbal* published an interview with Johnny Abdo, former Lebanese ambassador to France and former army intelligence chief, in which he criticized Lahoud's performance. According to *The Daily Star*, Abdo was quoted as saying that "under Lahoud's mandate, the Presidential Palace was turned into an unsuitable place to hold dialogue, and Lahoud's presence violates the constitution, because the constitution says the president is the symbol of unity." The journalists faced up to two years in prison. *Al-Mustaqbal*, owned by the al-Hariri family, said its journalists faced 12 charges related to defaming the president and members of Lebanon's parliament.

Like many of its neighbors, Lebanon suffered repercussions from the worldwide controversy involving the September 2005 publication in a Danish newspaper of cartoons depicting the Prophet Muhammad. Public protests over the cartoons took place in Beirut in February and led to tension between Muslim and Christian communities. In Beirut, Muslim protesters set fire to the Danish embassy and rampaged through a predominantly Christian neighborhood. News photographers and cameramen at the scene were roughed up and some equipment was destroyed. *The New York Times* reported that a Dutch news photographer was beaten when several demonstrators mistook him for being Danish.

The government of Iran continued to demand information about two Iranian diplomats and a journalist who disappeared in 1982. In a May 18 interview with *As-Safir* newspaper, former Lebanese Forces head Samir Geagea said the militia abducted and killed the Iranians, including Tehran-based Islamic Republic News Agency photographer Kazem Akhavan. Akhavan disappeared in Lebanon on July 4, 1982, along with officials from the Iranian embassy in Beirut. They were believed to have been kidnapped at a checkpoint near the northern city of Byblos. Iran has maintained that the men might still be alive and held in Israel.

· · · · · · · · · · · · · · · · · · · **MOROCCO** ·

Morocco's robust independent press has few rivals in the Middle East, yet press freedom has eroded under what many journalists and human rights groups consider a government-inspired judicial assault against outspoken newspapers. During the year, several such publications were targets of criminal prosecutions that produced high damages and prison terms for journalists.

In a case that set the tone for the year, the Rabat Court of Appeals upheld record damages in April against the independent weekly newsmagazine *Le Journal Hebdomadaire* in a defamation suit brought by Claude Moniquet, head of the Brussels-based European Strategic Intelligence and Security Center. A lower court had awarded 3 million dirhams (US$359,700) in damages to Moniquet, who said *Le Journal Hebdomadaire* had defamed him in a six-page critique questioning the independence of his think tank's report on the disputed Western Sahara, which was annexed by Morocco three decades ago. The court also fined the magazine 100,000 dirhams (US$12,000). *Le Journal Hebdomadaire* withdrew from both the trial and the appeal after it was barred from introducing an expert witness. The courts provided no explanation for how they reached the damage award, which was unprecedented in such a case. The damages threatened the magazine's financial viability.

The independent weeklies *TelQuel*, *Al-Ousbouiya al-Jadida*, *Al-Ayam*, and *Al-Ahdath al-Maghribiya*, were convicted in May 2005 of defaming Touria Bouabid, head of a nongovernmental children's assistance organization, when they wrote that police officers had questioned Bouabid on suspicion of embezzlement. All four papers had relied on the same police source, but the information turned out to be false. The papers immediately issued corrections and apologies, but the suit proceeded. Each paper was fined a relatively small amount—except *TelQuel*, which was ordered by a lower court to pay 900,000 dirhams (US$107,900). A Casablanca appeals court upheld the conviction but reduced the damages to 500,000 dirhams (US$60,000) in February.

The outspoken *TelQuel* had been in the judicial system's crosshairs in the past. On December 29, 2005, the Casablanca Court of Appeals upheld the libel convictions of Publisher Ahmed Reda Benchemsi and Editor Karim Boukhari after they published an article saying that a female member of the Moroccan parliament was once a "chiekha," the equivalent of a cabaret dancer. The article referred to her by the pseudonym Asmaa. The court upheld the journalists' two-month suspended sentences and awarded the plaintiff 800,000 dirhams (US$95,900) in damages. Both Touria Bouabid and the member of parliament absolved *TelQuel* of having to pay the damages, allowing the weekly to continue publishing.

In May, Idris Shahtan, editor of the Arabic-language weekly *Al-Mishaal*, received a four-month suspended sentence and was fined 100,000 dirhams (US$12,000) after the Casablanca Court of Appeals upheld his conviction on charges of offending a foreign head of state. The charge stemmed from the weekly's publication in May 2005 of a cartoon of Algerian President Abdelaziz Bouteflika together with a satirical article about his private life.

Abdelaziz Koukas, publisher and editor of the independent weekly *Al-Ousbouiya al-Jadida*, went on trial in mid-March on charges of defaming the monarchy. Koukas published a June 2005 front-page interview with Nadia Yassine, the daughter of Sheikh Abd al-Salam Yassine, head of the outlawed Islamist organization Justice and Charity. Yassine criticized the monarchy, a constitutional offense, and said Morocco would fare better as a republic. Koukas faced three to five years in prison and a fine of up to 100,000 dirhams. The weekly faced possible closure. The court adjourned the trial indefinitely, but Koukas can be summoned at any time, CPJ sources said.

In February, Nour Eddine Miftah, editor of the independent weekly *Al-Ayam*, and Meriem Moukrim, a journalist for the weekly, were convicted by a Casablanca court of disturbing public order by publishing "false" articles. Both received a four-month suspended sentence and were fined 100,000 dirhams for a piece by Moukrim in which the king's personal doctor revealed details of the private lives of the monarchs he had served. The story detailed the activities of the royal harems during the reigns of Mohammed V and his son Hassan II.

The government also resorted to acts of intimidation against independent publications. Authorities appeared to orchestrate February protests against *Le Journal Hebdomadaire* after the weekly published a photograph of a reader holding an edition of the Paris daily *France Soir* that reproduced Danish cartoons of the Prophet Muhammad. *Le Journal Hebdomadaire* published the photograph as part of a 10-page chronology of events related to the controversial drawings.

The Casablanca magazine said that several minibuses with *J* license plates, which signify they belong to the Casablanca city government, brought about 100 people to demonstrate outside its offices for two days in mid-February. Reporters and photographers witnessed municipal employees giving the "protesters" placards and Moroccan flags. Photographs of the vehicles and the employees were taken by *Le Journal Hebdomadaire* and several other independent publications, including the Arabic-language dailies *Al-Ahdath al-Maghribiya* and *Assabah*.

THE MIDDLE EAST AND NORTH AFRICA

Le Journal Hebdomadaire accused the Interior Ministry, which oversees the Casablanca local government, of organizing the protests. The weekly interviewed several supposed protestors who acknowledged that authorities had recruited them. Nabil Benabdallah, minister of communications, denied the government played any part in the demonstrations.

Local journalists told CPJ that no members of the press were in prison in Morocco following the release of Anas Tadili, editor of the weekly *Akhbar al-Ousboue*. He was freed in January after completing a sentence for alleged currency violations; journalists and human rights groups believed the case was in reprisal for an April 2004 article alleging that Fathallah Oualalou, Morocco's minister of finance and privatization, was homosexual. The journalist had previously served a one-year sentence for defaming Oualalou.

The country's onerous 2002 Press Code leaves journalists working under the constant threat of prosecution. The press law criminalizes criticizing the king, "defaming" the monarchy, and challenging Morocco's claim to Western Sahara.

Despite a 2005 promise by Minister of Communications Benabdallah to end imprisonment as a punishment for these offenses, violators continue to face possible prison sentences of up to five years. The government also has the power to revoke publication licenses, suspend newspapers, and confiscate editions deemed to threaten public order.

Independent journalist Ali Lmrabet remains banned from writing in the Moroccan press following a 2005 conviction for defaming a previously unknown group called the Association of Relatives of Saharawi Victims of Repression. The group sued after he wrote an article for the Madrid-based daily *El Mundo* that referred to the Saharawi people in the Algerian city of Tindouf as refugees, contradicting the Moroccan government's position that they are prisoners of the rebel Polisario Front. The Polisario, which is fighting for the independence of neighboring Western Sahara, operates  mostly out of Algeria. Although neither the association nor its spokesman, Ahmed Khier, was mentioned in the article, the criminal court convicted Lmrabet in April 2005.

In February 2006, Moroccan censors banned an edition of *El Mundo* that carried an Lmrabet article alleging that King Mohamed VI was restricting the movements of the royal mother.

Medi 1 SAT, the country's first private satellite television channel, went on the air on December 1. The Tangiers-based channel is operated by Medi 1, a media group backed by French President Jacques Chirac and the late King Hassan II. It airs in Arabic and French, competing against the two state-owned TV channels, RTM and 2M. A CPJ source noted that Medi 1 SAT's backers are pro-government, so its arrival would not necessarily expand the range of information available to viewers.

SAUDI ARABIA

Prompted by post-9/11 criticism that Saudi Arabia's closed society had bred violent religious extremism, the government has eased constraints on the country's heavily censored domestic press, and local journalists have seized the initiative to produce more daring reports on crime, drug trafficking, unemployment, and religious extremism.

But progress has been uneven and limited, and the margin of freedom is one that "is given and taken away," according to Khaled al-Dakhil, a liberal academic whose columns for the Saudi-owned daily *Al-Hayat* of London were banned by the government after he questioned official reform efforts. The Saudi government, often acting under pressure from religious authorities, frequently reins in criticism by banning newspapers, blacklisting writers, ordering news blackouts, and pressuring journalists behind the scenes.

In February, a CPJ delegation headed by Chairman Paul Steiger visited Riyadh to meet with Saudi editors, journalists, and government officials. From those meetings emerged a picture of the opaque and often contradictory forces that regularly inhibit press freedom in the kingdom. CPJ's Joel Campagna detailed the situation in a special report, "Princes, Clerics, and Censors," released in May.

Those forces were on display in February, when the government temporarily shuttered the newly launched tabloid daily *Shams* for reproducing one of the controversial cartoons of the Prophet Muhammad that first appeared in the Danish daily *Jyllands-Posten* and subsequently caused outrage across the Muslim world. In a meeting with CPJ representatives in Riyadh, Iyad Madani, head of the Ministry of Culture and Information, said that he suspended the paper for two weeks for violating sacred religious strictures. But according to *Shams* editor Ahmed Fheed, the ministry's own censors had cleared the issue for distribution, and belatedly moved to halt publication 20 days later, when hard-line clerics and religious figures protested *Shams'* liberal approach. The paper was allowed to resume publishing once it agreed to dismiss its 32-year-old editor-in-chief, Batal al-Qaws, in late February.

Other journalists who ran afoul of the country's strict religious conservatives were similarly targeted. In April, police in the northern city of Hail detained journalist Rabah al-Quwai' for 13 days in retaliation for his writings about religious extremism. A writer for *Shams* who also contributed to several Saudi news sites, al-Quwai' was questioned about articles he wrote on the Web three years ago criticizing the strict religious interpretations of hard-line Wahhabi Islamists. Al-Quwai' told CPJ that before his release, he was compelled to sign a statement saying that he had denigrated Islamic beliefs in his writing, that he was not a true Muslim, and that he would defend Islamic values in his future work. Had he not signed the statement, al-Quwai' said, he would have faced a charge of *riddah*—a renunciation of Islam—which is punishable by death.

Pressures from religious figures took a violent form in February; during a Riyadh book fair, Islamists disrupted a panel on censorship that included leading pro-government editor Turki al-Sudeiri, whose newspaper *Al-Riyadh* had published critiques of religious extremists. Also on the panel were Muhammad Abdo Yamani, a former information minister, and other writers critical of religious hard-liners. Men in the audience shouted down the panelists, accused them of being un-Islamic, and urged that they be tried in religious courts for their liberal policies. The activists surrounded the panelists and roughed up at least one journalist.

Further underscoring the militant threat, Osama bin Laden purportedly issued a death threat against liberal Gulf writers and intellectuals, including the Saudi writer Turki al-Hamad, in an audiotape released in April.

Over the years, dozens of editors, writers, academics, and other media critics have been suspended, dismissed from their jobs, or banned from appearing in the Saudi press when they offended the government or important religious constituencies. During the year, CPJ received several new reports of journalists who were suspended from writing. In meetings with CPJ in February, Minister of Information and Culture Madani and his deputy, Saleh Namlah, acknowledged the government's practice of banning writers. Madani confirmed at least one existing ban, on the poet Abdel Mohsen Mosallam, who had lashed out at Saudi religious judges on the pages of *Al-Madina* newspaper four years earlier. Namlah said that bans are imposed when citizens complain to the king or high-ranking officials, and that such actions are intended to preserve the country's traditional, conservative society. "My main intent and concern is for journalists not to upset the conservative fabric," Namlah said. "If children fight with each other, you say go to your room. To the writer, you say please do not write. It's a way of calming things." Namlah said he was not aware of any journalist who had been permanently banned.

As often as not, journalists said, the Ministry of Culture and Information, which is commonly viewed as a progressive force in the kingdom, acts at the behest of more powerful political and religious figures. They said the Ministry of the Interior is the leading force in restricting the press, even though the agency's spokesman, Lt. Gen. Mansour al-Turki, said it had no official role. "It is not the Ministry of [the] Interior who makes a decision to ban a journalist," he told CPJ in Riyadh. But the ministry is seen as allied with hard-line religious forces and is widely believed to be behind many bans on journalists. Its security forces, known as the *mubahith*, monitor press coverage and keep tabs on writers in every major city, and frequently compel outspoken writers to sign confidential *ta'ahuds*, or written pledges, to refrain from certain criticisms or from writing at all.

With the press heavily constrained, Saudis take their frankest discussions to the Internet—though the government censors content there as well. Since the Internet made its debut in the kingdom in 1999, the government has enforced one of the most stringent Web-filtering schemes in the world. It systematically extracts content deemed at odds with the country's strict religious norms, as well as undesirable political content. A number of political discussion forums and news sites, such as the popular news Web site *Elaph*, were banned during the year.

While Saudi Arabia's government and religious establishment shoulder much of the blame for press restrictions, the media themselves are also culpable. Saudi writers are heavily critical of the country's chief editors, who they describe as government loyalists who have held their jobs for many years, and who have little interest in jeopardizing their privileged positions by challenging authority. Top editors are quick to suspend critical writers and to spike contentious columns. Even government officials criticize the lack of zeal of the mainstream press. "Some editors have been in their jobs for too long, but we cannot do anything about it," Madani said. "If it were up to me, I would change them tomorrow. I think these papers need young blood."

The Saudi Journalists Association, which was formed in February 2003 with government approval, is composed of the kingdom's leading editors but has been almost entirely inactive; in meetings with CPJ, the group's directors proudly declared that they had not received a single complaint from a Saudi journalist. Asked whether the association would advocate for colleagues banned by the government, association head Turki al-Sudeiri said such matters should be handled by the Ministry of Labor.

Most rank-and-file journalists have little idea of the association's agenda and are pessimistic it will ever be a force for change. Even Madani was unsparing in criticizing the association's leaders. "As far as we are concerned, they have done nothing," he said. "We are waiting for them to move, to register a presence, to do anything!"

The government has loosened restrictions on the foreign press; applications for visas and long-term accreditation for foreign journalists are being granted to international news organizations. Still, some foreign journalists have complained that the authorities use subtle intimidation against reporters' sources. In February, Saudi authorities apparently pressured the owner of a nightclub in Jeddah after *Forbes* published a story about the venue, where men and women socially mingle.

• TUNISIA •

Despite its election to the newly established U.N. Human Rights Council in May, Tunisia under the autocratic rule of President Zine El Abidine Ben Ali continued to pursue a policy of muzzling critical media and harassing independent journalists and their families.

In February, the U.N. vote approaching, Ben Ali pardoned Hamadi Jebali, editor of the now-defunct Islamist weekly newspaper *Al-Fajr*, and hundreds of other political prisoners. CPJ welcomed the release of Jebali, who spent more than 15 years in prison for publishing an article on the unconstitutionality of military tribunals and for membership in the banned Islamist Al-Nahda Movement.

But the pardon soon rang hollow. Shortly after leaving jail, Jebali and his family were targets of police harassment reminiscent of treatment he received before his 1991 arrest. Jebali and his wife were eventually charged with "attempting to bribe a civil servant" when he was still behind bars. Human rights lawyers said the charges were groundless.

Another reporter for *Al-Fajr*, Abdallah Zouari, remained under police surveillance in the southern city of Zarzis, more than 300 miles (480 kilometers) from his wife and children in Tunis. He was forcibly sent there after his release from prison in 2002 and has been prevented from working or using the Internet. Zouari, who was sentenced to 11 years in prison in 1992 by a military court for "belonging to an illegal organization" and "planning to change the nature of the state," has gone on several hunger strikes to protest his virtual house arrest since his release.

Imprisoned writer and human rights lawyer Mohamed Abbou and his family were also targets of harassment. Abbou was sentenced in April 2005 to three and a half years for work that "defamed the judicial process" and was "likely to disturb public order." Abbou's main crime, according to local and international human rights groups, was an opinion piece he wrote for the blocked news Web site *TunisNews* that compared torture in Tunisia's prisons to conditions in Iraq's infamous Abu Ghraib.

Abbou went on hunger strike several times to protest prison conditions and the harassment of his wife, whose weekly visits after long hours on the road to Le Kef Prison near the Algerian border were often arbitrarily ended after only two or three minutes. "It looks like they have instructions to destroy Abbou physically and morally. Sadly, we seem to be closer to the law of the jungle than the rule of law," human rights lawyer Abderrazak Kilani told CPJ.

CPJ wrote to Ben Ali on June 6 to express its deep concern about the "widening circle of repression of journalists in Tunisia as evidenced by the arbitrary imprisonment of Abbou; the harassment of his wife, and of Jebali and his family; and the brief detention on May 11, and again on June 3, of Lotfi Hajji, president of the independent Tunisian Journalists Syndicate." As a member of the U.N. Human Rights Council, Tunisia is required to "uphold the highest standards in the promotion and protection of human rights," according to the U.N. General Assembly resolution that established the council.

Hajji was targeted not only as head of the beleaguered Tunisian Journalists Syndicate, which was prevented from holding its first general assembly in September 2005, but also as a correspondent for Al-Jazeera. The Qatar-based satellite television channel is still denied accreditation in Tunisia.

On October 25, the government said it would close its embassy in Qatar to protest what it called a "hostile campaign by Al-Jazeera to harm Tunisia." The move followed the broadcast of an interview with democracy advocate Moncef Marzouki, who said he would return to Tunisia from exile to take part in peaceful civil resistance to Ben Ali's rule. The interview spurred court proceedings by the Tunisian authorities against Marzouki for "inciting civil disobedience." The government accused Al-Jazeera of ignoring "basic rules of journalism and ethics."

Another local target of the country's ubiquitous plainclothes police was Neziha Rejiba (also known as Um Ziad), editor of the blocked online magazine *Kalima* and vice president of the Observatory for Press Freedom, Publishing, and Creation.

After numerous anonymous threats to ruin her reputation and that of her family if she continued her critical journalism, Rejiba in March received a letter posted in France containing fabricated pornographic pictures featuring her husband, lawyer and former member of parliament Mokhtar Jellali.

On May 4, upon her arrival at the Tunis-Carthage airport from Cairo, where she had taken part in a conference on imprisoned Arab journalists, Rejiba was harassed for hours and her personal documents were confiscated.

Rejiba, *Kalima* co-editor Sihem Ben Sedrine, and freelancer Souhayr Belhassen have been frequently assaulted and harassed in recent years. On the eve of the World Summit on the Information Society in November 2005, they were harassed by plainclothes police and called "prostitutes." On July 21, 2006, Rejiba was prevented from attending a meeting at the office of a local rights group in Tunis and insulted by plainclothes police, who forced her into a cab. They told the cab driver she was a prostitute and ordered him to take her away.

A fifth fact-finding mission conducted by members of the International Freedom of Expression Exchange Tunisia Monitoring Group concluded in April that "violations of freedom of expression, freedom of the press, freedom of association, and other basic human rights are still rampant."

Although self-censorship is prevalent, government bodies and ministries often dictate newspaper content. Papers such as the opposition weekly *Al-Mawkif*, the most frequently harassed of the authorized publications, often disappeared from newsstands following instructions from the Interior Ministry. On October 2, *Al-Mawkif* editor and Progressive Democratic Party chief Ahmed Néjib Chebbi appeared before the assistant public prosecutor in Tunis on charges of changing printing houses without Interior Ministry authorization. Chebbi denied that *Al-Mawkif* used a different printing house. "This is part of an ongoing cycle of political and financial pressure on *Al-Mawkif* aimed at stifling its voice," Chebbi said.

The Interior Ministry also tightened its grip on foreign papers, banning several issues of the French dailies *Le Monde* and *France Soir*, the monthly *Le Monde Diplomatique*, and the London-based daily *Al-Quds al-Arabi*. Many other European publications and Arab papers such as *Al-Hayat* disappeared from Tunisian newsstands years ago.

The September 19 issue of the French daily *Le Figaro* was banned because it carried an opinion piece deemed defamatory of Islam in the wake of Pope Benedict's remarks on the Islamic faith. In a lecture that month in Germany, Benedict cited centuries-old texts asserting that Islam was spread by the sword. Use of the quotations, which the pope said did not reflect his own opinions, provoked widespread anger in Muslim countries.

Authorities also halted distribution of *Le Figaro*'s edition of October 18. The issue carried a story on the alleged involvement of a Ben Ali relative in the May theft of a yacht owned by Parisian banker Bruno Roger and the smuggling of stolen French luxury vessels to Tunisia.

Foreign journalists critical of Ben Ali are not welcome in the country. In September, French journalist Léa Labaye of the satirical news Web site *Bakchich* was denied entry upon her arrival from Paris at the Tunis airport. No official explanation was given to Labaye, who in August wrote a critical review of a book by Antoine Sfeir, a French writer close to the Tunisian authorities, that praises Ben Ali.

Journalists contributing to opposition papers, news Web sites, and foreign and Arab media were often denied press cards and harassed for covering issues such as torture, corruption, and the lack of judicial independence. Coverage of the Tunisian League for Human Rights, established in 1977 and the first organization of its kind in the Arab world, was also taboo.

The number of blocked news Web sites continued to rise. One of the latest victims was the online weekly *Le Maghrébin*, run by the Maghreb Alliance for Democracy. The pro-democracy group is headed by Omar Shabou, who, in 1991, became the first Tunisian journalist imprisoned for his work under Ben Ali. Shabou fled to France after his release.

Subscribers to *TunisNews*, circulated via e-mail and the main source of independent information for tens of thousands of Tunisians, unexpectedly received a British soccer report on August 19 instead of the journal's usual selection of news and opinion. The team in charge of *TunisNews* later explained that the site came under an electronic attack that also caused its mailing list to disappear.

TURKEY

A wave of criminal prosecutions against the press reignited doubts about Turkey's commitment to Western-style democracy and a free press just one year after the nation began formal talks for European Union membership. Journalists and writers found themselves the repeated targets of criminal lawsuits initiated under vaguely worded, restrictive statutes that remained on the books despite recent legislative reforms. Those who tackled controversial topics such as the country's ethnic Kurds, criticism of the military and the courts, the mass killing of Armenians under the Ottoman Empire, or criticism of the country's founder, Mustafa Kemal Atatürk, were the primary victims.

Over the last decade, Turkey made noticeable progress in improving its press freedom record. Among the world's leading jailers of journalists in the 1990s, Turkey has nearly ended the practice of putting reporters behind bars; at year's end, there was one reporter in prison for his work. Much of the improvement was the result of comprehensive legal reforms undertaken by the government in recent years. In an attempt to bring its laws in line with European legislation, Turkish authorities have amended or abolished restrictive statutes that had once been used to jail journalists by the dozens.

However, repressive laws remain on the books, and in 2006 they were frequently invoked to haul outspoken writers before the courts. Turkish nationalists opposed to EU membership were a driving force behind many of the prosecutions, which they hoped would derail accession. In doing so, they frequently sought out sympathetic public prosecutors across the country to launch criminal suits against journalists, writers, and academics.

In what was billed as a test case for the country's commitment to freedom of expression, prominent journalists Murat Belge, Haluk Sahin, Erol Katircioglu, and Ismet Berkan of the daily *Radikal*, and Hasan Cemal of the daily *Milliyet* stood trial in February, accused of attempting to influence the outcome of a trial and publicly denigrating "Turkishness" and the institutions of the Turkish state—crimes under Articles 288 and 301 of the Turkish penal code. CPJ Senior Editor Robert Mahoney monitored the court proceedings in Istanbul, producing a special report in March titled "Nationalism and the Press."

The charges were initiated by a group of nationalist lawyers in response to articles the five columnists wrote in 2005 challenging the decision of an Istanbul administrative court to ban an academic conference on the mass killing of Armenians under the Ottoman Empire from 1915 to 1917. The Ottoman authorities, allied with imperial Germany, killed or forcibly relocated Armenians whom they accused of sympathizing with Russia. The Armenian massacre is still taboo in Turkey. Armenians contend that the killings constituted the first genocide of the 20th century, a characterization that  Turkey rejects. The case against Sahin, Katircioglu, Berkan, and Cemal was dismissed in April, but the prosecution appealed the ruling. Belge was acquitted in June.

During the year, 17 journalists who discussed human rights cases, the Armenian conference ban, and torture cases were charged under Article 288, according to the press freedom group Bia. Criminal charges were brought against *Radikal* journalist Ismail Saymaz under Article 288 in response to a report alleging the torture of children by authorities. He was later fined 20,000 Turkish lira (US$13,600).

Another *Radikal* journalist, Murat Yetkin, was charged under the statute in relation to a 2005 column he wrote criticizing the prosecution of Nobel Prize winner Orhan Pamuk, who was tried for denigrating "Turkishness" but had the charge dropped in January. If convicted, Yetkin faced up to four and a half years in prison.

In July, Turkey's High Court of Appeals upheld the six-month suspended prison sentence of Turkish-Armenian journalist Hrant Dink for violating Article 301 in a case launched by nationalists. Dink is managing editor of the bilingual Turkish-Armenian weekly *Agos*. His prosecution followed a series of articles in early 2004 dealing with the collective memory of the Armenian massacres of 1915-17.

Dink said he would take the case to the European Court of Human Rights in Strasbourg, France, to clear his name. EU Commissioner for Enlargement Olli Rehn criticized the ruling and called on Turkey to amend its law to guarantee free expression. He said Turkey would have to rewrite its penal code again to meet EU standards.

Other repressive legal statutes were exploited by press freedom adversaries during the year. In June, Perihan Magden, a columnist for the weekly magazine *Yeni Aktuel*, was tried on a charge of violating Article 318 of the penal code when she defended conscientious objectors. The complaint was filed in response to a December 2005 article in which she took up the case of Mehmet Tarhan, who had received a record four-year sentence in a military jail for refusing to wear his uniform. Magden faced up to three years in prison if convicted. She was acquitted in July.

In yet another case, journalist Ipek Calislar was charged with insulting Atatürk during an interview about her upcoming book on Atatürk's wife. Calislar recounted an episode in which Atatürk wore women's clothing in order to escape assassination. She faced up to four and a half years in jail but was acquitted of the charge in December.

While none of those charged during the year was jailed, Turkish journalists said the rash of new criminal cases had a chilling effect on their work. "These cases lead to self-censorship. Before you write about issues like the army or the Kurds, you will think two or three times," said Turkish journalist and press freedom advocate Nadire Mater.

At least one newspaper was a casualty of the judicial crackdown. In August, a Turkish court ordered the 15-day closure of the pro-Kurdish daily *Ulkede Ozgur Gundem* for allegedly disseminating terrorist propaganda under a newly enacted antiterror law. It reopened after five days when the paper appealed the ruling.

Over the last two decades, attacks against Turkish media have been a disturbingly common occurrence. The trend continued in 2006 when the offices of the daily *Cumhuriyet*, the secular, republican flagship of Atatürk's followers, were targeted in three separate hand grenade attacks. No one was injured in the attacks, and the suspects remained at large at year's end.

·   **YEMEN**   ·

Presidential elections provided the backdrop for a series of troubling attacks against Yemen's increasingly vocal independent and opposition press. As expected, President Ali Abdullah Saleh extended his nearly three decades in power by another six years, but the run-up to the September vote saw an upsurge in violence, intimidation, and legal harassment, along with a smear campaign directed by the state-controlled press against independent journalists.

Yemen's outspoken press is one of the country's most important centers of dissent and political debate, and over the last two years, it has become noticeably bolder in exposing high-level corruption and tackling sensitive political issues. Newspapers questioned the wisdom of Saleh staying in power, and they challenged the grooming of the president's son, Ahmed, as his successor. Some criticized Yemeni officials for supporting religious militant groups at the same time Saleh cast himself as an ally in Washington's war on terrorism. Others criticized the president for harshly combating a regional insurgency led by tribal and religious figures in the northern Saada region that began in 2004. Authorities and suspected state agents responded aggressively to the critical coverage.

A series of brutal, unsolved assaults against independent journalists in 2005 prompted CPJ to send a delegation that included board members Clarence Page of the *Chicago Tribune* and Dave Marash of Al-Jazeera English to the capital, Sana'a, in January. Journalists, human rights lawyers, and civil-society activists described a climate of intimidation and mounting restrictions on Yemeni journalists. In six cases of violent attacks documented by CPJ in 2005, the Yemeni government failed to conduct serious investigations or bring perpetrators to justice, while officials conspicuously failed to denounce the assaults. Witnesses and evidence point to involvement by government forces and suspected state agents in a number of assaults. Those targeted were journalists who covered protests, reported on official corruption, criticized the president or government policies, or discussed the possibility of Saleh's son becoming president.

Yemeni officials who met with CPJ in January pledged to investigate attacks on the press, but they avoided explicitly denouncing the assaults on journalists. During a contentious meeting with the CPJ delegation, Prime Minister Abdelqader Bajammal said attacks against any Yemeni citizen were unacceptable, but he suggested that the assaults on journalists were unrelated to their work and had been staged to gain attention. "Some people are creating problems against themselves," Bajammal said. "They want to appear as fighters for press freedom. A journalist is drunk and then he clashes with people."

Despite dismissing the attacks, Bajammal promised that the government would investigate and make its results public. Yet by year's end, no findings were forthcoming, and attacks continued apace.

Qaed al-Tairi, a journalist for the Socialist Party weekly *Al-Thawri*, told CPJ that several men kidnapped and assaulted him in March in apparent retaliation for his writings. He said an assailant attacked him with an electric prod, while another attempted to break the fingers of his writing hand. They told him his column about local political factions had crossed "red lines" intended to prevent criticism of public figures, and that he risked death by continuing to write the column. The perpetrators remained at large.

In April, Jamal Amer, editor of the weekly newspaper *Al-Wasat*, who was abducted and brutally assaulted by suspected government agents in August 2005 after writing about high-level corruption, continued to face intimidation and harassment. On April 10, a known political security officer and four other men asked Amer's neighbors to identify the editor's apartment, provide the cell phone numbers of his children, name the schools his children attended, and provide the license plate of his car, Amer told CPJ. The visit came while Amer was traveling in the United States. Amer's U.S. trip prompted the state-controlled newspaper *Al-Mithaq* to accuse him of being an agent of the West. In November, Amer was awarded CPJ's International Press Freedom Award in recognition of his commitment to independent journalism amid threats and harassment.

Also in April, Abed al-Mahthari, editor-in-chief of the independent weekly *Al-Deyar*, said he was targeted by suspected weapons traffickers in Saada, near the Saudi border, after he had investigated weapons trafficking and received several death threats as a result. Al-Mahthari said his car was being driven by a friend on April 19 when several gunmen took up pursuit. The assailants, apparently believing they had followed the editor, forced their way into the friend's house, threatened the friend's family at gunpoint, and stole the car, al-Mahthari said. The friend obtained the license plate of the perpetrators' car, and al-Mahthari reported it to the police. The attackers were not apprehended.

Yemeni journalists continued to face the threat of government legal action or spurious lawsuits for their critical coverage. Several journalists fell victim to an international wave of government reprisals related to the publication of cartoons of the Prophet Muhammad that caused outrage across the Muslim world after they first appeared in the Danish daily *Jyllands-Posten*. Mohammed al-Asaadi, editor-in-chief of the English-language *Yemen Observer*; Abdulkarim Sabra, managing editor and publisher of *Al-Hurriya*; Yehiya al-Abed, a reporter for *Al-Hurriya*; and Kamal al-Aalafi, editor-in-chief of the Arabic-language *Al-Rai al-Aam*, were all charged with violating a press law provision that prohibits "printing, publishing, circulating, or broadcasting ... anything that prejudices the Islamic faith and its lofty principles or belittles religions or humanitarian creeds." The journalists were detained for several days and their publications suspended. Al-Aalafi was convicted in November and sentenced to a year in prison; he was free on appeal. The next month, a Sana'a court fined al-Asaadi 500,000 rials (US$2,850). Sabra and al-Abed received suspended terms in December.

Meanwhile, other prosecutions moved steadily through the courts. In July, a Sana'a court ordered the opposition weekly *Al-Wahdawi* to pay 500,000 rials in compensation to the Ministry of Defense, fined the paper 50,000 rials (US$285), and banned Editor-in-Chief Ali Saqqaf from practicing journalism for six months. The case against *Al-Wahdawi* stemmed from an August 2005 article alleging improprieties by members of the Republican Guard in taking over land in Dhamar province. The Ministry of Defense, which brought the case against *Al-Wahdawi*, accused the newspaper of revealing military secrets. Saqqaf told CPJ he intended to appeal the ruling. At the time, the paper faced nine other trials stemming from its reporting on government corruption.

In other court cases, *Al-Thawri* faced 13 defamation cases—the largest number against a single paper, according to press freedom lawyers.

During the year, the Yemeni parliament debated a press bill that threatened increased restrictions. Government officials touted the measure as a step forward for press freedom because it removed provisions from the 1990 law that stipulated jail terms for purported press offenses. But Yemeni lawyers noted that the change would be irrelevant since journalists would still face jail time under provisions of the country's penal code. The draft prescribed stiffer professional requirements to practice journalism, including membership in the Yemeni Journalists Syndicate, and it stipulated that nonjournalists could not work in the press. It also demanded expensive capital requirements for launching publications. Potential fines also drew concern. The draft before parliament did not specify the amounts of potential fines, and journalists feared that exorbitant penalties would be inserted by lawmakers or left to the discretion of judges under the sway of the executive branch.

Aside from legal means, authorities have resorted to dirty tricks against the press. Security agents were believed to be responsible for several incidents, including a January case in which a recording of a private telephone conversation between Al-Jazeera correspondent Ahmed al-Shalafi and his wife was distributed to senior Al-Jazeera staff in Doha, Qatar, and to journalists in Yemen. Al-Shalafi was said to have discussed potentially embarrassing personal matters. Journalists interpreted the recording as an attempt to get al-Shalafi fired; they suspected al-Shalafi had angered Yemeni authorities by interviewing the kidnappers of Italian tourists and by reporting on corruption and human rights abuses.

ALGERIA

- Authorities arrested Kamel Bousaad, editor of the pro-Islamist weekly *Errissala*, on February 8 and Berkane Bouderbala, managing editor of the weekly *Essafir*, on February 11, after their newspapers published controversial Danish cartoons depicting the Prophet Muhammad. The editors faced charges under Article 144 of the penal code for insulting the Prophet and denigrating Islam, which carries a five-year prison sentence. The case was closed and they were released after four weeks in prison, but the publications were suspended, according to CPJ sources.

- On February 11, cartoonist Ali Dilem was sentenced to one year in prison and fined 50,000 dinars (US$730) on defamation charges stemming from a series of cartoons depicting President Abdelaziz Bouteflika that appeared in the French-language daily *Liberté* in 2003. An appeals court later found him not guilty of the charges. On February 2, the director of Canal Algérie, Lotfi Shriat, and the director of Thalita TV, Houriya Khateer, showed two of the cartoons during news broadcasts. They were later dismissed by state-owned Télévision Algérienne, which runs both channels, local sources told CPJ.

- The government approved a decree in February that effectively barred the media and families of victims from investigating crimes and human rights abuses that took place during the Algerian civil conflict of the 1990s. The blanket ban prevents investigation of the murders of at least 58 journalists by armed groups or unknown assailants between 1993 and 1996, and the disappearance of at least two reporters, Djameleddine Fahassi and Aziz Bouabdellah, widely believed to have been seized by members of the Algerian security forces. "The provisions of this decree are so sweeping that they amount to censorship and an attempt to control the writing of history," CPJ said in a letter to Bouteflika on March 22.

- Mohamed Benchicou, former publisher of the French-language daily *Le Matin*, was released June 14 from El-Harrache Prison outside Algiers after serving a two-year sentence for allegedly violating the country's currency laws in 2003. Journalists and human rights groups viewed his conviction as retaliation for *Le Matin*'s critical editorial line against the government. He was prosecuted shortly after *Le Matin* alleged that Interior Minister Yazid Zerhouni had tortured detainees while a military security commander in the 1970s. Several criminal defamation lawsuits remained pending against Benchicou. *Le Matin* was forced to close in 2004 when the state printer demanded the newspaper settle its outstanding debts immediately.

- On July 5, Algeria's Independence Day, Bouteflika pardoned all journalists convicted of defaming or insulting the president, public officials, and state institutions. The president had marked World Press Freedom Day on May 3 by offering amnesty to jailed journalists, but it applied only to journalists whose appeals had failed, Agence France-Presse reported.

- An Algiers court convicted Ali Fodil, executive editor of the Arabic-language newspaper *Ech-Chourouk*, and reporter Naila Berrahal on October 31 on charges of defaming Libyan leader Muammar Qaddafi, according to the newspaper. The defense planned an appeal, The Associated Press reported. The Libyan embassy in Algiers sued the newspaper after it published two articles in August suggesting the Libyan leader had a role in negotiations with Touareg leaders to create a new state in the Sahel region. The articles reported the hostile reaction of the Touareg in southern Algeria to the plan.

BAHRAIN

- In October, the High Criminal Court prohibited the "publication of all types of news, analyses, or information pertaining to the case of Salah al-Bandar," the Bahrain News Agency reported. Al-Bandar, an adviser to the Cabinet Affairs Ministry, authored a report for the Gulf Centre for Democratic Development alleging that certain government officials intended to deprive many Shiites of their voting rights. Police deported al-Bandar, a British citizen, to the United Kingdom. The government said he would be tried in absentia for sedition, The Associated Press reported. Senior editors of Bahrain's Arabic-language newspapers urged the country's highest court on October 15 to review the government's ban on reporting allegations of election fraud, according to AP.

JORDAN

- Security agents questioned Fahd al-Rimawi, editor of the weekly *Al-Majd*, for more than six hours on May 8 over an article criticizing the government's announcement that it had uncovered a Hamas arms cache, son Mothaffar al-Rimawi told CPJ. The editor was not allowed to call his family or newspaper.

- Two editors were sentenced on May 30 to two months in prison for publishing controversial cartoons of the Prophet Muhammad. Jihad Momani, former editor-in-chief of the weekly *Shihan*, and Hashem al-Khalidi, editor-in-chief of the weekly *Al-Mehwar*, were found guilty by an Amman court of offending religious feelings and beliefs. Both editors were released on bail pending appeal.

- On June 8, security services abruptly halted a live Al-Jazeera interview with Abu Musab al-Zarqawi's brother-in-law, briefly detaining interviewer Yasser Abu Hilala and his crew in al-Zarqa, north of Amman. Al-Jazeera was interviewing Abu Qudama, who praised his brother-in-law, an al-Qaeda leader killed by U.S. forces in Iraq, when Jordanian security officers interrupted the interview and arrested Qudama. A CBS freelance correspondent and cameraman waiting to interview Qudama after Al-Jazeera were also detained at the scene and had their equipment confiscated.

KUWAIT

- On November 21, state prosecutors briefly detained Khaled al-Obysan, a columnist for the daily *Al-Seyassah*, for defending former Iraqi leader Saddam Hussein in an article published in the paper's November 9 issue, The Associated Press reported. Al-Obysan said the death sentence imposed against Saddam by an Iraqi tribunal was a "medal on his chest and a brand of shame on the forehead of the American administration and its tools in the Arab world." Prosecutors also questioned Ahmed al-Jarrallah, the paper's editor-in-chief, according to AP. Prosecutors said the column threatened ties with Iraq and the United States. No charges were pressed.

LIBYA

- On August 20, Seif al-Islam Muammar Qaddafi, son of Libyan leader Muammar Qaddafi and president of the Qaddafi Institution for Development, said Libya has "no constitution, no press, and no democracy," while announcing in the city of Surt, east of Tripoli, a program to advance the country to levels achieved by other oil states. "In all frankness and transparency, there is no freedom of the press in Libya; actually there is no press, even, and there is no real 'direct people's democracy' on the ground," the younger Qaddafi said. "That is something all Libyans say, from simple individuals to officials. And the people are all in agreement that there is no democracy in Libya."

MAURITANIA

- Security authorities detained El-Moustapha Ould Aoufa, a correspondent for the Iranian Arabic-language satellite channel Al-Alam and chief editor of the state-run Mauritanian TV. The March 4 arrest followed a program by Al-Alam on unrest in the Azouad region of neighboring Mali. Mauritanian authorities believed the program had offended a friendly government, the local independent news agency Al-Akhbar reported. Aoufa and his guest on the show, El-Moukhtar el-Jaid, were arrested shortly after the broadcast. Aoufa was accused of aiding someone hostile to a friendly government. Security agents handed over el-Jaid, an Azaouad activist, to Malian authorities. In the program, el-Jaid accused the Malian government of carrying out extrajudicial killings of Azouad opposition activists, Al-Akhbar reported. The Azaouad region, located in northwestern Mali, is inhabited by Touareg herders who are fighting the central government in Bamako. Mauritanian TV sacked Aoufa a few hours after his release on March 7, according to Al-Akhbar.

SUDAN

- Defense Minister Abdel Rahim Mohammed Hussein lashed out at foreign journalists attending a March 1 press conference in Khartoum, calling them "terrorists" and expelling them from the room. Hussein was angered by the international media's coverage of the crisis in Sudan's Darfur region. "The international media have escalated the problem ... because they sent incorrect information," he was quoted as saying.

- Pro-Sudanese government forces detained Paul Salopek, a two-time Pulitzer Prize-winning reporter for the *Chicago Tribune*, along with his Chadian interpreter, Suleiman Abakar Moussa, and driver Idriss Abdelrahman Anu, in Darfur on August 6. Salopek was on a freelance assignment for the U.S. magazine *National Geographic* to report on the culture, geography, and history of Africa's Sahel region. On August 26, a court in El-Fasher charged the three with espionage, illegally disseminating information, and writing "false news," in addition to a noncriminal count of entering the country without a visa. President Omar al-Bashir agreed on September 8 to free the men on humanitarian grounds following a personal appeal from Bill Richardson, governor of New Mexico and former U.S. ambassador to the United Nations.

- On August 30, Khartoum police beat Ibrahim Muhammad, a cameraman for the Qatar-based satellite channel Al-Jazeera, and seized his camera during a banned demonstration of opposition parties and their supporters against a rise in gasoline and sugar prices, Reuters reported. The police chased Muhammad, who had been filming the demonstration, and beat him with sticks while firing tear gas into the crowd. One of the tear gas canisters hit a Reuters vehicle, the agency reported.

- On September 5, masked gunmen kidnapped editor Mohammed Taha Mohammed Ahmed of the private daily *Al-Wifaq* outside his home in Khartoum. Police found his severed head next to his body the following day south of the capital. His hands and feet were bound. Taha, 50, was a pro-government Islamist who had offended the country's powerful Islamists by republishing an article from the Internet that questioned the ancestry of the Prophet Muhammad. He was detained, his newspaper suspended, and he was subsequently charged with blasphemy. Later in September, a purported leader of an al-Qaeda branch in Africa, Abu Hafs al-Sudani, claimed responsibility for the slaying, saying that Taha had insulted the Prophet. Some questioned the authenticity of the claim.

- Zuhayr al-Sarraj, a columnist for the private daily *Al-Sahafa*, was arrested by Sudanese security forces and held for 60 hours at Kober jail in Khartoum on January 3, a source at the paper told CPJ. Al-Sarraj was charged by the national security prosecutor with "insulting the president" in connection with a column questioning the president's performance. Charges were pending.

- Riot police beat three journalists—Imam Abdelbagi al-Khidir, a reporter for the private daily *Akhir Lahza*; Maha Mabruk, an intern for the paper; and Safa al-Salih, a correspondent for the BBC Arabic service—covering an August 30 demonstration in Khartoum about economic hardship. Al-Hindi Izzedine, *Akhir Lahza's* deputy editor, told CPJ that the three were held for about two hours at the central police station until their press credentials were verified.

- On September 18, Vice President Ali Osman Mohamed Taha announced the end of a wave of censorship against Khartoum papers. Seven private Arabic-language dailies—*Al-Ayam, Al-Adwoaa, Al-Sudani, Alwan, Al-Sahafa, Ray-al-Shaab,* and *Al-Watan*—were censored or confiscated beginning September 9. Authorities told editors that the issues were censored to avoid compromising an investigation into the murder of *Al-Wifaq's* Taha. Local journalists said the censored editions carried articles about the lack of democratic transformation and the suppression of demonstrations against fuel and sugar price increases.

- Abu Obeida Abdallah, a reporter for the pro-government daily *Al-Ra'y al-Aam*, was released on October 15 after being held incommunicado and without charge for more than two weeks by security forces. Reuters said that sources reported different reasons for the detention. Kamal Hassan Bakhiet, the paper's editor-in-chief, said he believed Abdallah was questioned as part of the Taha murder investigation. Abdallah may have had telephone contact with someone state security suspected in the slaying, he told the news agency.

- Sa'd al-Din Hassan-Abdallah, correspondent for the satellite channel Al-Arabiya, told CPJ he was arrested by security forces in Khartoum on October 15, questioned for several hours, and had his laptop confiscated. Hassan-Abdallah's arrest followed the broadcast of a report on the forced relocation of residents in the Amri region, 200 miles (320 kilometers) north of Khartoum, where the government is building the Merowe High Dam. He was summoned on October 17 and October 19 for further questioning, he told CPJ. He later stopped working under pressure from the pro-government Press and Publications Council.

SYRIA

- Sha'ban Abboud, Damascus correspondent for the leading Lebanese daily *Al-Nahar*, was detained by Syrian authorities on March 2, according to the paper. Abboud was accused by a military court of publishing false information following a February 28 article on nominations within the security and intelligence services, Syrian rights lawyer Anwar Bunni told Agence France-Presse. According to *Al-Nahar*, Abboud was released on bail March 7, following the intervention of fellow journalists and human rights groups. He faced three years in prison if convicted by a military court, according to news reports.

- On June 7, a military court found Muhammad Ghanem, editor of the news Web site *Surion*, guilty of insulting the president, undermining the state's dignity, and inciting sectarian divisions. Ghanem was sentenced to one year in jail, but the judge commuted his sentence to six months, *Surion* said, without offering further explanation. Ghanem had been detained since March 31, *Surion* and human rights organizations reported. He had written many articles advocating political and cultural rights for Syria's Kurdish minority and had been critical of the Baath Party's handling of domestic issues.

- Security agents arrested Palestinian-born Swedish journalist Rachid al-Hajeh at the Damascus airport on June 16 and threatened to charge him with insulting the Syrian state. The arrest stemmed from a Swedish television interview conducted 10 years earlier with a Syrian seeking asylum, according to Sweden's Foreign Ministry. In the interview, the Syrian was reported to have made critical comments about his home country, attracting the attention of Syria's secret service, news reports said. Throughout al-Hajeh's detention, Swedish Embassy officials were not allowed to see him, or to attend his interviews and court proceedings. He was released on June 27.

- Human rights activist and freelance journalist Ali Abdallah and his son Mohammad were released October 4 after completing six-month sentences for "disturbing public order," "spreading false information likely to harm the financial prestige of the state," and "insulting a high-ranking public employee," according to CPJ sources. Abdallah's son was arrested immediately after protesting his father's arrest in an interview with the satellite channel Al-Jazeera. According to CPJ sources, the questioning of Abdallah and his son by the president of a military tribunal focused on the journalist's opinion pieces and his son's interview with Al-Jazeera. Abdallah is a regular contributor to Lebanese papers, including the daily *Al-Nahar*, and to the London-based daily *Al-Quds al-Arabi*.

- Information Minister Muhsin Bilal ordered the closure of the country's only private satellite channel, Sham TV, eight months after it launched. The October 30 order was issued orally to owner Muhammad Akram al-Jundi, a member of parliament, and to Director Maamun al-Bunni, according to the independent AKI Press agency, which cited government sources. The closure came on the day Sham TV was scheduled to air its first news report and five weeks after it began broadcasting from outside Damascus, the U.N. news agency IRIN said. The report quoted al-Bunni as saying that problems with the paperwork for the station's broadcast rights had led to the government order. He said that Sham TV would be back on the air.

IN IRAQ, JOURNALIST DEATHS
SPIKE TO A RECORD

Violence in Iraq claimed the lives of 32 journalists in 2006, the deadliest year for the press in a single country that the Committee to Protect Journalists has ever recorded. In most cases, such as the killing of Atwar Bahjat, one of the best-known television reporters in the Arab world, insurgents specifically targeted journalists to be murdered, CPJ's analysis revealed.

Worldwide, CPJ found 55 journalists were killed in direct connection to their work in 2006, and it is investigating another 30 deaths to determine whether they were work-related. The figures reflect increases from 2005, when 47 journalists were killed in direct relation to their work, while 17 others died in circumstances in which the link to their profession was not clear. CPJ, founded in 1981, compiles and analyzes journalist deaths each year.

Afghanistan and the Philippines, with three deaths apiece, were the next most dangerous datelines in 2006. Russia, Mexico, Pakistan, and Colombia each saw two journalists killed. All are traditionally dangerous countries for the press, CPJ research shows.

But for the fourth consecutive year, Iraq was in a category all its own as the deadliest place for journalists. This year's killings bring to 92 the number of journalists who have died in Iraq since the U.S.-led invasion of March 2003. In addition, 37 media support workers—interpreters, drivers, fixers, and office workers—have been killed since the war began.

Only four journalists died in Iraq in 2006 as a result of crossfire or acts of war, CPJ's analysis found. The other 28 were murdered, half of them threatened beforehand. Three were kidnapped and then slain, CPJ found.

The viciousness of the onslaught in Iraq was shown on October 12 when masked gunmen attacked the Baghdad offices of the fledgling satellite TV channel Al-Shaabiya and executed 11 people, five of them journalists. It was the deadliest single assault on the press since the 2003 invasion.

Here are other trends about Iraq that emerged in CPJ's analysis:

- Thirty of 32 journalists killed were Iraqis, continuing a two-year trend in which local journalists made up an overwhelming proportion of the casualties. CBS cameraman Paul Douglas and soundman James Brolan, both London-based, were the only foreign journalists killed in Iraq in 2006. Among the Iraqi victims was Bahjat, correspondent for the satellite channel Al-Arabiya and former reporter for Al-Jazeera. CPJ honored Bahjat posthumously in November with its International Press Freedom Award.

- Murder accounts for 61 percent of deaths in Iraq since the war began. The incidence of murder began to increase in mid-2005 and accelerated in 2006. Crossfire and combat-related incidents had been a more frequent cause of media deaths in the first two years of the war.

- The 2006 toll jumped 45 percent from the 22 deaths recorded in 2005.
- The war in Iraq is the deadliest conflict CPJ has documented. Iraq has far surpassed the Algerian civil conflict of the 1990s, which took the lives of 58 journalists.
- The 2006 tally in Iraq is the highest in a single country since CPJ was founded in 1981. The second deadliest years were 2004 in Iraq and 1995 in Algeria, both of which saw 24 journalists killed.

JOURNALISTS KILLED WORLDWIDE, BY YEAR

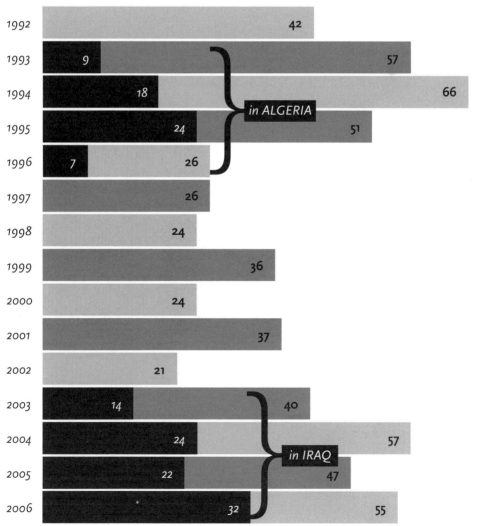

Year		
1992		42
1993	9 *in ALGERIA*	57
1994	18	66
1995	24	51
1996	7	26
1997		26
1998		24
1999		36
2000		24
2001		37
2002		21
2003	14	40
2004	24 *in IRAQ*	57
2005	22	47
2006	32	55

Worldwide, murder was the leading cause of journalist deaths in 2006, accounting for about 85 percent of cases. (About 11 percent of victims died in combat incidents and 4 percent while covering dangerous assignments such as protests.) CPJ research found that little progress was reported in investigations into the vast majority of cases, reinforcing long-term research showing that less than 15 percent of journalist murders result in convictions.

Among those slain was Russian Anna Politkovskaya, a leading investigative journalist and critic of President Vladimir Putin. She was shot, contract-style, in her Moscow apartment building on October 7.

Seven other female journalists were killed in 2006. In the Central Asian nation of Turkmenistan, reporter Ogulsapar Muradova of Radio Free Europe/Radio Liberty was killed in prison under unexplained circumstances in September. And in southern Lebanon, an Israeli missile killed freelance photographer Layal Najib in July as she was traveling by taxi to cover civilians fleeing north.

The deadliest nations include such disparate places as the Philippines and Afghanistan. Two of the victims in the Philippines were radio commentators, continuing a trend CPJ has documented over several years. In strife-ridden Afghanistan, two German broadcast journalists were among the three casualties.

In Latin America, two nations with long histories of violence against the press appeared on the 2006 list of dangerous places. In Colombia, two provincial journalists known for tough reporting on paramilitary activities were slain. In Mexico, a local crime reporter was murdered in the eastern city of Veracruz, and a U.S. freelance journalist was shot to death during civil unrest in the southern state of Oaxaca. CPJ is investigating the disappearance of a northern Mexican reporter and the slayings of five other Mexican journalists in circumstances that were not immediately clear.

In sub-Saharan Africa, one journalist was killed in direct connection to his work in 2006. Martin Adler, an award-winning Swedish photojournalist, was shot while filming a June demonstration in Somalia's capital, Mogadishu.

CPJ applies strict standards for each entry on its annual list of journalists killed; researchers independently investigate and verify the circumstances behind each death. CPJ considers a case as work-related only when its staff is reasonably certain that a journalist was killed in direct reprisal for his or her work; in crossfire; or while carrying out a dangerous assignment.

If the motives in a killing are unclear, but it is possible that a journalist died in direct relation to his or her work, CPJ classifies the case as "unconfirmed" and continues to investigate. CPJ's list does not include journalists who are killed in accidents—such as car or plane crashes—unless the crash was caused by hostile action (for example, if a plane were shot down or a car crashed trying to avoid gunfire). Other press organizations using different criteria cite higher numbers of deaths than CPJ.

A database of all journalists killed since 1992 is available at: *www.cpj.org/killed/killed_archives/stats.html*

55 JOURNALISTS KILLED: MOTIVE CONFIRMED

AFGHANISTAN: 3

Abdul Qodus, Aryana TV
July 22, 2006, Kandahar

Qodus, a cameraman for the private station, was killed in a double suicide bombing in the city of Kandahar. He had arrived at the scene of a suicide car bomb when a second attacker with explosives strapped to his body blew himself up, according to the Kabul-based Committee to Protect Afghan Journalists (CPAJ) and news reports. Qodus died of head injuries at a local hospital.

A Taliban spokesman claimed responsibility for the two explosions, which also killed two Canadian soldiers and several civilians, according to news reports.

Qodus, 25, had worked for the Kabul-based station for eight months, according to CPAJ. Fighting between Taliban militants and U.S.-led coalition forces, which invaded Afghanistan in 2001, had led to the deaths of hundreds of people in the preceding months.

Karen Fischer, freelance
Christian Struwe, freelance
October 7, 2006, Baghlan

Fischer, 30, and Struwe, 39, Deutsche Welle journalists doing research for a freelance documentary, were shot in a tent they had pitched along a road near Baghlan, about 95 miles (150 kilometers) northwest of Kabul.

Deutsche Welle said the two had recently visited several United Nations Children's Fund projects in northern Afghanistan and were en route to the central province of Bamiyan.

News reports said the pair's personal possessions were not taken. The area, though considered safer than other parts of the country, was still poorly controlled by the government and NATO forces in charge of security. Local police detained two people for questioning, the Kabul-based daily *Cheragh* reported on October 12.

CHINA: 1

Wu Xianghu, *Taizhou Wanbao*
February 2, 2006, Taizhou

Wu, deputy editor of *Taizhou Wanbao*, died from serious injuries sustained when traffic police in the eastern coastal city of Taizhou, Zhejiang province, attacked him in October 2005 for an exposé that embarrassed them, according to international news reports.

Wu, 41, died of liver and kidney failure after months of hospitalization. State-run Xinhua News Agency reported that the assault had damaged his liver, which was already compromised due to a previously existing medical condition.

On October 20, 2005, dozens of uniformed traffic officers arrived at the offices of the *Taizhou Wanbao* evening newspaper, assaulted Wu, carried him from the building, and forced him into a police van. The attack stemmed from a report in the previous day's newspaper on high fee collections for electric bicycle licenses, according to local news reports.

Senior officer Li Xiaoguo was removed from his post for his role in the attack, Xinhua reported in October. Li had called the other police officers to the scene after his demands for an apology for the October 19 report had led to an argument with Wu. "I am not a policeman today," Li said during the attack, according to local news reports.

Taizhou Wanbao defended the report, saying that it was done in cooperation with local government agencies.

The Hong Kong-based *South China Morning Post* quoted an unnamed staff member at the Taizhou News Group who said that authorities had prevented local media from reporting on Wu's death, and that his colleagues believed that criminal charges should be filed in the case.

Journalists who report on local crime and corruption in China's newly competitive media environment face increasing incidence of violent attack in retribution for their work, according to CPJ research.

COLOMBIA: 2

Gustavo Rojas Gabalo, Radio Panzenú
March 20, 2006, Montería

Rojas, 56, host of "El Show de El Gaba" on Radio Panzenú, was shot by unidentified gunmen on February 4 in the northwestern city of Montería, Córdoba province.

He died on March 20 from complications at a hospital in Medellín, capital of the central Antioquia province.

Two men aboard a motorcycle approached Rojas as he opened his car outside a liquor store he owned in Montería. Witnesses said one of the assailants got off the motorcycle, argued with Rojas, and shot him twice at close range, the local press reported. One bullet shattered Rojas' collarbone, while the other caused severe head injuries.

Rojas underwent repeated surgery for head injuries in Montería, his physician, Jesús Jímenez Isaza, told CPJ. On March 18, Rojas was moved to the Salucoop Clinic in Medellín to receive specialized medical attention, his daughter Erly Rojas said.

Known as "El Gaba," Rojas had been on the air for more than 30 years. His popular "El Show de El Gaba" featured music, news, and commentary that often focused on government corruption. He had earned a regional reputation for voicing listeners' social and political concerns.

In April, local police arrested four men in connection with the murder. Luis Armando Díaz Berrocal, the local prosecutor in charge of the case, told CPJ that two were paramilitary fighters. The four denied involvement in the slaying, he said. Díaz said that Rojas' journalism—especially his criticism of local officials and paramilitary forces—was considered a strong motive. Local reporters told CPJ that they believe his commentary had sparked retaliation.

Atilano Segundo Pérez Barrios
Radio Vigía de Todelar
August 22, 2006, Cartagena

Pérez, 52, host of the weekly program "El Diario de Marialabaja," was killed by an unidentified assailant who forced his way into the journalist's Cartagena apartment at around 9 p.m. and shot him twice in the abdomen, a family member told CPJ. The assailant then fled on the back of a motorcycle. Pérez was pronounced dead at the Hospital Universitario del Caribe.

Local journalists said Pérez had been consistently critical of local paramilitary activity. He leased a one-hour, Sunday-morning time slot from Radio Vigía de Todelar for his program, Station Manager Doris Jiménez told CPJ. The show focused on news from Pérez's hometown of Marialabaja, 37 miles (60 kilometers) south of Cartagena.

Ricardo Carriazo, the local prosecutor in charge of the case, told CPJ that Pérez had fled his hometown because of work-related threats. Authorities believed the murder was linked to Pérez's comments on local paramilitary activities, although they had not conclusively ruled out other motives, Carriazo said.

Jairo Baena, president of a local journalists union, told CPJ that Pérez often denounced government corruption and paramilitary influence in Marialabaja. In his last show, on August 20, he accused the five candidates for mayor of Marialabaja of being financed by right-wing paramilitary groups, the local press reported. The family member told CPJ that Pérez had received recent death threats.

Pérez had been a member of the Marialabaja town council and a deputy in the Bolívar provincial assembly a decade earlier, but he was no longer involved in politics, the Cartagena-based daily El Universal reported. Pérez, while not a lawyer, also provided assistance in legal cases related to the public transportation system, according to the local press freedom group Fundación para la Libertad de Prensa.

Investigators identified two men with links to local paramilitary groups as the likely perpetrators, provincial police Cmdr. Luís Angulo told CPJ. Police found the two men dead a few days after the murder, he said.

INDIA: 1

Prahlad Goala, *Asomiya Khabar*
January 6, 2006, Golaghat

Goala was murdered near his home in Golaghat district in India's northeastern state of Assam after writing a series of articles in the Assamese-language daily *Asomiya Khabar* that linked local forestry service officials to timber smuggling.

Local journalists told CPJ that police arrested forest warden Zamman Jinnah in connection with the death. He was released on bail. Two other suspects, who were not forestry service employees, were also taken into custody, the journalists said.

Jinnah had made death threats against Goala soon after his articles on corruption in the forestry service appeared, *The Assam Tribune* reported.

Goala, 32, was riding a motorcycle near his home some 160 miles (260 kilometers) east of the state capital, Guwahati, when he was apparently rammed by a truck. When police arrived at the scene, they found that Goala had been stabbed several times.

Local journalist organizations and civic groups staged a protest in Golaghat on January 10 and called for a full investigation into the slaying.

INDONESIA: 1

Herliyanto, *Radar Surabaya* and *Jimber News Visioner*
April 29, 2006, Probolinggo

Reporter Herliyanto was killed by a group of assailants while riding his motorcycle in a forested area connecting the villages of Tulupari and Tarokan in the Banyuanyar district of East Java province. Herliyanto, 40, was stabbed in the stomach, neck, and head shortly after evening prayers, according to the Probolinggo General Hospital's autopsy report.

Banyuanyar police investigators found the slain journalist's motorcycle, wallet, camera, and notebook about 100 feet (30 meters) away, according to CPJ sources. Five days later, a villager found and turned over to police investigators the slain reporter's cell phone with the SIM card missing, CPJ sources said.

On September 26, Probolinggo police arrested three suspects identified as Slamet, 35, Nipa Cipanjar, 27, and Su'id, 50, all of whom were residents of Alun-alun village in nearby Ranuyoso district, according to CPJ sources. Police also publicly identified four additional suspects identified as Juri, Leung, Slamet, and Abdul Basyir, none of whom were immediately apprehended. It is customary for many Indonesians to use only one name.

According to public statements made on September 29 by Probolinggo Resort Police Chief Nana Sudjana, Herliyanto's murder was directly related to the journalist's April 9 newspaper report concerning official corruption in a bridge project in the nearby village of Rejing. Herliyanto's report alleged that 120 million rupiah (US$13,165) was pilfered from a local infrastructure fund, CPJ sources said.

Sudjana accused Basyir, the village official who oversaw the Reijing bridge project, of both planning and participating in the murder. The police official said he drew his conclusions from the statements of the three detained witnesses. Probolinggo police said they recovered Herliyanto's missing SIM card from a local villager and discovered that Basyir had called him in the afternoon of the day that he was killed.

IRAQ: 32

Mahmoud Za'al, Baghdad TV
January 25, 2006, Ramadi

Za'al, 35, a correspondent for Baghdad TV, was shot during clashes between U.S. forces and Sunni rebels in Ramadi, an insurgent stronghold 70 miles (110 kilometers) west of Baghdad.

Reuters quoted witnesses as saying Za'al was covering an insurgent attack on two U.S.-held buildings when he was wounded in the legs and then killed moments later in a U.S. air strike. The U.S. military denied it had launched an air strike in Ramadi that day and declined comment on the clashes or Za'al's death, the agency reported.

Staff at Baghdad TV told CPJ that U.S. soldiers briefly questioned Za'al 15 minutes before he was shot.

Staff said several of the station's correspondents had been detained by U.S. troops in the preceding few months. Baghdad TV is owned by the Iraqi Islamic Party, the biggest Sunni political group. Za'al had worked for the station for one year.

Atwar Bahjat, Al-Arabiya
Adnan Khairallah
Wasan Productions and Al-Arabiya
Khaled Mahmoud al-Falahi
Wasan Productions and Al-Arabiya
February 23, 2006, Samarra

The bodies of correspondent Bahjat, cameraman al-Falahi, and engineer Khairallah were found near Samarra, a day after the station lost contact with the crew, editors at Al-Arabiya told CPJ. Bahjat, 30, was a well-known on-air figure. Al-Arabiya said she had recently joined the channel after working as a correspondent for the Arabic satellite channel Al-Jazeera.

Al-Falahi, 39, and Khairallah, 36, were employees of Wasan Productions who were on assignment for Al-Arabiya. The crew was on the outskirts of the city covering the bombing of the Shiite shrine Askariya, also known as the Golden Mosque.

Al-Arabiya Executive Editor Nabil Khatib said the station lost phone contact with the crew on the evening of February 22. A fixer for Wasan Productions told the station later that armed men driving a white car had attacked the crew after demanding to know the whereabouts of the on-air correspondent.

Munsuf Abdallah al-Khaldi
Baghdad TV
March 7, 2006, Baghdad

Unidentified gunmen in west Baghdad shot al-Khaldi, 35, a presenter for the Iraqi television station Baghdad TV. Al-Khaldi was driving to the northern city of Mosul to interview poets when assailants stopped the car and fired three shots, Baghdad TV Deputy Director Thaer Ahmad said. One passenger was killed and two others were injured. Al-Khaldi presented an educational and cultural show focusing on Middle Eastern poetry.

On March 1, Baghdad TV came under artillery fire by insurgents, according to Ahmad. Four employees were injured by two shells, which hit a parking area. The station had received e-mail threats because of its criticism of insurgent attacks, Ahmad added.

Baghdad TV is owned by the Iraqi Islamic Party, the biggest Sunni political group.

Amjad Hameed, Al-Iraqiya
March 11, 2006, Baghdad

Hameed and his driver Anwar Turki were shot and killed by gunmen apparently affiliated with al-Qaeda in an ambush in central Baghdad. Hameed had been head of programming for Iraq's state television channel Al-Iraqiya since July 2005.

Hameed, 45, the father of three children, had just left home for work when he was shot several times in the head and chest. Al-Iraqiya, which receives funding from the U.S. government, suspended regular programming and aired verses from the

Quran after the widely condemned attack.

Al-Qaeda's affiliate in Iraq claimed responsibility for the attack in Internet postings, but those claims could not be independently verified. "Your brothers in the military wing of the Mujahedeen Council assassinated on Saturday Amjad Hameed, the editor of Iraqiya ... which always broadcasts lies about jihad to satisfy crusader masters," said a statement posted on a Web site often used by militant groups and attributed to the group, Reuters reported. According to the statement, the station was "the mouthpiece of the apostate government."

About two dozen employees of the state-run Iraq Media Network, which includes Al-Iraqiya, had been killed in the war, most by insurgents. Al-Iraqiya offices had repeatedly come under mortar attack.

Muhsin Khudhair, *Alef Ba*
March 13, 2006, Baghdad

Khudhair, editor of the newsmagazine *Alef Ba*, was killed by unidentified gunmen near his home in Baghdad, the third journalist killed in Iraq in a week, Reuters and Agence France-Presse reported.

The shooting took place just hours after Khudair attended a meeting of the Iraqi Journalists Union, which discussed the targeting of local journalists in Iraq, Reuters said. The killing continued two trends in Iraq: The vast majority of victims were Iraqi citizens; and most cases were targeted assassinations.

Kamal Manahi Anbar, freelance
March 26, 2006, Baghdad

Anbar, 28, a freelance journalist and former trainee with the Institute for War and Peace Reporting (IWPR), was killed by Iraqi forces' fire during a clash with insurgents. The shooting broke out near Al-Mustafa al-Husseiniyah mosque in Baghdad's Ur neighborhood, according to CPJ sources. Iraqi forces, backed by U.S. military, opened fire after shots were fired from a building adjacent to the mosque. Civilians rushed for cover, among them Anbar, who was found shot several times in the face and neck, according to IWPR. According to CPJ sources, Anbar was among 16 people killed in the fighting.

Anbar had completed a two-week IWPR course on economics reporting and was writing an article on the displacement of Iraqi families and the volatile housing market. He was at the mosque to interview Sheikh Safaa al-Timimi, head of Shiite cleric Muqtada al-Sadr's local political movement and an authority on displaced families seeking shelter in Ur, according to IWPR.

So'oud Muzahim al-Shoumari
Al-Baghdadia
April 4, 2006, Baghdad

Al-Shoumari, a correspondent for the Egypt-based satellite channel Al-Baghdadia, was found shot in Baghdad's southern district of Doura on April 4 by Iraqi police and taken to Yarmouk hospital morgue, his father told CPJ. Al-Shoumari, also know as al-Hadithi (the name of his family's hometown), was abducted on April 3.

Al-Shoumari was alone when he was seized, and his killers were not identified, sources told CPJ. Abdelhamid al-Sa'eh, director of news at the channel, said he suspected that al-Shoumari, a Sunni Muslim, was kidnapped by elements within the Shiite-dominated Iraqi police, but could not provide details.

Al-Shoumari had worked for Al-Baghdadia for seven months. According to the *Los Angeles Times*, al-Shoumari regularly confronted Iraqi police about suspicions that they were committing extrajudicial killings. The channel's Baghdad director, Muhammad Fitian, and al-Shoumari's father both told CPJ they were not aware of confrontations with the police.

A colleague at Al-Baghdadia said al-Shoumari regularly interviewed authorities about human rights violations and the daily suffering of the Iraqi people. Al-Shoumari did on-camera reporting and anchored a news program.

Al-Baghdadia was critical of the Iraqi government and the U.S. military presence in Iraq, according to The Associated Press.

Laith al-Dulaimi, Al-Nahrain
May 8, 2006, south of Baghdad

Al-Dulaimi, a reporter for the privately owned TV station Al-Nahrain, and Muazaz Ahmed Barood, a telephone operator for the station, were kidnapped by men dressed as police officers at Diyala Bridge. The two were driving home to Madain, a town 12 miles (19 kilometers) southeast of Baghdad, Abdulkarim al-Mehdawi, the station's general manager, told CPJ.

Their bodies were discovered in Al-Wihda district, 20 miles (32 kilometers) south of Baghdad. Both men, in their late 20s,

were shot in the chest, al-Mehdawi told CPJ. Al-Dulaimi had become a reporter for Al-Nahrain four months earlier.

James Brolan, CBS
Paul Douglas, CBS
May 29, 2006, Baghdad

Cameraman Douglas and soundman Brolan were killed when a car bomb exploded while they were on patrol in Baghdad with Iraqi and American soldiers. Correspondent Kimberly Dozier, the third member of the CBS crew, was seriously injured in the attack.

The CBS journalists, embedded with the U.S. Army's 4th Infantry Division, were reporting from outside their Humvee and were believed to have been wearing protective gear when a car packed with explosives detonated, CBS said in a statement. An Iraqi contractor and an American soldier also were killed, and six soldiers were injured, according to news reports.

Douglas, 48, based in London, had worked for CBS News in Iraq, Afghanistan, Pakistan, Rwanda, and Bosnia since the early 1990s, CBS said. Brolan, 42, also based in London, was a freelancer who worked with CBS News in Baghdad and Afghanistan over the preceding year, according to the network.

Ali Jaafar, Al-Iraqiya
May 31, 2006, Baghdad

Jaafar, 24, a well-known sports correspondent and anchor at Iraq's state television channel Al-Iraqiya, was shot by unidentified gunmen as he opened his recently deceased brother's auto shop near his home in Al-Shorta al-Rabaa in southwest Baghdad, according to CPJ sources and international news reports. His colleagues believe he was killed because he worked for Al-Iraqiya.

Insurgents frequently targeted Al-Iraqiya and its staff because of the station's ties to the U.S.-supported Iraqi government. About two dozen employees of the state-run Iraq Media Network, which includes Al-Iraqiya, had been killed in the war, most by insurgents. Al-Iraqiya offices had repeatedly come under mortar attack.

Ibrahim Seneid, *Al-Bashara*
June 13, 2006, Fallujah

Seneid, an editor for the local newspaper *Al-Bashara*, was murdered in an evening drive-by shooting, Fallujah police Lt. Mohammed Ali told The Associated Press. Insurgents accused the paper of publishing U.S. propaganda, and they demanded its closure in leaflets distributed in Fallujah, AP reported.

Al-Bashara was established following the battle for Fallujah in November 2004, according to a CPJ source. It was perceived by many local residents as a mouthpiece for the United States, the source said.

Adel Naji al-Mansouri, Al-Alam
July 29, 2006, Baghdad

Unidentified gunmen intercepted al-Mansouri, 34, a correspondent for the Iranian state-run Arabic language satellite channel Al-Alam, as he was driving in the Al-Amariyeh neighborhood of western Baghdad, colleague Abdullah Hamdullah Bardan Ruba'i told CPJ. Al-Mansouri was driving to the station's offices when he was attacked, Ruba'i said.

The gunmen took al-Mansouri's mobile phone, satellite phone, press card, and money, Ruba'i said. He said his colleague was rushed to a hospital but died shortly afterward. Ruba'i and CPJ sources said they believe al-Mansouri was killed because he was a journalist.

Al-Mansouri, a Shiite, received death threats a year earlier when he resided with his family in Baghdad, where sectarian violence had intensified, according to Ruba'i. The Associated Press reported that the journalist moved his wife and daughter to the Shiite-dominated city of Karbala following the threats, but he chose to stay in Baghdad himself. He had dropped off his visiting wife at her parent's house in Al-Amariyeh around 7 p.m. the night of the attack, sources said.

Al-Mansouri was the first journalist from the Arabic-language Iranian satellite channel to be murdered. The station, which started regular broadcasting in March 2003, was based in Tehran and run by IRIB, the Iranian state radio and TV service. It opposed the U.S.-led invasion of Iraq and, in hourly news bulletins, showed extensive footage of Iraqi civilians lying dead in residential areas or being treated in hospitals.

Riyad Muhammad Ali, *Talafar al-Yawm*
July 30, 2006, Mosul

Ali, a reporter for the weekly *Talafar al-Yawm*, was murdered by unidentified gunmen in Mosul's Wadi Aqab area late at night. The killers took the journalist's cell phone and the money he was carrying to pay the paper's printers, Editor-in-Chief Tareq Muhammad Ali told CPJ.

Ali gathered news from official sources, including the police and security forces, and enjoyed good relations with them, his editor said. Insurgents target journalists dealing with official sources, especially the police, he added. Ali, who is also the victim's brother, spoke with the killers via the stolen cell phone. They said they had killed him because he was an infidel and journalist.

Ali described *Talafar al-Yawm* as pro-Iraqi government and pro-democracy, adding that the paper's reports had not refered to U.S. forces as occupiers. As a result, he said, the paper had received multiple threats from insurgents.

Mohammad Abbas Mohammad
Al-Bayinnah al-Jadida
August 7, 2006, Baghdad

Unidentified gunmen shot Mohammad, 28, an editor for the Shiite-owned newspaper *Al-Bayinnah al-Jadida*, as he left his home in the Adil section of western Baghdad to go to work early the morning of August 7, according to The Associated Press and CPJ sources.

Mohammad was highly critical of politicians and Iraqi officials regardless of sect or affiliation, a local source told CPJ. The journalist had received several death threats because he worked for the paper, local journalists said.

Ismail Amin Ali, freelance
August 7, 2006, Baghdad

The body of freelance journalist Ali, 30, was discovered in late evening by police in the eastern section of Baghdad known as al-Sadr City, according to a CPJ source. His body was riddled with bullets, and Iraqi police said they found signs of torture, The Associated Press reported.

A local source told CPJ that the journalist had been abducted while he was at a gas station in Al-Shaab neighborhood of Baghdad two weeks earlier. The kidnappers had demanded ransom, but his family was unable to pay.

A local source said Ali, a well-known Sunni columnist for several Baghdad-based papers, including *Al-Sabah* and *Al-Qarar*, may have been targeted because he was highly critical of the Shiite-dominated security forces.

Abdel Karim al-Rubai, *Al-Sabah*
September 9, 2006, Baghdad

Al-Rubai, 40, a design editor for Iraq's state-run daily *Al-Sabah*, was shot by several gunmen while traveling to work in the eastern Baghdad neighborhood known as Camp Sara. The driver of the car was seriously wounded, media sources told CPJ.

Al-Sabah reported two weeks earlier that it had received an e-mailed death threat against al-Rubai and his family, which was signed by the military wing of the Mujahedeen Council, an al-Qaeda affiliate in Iraq. According to the e-mail, the group was angered by the editor's accusation that it was behind a car bomb attack on *Al-Sabah* on

August 27, which killed a guard and an un-identified man.

"We have our reservations about this newspaper despite the fact that there are Iraqis working in it, but we condemn those false accusations against our resisting army, which issued just a few days ago a state-ment that forbids the killing of Muslims, especially Iraqis of any background or be-liefs. But these allegations and accusations will not go unpunished, and we hold ... al-Rubai responsible for what will happen to him and his family since with the help of God we obtained their names and ad-dresses. We will set an example out of him to those who think of destroying the unity of the Iraqi nation that is fighting the occu-pation," the e-mail published by *Al-Sabah* read.

Insurgents frequently targeted *Al-Sabah* and other state-run media because of their ties to the U.S.-supported Iraqi govern-ment. About two dozen employees of the state-run Iraq Media Network, which in-cludes *Al-Sabah*, had been killed in the war, most by insurgents.

Safa Isma'il Enad, freelance
September 13, 2006, Baghdad

Enad, 31, a freelance photographer for several outlets including the defunct newspaper *Al-Watan*, was shot in a photo print shop in Baghdad's Ur neighborhood, according to the Journalistic Freedoms Observatory, an Iraqi press freedom or-ganization run by local journalists. Two gunmen entered the store on Sabah al-Khayat circle and asked for Enad by his first name, a source told CPJ. When the

photographer replied, they shot him. They dragged his body to their car and dumped it east of Baghdad, the source said.

Al-Watan, based in Tikrit, was affiliated with the Iraqi National Movement, a party established in 2001 that receives funds from the United States. The paper closed two months earlier for lack of money and was trying to re-establish itself as a magazine.

Ahmed Riyadh al-Karbouli
Baghdad TV
September 18, 2006, Ramadi

Six gunmen in two cars shot al-Karbouli, a reporter and cameraman, as he chatted with friends after midday prayers outside a mosque, CPJ sources said.

Al-Karbouli, 25, had received numerous death threats from insurgents over the past four months warning him to leave the sat-ellite channel. Baghdad TV is owned by the Iraqi Islamic Party, a major Sunni po-litical group in the country.

Ramadi, 70 miles (110 kilometers) west of Baghdad, forms the southwestern point of the Sunni Triangle, a focus of Sunni Muslim opposition to the U.S. presence in Iraq. Many journalists with Baghdad TV, including the channel's other correspon-dent in Ramadi, received death threats, a source at the station said.

Al-Karbouli worked at Baghdad TV for two years covering security and the plight of the residents of Ramadi. According to CPJ sources, his features offended some insurgents in Ramadi. A month earlier, gunmen stormed into his house and threat-ened him in front of his family.

Hussein Ali, Al-Shaabiya
Abdul-Rahim Nasrallah al-Shimari
Al-Shaabiya
Noufel al-Shimari, Al-Shaabiya
Thaker al-Shouwili, Al-Shaabiya
Ahmad Sha'ban, Al-Shaabiya
October 12, 2006, Baghdad

Masked gunmen in at least five vehicles drove up to the fledgling satellite TV channel Al-Shaabiya in the eastern district of Zayouna around 7 a.m., burst into the offices, executed 11 people, and wounded two others. It was the deadliest single assault on the press in Iraq since the U.S.-led invasion in March 2003. Five of the victims were journalists.

Al-Shaabiya is owned by the National Justice and Progress Party, headed by Abdul-Rahim Nasrallah al-Shimari, who was killed in the attack, according to Reuters and CPJ sources. The small party ran in the preceding election but failed to win any seats. Al-Shaabiya had not yet gone on the air and had run only test transmissions. Executive Manager Hassan Kamil told Reuters that the station had no political agenda and that the staff had been a mix of Sunnis, Shiites, and Kurds. The station had not been threatened previously.

Kamil said some of the gunmen wore police uniforms, and all were masked. News reports said the gunmen's cars resembled police vehicles.

A local press freedom group, The Journalistic Freedoms Observatory, named the dead as Chairman and General Manager Abdul-Rahim Nasrallah al-Shimari and his bodyguard, Ali Jabber; Deputy General Manager Noufel al-Shimari; presenters Thaker al-Shouwili and Ahmad Sha'ban; administrative manager Sami Nasrallah al-Shimari; video mixer Hussein Ali; and three guards identified by first names only: Maher, Ahmad, and Hassan. The station's generator operator, whose name was not available, was also killed. A source at Al-Shaabiya confirmed the names.

Program Manager Mushtak al-Ma'mouri and news chief Muhammad Kathem were hospitalized with gunshot wounds.

Saed Mahdi Shlash, *Rayat al-Arab*
October 26, 2006, Baghdad

Unidentified gunmen murdered Shlash and his wife as they drove up to their home in Baghdad's western neighborhood of Al-Aamariyeh, according to Abdullah al-Lamy, former head of the Iraqi Journalists Syndicate.

Al-Lamy, a friend of Shlash, said the journalist was a reporter for *Rayat al-Arab*, a newspaper associated with the Movement of Arab Nationalists. Shlash often wrote critically about the U.S. occupation of Iraq and called on Iraqis to set religious and political differences aside and unite for a free Iraq. He received several warnings to stop practicing journalism or leave Iraq, al-Lamy told CPJ. Al-Amariyah neighborhood is an insurgency stronghold where journalists are often targeted, CPJ research shows.

Naqshin Hamma Rashid, Atyaf
October 29, 2006, Baghdad

Unidentified gunmen killed Rashid, 30, a presenter for the Iraqi state television channel Atyaf, and her driver, Anis Qas-

JOURNALISTS KILLED IN 2006

sem, as the two were driving to work near Haifa Street in central Baghdad, according to CPJ sources.

Rashid, a Kurd also known by colleagues as Sherin Rashid, presented Kurdish-language news on Atyaf. Atyaf is part of the Iraqi Media Network and broadcasts in several languages, including Kurdish and English, according to CPJ sources. Colleagues at Al-Iraqiya, the main state television channel, said the murders were part of continued targeting of employees of the Iraqi Media Network.

About two dozen employees of the state-run Iraq Media Network, which includes Atyaf, were killed in the war, most by insurgents.

Muhammad al-Ban, Al-Sharqiya
November 13, 2006, Mosul

Unidentified gunmen shot al-Ban, 58, a reporter and cameraman for the privately owned Al-Sharqiya television station, as he was leaving his home in Mosul's Al-Nour neighborhood around 8 a.m., according to CPJ sources.

The gunmen used a Russian-made BKC machine gun mounted on the back of a pickup truck, a standard weapon used by Iraqi police and security, a CPJ source said. Four men then got out of the vehicle and shot several more times, the source said. Al-Ban's wife was wounded in the attack, The Associated Press reported.

According to a CPJ source, al-Ban received several death threats warning him not to cover Kurdish activities in the north. The source said that al-Ban's last report, on a Kurdish educational festival in Arbil, was done in defiance of the death threats.

Al-Ban worked for three years at Al-Sharqiya, according to a CPJ source. He had also been deputy editor of the leading local daily Al-Masar but had resigned seven months earlier to focus on his work for Al-Sharqiya.

Luma al-Karkhi, Al-Dustour
November 15, 2006, Baqubah

Al-Karkhi, 25, a reporter for the Baghdad-based daily Al-Dustour, was gunned down in the Tahreer neighborhood of Baqubah, northeast of Baghdad, while on her way to work. She stopped at a cell phone shop where several gunmen shot her, a source at the paper told CPJ.

Al-Karkhi had received several death threats from insurgents in Diyala province warning her to stop reporting, the source said. He said she had grown increasingly apprehensive about reporting in the province.

Nabil Ibrahim al-Dulaimi, Radio Dijla
December 4, 2006, Baghdad

Unidentified gunmen killed al-Dulaimi, 36, a news editor for the privately owned station, shortly after he left his home in Baghdad's Al-Washash neighborhood to go to work, sources at the station told CPJ. The station learned of the killing when a colleague called al-Dulaimi's home to inquire about the editor's whereabouts, the sources added. Radio Dijla had been targeted earlier in the year, when a broadcaster was kidnapped.

Aswan Ahmed Lutfallah
Associated Press Television News
December 12, 2006, Mosul

Gunmen killed Lutfallah, 35, an Iraqi cameraman for APTN, as he covered clashes between insurgents and police in the northern city of Mosul. The Associated Press reported that Lutfallah was having his car repaired in the city's eastern Al-Karama neighborhood when insurgents and police began fighting nearby. He rushed to cover the clash. Police Brig. Abdul-Karim Ahmed Khalaf said insurgents spotted him filming, approached him, and shot him to death, AP reported. Lutfallah had not reported any prior threats against him, the news agency added.

Lutfallah began his career at the Patriotic Union of Kurdistan-backed Kirkuk TV. He then worked for several other local television channels before joining APTN as a cameraman in 2005. Lutfallah is the second APTN cameraman to be killed under similar circumstances in Mosul. On April 23, 2005, cameraman Saleh Ibrahim was killed by gunfire near the city's Al-Yarmouk Circle, the scene of an earlier explosion that he and his brother-in-law, AP photographer Mohamed Ibrahim, had gone to cover.

LEBANON: 1

Layal Najib, freelance
July 23, 2006, Sadiqeen

Najib, 23, a freelance photographer for the Lebanese magazine *Al-Jaras* and Agence France-Presse, was the sole journalist to be killed when Israel began attacks on Lebanon in response to a cross-border raid by the Lebanese Shiite group Hezbollah.

Najib was hit by shrapnel from a missile while in a taxi on the road between the villages of Sadiqeen and Qana, according to news reports. Najib, who died at the scene, was trying to meet a convoy of villagers fleeing the Israeli bombardment of south Lebanon.

MEXICO: 2

Bradley Will, freelance
October 27, 2006
Santa Lucía del Camino

Will, 36, an independent documentary filmmaker and reporter for the news Web site *Indymedia*, was shot at 5:30 p.m. on October 27, while covering clashes between activists of the antigovernment Popular Assembly of the People of Oaxaca (APPO) and armed assailants.

Oswaldo Ramírez, a photographer for the Mexico City-based daily *Milenio* who was with Will and other Mexican journalists, told CPJ that armed men fired at the protesters. Will, who was standing nearby, was hit in the neck and abdomen.

Will had been covering the conflict in Oaxaca for at least six weeks. He had interviewed witnesses and activists, and shot footage of protests for a documentary on the conflict, the local human rights group, Red Oaxaqueña de Derechos Humanos, said in a statement.

The conflict in the colonial city started

May 22, when a strike by the local teachers union sparked a wave of antigovernment protests. After Oaxaca Gov. Ulises Ruiz Ortiz ordered police to disperse protesters with tear gas on June 14, leftist, indigenous, and student groups joined the protests, which became violent. APPO protesters had been calling for the ouster of Ruiz since the confrontation began. Several journalists covering the unrest were beaten and harassed by protesters and by police in civilian clothes, CPJ research showed.

Two local officials were detained in connection with Will's killing, but they were released within weeks. Mexican press reports said photographs and video footage documented the killing.

Roberto Marcos García, *Testimonio* and *Alarma*, November 21, 2006 Mandinga y Matoza

García, a reporter for the Veracruz-based publication *Testimonio* and local correspondent for the Mexico City weekly *Alarma*, was found murdered near the town of Mandinga y Matoza.

Traveling by motorcycle from Veracruz to the nearby city of Alvarado, García was run down by a stolen car with Mexico City plates at 1 p.m., the Mexican press reported. Unidentified assailants shot García while he was on the ground, twice in the head and at least four times in the chest, according to press reports and a CPJ source.

Marco Antonio Aguilar Yunes, a regional deputy prosecutor, told the U.S.-based Univisión that authorities found bullet casings from at least two guns at the scene and recovered the attackers' car.

García had reported for 13 years on violent crime and drug trafficking in Veracruz, a colleague told CPJ. García's last report, published a week before his death in the bimonthly *Testimonio*, detailed the activities of a gang of thieves who stole containers coming into the port of Veracruz, the colleague said. Other reporters in Veracruz said that García had previously received death threats on his cell phone.

State police arrested José Cortés Terrones, known as "El Loro," on December 1. Two weeks before the killing, Cortés allegedly warned García that two men angry with his crime reporting were going to kidnap him, the Veracruz daily *El Dictamen* reported. Cortés acknowledged he knew García but denied any involvement in the murder, local press reports said.

Cortés' arrest led to the detention of another suspect, Sergio Muñoz López, known as "El Drácula." Local press reports alleged that Muñoz was among a group of people who severely beat García three years ago in a work-related attack.

Colleagues told CPJ that they believe the killing was connected to García's crime reporting. Veracruz's top state prosecutor, Emeterio López Márquez, told CPJ in December that journalism and other motives were being considered.

PAKISTAN: 2

Munir Ahmed Sangi Kawish Television Network (KTN) May 29, 2006, Larkana

Sangi, a cameraman for the Sindhi-language KTN, was shot while covering a gunfight between members of the Unar and Abro tribes in the town of Larkana, in southeast Pakistan's Sindh district, according to local media reports. At least one other person was killed in the clash, which Sangi recorded before he died. KTN broadcast his video.

Police said Sangi was killed in crossfire, although some colleagues believe he may have been deliberately targeted for the station's reporting on a *jirga*, or tribal council, held by leaders of the Unar tribe, according to the Pakistan Federal Union of Journalists (PFUJ). An uncle and colleague of Sangi had recently been attacked in connection with KTN's reports that two children had been punished by the tribal court, PFUJ said.

Mazhar Abbas, secretary-general of the PFUJ, said Sangi's body was not recovered for several hours after he was shot. The local police chief suspended at least one police officer for negligence, according to media reports. Journalists in Larkana staged a sit-in to protest the killing.

Hayatullah Khan, freelance
June 16, 2006, Mir Ali

Khan's body was found by villagers in the North Waziristan town of Mir Ali, where he had been kidnapped six months earlier. Khan was abducted on December 5, 2005, by five gunmen who ran his car off the road as his younger brother, Haseenullah, watched helplessly. Local government officials and family members said Khan, 32, had been found handcuffed and shot several times. His body appeared frail and he

had grown a long beard since he was last seen, Pakistani journalists told CPJ.

The day before his abduction, Khan had photographed the apparent remnants of a U.S.-made missile said to have struck a home in the tribal region's main town, Miran Shah, on December 1, 2005, killing senior al-Qaeda figure Hamza Rabia. The pictures—widely distributed by the European Pressphoto Agency on the same day they were shot—contradicted the Pakistani government's explanation that Rabia had died in a blast caused by explosives located within the house. International media identified the fragments in the photographs as part of a Hellfire missile, possibly fired from a U.S. drone.

Khan, who was also a reporter for the Urdu-language daily *Ausaf*, had received numerous prior threats from Pakistani security forces, Taliban members, and local tribesmen because of his reporting.

During his six-month disappearance, government officials provided Khan's family with numerous and often contradictory accounts of his whereabouts: Khan was in government custody, soon to be released; Khan had been abducted by "miscreants;" he had been taken by Waziristan mujahedeen; he had been flown to the military base at Rawalpindi and then detained in Kohat air base.

After the body was found, Khan's relatives were told by hospital workers that he had suffered five or six bullet wounds and that one hand had been manacled in handcuffs typically used by Pakistan's powerful Inter-Services Intelligence agency. Mahmud Ali Durrani, Pakistan's ambassador to the United States, dismissed the reported presence of the handcuffs as circumstantial and said the cuffs could have been planted to incriminate the government. No autopsy was performed.

An investigation led by High Court Justice Mohammed Reza Khan was conducted, but the results were not made public. Khan's family said they were not interviewed by the judge or other investigators. North West Frontier Gov. Ali Mohammad Jan Orakzai told CPJ that North Waziristan was not secure enough to risk exposing a judicial figure to kidnapping or death.

PHILIPPINES: 3

Fernando Batul, DZRH and DYPR
May 22, 2006, Puerto Princesa

Batul, 37, a radio commentator with DZRH and DYPR radio, was shot six times by motorcycle-riding gunmen while he was driving to work in the provincial town of Puerto Princesa on the island of Palawan.

Police officer Aaron Madamay Golifardo was charged in the murder two days later, after being identified by eyewitnesses, according to news reports. In a May 11 broadcast, Batul had criticized Golifardo for allegedly showing a weapon during a disagreement with a waitress in a karaoke bar, according to news reports. Hearings in Golifardo's trial began in September. The other person on the motorcycle was not immediately identified.

Batul, a former vice mayor, was also highly critical of city government, and his reporting often touched on alleged government corruption and nepotism. In April, two unexploded hand grenades and a threatening letter were left at Batul's home, according to news reports and CPJ sources. The letter demanded that Batul stop his critical radio broadcasts, and he later told National Bureau of Investigation officials that he thought local police were behind the threat. He also sent text messages and spoke with media colleagues about the threat, CPJ sources said.

Two local journalists who worked with Batul and who were investigating his murder told CPJ that they had been threatened. In June, they said, they fled Palawan due to concerns about their safety.

George Vigo
Union of Catholic Asian News
Maricel Vigo, DXND
June 19, 2006, Mindanao

Two unidentified gunmen shot radio journalists George and Maricel Vigo near their home on the southern island of Mindanao. The married couple were walking home from a public market when they were shot at around 5:15 p.m. by men on a motorcycle. They died on the way to the hospital.

George Vigo was a contributor to the Bangkok-based church news agency Union of Catholic Asian News and was active in a local nongovernmental organization that helped rehabilitate internally displaced people. Maricel Vigo hosted a radio program on local station DXND.

The couple's recent reporting and commentary was considered uncontroversial, according to colleagues and local media groups. But the two had long careers reporting on alleged government corruption and right-wing militias. Offices of a tabloid newspaper founded by the Vigos, *The Headliner*, were the target of an apparent arson attack in 2001.

The couple had previously been active in left-wing student groups and in recent years had cultivated contacts within the militant Communist rebel organization, the New People's Army (NPA), as part of their reporting, according to colleagues. In 2003, George Vigo reported on the NPA for a BBC documentary titled "One Day of War," according to journalist Orlando Guzman, a friend who did reporting for the documentary.

Some of George Vigo's colleagues believe that the couple's murder may be connected to a video CD he received from the NPA, which showed a raid on a police station, according to Guzman. He told several colleagues that he had been followed after receiving the video and had expressed fear that military or local officials would target him.

German Doria, the central Mindanao police chief, told reporters that an NPA member had been identified as one of the gunmen and that the killing appeared to be in retaliation for George Vigo's cooperation with the Philippine military. The Philippine government announced a heightened military campaign against the rebels in early June. An NPA spokesman, however, denied involvement in the killing, according to news reports.

RUSSIA: 2

Vagif Kochetkov
Trud and *Tulsky Molodoi Kommunar*
January 8, 2006, Tula

Kochetkov, 31, a reporter in Tula, 125 miles (200 kilometers) south of Moscow, died in the Tula city hospital after undergoing surgery for a serious head injury he sustained in an attack two weeks before, according to CPJ interviews and local press reports.

Kochetkov was Tula correspondent for the Moscow daily *Trud* and a columnist for the local newspaper *Tulsky Molodoi Kommunar*, reporting on politics, social issues, and culture.

At least one assailant struck Kochetkov on the head with a blunt object and robbed him of a bag and cell phone as he approached his home in Tula on the evening of December 27, 2005, sources told CPJ. The bag was believed to have contained Kochetkov's passport, press card, credit card, and work-related documents. The attackers did not take Kochetkov's money or an expensive fur coat he was wearing. When a neighbor found Kochetkov's bag in her apartment building's basement, the bag contained everything but the documents related to Kochetkov's work, according to CPJ interviews with Kochetkov's parents, Valentina and Yuri, and Lena Shuletova, a friend and colleague.

On the night of the attack, the news agency ANN reported, Kochetkov told his parents he was meeting an unidentified person, after which he would return home to download his work onto his computer.

That evening, Valentina and Yuri Kochetkov told CPJ, the journalist called from a local coffee shop and told them that he'd be home in an hour. On the way, he was attacked.

Two neighbors found Kochetkov lying unconscious on the ground at around 2 a.m. on December 28. After regaining consciousness, Kochetkov walked home with the help of neighbors. He did not seek immediate medical attention or report the attack to the police.

Kochetkov was not admitted to the hospital until the next day, when doctors diagnosed him with two hematomas and said his condition was not life-threatening, Yuri Kochetkov told CPJ. Kochetkov's health began deteriorating January 1. He underwent brain surgery on January 5 and fell into a coma and died three days later. An autopsy showed Kochetkov had suffered a skull fracture, a concussion, multiple chest bruises, and other head injuries, according to press reports and CPJ interviews. Kochetkov never identified his attackers.

The Kochetkovs reported the attack on January 7, and police opened a criminal investigation, the parents told CPJ. By January 9, police said that they had identified a suspect.

On April 3, Tula prosecutors announced they had completed their investigation and determined Kochetkov's death to be the result of a robbery. That same day, prosecutors filed robbery and manslaughter charges against Yan Stakhanov, a 26-year-old Tula businessman.

Police did not focus on Kochetkov's work as a motive. Investigators did not question colleagues about Kochetkov's recent assign-

ments, nor did they look at the reporter's computer or notebooks for leads. CPJ research shows that Kochetkov had worked on sensitive issues prior to his murder.

Just prior to the attack, Kochetkov wrote an article in *Trud* on the activities of a Tula drug-dealing group. The December 16 article was headlined, "Revenge of the Mafia?" In June 2005, Kochetkov criticized the aggressive business practices of a local pharmaceutical company in another article.

Journalists at *Tulsky Molodoi Kommunar* said in late March that Kochetkov had received telephone threats in retaliation for his reporting, the Moscow-based news Web site *Newsinfo* said.

The trial of Stakhanov opened on April 17 in the Proletarski district court in Tula. Although the trial was said to be open, only one journalist at a time was admitted to the hearings. Officials cited lack of space in the courtroom, Valentina and Yuri Kochetkov told CPJ. Before the trial, Stakhanov allegedly confessed to killing Kochetkov but said later that the confession was coerced, local press reports said. During the trial, prosecutors said the assault on Kochetkov was part of a string of robberies in Tula, according to local press reports. The trial was recessed in September without an immediate date to reconvene, colleague Shuletova said.

Anna Politkovskaya, *Novaya Gazeta*
October 7, 2006, Moscow

Politkovskaya, 48, a journalist renowned for her critical coverage of the Chechen conflict, was found slain in her apartment building in Moscow, according to international news reports. The Interfax news agency, citing police, said Politkovskaya had been shot and that a pistol and four bullet casings had been found.

Politkovskaya, special correspondent for the independent Moscow newspaper *Novaya Gazeta*, was well known for her investigative reports on human rights abuses by the Russian military in Chechnya. In seven years covering the second Chechen war, Politkovskaya's reporting repeatedly drew the wrath of Russian authorities. She was threatened, jailed, forced into exile, and poisoned during her career, CPJ research shows.

Igor Korolkov, a colleague, told the *Regnum* news Web site that Politkovskaya had been reporting on alleged torture in Chechnya for a coming story.

CPJ had named Politkovskaya one of the world's top press freedom figures of the past 25 years in the fall 2006 edition of its magazine, *Dangerous Assignments*. In an interview for that profile, Politkovskaya noted the government's obstruction and harassment of journalists trying to cover the Chechen conflict and pointed to the deadly 2004 hostage crisis in the North Ossetian town of Beslan. "There is so much more to write about Beslan," she told CPJ, "but it gets more and more difficult when all the journalists who write are forced to leave."

Politkovskaya was poisoned on her way to cover the Beslan crisis. After drinking tea on a flight to the region, she became seriously ill and was hospitalized—but the toxin was never identified because the medical staff was instructed to destroy her blood tests.

Politkovskaya had been threatened and attacked numerous times in retaliation for her work. In February 2001, CPJ research shows, security agents detained her in the Vedeno district in Chechnya, accusing her of entering Chechnya without accreditation. She was kept in a pit for three days without food or water, while a military officer threatened to shoot her. Seven months later, she received death threats from a military officer accused of crimes against civilians. She was forced to flee to Vienna after the officer sent an e-mail to *Novaya Gazeta* promising that he would seek revenge.

When Politkovskaya covertly visited Chechnya in 2002 to investigate new allegations of human rights abuses, CPJ research shows, security officers arrested her, kept her overnight at a military base, and threatened her.

SOMALIA: 1

Martin Adler, freelance
June 23, 2006, Mogadishu

Adler, 47, an award-winning Swedish journalist and photographer, was shot by an unidentified gunman while filming a demonstration in the Somali capital. He was a longtime contributor to Britain's Channel 4 News. At the time of death, he was freelancing for several newspapers including the Swedish daily *Aftonbladet*.

An Associated Press reporter who witnessed the murder said the gunman came up from behind Adler and shot him in the back at close range before disappearing into the crowd. Adler died instantly. He was covering a demonstration organized by the Islamic Courts Union, which seized control of Mogadishu on June 5 from warlords backed by the United States. Several reports said he was filming demonstrators burning U.S. and Ethiopian flags. The National Union of Somali Journalists reported that Adler was standing in the crowd, not in the heavily guarded area where many other journalists and Islamic courts leaders were standing.

The rally, attended by thousands, was in support of a peace agreement reached June 22 in the Sudanese capital, Khartoum, between the Islamic courts and Somalia's transitional government. Demonstrators also protested against suggestions that foreign peacekeepers be sent to Somalia, according to the BBC. Anti-foreigner sentiment had been stoked by reports that some warlords had gotten CIA financing to help capture suspected al-Qaeda members in Somalia. International journalists had been stoned and harassed while reporting on demonstrations, AP said.

In a statement, Britain's Independent Television News company called Adler "a long-term friend" who had "contributed outstanding journalism and filmmaking." Adler won many international awards, including the 2001 Amnesty International Media Award, a Silver Prize for investigative journalism at the 2001 New York Film Festival, and the 2004 Rory Peck Award for hard news for a report that that exposed abuses by U.S. troops in Iraq. He had worked in more than two dozen war zones, including Iraq, Afghanistan, Bosnia, Rwanda, Congo, and Sierra Leone.

Adler was the 14th journalist killed in Somalia since the fall of former dictator Siad Barre in 1991, according to CPJ research. The country has had no effective central government since that time.

SRI LANKA: 1

Subramaniyam Sugitharajah
Sudar Oli
January 24, 2006, Trincomalee

An unidentified gunman killed Tamil journalist Sugitharajah as the reporter was on his way to work in the eastern port town of Trincomalee.

Sugitharajah, a part-time reporter for the Tamil-language daily *Sudar Oli*, was killed just weeks after he reported on the January 2 killing of five Tamil students in Trincomalee, according to news Web site *Tamil-Net*. Military spokesmen initially said that the men were killed by their own grenade in a botched attack on the army, but photographs taken by Sugitharajah showed that the men had died of gunshot wounds. The government ordered a probe into the deaths.

"Mr. Sugitharajah was a fearless reporter and we believe he was killed to demoralize journalists working in the northeast," *Sudar Oli* Managing Director E. Saravanapavam told The Associated Press.

The offices of *Sudar Oli* had been attacked repeatedly in the preceding months. On August 29, 2005, a grenade attack at the printing press killed a security guard. Just days earlier, activists from the People's Liberation Front (JVP) political party turned over to police a photographer for the newspaper and accused him of spying for the Liberation Tigers of Tamil Eelam (LTTE). The newspaper and its Jaffna-based sister publication *Uthayan* came under attack by both LTTE and anti-LTTE forces in political violence.

SUDAN: 1

Mohammed Taha Mohammed Ahmed
Al-Wifaq
September 6, 2006, Khartoum

Masked gunmen bundled Taha, editor-in-chief of the private daily *Al-Wifaq*, into a car outside his home in east Khartoum late on September 5. Police found his severed head next to his body in an area south of the capital the following day. His hands and feet were bound, according to a CPJ source and news reports.

Taha had angered Islamists by running an article about the Prophet Muhammad. He had also written critically about the political opposition and armed groups in Sudan's western Darfur region, according to press reports. No group claimed responsibility for the killing, Reuters reported.

Taha, 50, was an Islamist and former member of the National Islamic Front. But in May 2005, he was detained for several days, fined 8 million Sudanese pounds (US$3,200), and his paper closed for three months after he offended the country's powerful Islamists by republishing an article from the Internet that questioned the ancestry of the Prophet Muhammad. Demonstrators outside the courthouse demanded he be sentenced to death for blasphemy. Sudan is religiously conservative and penalizes blasphemy and insulting Islam with the death penalty.

Six months before the slaying, unidentified assailants set fire to the offices of *Al-Wifaq*, badly damaging the building. The perpetrators were never identified, a CPJ source said.

Several Sudanese journalists gathered at the Khartoum morgue to protest the murder and demand government protection for the press. The Arabic-language satellite news channel Al-Jazeera said Taha had fought many battles with the government and opposition parties over his writings and had made many political enemies.

TURKMENISTAN: 1

Ogulsapar Muradova
Radio Free Europe/Radio Liberty
September 2006, Ashgabat

Muradova, a reporter for the Turkmen service of Radio Free Europe/Radio Liberty (RFE/RL), died in prison sometime in September. Her body was released to her family on September 14, 2006. One Turkmen human rights group that had spoken with relatives said Muradova had suffered head and neck injuries.

Authorities in the capital, Ashgabat, handed over the body only after Western diplomats accompanied Muradova's children to the morgue, RFE/RL Turkmen Service Director Aleksandr Narodetsky told CPJ. Authorities refused the family's request for an autopsy and did not disclose the cause or date of death. Security forces later surrounded the Muradova home and prevented people from seeing the body or contacting Muradova's relatives.

Muradova, 58, had been convicted of possessing ammunition and sentenced to six years in jail after a closed-door trial that lasted only minutes. She had been denied legal counsel.

The Turkmenistan Helsinki Foundation, a human rights organization operating from Bulgaria, released a statement saying that Muradova's body showed a large head wound and bruises around the neck. The foundation, which also said Muradova had been drugged and tortured in jail, had spoken with her adult children before the telephone connection was abruptly cut. RFE/RL's Narodetsky also said that the children reported that their mother had a head wound.

VENEZUELA: 1

Jorge Aguirre, Cadena Capriles (*El Mundo*), April 5, 2006, Caracas

Aguirre, 60, a photographer with the newspaper chain Cadena Capriles, which publishes *El Mundo*, was shot as he approached an anticrime demonstration in Caracas. He was initially assigned to take pictures of stadium renovations, *El Mundo* Editor Enrique Rondón told CPJ.

The stadium is near Universidad Central de Venezuela, where demonstrators were protesting the recent killing of three young brothers. The slayings ignited street protests demanding a crackdown on crime, the Venezuelan press said.

After completing the stadium assignment, Aguirre decided to cover the nearby protest. He got into a white Toyota Corolla, provided by *El Mundo* and marked with the paper's logo. As Aguirre's car neared the protest around 3:30 p.m., a man driving a blue Yamaha motorcycle approached. The motorcyclist demanded that driver Julio Canelón stop the car, Rondón said. When Canelón asked why, the motorcyclist responded that he was with the authorities but did not show any identification, the editor told CPJ.

Rondón said the driver did not stop and proceeded to the protest scene. The motorcyclist followed and shot Aguirre four times as he was getting out of the car with his camera. Aguirre managed to take a picture of the killer's back fleeing the scene on his motorcycle, Rondón said. With the help of bystanders, the driver put Aguirre in the car and took him to a local hospital. The journalist died a few hours later.

Boris Lenis Blanco, a former Chacao police officer, was arrested in the killing on April 13. Members of the national crime police apprehended Blanco when a former colleague identified him as the driver of the motorcycle, the Caracas-based daily *El Universal* reported.

30 JOURNALISTS KILLED: MOTIVE UNCONFIRMED

COLOMBIA: 1

Milton Fabián Sánchez
Yumbo Estéreo
August 9, 2006, Yumbo

Sánchez, 38, a host on local radio station Yumbo Estéreo, was shot three times by a masked assailant outside his home in Yumbo, in southwestern Valle del Cauca province, at around 9:45 p.m., colleague Leonardo Orozco told CPJ.

Witnesses said the assailant had been waiting in the bushes behind Sánchez's home, he said. Sánchez was taken to a local hospital and then to Valle University Hospital in the provincial capital, Cali, before dying at around midnight, Orozco said.

Sánchez was host of three weekly programs. "Notas de Gestión" and "La Personería," were civic education programs funded by the local government. The third, "Mesa Redonda," was a community-based opinion program, Orozco told CPJ.

During "Mesa Redonda" broadcasts, Orozco said, Sánchez sometimes criticized the performance of the local government. Sánchez once had been spokesman for the local mayor, according to the mayor's press office. Orozco said that Sánchez had not mentioned getting threats.

Cali Police Cmdr. José Roberto León told CPJ that a joint investigation with the Cali state prosecutor had been opened. There were no concrete leads, he said.

DEMOCRATIC REPUBLIC OF CONGO: 1

Bapuwa Mwamba, freelance
July 8, 2006, Kinshasa

Mwamba, a Congolese journalist who worked for several local publications, was killed by unidentified gunmen who burst into his home in the capital, Kinshasa. He was shot in the leg and died from loss of blood on the way to the hospital, the local press freedom organization Journaliste en Danger (JED) reported.

Information Minister Henri Mova Sakanyi condemned the killing in an interview with the U.N.-backed Radio Okapi, announcing that he would meet with President Joseph Kabila and other high-ranking government officials "to speed the investigation." In March, men wearing military uniforms had raided Mwamba's house, stealing a cell phone and $850 in cash, JED reported.

The killing occurred amid campaigning for July 30 presidential and parliamentary elections, the first since independence in 1960.

ECUADOR: 1

José Luis León Desiderio
Radio Minutera
February 13 or 14, 2006, Guayaquil

León, 43, host of a daily news program "Opinión" on local Radio Minutera, was shot in the coastal city of Guayaquil. León often denounced gang violence and police inaction in the city, Alejandro Alvarez, a reporter for the daily *El Universo*, told CPJ.

León left his home at 11 p.m. on February 13 to meet his wife, Jenny Piza, at a nearby bus stop, but the two never met. León's wife and daughter found his body near their home early the next day, February 14. Press reports initially said that León had been shot three times, but his wife told CPJ that León was shot once in the head. He was not robbed.

Piza told CPJ that León had received a text message on his cell phone threatening him with death a few days before his murder. According to Hugo Asencio, news director for the radio program, a few weeks before the murder León had told him that a group of unidentified men hurled stones at his house.

León often reported on gang violence, drug trafficking, and the lack of police in Guayaquil's suburbs, local press reports said. León also worked at a printing press and was studying journalism, Piza told CPJ. On March 2, Guayaquil prosecutor Manuel Alvear Hernández ordered the national police to launch an investigation into the murder. The prosecutor asked Radio Minutera to provide audiotapes of the program to investigators.

In June, three men were accused in the killing, according to *El Universo*. In a report made public on October 27, local prosecutor Miriam Rosales Riofrío cited insufficient evidence in clearing two of the men. *El Universo* reported that the third man, Medardo Bone Bone, was held after two witnesses identified him as the gunman. No motive was immediately established.

GUATEMALA: 1

Eduardo Maas Bol, Radio Punto
September 9, 2006, Cobán

Maas, 58, Cobán correspondent for the Guatemala City-based Radio Punto, was found dead at around 4 a.m. in his parked car near the road that connects central Cobán to Guatemala City.

Maas was shot four times, in the head, left arm, back, and chest, local prosecutor Genaro Pacheco told CPJ. The reporter was on his way to his house after driving a colleague home from a party, his brother Félix Maas Bol told CPJ. Pacheco said the journalist's wallet and gold jewelry were found intact. Maas reported news from the Alta Verapaz region. Félix Maas told CPJ that his brother had not been threatened.

Maas also worked as a supervisor for the Ministry of Education, as a spokesman for the local journalists union, and as a human rights advocate, according to his brother. Until three months prior to his death, Maas had directed the daily news program "Correo del Norte" on local Radio Mía, which he left after a change in the station's administration, said Eduardo Fam Chun, the vice president of the local journalists union.

Local authorities detained a suspect in September, according to local press accounts. Hugo Pop, a spokesman for the special prosecutor for human rights, told CPJ that a motive had not been determined, but investigators were looking into Maas' reporting as a possible reason.

INDIA: 1

Arun Narayan Dekate, *Tarun Bharat*
June 10, 2006, Nagpur

Up to four unidentified men attacked Dekate on June 8 as he was riding with a friend on a motorcycle, according to *The Hindu* newspaper. He was pounded with rocks and died from his injuries in a hospital in Nagpur on June 10. Dekate was a reporter with the Marathi-language daily *Tarun Bharat* in Nagpur, central India.

Police did not cite a motive for the attack. Indian media reports said Dekate had recently written articles about illegal gambling in Takalghat village, about 19 miles (30 kilometers) from Nagpur. Dekate also cooperated with police from the nearest town, Bori, in their investigations, which had apparently resulted in several arrests.

IRAQ: 8

Abdel Majid al-Mehmedawi, freelance
May 5, 2006, Baghdad

Al-Mehmedawi, who had reported on social issues, was murdered by unidentified gunmen in Baghdad's center, according to local sources. The motive was unknown.

Alaa Hassan, Inter Press Service
June 28, 2006, Baghdad

Hassan, 35, an Iraqi freelance reporter for Inter Press Service (IPS), was killed by assailants who sprayed his car with gunfire as he crossed Baghdad's Al-Muthana Bridge, a spot notorious for insurgent attacks.

"It appears he was not targeted but was just in the wrong place at the wrong time, part of the senseless violence engulfing Iraq since the U.S.-led invasion in March 2003," the news agency reported in July.

Hassan had only recently begun freelancing for the news service. He also managed a stationery store, according to Editor Sanjay Suri. Hassan was not on assignment for IPS at the time of his death, Suri said. "The only way from his neighborhood to central Baghdad was to cross the Al-Muthana Bridge over the Tigris River, a regular spot for insurgent attacks," wrote reporter Aaron Glanz, who worked with Hassan. "Because of an Iraqi police checkpoint and a bend, every car passing over the bridge has to slow down. Killings occur here many times a week."

Osama Qadir, freelance
June 29, 2006, Baghdad

The body of Qadir, a freelance cameraman who worked occasionally for Fox News and other media organizations in Iraq, was found on or about June 29 with several bullet wounds, according to the Journalistic Freedoms Observatory, a local Iraqi press freedom group.

He had been abducted by unknown assailants in Baghdad about a week earlier. The circumstances surrounding his death were unclear. John Stack, a Fox News vice president, confirmed Qadir's death but said the journalist was not on assignment for the network at the time of his abduction. He said the station had no indication that the murder was in retaliation for his work.

Hadi Anawi al-Joubouri, freelance
September 12, 2006, Diyala

Al-Joubouri, 56, a freelancer and representative of the Iraqi Journalists Syndicate in the eastern province of Diyala, was ambushed as he drove between Baquba and Khalis, about 125 miles (200 kilometers) northeast of Baghdad, according to the Journalistic Freedoms Observatory. His body was found riddled with bullets.

Azad Muhammad Hussein
Radio Dar Al-Salam
October 10, 2006, Baghdad

The body of Hussein, 29, a reporter for the Iraqi Islamic Party-owned Radio Dar Al-Salam, was identified in the Baghdad morgue on October 10, according to the Journalistic Freedoms Observatory, an Iraqi press freedom organization.

The journalist had been kidnapped from Al-Shaab neighborhood in northern Baghdad on October 3. The motive for the abduction and killing was not clear.

Raed Qays, Sawt al-Iraq
October 13, 2006, Baghdad

Unidentified gunmen murdered Qays, a journalist for radio station Sawt al-Iraq, according to CPJ sources. The assailants intercepted the journalist's vehicle in Baghdad's northern neighborhood of Al-Dura, the Journalistic Freedoms Observatory reported, citing the independent news agency Aswat al-Iraq.

Qays' sister, a passenger, was unharmed, the observatory said. Qays, 28, also worked for Radio Sumer, part of the Iraqi satellite network Al-Sumaria.

Ahmad al-Rashid, Al-Sharqiya
November 3, 2006, Baghdad

Al-Rashid, 28, an Al-Sharqiya correspondent, was shot in north Baghdad's Al-Aathamiya neighborhood, according to CPJ sources. Al-Rashid, who began working for Al-Sharqiya three months earlier, was visiting family when he was stopped by gunmen, asked to exit his car, and shot in front of witnesses, CPJ sources said. Al-Sharqiya is owned by the London-based Azzaman Group, which also publishes the Iraqi daily *Azzaman*.

Yasin al-Dulaimi, Radio Al-Mustaqbal
December 26, 2006, Baghdad

Al-Dulaimi, a Ramadi-based reporter for Radio Al-Mustaqbal, was killed in a bombing in Baghdad's Al-Kahdimiya neighborhood, where his parents lived, according to al-Dulaimi's colleagues. It was unclear whether al-Dulaimi was on assignment at the time. CPJ is investigating the circumstances.

MEXICO: 5

Jaime Arturo Olvera Bravo, freelance
March 9, 2006, La Piedad

Olvera, a freelance photographer and former correspondent for the Morelia-based daily *La Voz de Michoacán*, was shot outside his home in La Piedad in the central state of Michoacán.

Olvera left his home around 8 p.m. with his 5-year-old son. While they were waiting at a bus stop, an unknown assailant approached Olvera and fired at close range, according to local press reports. A bullet struck Olvera in the neck, and he died at the scene. His son was unharmed.

Olvera worked for *La Voz de Michoacán* until April 2002 when he resigned to become a salesman for a processed meat company, the paper reported. Olvera continued working as a freelancer, providing photographs and crime tips to local media, the Mexico City-based *El Universal* said.

Enrique Perea Quintanilla
Dos Caras, Una Verdad
August 9, 2006, Chihuahua

The body of Perea, a longtime police reporter who became editor of a crime magazine, was found at 2 p.m. on the side of a road about 9 miles (15 kilometers) south of Chihuahua, Eduardo Esparza, a spokesman for the Chihuahua state prosecutor, told CPJ. Perea was shot once in the head and once in the back with a .45-caliber gun.

Perea was editor of a monthly magazine, *Dos Caras, Una Verdad* (Two Sides, One Truth), which specialized in reporting on closed murder cases and local drug trafficking. He had worked for 20 years as a police reporter for the dailies *El Heraldo* and *El Diario* until becoming the magazine's editor in 2005, his former colleague and editor at *El Heraldo*, César Ibarra, told CPJ.

Esparza said the journalist was last seen leaving his office in his car at 11 a.m. on Au-

gust 8, but the car was found abandoned in Chihuahua's center that night. Perea's two sons reported the journalist missing.

Esparza said the state prosecutor's office believed the murder was the work of organized crime. While the motive was not immediately clear, he said, Perea's journalism was one of the investigation's leads.

Misael Tamayo Hernández
El Despertar de la Costa
November 10, 2006, Ixtapa

A security guard at the Venus Motel near the southern city of Ixtapa found Tamayo's body at 7:30 a.m., local police Cmdr. Mario Cruz Gallardo told CPJ. Motel staff said that Tamayo, editor and owner of the daily *El Despertar de la Costa* in the nearby city of Zihuatanejo, arrived at the motel at about 1:30 a.m., according to local press reports. The car in which he was believed to have arrived left the motel parking lot two hours before the body was found, *El Despertar de la Costa* reported.

Tamayo had left his office at 9 a.m. the day before, November 9, to have breakfast with the manager of a local bus company, said his sister, Rebeca Tamayo. The editor called the office at 10:30 a.m. to give instructions to a reporter looking into a story on water quality in a nearby town. Tamayo didn't return to work that day, and he did not answer cell phone calls from colleagues. At 3 a.m. on November 10, Tamayo's family notified authorities that he was missing.

Ruth Tamayo, another sister, said the local coroner told her that a preliminary autopsy found that her brother died from a massive heart attack. In an interview with

CPJ, Ruth Tamayo said she viewed the body and saw what appeared to be three small puncture marks in one arm. Both Ruth and Rebecca Tamayo work at the family-run *El Despertar de la Costa*.

Tamayo's family and colleagues said that he was critical of local government corruption and criminal activities. Tamayo's sisters told CPJ that their brother had received a threatening call from an unidentified individual two months prior to his death, but Tamayo did not take the threat seriously.

José Manuel Nava Sánchez
El Sol de México
November 16, 2006, Mexico City

Nava's body was found around 9 a.m. by a cleaner in his Mexico City apartment, according to local press reports. Columnist for the national daily *El Sol de México* and former director of the Mexico City-based daily *Excélsior*, he had been stabbed at least seven times in the neck and chest. Local authorities told reporters that a number of valuable items were apparently missing from the journalist's home.

Nava had been *Excélsior's* director from February 2002 until December 2005, when the paper was bought by Grupo Imagen, owner of several Mexican radio stations. Until then, *Excélsior* had been run by employees as a cooperative. Before taking over as director, Nava had been *Excélsior's* Washington correspondent for 16 years.

In September, Nava began writing the daily column "Nuevo Poder" (New Power) for *El Sol de México*, said Guillermo Chao, information director for the Mexican Editorial Organization, which owns the daily.

Nava's columns focused on political and social analysis, Chao told CPJ.

On November 6, Nava published a book titled *Excélsior, el Asalto Final* (Excélsior, the Final Assault), which criticized government officials, *Excélsior* employees, and business people for their roles in the demise of *Excélsior* as a cooperative, the local press reported. Nava accused several individuals of dishonesty, The Associated Press quoted Octavio Colmenares, a spokesman for the book's publisher Libros para Todos Editorial, as saying. Both Colmenares and Chao said that they knew of no threats against Nava.

Authorities believe Nava knew his murderer and that he was killed for personal reasons, according to a spokesman for the special prosecutor for crimes against journalists. The spokesman told CPJ in December that investigators had put aside theories related to Nava's book.

Adolfo Sánchez Guzmán
Orizaba en Vivo
November 30, 2006, Mendoza

Sánchez, 31, a reporter for the Mexican news Web site *Orizaba en Vivo*, was found shot to death on the banks of the Blanco River near Mendoza in the southeastern state of Veracruz on November 30.

On November 28, Sánchez and three friends left his home in Orizaba, just east of Mendoza, said Rodolfo Mendoza, administrative director of *Orizaba en Vivo*. Local authorities found the journalist's car abandoned the next day.

His body was found with two gunshots to the back of the head. Sánchez had bruises and stab wounds to the chest, a police source in Mendoza told CPJ. Nearby was the body of another man, César Martínez López, alias "El Pollo," who had also been shot in the head, the source said.

The reporter's family and colleagues did not know of any threats against Sánchez, who normally covered regional politics, Rodolfo Mendoza told CPJ. Two suspects were detained on December 4. Investigators said the men targeted Martínez because they thought he had stolen their truck, The Associated Press said.

well as the *African Guardian* which was shut down in 1994 by the military regime of Sani Abacha. In 1996, still under the Abacha regime, Agbroko spent several months in jail for his work. In 1997, PEN American Center awarded him its prestigious Barbara Goldsmith Freedom to Write Award. At *ThisDay*, he was not only board chairman but also a prominent columnist with a weekly column, "This Nation." His last column was a political satire on the presidential primaries of the ruling PDP party.

NIGERIA: 1

Godwin Agbroko, *ThisDay*
December 22, 2006, Lagos

Agbroko, editorial board chairman of the private daily *ThisDay*, was found shot to death in his car, according to local and international media reports.

The circumstances of the killing were not immediately clear. Several initial reports quoted a *ThisDay* statement as saying that Agbroko was slain when he encountered the scene of a robbery. CPJ sources were unable to confirm that description. *ThisDay* later distanced itself from the original statement, saying it would await the results of a police investigation. A police spokesman contacted by CPJ declined to provide details, citing the pending investigation.

Local journalists told CPJ that Agbroko was killed by a single shot to the neck, and that his valuables were untouched.

Agbroko, 53, was a former editor of *Newswatch* and *The Week* magazines, as

PAKISTAN: 1

Mohammad Ismail
Pakistan Press International
November 1, 2006, Islamabad

Ismail, Islamabad bureau chief for Pakistan Press International, was found on the morning of November 1 near his home in Islamabad with his head "smashed with some hard blunt object," according to Mazhar Abbas, secretary-general of the Pakistan Federal Union of Journalists. The Associated Press reported that a police investigator said an iron bar may have been used as a weapon.

Ismail, nearing retirement, was last seen the previous night as he was leaving his house to take a walk. Doctors who received the body when it was taken to a local hospital told PFUJ that Ismail had been dead a few hours before being discovered.

Ismail's family told Abbas that they were at a loss as to what could have prompted the attack. They told him Ismail was carrying little of value when he was assaulted. Ismail's news agency is not known for particularly critical reporting of the government, CPJ research shows.

PHILIPPINES: 5

Rolly Cañete, freelance
January 20, 2006, Pagadian City

Unidentified gunmen killed radio broadcaster and political publicist Cañete on a busy street in the southern city of Pagadian. International news reports said the attackers fled on a motorcycle.

Cañete was a block-time broadcaster on three radio stations. Two of the stations, DXPA and DXBZ, were controlled by Congressman Antonio Cerilles and his wife, provincial Gov. Aurora Cerilles, the reports said. Both politicians employed Cañete as their publicist and paid for his radio programs.

Cañete frequently criticized opponents of Cerilles on his daily radio programs, and police believe that his work for the politicians may have been a motive in his killing. Philippine National Police Chief Arturo C. Lomibao told reporters that charges were filed against two suspects.

Cañete leased airtime under a practice known as block-timing, in which commentators also solicit their own advertisers. A number of block-time broadcasters have been killed in recent years.

Orlando Tapios Mendoza, freelance
April 4, 2006, Tarlac

Mendoza, a part-time newspaper editor and columnist, was shot several times by unidentified men as he was returning home in Tarlac, 65 miles (110 kilometers) north of Manila. He was pronounced dead at the scene, according to local media reports.

Mendoza, 58, reported and edited for small local newspapers—the *Tarlac Profile* and *Tarlac Patrol*—and wrote several pieces on land disputes before his death, according to the Manila-based Center for Media Freedom and Responsibility (CMFR).

Philippine National Police Chief Arturo Lomibao told reporters that "information on the killing of Orlando Mendoza points to the victim's involvement in land disputes as the motive for the crime."

Before Mendoza became a journalist in 1998, he was responsible for implementing the government's land reform program. Land ownership claims are often highly contested and result in animosity in the Philippines.

Armando Pace, DXDS
July 18, 2006, Digos City

Pace, 51, an outspoken block-time commentator on Radyo Ukay DXDS, was shot in the head and chest by two motorcycle-riding assailants while traveling home from work on a busy street in Digos City on the island of Mindanao. He died shortly after arriving at a local hospital.

On July 20, Digos City police arrested Joy Anticamara in the murder. Police said a young woman witnessed the shooting from 15 to 30 feet away and identified Anticamara in a lineup. Digos City Police Director Caesar Cabuhat said that Pace's killing could have been "a personal or work-related crime," according to news reports.

Police investigators also questioned Jesus Saraum, who allegedly owned the motorcycle used in the killing. Isidro Lapeña, Philippine National Police deputy director-general, said blood found on Saraum's motorcycle matched that of the victim.

Pace was known for stinging radio commentaries that often targeted local politicians. News reports noted that he had been the target of a number of libel lawsuits filed by politicians, business people, and others.

Ponciano Grande, DWJJ
December 7, 2006, Cabantuan City

Two unidentified gunmen killed Grande, 53, a former newspaper columnist and occasional co-host of a radio variety show, at his farm in Cabantuan City, central Luzon. The assailants shot Grande five times and chased his wife, Annie Luwag-Grande, but did not harm her, according to the online news site *INQ7* and the National Union of Journalists of the Philippines.

Grande, former director of the Nueva Ecija Press Club, wrote columns for the local weeklies *The Recorder* and *Nueva Ecija Times* until 2002, and had recently co-hosted a radio program with his wife on radio station DWJJ.

Grande had retired from writing columns in order to manage the family farm, *INQ7* reported. Police were investigating the motive for the attack, according to Deutsche Presse-Agentur.

Andres Acosta, DZJC
December 20, 2006, Batac

An unidentified attacker stabbed commentator Acosta in the town of Batac, 240 miles (390 kilometers) north of Manila. Stabbed in the head and body, Acosta collapsed on his motorcycle while trying to get to a hospital.

Batac Police Chief Bienvenido Rayco told local reporters that the killing might have been work-related. "He had been receiving death threats," Rayco said, without giving further details. He also noted that Acosta had been a witness in a court case and could have been targeted in revenge. Another DZJC commentator, Roger Mariano, was killed in 2004.

RUSSIA: 2

Ilya Zimin, NTV
February 26, 2006, Moscow

Zimin, 33, a correspondent for the national television station NTV, was found murdered in his Moscow apartment. Colleagues went to Zimin's home on February 27 after the reporter failed to show up for work or answer his phone, according to local press reports. They found his heavily beaten corpse lying face down in a pool of blood and much of the furniture overturned in what appeared to be a sign of a violent struggle, according to local and international press reports.

Medical experts determined that Zimin probably died around 3 p.m. the day before, February 26, as a result of head trauma. The Moscow city prosecutor opened a murder investigation. A laptop computer and cell phone were stolen from the apartment, and a bloody fingerprint belonging to someone other than the victim was found on a light switch, local news outlets reported.

Authorities said the killing was probably not related to Zimin's work at NTV. Prosecutor Anatoly Zuyev said the murder was most likely a common crime resulting from an argument. He said there was no sign of forced entry, suggesting that Zimin knew his assailant, according to press reports.

NTV News Editor Tatyana Mitkova said she did not rule out the possibility that the murder was linked to Zimin's work for the station, the news Web site *Polit* reported. Zimin worked as a correspondent for NTV's investigative program "Profession: Reporter." Colleague Vadim Takmenev said Zimin had recently used hidden cameras to prepare an exposé of health violations at expensive Moscow restaurants, *Polit* reported.

Authorities did not immediately identify a suspect, according to the Moscow daily *Kommersant*. A concierge at Zimin's apartment building initially reported that three men with police identifications visited the reporter at 10 a.m. on February 26 and left an hour later, but authorities said they determined the three had visited another apartment in the building, according to *Kommersant*.

Zimin was assaulted, robbed, and hospitalized with a broken leg in April 2005, but he did not link the attack to his work, the Moscow daily *Novoye Izvestiya* reported. Born in the far eastern city of Vladivostok, he had worked as a local correspondent for state television GTRK and NTV before moving to Moscow in 2000.

Yevgeny Gerasimenko
Saratovsky Rasklad
July 26, 2006, Saratov

Gerasimenko, a correspondent for the independent weekly *Saratovsky Rasklad*, was found dead in his apartment in Saratov in southeastern Russia, according to local press reports. Saratov Department of Interior spokesman Denis Zheltov said forensic evidence indicated that Gerasimenko had been killed around 1 a.m., the local television channel GTRK Saratov reported.

Gerasimenko's mother found the journalist with a plastic bag over his head and multiple bruises on his body. Police found no signs of forced entry, but Gerasimenko's computer was missing, local reports said. Gerasimenko had been investigating the corporate takeover of a local commercial enterprise, *Saratovsky Rasklad* Editor-in-Chief Vladimir Spiryagin told the *United Volga* news Web site.

In November, a regional court in Saratov convicted a local man, Sergei Finogeyev, in the killing and sentenced him to 18 years in prison. In a statement, the prosecutor's office said the slaying occurred during a robbery.

SRI LANKA: 2

Sampath Lakmal, *Sathdina*
July 1, 2006, Colombo

The body of reporter Lakmal, a contributor to the Sinhala-language weekly *Sathdina*, was found in suburban Colombo on July 2. He had been shot after leaving his house to meet a contact on July 1, according to local media reports and the Colombo-based Free Media Movement (FMM).

Lakmal, 24, had gathered news for several media outlets in Colombo, according to FMM. He reported on crime and the conflict between the government and the Liberation Tigers of Tamil Eelam rebel group. His colleagues told the Colombo-based newspaper *Morning Leader* that he had received threats from intelligence agents, Tamil and Sinhalese politicians, and members of the criminal underworld.

Sinnathamby Sivamaharajah
Namathu Eelanadu
August 20, 2006, Jaffna

Sivamaharajah, a Tamil newspaper editor and former member of parliament, was killed outside his home on the besieged Jaffna peninsula, international and local media reported. Sivamaharajah, managing director of the Tamil-language *Namathu Eelanadu*, was shot dead in Vellippalai. The motive was unclear.

Sivamaharajah, 68, was a former MP of the Tamil United Liberation Front, and a member of the Tamil National Alliance, a pro-separatist party thought to be the political wing of the Liberation Tigers of Tamil Eelam rebels. *Namathu Eelanadu* was considered sympathetic to the Tamil nationalist cause.

VENEZUELA: 1

Jesús Rafael Flores Rojas, *La Región*
August 23, 2006, El Tigre

Flores, 66, columnist and Anzoátegui coordinator for the Cumaná-based daily *La Región*, was shot by an unidentified assailant in front of his house.

At 9 p.m., as Flores and his daughter Nancy were putting their car into the garage, an armed man approached the journalist. The daughter said that she implored the attacker to take their car and money, but the assailant told her that he wasn't there for either and shot the journalist repeatedly. Flores was struck eight times, in the face, neck, and arm, Luis Marcano Barrios, editor of *La Región*, told CPJ.

Flores wrote a weekly column in which he often criticized local government officials. Marcano said Flores had told him that he had received several death threats, the most recent coming a month earlier when an unidentified caller told Flores to stop criticizing the municipal government. Family members said they didn't know of any threats against Flores, the local press reported.

Police Commissioner José Rivero Alfonzo told reporters that the murder appeared to be the work of a professional hit man. Rivero said that police were reviewing Flores' columns in search of a motive or suspects.

INTERNET FUELS RISE IN NUMBER
OF JAILED JOURNALISTS

T he number of journalists jailed worldwide for their work increased for the second consecutive year, and one in three was an Internet blogger, online editor, or Web-based reporter. CPJ's annual worldwide census found 134 journalists imprisoned on December 1, an increase of nine from the 2005 tally. China, Cuba, Eritrea, and Ethiopia were the top four jailers among the 24 nations who imprisoned journalists.

Print reporters, editors, and photographers continued to make up the largest professional category, with 67 cases in 2006, but Internet journalists were a growing segment of the census and constituted the second largest category, with 49 cases. The number of imprisoned journalists whose work appeared primarily on the Web, via e-mail, or in another electronic form has increased each year since 1997, when CPJ recorded the first jailed Internet writer in its annual census. The 2006 roster of imprisoned Internet journalists included China's "citizen reporters," independent Cuban writers who filed reports for overseas Web sites, and American video blogger Joshua Wolf, who refused to hand over footage to a grand jury.

Over all, "antistate" allegations such as subversion, divulging state secrets, and acting against the interests of the state were the most common charges used to imprison journalists worldwide. Eighty-four journalists were jailed under these charges, many by the Chinese, Cuban, and Ethiopian governments.

But CPJ also found an increasing number of journalists held without any charge or trial at all. Twenty imprisoned journalists, or 15 percent, had been denied even the most basic elements of due process, CPJ found. Eritrea, which accounted for more than half of these cases, kept journalists in secret locations and withheld basic information about their well-being. The United States imprisoned two journalists without charge or trial: Associated Press photographer Bilal Hussein, in Iraq; and Al-Jazeera cameraman Sami al-Haj, at the U.S. Naval Base at Guantánamo Bay, Cuba.

For the eighth consecutive year, China was the world's leading jailer of journalists, with 31 imprisoned. About three-quarters of the cases in China were brought under vague "antistate" laws; 19 cases involved Internet journalists. China's list included Shi Tao, an internationally recognized journalist serving a 10-year sentence for posting notes online detailing propaganda department instructions on how to cover the anniversary of the Tiananmen Square crackdown. The government declared the instructions a "state secret."

Cuba ranked second, with 24 reporters, writers, and editors behind bars, most of them jailed in the country's massive March 2003 crackdown on dissidents and the independent press. Nearly all of those on Cuba's list had filed news and commentary with overseas Web sites. These journalists used phone lines and faxes, not computers, to transmit their reports; once posted, their articles were seen across the world but almost never in Cuba, where the government heavily restricts Internet access.

Eritrea was the leader among African countries, with 23 journalists in prison. These prisoners were being held incommunicado, and their well-being was a growing source of concern. A non-bylined report, circulated on several Web sites in August and deemed by CPJ sources to be generally credible, claimed that three of the journalists may have died. CPJ and other international organizations urgently sought information from officials in Asmara, but the government refused to provide basic facts about the journalists' whereabouts, their health, or whether they were still alive.

Neighboring Ethiopia imprisoned 18 journalists, most of whom were being tried for treason after being swept up by authorities in a November 2005 crackdown on dissent. A CPJ investigation in April found no basis for the government's treason charges. Burma, which held seven journalists, was fifth among nations, followed by Uzbekistan, which imprisoned five. Azerbaijan, Burundi, and the United States were seventh on the list of nations, each having jailed three journalists.

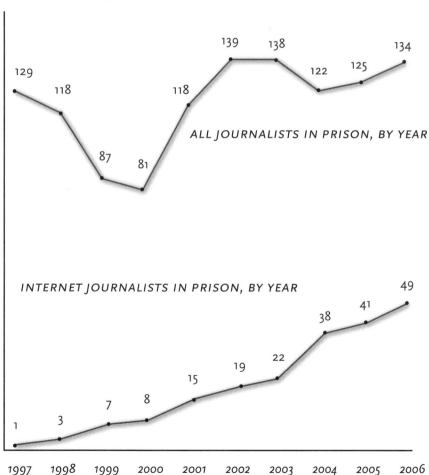

ALL JOURNALISTS IN PRISON, BY YEAR

129 118 87 81 118 139 138 122 125 134

INTERNET JOURNALISTS IN PRISON, BY YEAR

1 3 7 8 15 19 22 38 41 49

1997 1998 1999 2000 2001 2002 2003 2004 2005 2006

Here are other trends and details that emerged in CPJ's analysis:

- In about 10 percent of cases, governments used a variety of charges unrelated to journalism to retaliate against critical writers, editors, and photojournalists. Such charges ranged from property damage and regulatory violations to drug possession and association with extremists. In the cases included in this census, CPJ determined that the charges were most likely lodged in reprisal for the journalist's work.

- Spreading ethnic or religious "hatred" was the next most common charge used to imprison journalists worldwide. Such charges were lodged in about 4 percent of cases.

- Criminal defamation charges were filed in about 3 percent of cases, a slight decline from the rate recorded in previous years. A growing number of nations, particularly in Western Europe, have moved to decriminalize defamation and insult.

- Violations of censorship rules accounted for another 3 percent of cases. Burma, for example, jailed two journalists in March for violating prohibitions on photographing or filming the country's new capital, Pyinmana.

- Television journalists accounted for eight cases on the CPJ census; radio journalists eight; documentary filmmakers two.

- The longest-serving journalists in CPJ's census were Chen Renjie and Lin Youping, who were jailed in China in July 1983 for publishing a pamphlet titled *Ziyou Bao* (Freedom Report). Co-defendant Chen Biling was executed.

CPJ believes that journalists should not be imprisoned for doing their jobs. The organization sent letters expressing its serious concerns to each country that imprisoned a journalist. In addition, CPJ sent requests during the year to Eritrean and U.S. officials seeking details in the cases in which journalists were held without publicly disclosed charges.

This census is a snapshot of those incarcerated as of midnight on December 1, 2006. It does not include the many journalists imprisoned and released throughout the year; accounts of those cases can be found at www.cpj.org. Journalists remain on CPJ's list until the organization determines with reasonable certainty that they have been released or have died in custody.

Journalists who either disappear or are abducted by nonstate entities, including criminal gangs, rebels, and militant groups, are not included on the imprisoned list. Their cases are classified as "missing" or "abducted." Details of these cases are also available on CPJ's Web site.

134 JOURNALISTS IMPRISONED AS OF 12/1/2006

ALGERIA: 2

Djamel Eddine Fahassi, Alger Chaîne III
IMPRISONED: May 6, 1995

Fahassi, a reporter for the state-run radio station Alger Chaîne III and a contributor to several Algerian newspapers, including the now-banned weekly of the Islamic Salvation Front, *Al-Forqane*, was abducted near his home in the al-Harrache suburb of the capital, Algiers, by four well-dressed men carrying walkie-talkies. According to eyewitnesses who later spoke with his wife, the men called out Fahassi's name and then pushed him into a waiting car. He has not been seen since, and Algerian authorities have denied any knowledge of his arrest.

Prior to Fahassi's "disappearance," Algerian authorities had targeted him on at least two occasions because his writing criticized the government. In late 1991, he was arrested after an article in *Al-Forqane* criticized a raid conducted by security forces on an Algiers neighborhood. On January 1, 1992, the Blida Military Court convicted him of disseminating false information, attacking a state institution, and disseminating information that could harm national unity.

He received a one-year suspended sentence and was released after five months. On February 17, 1992, he was arrested a second time for allegedly attacking state institutions and spreading false information. He was transferred to the Ain Salah Detention Center in southern Algeria, where hundreds of Islamic suspects were detained in the months following the cancellation of the January 1992 elections.

In late January 2002, Algerian Ambassador to the United States Idriss Jazairy responded to a CPJ query, saying a government investigation had not found those responsible for Fahassi's abduction. The ambassador added that there was no evidence of state involvement.

Aziz Bouabdallah, *Al-Alam al-Siyassi*
IMPRISONED: April 12, 1997

Three armed men abducted Bouabdallah, a reporter for the daily *Al-Alam al-Siyassi*, from his home in the capital, Algiers. According to Bouabdallah's family, the men stormed into their home and, after identifying the journalist, grabbed him, put his hands behind his back, and pushed him out the door and into a waiting car. An article published in the privately owned daily *El-Watan* a few days after his abduction reported that Bouabdallah was in police custody and was expected to be released soon.

In July 1997, CPJ received credible information that Bouabdallah was being held in Algiers at the Châteauneuf detention facility, where he had reportedly been tortured. But Bouabdallah's whereabouts were unknown in 2006, and authorities have denied any knowledge of his abduction.

In late January 2002, Algerian Ambassador to the United States Idriss Jazairy responded to a CPJ query, saying a government investigation had not found those responsible for Bouabdallah's abduction. The ambassador added that there was no evidence of state involvement.

ARMENIA: 1

Arman Babadzhanian
Zhamanak Yerevan
IMPRISONED: June 26, 2006

The Yerevan prosecutor general summoned Babadzhanian, editor-in-chief of *Zhamanak Yerevan*, purportedly for questioning as a witness in a criminal case. Instead, authorities charged him with forging documents to evade military service in 2002 and took him into custody, according to international press reports.

At his trial, Babadzhanian pleaded guilty to draft evasion but said the charge was in retaliation for the paper's critical reporting. Days before his arrest, *Zhamanak Yerevan* published an article questioning the independence of the prosecutor general's office, according to the London-based Institute for War and Peace Reporting.

On September 8, a district court in Yerevan sentenced Babadzhanian to four years in prison on charges of forgery and draft evasion, according to the Armenian service of Radio Free Europe/Radio Liberty. The defense filed an appeal in September.

AZERBAIJAN: 3

Sakit Zakhidov, *Azadlyg*
IMPRISONED: June 23, 2006

Police arrested Zakhidov, a prominent reporter and satirist for the Baku-based opposition daily *Azadlyg*, and charged him with possession of heroin with intent to sell. Zakhidov denied the charge and said a police officer placed the drugs, about a third of an ounce, in his pocket during his arrest, according to local and international news reports.

CPJ sources said Zakhidov had previously told colleagues he feared retaliation. His arrest came three days after Executive Secretary Ali Akhmedov of the ruling Yeni Azerbaijan party publicly urged authorities to silence Zakhidov. At a June 20 panel on media freedom, Akhmedov said: "No government official or member of parliament has avoided his slanders. Someone should put an end to it," the news Web site *EurasiaNet* reported.

Zakhidov was held in a police pretrial detention unit until he was transferred to the Bailovsk Prison in Baku in July. On September 26, Public Prosecutor Shamil Guliyev announced that the prosecution could not prove the drug-selling count and revised the charge to drug possession.

On October 4, a court in Baku convicted Zakhidov and sentenced him to three years in prison. He was placed in the Bailovsk Prison.

Samir Sadagatoglu, *Senet*
Rafiq Tagi, *Senet*
IMPRISONED: November 15, 2006

Editor-in-Chief Sadagatoglu and reporter Tagi of the independent newspaper *Senet* were detained in connection with a November 1 article headlined "Europe and

JOURNALISTS IN PRISON: BURMA

Us." Tagi, the author, suggested that Islamic values were blocking development in the oil-rich Caspian Sea nation, according to international media reports. The article referred to Islam as a cause of infighting.

Tagi denied that he had slandered Islam. "There are no offensive words addressed to the Prophet," the local news Web site *Day* quoted him as saying. "On the other hand, we do not live in a religious state."

The Nasimi District Court in the capital, Baku, ordered Sadagatoglu and Tagi held for two months while authorities investigated the case, according to international press reports. If convicted of spreading national, ethnic, or religious hatred under Article 283 of the penal code, the journalists could face three to five years in prison, the online Russian news agency *Rosbalt* reported.

BANGLADESH: 1

Shafiqul Islam Shafiq, *Focus Bangla*
IMPRISONED: October 28, 2006

Shafiq, a photographer, was arrested on October 28 in Rajshahi, in northwestern Bangladesh. He was taken by plainclothes men believed to be members of the Rapid Action Battalion, an elite anticrime and antiterrorism force under the jurisdiction of the Ministry of Home Affairs.

Journalists from the *Dainik Prothom Alo* daily newspaper who were allowed to visit him on October 31 reported that he had been severely beaten, had burns on his body, and had broken bones in his hands. Shafiq told reporters that interrogators used an electric prod. He said police questioned him about the murders of police officers in Manda Chowbaria, in the western Bangladeshi area of Naoga, and forced him to sign blank confession papers.

During interrogation, police told Shafiq that other journalists would also be targeted. Colleagues alleged that he was being held without evidence on trumped-up charges as a warning to the press from the Rapid Action Battalion, which media and human rights groups have accused of extrajudicial killings and torture.

Bail was set on November 1, but Shafiq was immediately rearrested and accused in the murders. Police told reporters they had proof of Shafiq's contacts with Jamaat-ul-Mujahedeen terrorists through numbers saved on his mobile phone. Despite the claims of proof, Shafiq was charged under Section 54 of the Criminal Procedure Code, which allows the detention of people on the suspicion of criminal activity without an order from a magistrate or a warrant. The government regularly uses Section 54 to arrest people without formal charges or specific complaints.

The day after Shafiq's arrest, colleagues from the Rajshahi Journalists Union held a public rally to demand his release and specifically criticized the Rapid Action Battalion for harassing journalists.

BURMA: 7

U Win Tin, freelance
IMPRISONED: July 4, 1989

U Win Tin, former editor-in-chief of the

JOURNALISTS IN PRISON IN 2006

daily *Hanthawati* and chairman of Burma's Writers Club, was arrested and sentenced to three years hard labor in 1989 on the spurious charge of arranging a "forced abortion" for an opposition politician. While in prison, his sentence was extended twice, building to 20 years. U Win Tin suffered at least two heart attacks in prison and has been shuttled between the notorious Insein Prison and Rangoon Hospital's prisoner wing.

U Win Tin helped establish various pro-democracy publications during the 1988 uprisings that the ruling military junta violently crushed. As a former joint secretary to the main opposition National League for Democracy (NLD) political party, U Win Tin was considered a close adviser to NLD party leader and Nobel Laureate Daw Aung San Suu Kyi.

In 1992, his initial term drawing to an end, U Win Tin saw his sentence extended on charges of "writing and publishing pamphlets to incite treason against the state" and "giving seditious talks" during the 1988 uprisings. In 1996, military authorities extended his term yet again on charges that he secretly published "antigovernment propaganda" from prison, including notes drawn up for a U.N. special rapporteur detailing human rights abuses at Insein.

In 1996, U Win Tin was held for five months in crude solitary confinement in kennels designed for the prison's guard dogs.

Such deprivations contributed to the 76-year-old journalist's declining health, including a degenerative spine condition, heart disease, inflamed knee joints, dental problems, and a prostate gland disorder, according to the Assistance Association for Political Prisoners in Burma (AAP-PB), a prisoner assistance group based in Thailand.

A senior Burmese military official offered to release U Win Tin in 2003 in exchange for the journalist signing a document promising to cease political activities, according to a report in *Le Monde*. U Win Tin refused.

Two years later, U Win Tin was subjected to a cruel manipulation, according to news reports. The Associated Press reported that the journalist was told he would be among the political prisoners released on July 6, 2005. In all, nearly 250 such prisoners were freed at the time. But after gathering his belongings and attending a briefing on the conditions of release, U Win Tin was instead directed to a nearby office, according to a freed prisoner quoted in a Radio Free Asia dispatch. For unknown reasons, U Win Tin was not freed.

Amnesty International reported that U Win Tin should have been eligible for early release in July.

Maung Maung Lay Ngwe
Pe-Tin-Than
IMPRISONED: September 1990

Maung Maung Lay Ngwe was arrested and charged in 1990 with writing and distributing undisclosed publications that the authorities deemed to "make people lose respect for the government."

The publications were titled collectively *Pe-Tin-Than*, which from the Burmese translates loosely to "Echoes." CPJ has been unable to confirm his current whereabouts, legal status, or records of his original sentencing 16 years ago.

Aung Htun, freelance
IMPRISONED: February 17, 1998

Aung Htun, a writer and activist, was imprisoned in February 1998 for writing and publishing a seven-volume book that documented the history of the student movement that led to the pro-democracy uprisings of 1988. He was sentenced to a total of 17 years in prison, according to information compiled by the Assistance Association for Political Prisoners in Burma (AAPPB), a prisoner assistance group based in Thailand.

He was sentenced to three years for violating the 1962 Printers and Publishers Registration Act, the military government's main legal instrument of official censorship; seven years under the 1950 Emergency Provisions Act, which is used broadly to suppress any dissent against the regime; and another seven years under the 1908 Unlawful Associations Act, a draconian holdover law from Burma's colonial era under British rule, according to the AAPPB.

The writer's health deteriorated during his detention.

In 2002, Amnesty International issued an urgent appeal requesting that Aung Htun be granted access to medical treatment for complications related to growths on his feet, which had apparently inhibited his ability to walk, as well as a severe asthma condition. It is believed that his health has deteriorated further in subsequent years, according to the Burma Media Association, an exiled press freedom advocacy group.

Thaung Tun (Nyein Thit), freelance
IMPRISONED: October 4, 1999

Thaung Tun, an editor, filmmaker, and poet better known as Nyein Thit, was arrested on October 4, 1999, and subsequently sentenced on December 3, 1999, to eight years in prison for collecting and disseminating human rights-related information outside of the country, according to the Assistance Association for Political Prisoners in Burma (AAPPB), a prisoner assistance group based in Thailand.

The films depicted topics that exposed chronic mismanagement and human rights abuses under military rule, including footage of forced labor and images of grinding poverty in rural areas. His videotapes were circulated through underground networks inside and outside the country, and copies were eventually captured by military intelligence officials, according to the Burma Media Association, an exiled press freedom advocacy group.

The 47-year-old Thaung Tun was a longtime journalist with the *Padaut Pwint Thit* magazine, which the government shuttered in 1995. He was also a member of the opposition National League for Democracy party and spent three years in prison for his political activities in the late 1970s. He was detained in 2006 at Moulmein Prison in southern Burma, 625 miles (1,000 kilometers) away from his family in Mandalay, according to the AAPPB.

CPJ honored Thaung Tun and his videographer colleague Aung Pwint, who was also imprisoned for his role in making the unauthorized documentaries, with 2004 International Press Freedom Awards.

Aung Pwint was released in 2005.

Ne Min (Win Shwe), freelance
IMPRISONED: May 7, 2004

Ne Min, a lawyer and former stringer for the BBC, was sentenced to 15 years in prison on charges that he illegally passed information to "antigovernment" organizations operating in border areas, according to the Assistance Association for Political Prisoners in Burma (AAPPB), a prisoner assistance group based in Thailand.

It represented the second time Burma's military government had imprisoned the well-known journalist, also known as Win Shwe, on charges related to disseminating information to news sources outside of Burma. In 1989, a military tribunal sentenced Ne Min to 14 years hard labor for "spreading false news and rumors to the BBC to fan further disturbances in the country" and the "possession of documents including antigovernment literature, which he planned to send to the BBC," according to official radio reports.

He served nine years at Rangoon's Insein Prison before being released in 1998. Exiled Burmese journalists who spoke with CPJ said that Ne Min sent news and information to political groups and exile-run news publications after his release from prison.

Thaung Sein (Thar Cho), freelance
Kyaw Thwin (Moe Tun), *Dhamah Yate*
IMPRISONED: March 27, 2006

Thaung Sein, a freelance photojournalist, and Kyaw Thwin, a columnist at the Burmese-language magazine *Dhamah Yate*, were arrested on March 27, 2006, and sentenced the following day to three years in prison for photographing and videotaping while riding on a public bus near the new capital city, Pyinmana.

The two journalists were charged under the 1996 Television and Video Act, which bars the distribution of film material without official approval. Under the law, every videotape in Burma must receive a certificate, which may be revoked at any time, from the government's censorship board.

Burmese security officials were under strict orders to stop and detain anyone found taking photographs near the mysterious new capital. Thaung Sein, also known as Thar Cho, and Kyaw Thwin, more widely known by his Moe Tun pen name, were placed at Yemethin Prison in central Burma, according to the Assistance Association for Political Prisoners in Burma (AAPPB), a prisoner assistance group based in Thailand.

Both journalists appealed the decision on the argument that they had not taken film or video footage of restricted areas. On June 21, an appeals court based in the central Burma town of Yemethin upheld the lower court's verdict without allowing defense witnesses to testify, according to information from their lawyer that was received by the Burma Media Association, an exile-run press freedom advocacy group.

Burma's secretive military government abruptly moved the national capital in November 2005 to a newly built administrative center located 250 miles (400 kilometers) north of Rangoon. Regional news reports, citing official government documents, said the junta's decision to move the capital was motivated by fears of supposed military strikes.

BURUNDI: 3

Serge Nibizi
Domitile Kiramvu
Radio Publique Africaine
IMPRISONED: November 22, 2006

Editor Nibizi and reporter Kiramvu of the independent radio station Radio Publique Africaine (RPA) were arrested in connection with a story about an alleged coup plot, according to their lawyer and other local sources. The two were summoned for questioning, served with arrest warrants, and imprisoned on charges that included threatening state security, lawyer François Nyamoya said.

Nibizi and Kiramvu were accused of violating judicial secrecy by commenting on a story in the pro-government newspaper *Intumwa* claiming evidence of a coup plot, according to Nyamoya. No action was taken against *Intumwa*. Several leading opposition figures have been jailed since August in connection with the alleged coup plot.

Reports on RPA and two other independent radio stations, Radio Isanganiro and Radio Bonesha, cast doubt on whether a plot truly existed.

Station Director Alexis Sinduhije, a 2004 International Press Freedom Awardee, said he believed authorities were trying to close RPA because of its reporting on human rights abuses. Sinduhije went into hiding in September amid what he called a campaign of intimidation against RPA.

Matthias Manirakiza
Radio Isanganiro
IMPRISONED: November 29, 2006

Manirakiza, director of Radio Isanganiro, was held in the central prison in the capital, Bujumbura, in connection with a story broadcast in August. The report cited police sources as saying authorities planned to stage fake attacks on the homes of top officials to bolster their claims of a coup plot.

Several top opposition leaders, including the former president, were on trial in late year for alleged participation in the plot. Reports on Radio Isanganiro and other independent radio stations cast doubt on whether a plot truly existed.

Agence France-Presse quoted Manirakiza's lawyer, Raphael Gahungu as saying that his client was jailed for allegedly "authorizing the broadcast of information threatening to state and public security." It was not immediately clear whether any formal charges were filed.

Radio Isanganiro is backed by the U.S.-based nongovernmental organization Search for Common Ground.

CAMBODIA: 1

Hem Choun, *Samrek Yutethor*
IMPRISONED: June 7, 2006

Hem Chuon, a reporter with the Khmer-language newspaper *Samrek Yutethor*, was arrested by military police while reporting on the forced eviction of land squatters by military police from Sambok Chap village on the outskirts of the capital, Phnom Penh.

He was arrested along with three other villagers for their alleged role in leading a violent protest on May 31 against a private security company that had been hired to secure the land. That day, protestors dismantled metal fences erected around the village and burned down the village chief's empty house.

Chuon's lawyer said that he covered the riot as a reporter and did not participate in the melee. The Cambodian Center for Human Rights (CCHR), a rights advocacy group that has provided legal counsel to the jailed journalist, told CPJ that police arrested Chuon without a proper warrant and that they had refused to recognize him as a practicing journalist.

On June 8, Phnom Penh Municipal Court Investigation Judge Ke Sokhan charged Chuon under Article 52 of the U.N. Transitional Authority in Cambodia criminal law, which relates to wrongful damage of property. On June 9, Sokhan denied Chuon's bail petition submitted through his lawyer. Cambodian law allows the government to hold a person for six months without bail.

Chuon was being held in crowded conditions at Phnom Penh's notorious Prey Sar Prison. According to CCHR, Chuon has developed respiratory complications during his detention, and prison authorities on at least one occasion denied him outside medical treatment. The court did not immediately set a trial date.

CHINA: 31

Chen Renjie
Lin Youping
Ziyou Bao
IMPRISONED: July 1983

Twenty-three years after their imprisonment in the early days of China's economic reform, Chen and Lin are the longest-serving journalists in CPJ's worldwide census. The two men, along with Chen Biling, wrote and published a pamphlet titled *Ziyou Bao* (Freedom Report). They distributed only 300 copies of the pamphlet in the southern Chinese city of Fuzhou, Fujian province, in September 1982. The following July, they were arrested and accused of making contact with Taiwanese spy groups and publishing a counterrevolutionary pamphlet. According to official government records of the case, the men used "propaganda and incitement to encourage the overthrow of the people's democratic dictatorship and the socialist system."

In August 1983, Chen Renjie was sentenced to life in prison, and Lin Youping was sentenced to death with reprieve. Chen Biling was sentenced to death and later executed.

Fan Yingshang, *Remen Huati*
CHARGED: October 16, 1995

In 1994, Fan and Yang Jianguo printed more than 60,000 copies of the magazine *Remen Huati* (Popular Topics). The men had allegedly purchased fake printing authorizations from an editor of the *Journal of European Research* at the Chinese Academy of Social Sciences, according to official Chinese news sources. Printing authorizations are a prior restraint used to curtail independent publishing in China.

CPJ was unable to determine the date of Fan's arrest, but on October 16, 1995, he was indicted on charges of profiteering. On January 31, 1996, the Chang'an District Court in Shijiazhuang City sentenced him to 13 years in prison, with three years' subsequent deprivation of political rights, for publishing and distributing illegal "reactionary" publications. Yang escaped arrest and was not sentenced.

Fan's appeal was rejected on April 11, 1996, according to the Chinese government's response to a query by the San Francisco-based prisoner advocacy group Dui Hua.

Hua Di, freelance
IMPRISONED: January 5, 1998

The imprisonment of Hua, a Stanford University scientist and permanent resident of the United States, raised objections from former U.S. President Bill Clinton, colleagues at Stanford University, and others. But eight years later, he remained in jail.

Hua was arrested while visiting China and charged with revealing state secrets, a charge used frequently against journalists who write about controversial matters. Charges are believed to stem from articles that Hua had written in academic journals about China's missile defense system.

On November 25, 1999, the Beijing No. 1 Intermediate People's Court held a closed trial and sentenced Hua to 15 years in prison, according to the Hong Kong-based

Information Center for Human Rights and Democracy. In March 2000, the Beijing High People's Court overturned Hua's conviction and ordered that the case be retried. This judicial reversal was extraordinary, and it appeared to be a response to international pressure. But the decision did not mean that he was freed.

Instead, after a retrial, the Beijing No. 1 Intermediate People's Court issued a modified verdict, sentencing Hua to 10 years in prison in November 2000. News of Hua's sentencing did not break until three months later, when a relative gave the information to foreign correspondents based in Beijing.

Requests for medical parole have been rejected. Hua suffers from a rare form of male breast cancer.

Gao Qinrong, Xinhua News Agency
IMPRISONED: December 4, 1998

Gao, an investigative reporter for China's state news agency, Xinhua, was jailed for reporting on a corrupt irrigation scheme in drought-plagued Yuncheng, Shanxi province. Xinhua never carried Gao's article, which was finally published on May 27, 1998, in an internal reference edition of the official *People's Daily* that is distributed only among a select group of party leaders. But by fall 1998, the irrigation scandal had become national news, with reports appearing in the Guangzhou-based *Nanfang Zhoumo* (Southern Weekend) and on China Central Television. Gao's wife, Duan Maoying, said that local officials blamed Gao for the flurry of media interest and arranged for his prosecution on false charges.

Gao was arrested on December 4, 1998, and eventually charged with crimes including bribery, embezzlement, and pimping, according to Duan. On April 28, 1999, he was sentenced to 12 years in prison after a closed one-day trial.

In September 2001, Gao wrote to Mary Robinson, then the U.N. high commissioner for human rights, and asked her to intercede with the Chinese government on his behalf. Gao has received support from several members of the Chinese People's Political Consultative Conference of the National People's Congress, which issued a motion at its annual parliamentary meeting in March 2001 urging the Central Discipline Committee and Supreme People's Court to reopen his case.

In 2002, Gao received a sentence reduction of 21 months, and in 2004 received a further reduction of two years, the San Francisco-based Dui Hua Foundation reported. Though Gao's imprisonment was frequently listed as a case of concern by foreign governments in dialogue with China, the reductions were not publicly disclosed until 2006. Gao finally won his release on December 12. He told Agence France-Presse he hoped to clear his name.

Yue Tianxiang
Zhongguo Gongren Guancha
IMPRISONED: January 1999

Along with his colleagues Wang Fengshan and Guo Xinmin, Yue started a journal campaigning for workers' rights after they were unable to get compensation from the Tianshui City Transport Agency follow-

ing their dismissal from the company in 1995. The first issue of *Zhongguo Gongren Guancha* (China Labor Watch) exposed extensive corruption among officials at the company, according to international media reports. Only two issues were ever published.

On July 5, 1999, the Tianshui People's Intermediate Court in Gansu province sentenced Yue to 10 years in prison on charges of "subverting state authority," according to the Hong Kong-based Information Center for Human Rights and Democracy. His colleagues Wang and Guo were sentenced to two years in prison and have since been released. All three men reportedly belonged to the outlawed China Democracy Party, a dissident group, and were forming an organization to protect the rights of laid-off workers.

In 2006, the U.S.-based prisoner advocacy group Dui Hua Foundation reported that Yue's sentence was reduced to nine years in March 2005. He turned 50 in Lanzhou Prison in December 2006.

Wu Yilong, *Zaiye Dang*
IMPRISONED: April 26, 1999
Mao Qingxiang, *Zaiye Dang*
IMPRISONED: June 1999

Wu and Mao, both organizers for the banned China Democracy Party (CDP), were detained in the run-up to the 10-year anniversary of the military crackdown on demonstrators at Tiananmen Square. A few months later, authorities detained two more leading CDP activists, Zhu Yufu and Xu Guang. The four were later convicted of subversion for, among other things, establishing a magazine called *Zaiye Dang* (Opposition Party) and circulating pro-democracy writings online.

On October 25, 1999, the Hangzhou Intermediate People's Court in Zhejiang province conducted what *The New York Times* described as a "sham trial." On November 9, 1999, Wu was sentenced to 11 years in prison, and Mao was sentenced to eight years. Their political rights were suspended for three years each upon release. Xu was sentenced to five years in prison and was later released. Zhu was sentenced to seven years and was released in September 2006. After his release, Zhu told journalists that he had been abused and deprived of sleep while in prison.

"The guards would tell three or four criminals to beat me, saying it was a private matter between prisoners," Zhu told The Associated Press.

Xu Zerong, freelance
IMPRISONED: June 24, 2000

Xu is serving a 13-year prison term on charges of "leaking state secrets" through his academic work on military history and of "economic crimes" related to unauthorized publishing on foreign policy issues. Some observers believe that his jailing may have been related to an article he wrote for the Hong Kong-based *Yazhou Zhoukan* (Asia Weekly) magazine revealing clandestine Chinese Communist Party support for a Malaysian insurgency in the 1950s and 1960s.

Xu, a permanent resident of Hong Kong, was arrested in Guangzhou and held incommunicado for 18 months until his trial. He was tried by Shenzhen Intermediate Court in December 2001, and his appeal to Guangzhou Higher People's Court was rejected in 2002.

According to court documents, the "state secrets" charges against Xu stemmed from his use of historical documents for academic research. Xu, also known as David Tsui, was an associate research professor at the Institute of Southeast Asian Studies at Zhongshan University in Guangzhou. In 1992, he photocopied four books published in the 1950s about China's role in the Korean War, which he then sent to a colleague in South Korea. The verdict stated that the Security Committee of the People's Liberation Army of Guangzhou later determined that the books had not been declassified 40 years after being labeled "top secret." After his arrest, St. Antony's College at Oxford University, where Xu earned his doctorate and wrote his dissertation on the Korean War, was active in researching his case and calling for his release.

He was also the co-founder of a Hong Kong-based academic journal *Zhongguo Shehui Kexue Jikan* (China Social Sciences Quarterly). The "economic crimes" charges were related to the "illegal publication" of more than 60,000 copies of 25 books and periodicals, including several books about Chinese politics and Beijing's relations with Taiwan.

Xu was arrested just days after an article appeared in the June 26, 2000, issue of *Yazhou Zhoukan* in which he accused the Chinese Communist Party of hypocrisy by condemning other countries for interfering in its internal affairs by criticizing its human rights record.

Xu began his sentence in Dongguan Prison, outside of Guangzhou, but was later transferred to Guangzhou Prison, where it was easier for his family to visit him. He has been spared from hard labor and has been allowed to read, research, and teach English in prison, according to the U.S.-based prisoner advocacy group Dui Hua Foundation. He has suffered from high blood pressure and diabetes.

In 2006, Xu's family members were informed that he had received a nine-month reduction in his sentence, according to Dui Hua. Based on that, he would be scheduled for release in 2012.

Yang Zili, *Yangzi de Sixiang Jiayuan*
Xu Wei, *Xiaofei Ribao*
Jin Haike, freelance
Zhang Honghai, freelance
IMPRISONED: March 13, 2001

The four members of an informal discussion group called Xin Qingnian Xuehui (New Youth Study Group) were detained and accused of "subverting state authority." Prosecutors cited online articles and essays on political and social reform as proof of their intent to overthrow the Chinese Communist Party leadership.

Yang, Xu, Jin, and Zhang were charged with subversion on April 20, 2001. More than two years later, on May 29, 2003, the Beijing No. 1 Intermediate People's Court sentenced Xu and Jin to 10 years in prison each, while Yang and Zhang each received sentences of eight years. Each of the sentences was to be followed by two years' deprivation of political rights.

The four young men were students and recent university graduates who gathered occasionally to discuss politics and reform with four others, including an informant for the Ministry of State Security. The most prominent in the group, Yang, posted his own thoughts and reports by the others on topics such as rural poverty and village elections, along with essays advocating democratic reform on a popular Web site, *Yangzi de Sixiang Jiayuan* (Yangzi's Garden of Ideas).

Xu was a reporter at *Xiaofei Ribao* (Consumer's Daily). Public security agents pressured the newspaper to fire him before his arrest, a friend, Wang Ying, reported online.

The court cited a handful of articles, including Jin's "Be a New Citizen, Reform China" and Yang's "Choose Liberalism," in the 2003 verdict against them. Beijing Higher People's Court rejected their appeal without hearing defense witnesses in November 2003. Three of the witnesses who testified against the four men were fellow members of the group who later tried to retract their testimonies.

Yang, Xu, and Jin were imprisoned at Beijing's No. 2 Prison. Yang's wife, Lu Kun, who was also initially detained and questioned, was unable to visit him for four years after his imprisonment, she told reporters in 2005. Zhang, who initially suffered from ill health in detention, was jailed at Lishui Prison in Zhejiang province, where he makes sweaters, his brother told CPJ.

Tao Haidong, freelance
IMPRISONED: July 9, 2002

Tao, an Internet essayist and pro-democracy activist, was arrested in Urumqi, the capital of the Xinjiang Uighur Autonomous Region (XUAR), and charged with "incitement to subvert state power." According to the *Minzhu Luntan* (Democracy Forum) Web site, which had published Tao's recent writing, his articles focused on political and legal reform. In one essay, titled "Strategies for China's Social Reforms," Tao wrote that "the Chinese Communist Party and democracy activists throughout society should unite to push forward China's freedom and democratic development or else stand condemned through the ages."

Previously, in 1999, Tao was sentenced to three years of "re-education through labor" in Xi'an, Shaanxi province, according to the New York-based advocacy group Human Rights in China, because of his essays and work on a book titled *Xin Renlei Shexiang* (Imaginings of a New Human Race). After his early release in 2001, Tao began writing essays and articles and publishing them on various domestic and overseas Web sites.

In early January 2003, the Urumqi Intermediate Court sentenced Tao to seven years in prison. His appeal to the XUAR Higher Court later in 2003 was rejected.

Zhang Wei, *Shishi Zixun* and *Redian Jiyao*
IMPRISONED: July 19, 2002

Zhang was arrested and charged with illegal publishing after producing and selling two underground newspapers in Chongqing, in central China. According to an account published on the Web site of the Chongqing Press and Publishing Administration, a provincial government body that governs all local publications, beginning in April 2001 Zhang edited two newspapers, *Shishi Zixun* (Current Events) and *Redian Jiyao* (Summary of the Main Points), which included articles and graphics he had downloaded from the Internet.

Two of Zhang's business associates, Zuo Shangwen and Ou Yan, were also arrested on July 19, 2002, and indicted for their involvement with the publications. Zuo printed the publications in neighboring Sichuan province, while Ou managed the publications' finances. At the time of their arrests, police confiscated 9,700 copies of *Shishi Zixun*.

The official account of their arrests stated that the two publications had "flooded" Chongqing's publishing market. The government declared that "the political rumors, shocking 'military reports,' and other articles in these illegal publications misled the public, poisoned the youth, negatively influenced society, and sparked public indignation."

Zhang, Zuo, and Ou printed more than 1.5 million copies of the publications and sold them in Chongqing, Chengdu, and other cities.

On December 25, 2002, the Yuzhong District Court in Chongqing sentenced Zhang to six years in prison and fined him 100,000 yuan (US$12,000), the amount that police said he had earned in profits from the publications. Zuo was sentenced to five years and fined 50,000 yuan (US$6,000), while Ou was sentenced to two years in prison.

Abdulghani Memetemin
East Turkistan Information Center
IMPRISONED: July 26, 2002

Memetemin, a writer, teacher, and translator who had actively advocated for the Uighur ethnic group in the northwestern Xinjiang Uighur Autonomous Region, was detained in Kashgar, a city in Xinjiang, on charges of "leaking state secrets."

In June 2003, the Kashgar Intermediate People's Court sentenced him to nine years in prison, plus a three-year suspension of political rights. Radio Free Asia provided CPJ with court documents listing 18 specific counts against Memetemin, including translating state news articles into Chinese from Uighur; forwarding official speeches to the Germany-based East Turkistan Information Center (ETIC), a news outlet that advocates for an independent state for the Uighur ethnic group; and conducting original reporting for the center. The court also accused him of recruiting additional reporters for ETIC, which is banned in China.

Memetemin did not have legal representation at his trial.

Huang Jinqiu, *Boxun News*
IMPRISONED: September 13, 2003

Huang, a columnist for the U.S.-based citizen journalist Web site *Boxun News*, was arrested in Jiangsu province. Huang's family was not officially notified of his arrest for more than three months. On September 27, 2004, Changzhou Intermediate People's Court sentenced him to 12 years in prison on charges of "subversion of state authority," plus four years' deprivation of political rights. The sentence was unusually harsh and appeared linked to his intention to form an opposition party.

Huang worked as a writer and editor in his native Shandong province, as well as in Guangdong province, before leaving China in 2000 to study journalism at the Central Academy of Art in Malaysia. While he was overseas, Huang began writing political commentary for *Boxun News* under the pen name "Qing Shuijun." He also wrote articles on arts and entertainment under the name "Huang Jin." Huang's writings reportedly caught the attention of the government in 2001. Huang told a friend that authorities had contacted his family to warn them about his writing, according to *Boxun News*.

In January 2003, Huang wrote in his online column that he intended to form a new opposition party, the China Patriot Democracy Party. When he returned to China in August 2003, he eluded public security agents just long enough to visit his family in Shandong province. In the last article he posted on *Boxun News*, titled "Me and My Public Security Friends," Huang described being followed and harassed by security agents.

Huang's appeal was rejected in December 2004.

Huang's lawyer told CPJ in early 2005 that the journalist had been mistreated in prison and was in poor health. By late 2006, his family told *Boxun News* that his health had improved.

Kong Youping, freelance
IMPRISONED: December 13, 2003

Kong, an essayist and poet, was arrested in Anshan, Liaoning province. A former trade union official, he had written articles online that supported democratic reforms, appealed for the release of then-imprisoned Internet writer Liu Di, and called for a reversal of the government's "counterrevolutionary" ruling on the pro-democracy demonstrations of 1989.

Kong's essays included an appeal to democracy activists in China that stated, "In order to work well for democracy, we need a well-organized, strong, powerful, and effective organization. Otherwise, a mainland democracy movement will accomplish nothing." Several of his articles and poems were posted on the *Minzhu Luntan* (Democracy Forum) Web site.

In 1998, Kong served time in prison after he became a member of the Liaoning province branch of the China Democracy Party (CDP), an opposition party. In 2004, he was tried on subversion charges along with co-defendant Ning Xianhua, who was accused of being the vice chairman of the CDP branch in Liaoning, according to the U.S.-based advocacy organization Human Rights in China and court documents obtained by the San Francisco-based Dui Hua Foundation. On September 16, 2004, the Shenyang Intermediate People's Court sentenced Kong to 15 years in prison, plus four years' deprivation of political rights. Ning received a 12-year sentence. Kong's family has never seen the verdict in the case, according to CPJ sources in China.

Kong suffered from hypertension and was imprisoned in the city of Lingyuan far from his family, making visits difficult. In a letter written to his family from prison,

Kong said that he had received a sentence reduction to 10 years in his appeal, but that information could not be confirmed.

Yu Huafeng, *Nanfang Dushi Bao*
Li Minying, *Nanfang Dushi Bao*
IMPRISONED: January 2004

Yu, deputy editor-in-chief and general manager of *Nanfang Dushi Bao* (Southern Metropolis News), and Li, the newspaper's former editor, were detained less than a month after the newspaper reported a suspected SARS case in Guangzhou, the first case since the epidemic died out in July 2003. Their imprisonment was followed in March 2004 by the jailing of *Nanfang Dushi Bao* former editor-in-chief Cheng Yizhong, who was held for five months.

The arrests appeared to be a part of a crackdown on the newspaper, which became popular for its aggressive investigative reporting on social issues and wrongdoing by local officials. The paper broke news that a young graphic designer, Sun Zhigang, was beaten to death in March 2003 while being held in police custody in Guangzhou. Public outcry over Sun's death led to the arrest of several local government and police officials, along with a change in national laws on detention.

On March 19, 2004, Dongshan District Court in Guangzhou, Guangdong province, sentenced Yu to 12 years in prison on corruption charges. Li, who also served on the Communist Party Committee of the newspaper's parent group Nanfang Daily Group, was sentenced to 11 years on bribery charges. In an appellate trial held in June 2004, Li's sentence was reduced to six years in prison, while Yu's sentence was reduced to eight years.

According to the official Xinhua News Agency, Yu was convicted of embezzling 580,000 yuan (US$70,000) and distributing the money to members of the paper's editorial committee. The court also accused Yu of paying Li a total of 800,000 yuan (US$97,000) in bribes while Li was editor of Nanfang Dushi Bao. Li was accused of accepting bribes totaling 970,000 (US$117,000).

Both men maintained that the money was acquired legally and was distributed in routine bonus payments to the staff. Chinese journalists familiar with the case have told CPJ that evidence presented in court did not support the corruption charges.

In 2005, Cheng was named the recipient of the 2005 UNESCO/Guillermo Cano World Press Freedom Prize. He was not permitted to attend, but in his acceptance statement he asked to share the honor with Li and Yu: "Your suffering is the shame of China," he said. Later that year, more than 2,000 journalists in China signed an open letter to the Guangdong High People's Court appealing for the release of Yu and Li. Observers could remember no precedent in this show of support.

Yu's wife told CPJ that she travels monthly to Beijing to petition for the release of her husband.

Zhao Yan, *The New York Times*
IMPRISONED: September 17, 2004

Zhao, a news researcher at the Beijing bureau of *The New York Times* and a former investigative reporter for the Beijing-based *China Reform* magazine, was detained in Shanghai less than two weeks after *The Times* ran an article correctly predicting the retirement of President Jiang Zemin from his final leadership post.

Zhao was held under suspicion of "providing state secrets to foreigners," a charge that denied him access to a lawyer for nine months after his initial detention, prolonged his pretrial detention, and cloaked his case in official secrecy. Leaked state security documents confirmed that Zhao was detained in connection with the September 7 article on Jiang's retirement, but indicated that the sparse evidence against him comprised only a brief handwritten note taken through unknown means from the Beijing office of *The Times*. A fraud charge was added in April 2005. After a series of delays, Zhao was tried in June 2006 in closed proceedings in which he was not permitted to call defense witnesses.

On August 25, 2006, Beijing No. 2 Intermediate People's Court convicted Zhao of fraud charges, but in a very rare move for criminal cases brought to trial in China, acquitted him of the more serious state secrets charges due to "insufficient evidence." Zhao was sentenced to three years in prison.

The fraud charge stemmed from an accusation that Zhao took 20,000 yuan (US$2,500) from a local official with the promise of helping him get released from a work camp in 2001. Zhao was known as an aggressive investigative reporter and activist before joining *The Times*. Sources familiar with the situation told CPJ that the allegation against him was unsubstantiated.

Zhao's detention fueled an international outcry, and it was raised with high-ranking U.S. officials in talks with Chinese counterparts. The state secrets' charge against Zhao was briefly dropped ahead of Chinese President Hu Jintao's April 2006 visit to the White House, prompting premature speculation that the journalist would soon be released from prison. But all charges were reinstated after Hu's visit.

After his sentencing, Zhao's lawyers petitioned for a fully open appeal hearing with a right to call defense witnesses, something denied him in the first trial. But authorities denied this request and rejected his appeal after reviewing it behind closed doors in November.

Shi Tao, freelance
IMPRISONED: November 24, 2004

Shi, the former editorial director at the Changsha-based newspaper *Dangdai Shang Bao*, was detained near his home in Taiyuan, Shanxi province.

He was formally arrested and charged with "providing state secrets to foreigners" by sending an e-mail on his Yahoo account to the U.S.-based editor of the Web site *Minzhu Luntan* (Democracy Forum). In the anonymous e-mail sent several months before his arrest, Shi transcribed his notes from local propaganda department instructions to his newspaper, which included directives on coverage of the Falun Gong and the upcoming 15th anniversary of the military crackdown on demonstrators at Tiananmen Square. The official Xinhua News Agency reported that the National Administration for the Protection of State

Secrets later certified the contents of the e-mail as classified.

On April 27, 2005, the Changsha Intermediate People's Court found Shi guilty and sentenced him to a 10-year prison term. In June, the Hunan Province High People's Court rejected his appeal without granting a hearing.

Court documents in the case revealed that Yahoo had supplied information to Chinese authorities that helped them identify Shi as the sender of the e-mail. Yahoo's participation in the identification of Shi and other jailed Internet writers and dissidents in China raised questions about the role that international Internet companies are playing in the repression of online speech in China and elsewhere.

In November 2005, CPJ honored Shi in absentia with its annual International Press Freedom Award for his courage in defending the ideals of free expression. Shi's mother, Gao Qinsheng, was invited to attend the ceremony in New York but declined the invitation after police told her that her son's conditions in high-security Chisan Prison would improve if she stayed home. Instead, Shi's conditions stayed the same through 2006. He was forced to work cutting and polishing gems, lost weight, and was not allowed to read newspapers or write.

Zheng Yichun, freelance
IMPRISONED: December 3, 2004

Zheng, a former professor, was a regular contributor to overseas online news sites including the U.S.-based Web site *Dajiyuan* (Epoch Times), which is affiliated with the banned religious movement Falun Gong. Zheng wrote a series of editorials that directly criticized the Communist Party and its control of the media.

Because of police warnings, Zheng's family remained silent about his detention in Yingkou, Liaoning province, until state media reported that he had been arrested on suspicion of inciting subversion. Zheng was initially tried by Yingkou Intermediate People's Court on April 26, 2005. No verdict was announced, and on July 21 he was tried again on the same charges. As in the April 26 trial, proceedings lasted just three hours. Though officially "open" to the public, the courtroom was closed to all observers except close family members and government officials. Zheng's supporters and a journalist were prevented from entering, according to a local source.

Prosecutors cited dozens of articles written by the journalist, and listed the titles of several essays in which he called for political reform, increased capitalism in China, and an end to the practice of imprisoning writers.

On September 20, the court sentenced Zheng to seven years in prison, to be followed by three years' deprivation of political rights.

Sources familiar with the case believe that Zheng's harsh sentence may be linked to Chinese leaders' objections to the *Dajiyuan* series "Nine Commentaries on the Communist Party," which called the Chinese Communist Party an "evil cult" with a "history of killings" and predicted its demise.

Zheng is diabetic, and his health suffered a decline after his imprisonment. After his first appeal was rejected, he intended to pursue an appeal in a higher court, but his defense lawyer, Gao Zhisheng, was himself imprisoned in August 2006. Zheng's family has been unable to find another lawyer willing to take the case.

Zhang Lin, freelance
IMPRISONED: January 29, 2005

Zhang, a freelance writer and political essayist who made a living by writing for banned overseas Web sites, was convicted of "inciting subversion of state power" and misrepresenting national authorities in his articles and in a radio interview.

Zhang, who spent years in jail in the 1990s for his pro-democracy activism and for organizing a labor union, was detained at a train station near his home in Bengbu, in central China's Anhui province. Police apprehended him as he was returning from Beijing, where he had traveled to mourn the death of ousted Communist Party leader Zhao Ziyang. He was initially accused of "disturbing public order" but police formally arrested him on charges of inciting subversion after confiscating the computer he was using.

Bengbu Intermediate People's Court tried him on June 21, 2005, in proceedings that lasted five hours, his lawyer, Mo Shaoping, told CPJ. The defense argued that the six articles and one interview cited by the prosecution were protected free expression. Zhang's wife told reporters that his imprisonment was also connected to essays he wrote about protests by unemployed workers and official scandals. On July 28, 2005, the court convicted Zhang and sentenced him to five years in prison.

For 28 days in September 2005, Zhang waged a hunger strike to protest his unjust sentence and the harsh conditions at Bengbu No. 1 Detention Center. Officials there subjected him to long hours of forced labor making Christmas ornaments and refused to allow him to read newspapers or other material, according to his lawyer. During his hunger strike, he was fed through his nose, and was hospitalized briefly before returning to the detention center.

Zhang's appeals were rejected without a hearing, and he was moved to a prison in Anhui province. Zhang's wife told CPJ that his health has suffered during his imprisonment. They have a young daughter.

Li Changqing, *Fuzhou Ribao*
IMPRISONED: February 2005

Li, deputy news director of *Fuzhou Ribao* (Fuzhou Daily), was arrested in southern China's Fujian province in connection with an investigation of whistleblower Huang Jingao, a Communist Party official in Fujian province who wrote an open letter to the state-run *People's Daily* in 2004 denouncing corruption among local officials.

Huang won public support after describing death threats that he said forced him to wear a bulletproof vest. But in November 2005 he was convicted of accepting bribes and sentenced to life in prison. Supporters said that the charges against Huang were politically motivated.

Li was initially accused of inciting subversion. He told his lawyer that he was tortured in detention, and interrogated repeatedly about his defense of Huang in newspaper and online articles.

The unexplained subversion charge was later dropped and authorities filed a charge of "deliberately fabricating and spreading alarmist information." The new charge was related to an October 13, 2004, report in the U.S.-based Chinese-language Web site *Boxun News* reporting an outbreak of dengue fever, a viral mosquito-borne disease, in Fuzhou.

The author, identified by his lawyer as Li, anonymously reported more than 20 cases, according to *Boxun News*. In seeking to confirm the information, the Web site did its own research and updated the story to reflect 100 cases.

Li was tried in Fuzhou on January 19, 2006. On January 24, Gulou district court convicted Li and sentenced him to three years in prison. His appeal was rejected.

Ching Cheong, *The Straits Times*
IMPRISONED: April 22, 2005

Ching, a veteran Hong Kong reporter who was the China correspondent for the Singapore daily *The Straits Times*, was detained in Guangzhou while attempting to meet with a source to obtain transcripts of interviews with the late ousted leader Zhao Ziyang. He was held under house arrest in Beijing without access to a lawyer or his family until a formal arrest order was issued in August 2005 on espionage charges.

Official Xinhua News Agency reports in 2005 accused Ching of collecting millions of Hong Kong dollars to spy for Taiwan. Specific charges against him were not made clear until after his trial in a closed hearing in Beijing on August 15, 2006. On August

JOURNALISTS IN PRISON IN 2006

31, the Beijing No. 2 Intermediate People's Court convicted Ching of espionage and sentenced him to five years in prison, plus an additional year's deprivation of political rights.

The verdict in the case later appeared online and was published by several Hong Kong newspapers. The document accused Ching of accepting around 300,000 Hong Kong dollars (not millions as first reported by Xinhua) in fees to submit classified reports on political affairs, economics, and international relations for a Taiwan-based organization called the Foundation of International and Cross-Strait Studies, which authorities said was a cover for a Taiwan intelligence organization. Prosecutors said that Ching had met two representatives from the organization at a current events conference and had done research for them, including sending them reporting by himself and others for *The Straits Times*.

In his defense, Ching argued that he had no knowledge that the organization was a front for Taiwan intelligence—a charge the foundation itself has strongly denied—and that he had provided no state secrets. Ching's appeal was rejected in November.

Li Jianping, freelance
IMPRISONED: May 27, 2005

Li, a writer and businessman, was detained by police in Zibo, in northeast China's Shandong province. Initially held on suspicion of defamation for articles critical of former president Jiang Zemin and current President Hu Jintao, he was tried on more serious charges of "inciting subversion of state authority" on April 12, 2005. Before going forward with the case, state prosecutors sent it back to police twice on grounds of insufficient evidence, according to the U.S.-based advocacy group Human Rights in China.

In his trial, prosecutors cited 31 articles from banned U.S.-based Chinese-language Web sites *Yi Bao* (ChinaEWeekly), *Dajiyuan* (Epoch Times), and *Minzhu Luntan* (Democracy Forum). The verdict cited 18 of those articles, but his wife told CPJ it was not clear that her husband even wrote all of the stories.

On October 25, more than six months after Li's trial, Zibo Intermediate People's Court found him guilty and sentenced him to two years in prison, plus an additional two years' deprivation of political rights. He planned to appeal his verdict, his wife said.

Li Yuanlong, *Bijie Ribao*
IMPRISONED: September 2005

Li, a reporter for *Bijie Ribao* daily newspaper in Guizhou province, was detained in September 2005. He was tried on May 11, 2006, in a five-hour hearing on charges of "inciting subversion of state authority" for online articles criticizing the Chinese Communist Party. In July, Bijie Intermediate People's Court sentenced him to two years in prison.

Li's articles about poverty and unemployment in his home province angered local officials, according to the U.S.-based advocacy group Human Rights in China.

He told his lawyer that he began writing essays and posting them online after becoming increasingly frustrated with the "lies and clichés" he was writing for his state-controlled newspaper, and felt that it was his responsibility as a reporter to expose injustice and inequality. Under the name Ye Lang (Night Wolf), Li wrote articles that were very critical of Chinese Communist Party and local government actions, posting them on banned U.S.-based Web sites *Boxun News*, *Dajiyuan* (Epoch Times), *Yi Bao* (ChinaEWeekly) and *New Century Net*.

He is expected to be released from prison in September 2007.

Yang Tongyan (Yang Tianshui)
freelance
IMPRISONED: December 23, 2005

Yang, commonly known by his pen name, Yang Tianshui, was detained along with a friend in Nanjing, eastern China. He was tried on charges of "subverting state authority" and on May 17, 2006, the Zhenjiang Intermediate People's Court sentenced him to 12 years in prison.

Yang is a well-known writer and a member of the Independent Chinese PEN Center. He was a frequent contributor to U.S.-based Web sites banned in China, including *Boxun News* and *Epoch Times*. He often wrote critically about the ruling Communist Party, and he advocated the release of Internet writers Zheng Yichun and Zhang Lin.

According to the verdict in Yang's case, which was translated into English by the San Francisco-based Dui Hua Foundation, the harsh sentence against him was related to a fictitious online election, established by overseas Chinese citizens, for a "democratic Chinese transitional government." Yang's colleagues say that without his prior knowledge, he was elected "secretariat" of the fictional government.

Yang later wrote an article in *Epoch Times* in support of the model.

Prosecutors also accused Yang of transferring money from overseas to Wang Wenjiang, who had been convicted of endangering state security. Yang's defense lawyer argued that this money was humanitarian assistance to the family of a jailed dissident, and the transfer should not have constituted a criminal act.

Believing that the proceedings were fundamentally unjust, Yang did not appeal. Yang spent 10 years in prison for his opposition to the military crackdown on demonstrators at Tiananmen Square in 1989.

Guo Qizhen, freelance
IMPRISONED: May 12, 2006

Guo was detained as he prepared to join a rolling hunger strike by the lawyer Gao Zhisheng, who was later jailed. He was later formally arrested on charges related to his prolific writing for U.S.-based Chinese-language Web sites *Minzhu Luntan* (Democracy Forum) and *Epoch Times*.

The Cangzhou Intermediate People's Court tried Guo on charges of "inciting subversion of state authority" on September 12, 2006. He was convicted and sentenced to four years in prison, plus an additional two years' deprivation of political rights.

In its opinion presented to the prosecutor on June 16, the Cangzhou Public Security

Bureau cited several online essays as proof of Guo's crimes, including one titled "Letting some of the people first get rich while others cannot make a living," in which he accused the Communist Party government of using its policies to support an "autocratic" and "despotic" regime. Guo was critical of corruption and widespread poverty in the country.

In his defense, Guo argued that his criticism of the Communist Party was protected by the Chinese constitution. He appealed his sentence. Guo is married with a 16-year-old son.

Zhang Jianhong, freelance
IMPRISONED: September 6, 2006

The founder and editor of the popular news and literary Web site Aiqinhai (Aegean Sea) was taken from his home in Ningbo, in eastern China's Zhejiang province. In October, he was formally arrested on charges of "inciting subversion."

Authorities did not clarify their allegations against Zhang, but supporters believed they were linked to his online articles critical of government actions. An editorial he wrote two days before his detention called attention to international organizations' criticism of the government's human rights record and in particular the poor treatment of journalists and their sources two years before the start of the Olympics. Zhang referred to the situation as "Olympicgate."

Zhang was an author, screenwriter, and reporter who served one and a half years of "re-education through labor" in 1989 on counter-revolutionary charges for his writing in support of protesters. He was dismissed from a position on the local Writers Association and began working as a freelance writer.

His Web site Aiqinhai was closed in March 2006 for unauthorized posting of international and domestic news. He had also been a recent contributor to several U.S.-based Chinese-language Web sites, including Boxun News, the pro-democracy forum Minzhu Luntan, and Dajiyuan (Epoch Times).

COLOMBIA: 1

Fredy Muñoz Altamiranda, Telesur
IMPRISONED: November 19, 2006

Muñoz, Colombian correspondent for the regional television network Telesur, was detained by agents of the Colombian national intelligence service, the Administrative Department of Security (DAS), at Eldorado International Airport in Bogotá as he returned from Telesur headquarters in Caracas, Venezuela. The arrest warrant charged him with "rebellion and terrorism," Rodrigo Barrera Barinas, a spokesman for the attorney general, told CPJ.

The DAS said in a statement that a three-year investigation led authorities to link Muñoz to a series of explosions in 2000 and 2002 that destroyed electrical towers in the northern cities of Barranquilla and Cartagena. The explosions have been linked to the left-wing Revolutionary Armed Forces of Colombia (FARC).

The DAS statement said the arrest relied on witness testimony and intelligence reports. Barrera said evidence would not be made public until the investigation was concluded, but he said the arrest was not related to Muñoz's work as a journalist.

In a statement issued from prison on November 20, Muñoz denied the charges.

Esther Hernández, Telesur's director of institutional affairs, said in an interview with CPJ that the arrest was in reprisal for the correspondent's work. Muñoz primarily covered human rights issues, but he had recently reported on the arrests of several congressmen accused of links to paramilitary fighters. That issue is very sensitive because the government has repeatedly denied any official connections to paramilitaries.

Muñoz has had a long career in the Colombian media as a television producer and as an editor for Cartagena and Bogotá newspapers.

The Colombian government has accused Telesur of fomenting terrorism since it began broadcasting in 2005, Hernández told CPJ. In one of Telesur's initial broadcasts, the network showed images of FARC leader Manuel Marulanda, prompting criticism from President Álvaro Uribe Vélez's administration. The network was created at the urging of Venezuelan President Hugo Chávez Frías to promote his perspective throughout the hemisphere.

Muñoz was initially taken to DAS headquarters in Bogotá then moved to the agency's offices in the northern city of Barranquilla, about 590 miles (950 kilometers) away, a Telesur source told CPJ. On November 27, Muñoz was transferred to Cartagena, where he was being held when CPJ conducted its annual census on December 1.

CUBA: 24

Pedro Argüelles Morán, Cooperativa Avileña de Periodistas Independientes
IMPRISONED: March 18, 2003

Argüelles Morán, the director of the independent news agency Cooperativa Avileña de Periodistas Independientes in central Ciego de Ávila province, was tried under Law 88 for the Protection of Cuba's National Independence and Economy. In April 2003, he was sentenced to 20 years in prison.

Argüelles Morán was transferred several times from prison to prison, according to CPJ research. In November 2005, he was sent to Canaleta Prison in Ciego de Ávila province, according to press reports.

During his imprisonment, the journalist developed emphysema, his wife, Yolanda Vera Nerey, told CPJ. She said that a previously existing eye problem had worsened to the point of near blindness. She added that the journalist, who had been diagnosed with arthritis, suffered from inflammation in both knees. In February 2005, Argüelles Morán was hospitalized with inflammation of the liver.

Víctor Rolando Arroyo Carmona
Unión de Periodistas y Escritores de Cuba Independientes
IMPRISONED: March 18, 2003

Arroyo Carmona worked as a journalist for the independent news agency Unión de Periodistas y Escritores de Cuba Independientes (UPECI) in the western province of Pinar del Río. He was tried in April

2003 under Article 91 of the Cuban penal code, which imposes lengthy prison sentences or death for those who act against "the independence or the territorial integrity of the state," and sentenced to 26 years in prison.

The journalist was jailed at the Guantánamo Provincial Prison until September 2005 when he staged a hunger strike to protest mistreatment. In October, he was transferred to a hospital in nearby Holguín province. Ten days later, he was moved to the Holguín Provincial Prison, where he is currently jailed. Arroyo's prison conditions have since improved, his wife, Elsa González Padrón, told CPJ. However, the journalist has been diagnosed with pulmonary emphysema and hypertension, and he was not receiving adequate medical attention, she said.

González Padrón said she had to travel a long distance to visit her husband in prison, and she was allowed to visit him only once every four months. She said that she requested a transfer for her husband but heard no response.

Miguel Galván Gutiérrez
Havana Press
IMPRISONED: March 18, 2003

Galván Gutiérrez, a journalist with the independent news agency Havana Press, was tried under Article 91 of the penal code for acting against "the independence or the territorial integrity of the state." In April 2003, he was sentenced to 26 years in prison, which he was serving at the maximum security Agüica Prison in western Matanzas province.

In May 2004, news reports said that Galván Gutiérrez told his family that he had been jailed in a cell with hardened criminals, whom he said prison officials were inciting to attack him. News reports in 2005 indicated that Galván Gutiérrez was denied medical attention for a urinary ailment. In October 2006, he told Laura Pollán, wife of fellow imprisoned journalist Héctor Maseda Gutiérrez, that he was in good condition.

Julio César Gálvez Rodríguez
freelance
IMPRISONED: March 18, 2003

A Havana-based freelance reporter, Gálvez Rodríguez was tried and convicted in April 2003 under Law 88 for the Protection of Cuba's Independence and Economy, which punishes anyone who commits acts "aiming at subverting the internal order of the nation and destroying its political, economic, and social system." He was sentenced to 15 years in prison.

Gálvez Rodríguez was imprisoned at La Pendiente Prison in Villa Clara, where his wife, Beatriz del Carmen Pedroso, said that he served a year and a half. In 2004, Gálvez Rodríguez was transferred to Combinado del Este Prison in Havana.

The 62-year-old journalist was hospitalized and underwent gall bladder surgery in 2004. Pedroso told CPJ that the surgery had eased her husband's hypertension problems, but she added that he developed a chronic respiratory problem for which he was not receiving proper care. In October 2006, Gálvez Rodríguez was admitted to the Carlos J. Finlay Military

Hospital in Havana, according to news reports.

José Luis García Paneque, Libertad
IMPRISONED: March 18, 2003

García Paneque, director of the independent news agency Libertad in the eastern province of Las Tunas, was sentenced to 24 years in prison in April 2003. The journalist was convicted under Article 91 of the penal code for acting "against the independence or the territorial integrity of the state."

After a series of prison transfers, García Paneque was moved to Las Mangas Prison in Granma province in November 2005. As a result of serious intestinal ailments, he was initially housed in the infirmary. He was diagnosed with internal bleeding and severe malnutrition, said his wife, Yamilé Llánez Labrada. In late September, the journalist, who was still undernourished but in stable condition, was transferred into a cell with 16 hardened prisoners, his wife told CPJ.

Ricardo González Alfonso, freelance
IMPRISONED: March 18, 2003

González Alfonso, freelance journalist and Havana correspondent for the Paris-based press freedom group Reporters Without Borders, was tried in April 2003 under Cuba's Article 91, which imposes lengthy prison sentences or death for those who act against "the independence or the territorial integrity of the state." He was sentenced to 20 years in prison.

González Alfonso was initially incarcerated in Camagüey's Kilo 8 Prison, where he was harassed and punished after staging a hunger strike in December 2003, said his sister Graciela González-Degard.

The journalist's health began to deteriorate in July 2004; he was transferred to a hospital in Camagüey after doctors diagnosed hepatitis. In January 2005, he was admitted to the hospital at Combinado del Este Prison in Havana for gall bladder surgery.

Jailed in 2006 at Combinado del Este, González Alfonso gradually recovered from a series of infections caused by lack of medical attention to his surgical wounds, González-Degard told CPJ. He was imprisoned with common criminals and had lost weight, his sister said.

Léster Luis González Pentón
freelance
IMPRISONED: March 18, 2003

An independent journalist in the central Villa Clara province, González Pentón was tried under Article 91 of the penal code, which imposes lengthy prison sentences or death for those who act against "the independence or the territorial integrity of the state." In April 2003, he was sentenced to 20 years in prison.

He was transferred a number of times before he was jailed at the Villa Clara Provincial Prison, near his home. Mireya de la Caridad Pentón, the journalist's mother, told CPJ that she visited her son every week.

She said that González Pentón shared a cell with four other prisoners and was in relatively good health.

Alejandro González Raga, freelance
IMPRISONED: March 18, 2003

González Raga, an independent freelance journalist based in central Camagüey province, was tried and convicted under Article 91 of the penal code, which punishes those who act against "the independence or the territorial integrity of the state." In April 2003, he was sentenced to 14 years in prison and taken to Canaleta Prison in central Ciego de Ávila province.

González Raga was transferred to Kilo 7 Prison in central Camagüey province in 2004. In early February 2006, he sent an open letter to overseas news Web sites pleading for his freedom. González Raga said in the letter that prison conditions were poor and that his health was deteriorating, according to news reports.

Iván Hernández Carrillo, Patria
IMPRISONED: March 18, 2003

In April 2003, Hernández Carrillo, a journalist with the independent news agency Patria in western Matanzas province, was tried under Law 88 for the Protection of Cuba's National Independence and Economy and sentenced to 25 years in prison.

Originally placed at the Holguín Provincial Prison, Hernández Carrillo waged hunger strikes in 2003 and 2004 to protest inadequate food and medical care. He also complained after prison authorities threatened him and other prisoners.

In 2004, the journalist was transferred to Cuba Sí Prison in eastern Holguín province, hundreds of miles from his home. In January 2005, he was moved to the Pre

Prison in central Villa Clara province, which was closer to his home. He was allowed family visits every two months and marital visits every four months, according to press reports.

Alfredo Pulido López, El Mayor
IMPRISONED: March 18, 2003

Pulido López, director of the Camagüey-based independent news agency El Mayor, was tried under Article 91 of the Cuban penal code for "acting against the independence or the territorial integrity of the state." In April 2003, he was sentenced to 14 years in prison.

Pulido López had been held in solitary confinement for a year at Combinado del Este Prison in Havana, where he was first imprisoned, his wife, Rebeca Rodríguez Souto, told CPJ. In August 2004, Pulido López was transferred to Kilo 7 Prison in his native Camagüey, where he was held in a room with at least 100 hardened prisoners.

Rodríguez Souto said her husband was depressed and was suffering from a series of ailments that seriously weakened him. Among other things, Pulido López has been diagnosed with chronic bronchitis, chronic gastritis, chronic tonsillitis, high blood pressure, severe headaches, hypoglycemia, and loss of eyesight, according to his wife.

José Gabriel Ramón Castillo
Instituto Cultura y Democracia Press
IMPRISONED: March 18, 2003

In April 2003, Ramón Castillo, director of the independent news agency Instituto

Cultura y Democracia Press, was tried under Article 91 of the penal code for acting against "the independence or the territorial integrity of the state." He was given a 20-year prison sentence.

In February 2005, Ramón Castillo was transferred to Boniato Prison in Santiago de Cuba from a military hospital in Havana, where he was treated for various ailments. In 2006, the journalist shared a cell with several hardened convicts, his wife, Blanca Rosa Echavarría, told CPJ. He suffered from high blood pressure, chronic cirrhosis, and severe anxiety, but he was not receiving medical attention, Echavarría said.

Echavarría and her daughter visited Ramón Castillo every 45 days. In January 2006, prison authorities told Echavarría that she would no longer be allowed to bring food. In July, they forbid medicine; in September, they cut by more than half the number of personal hygiene items that Ramón Castillo was allowed to receive.

Omar Rodríguez Saludes
Nueva Prensa Cubana
IMPRISONED: March 18, 2003

The director of the Havana-based independent news agency Nueva Prensa Cubana, Rodríguez Saludes, was tried under Article 91 of the penal code, which imposes lengthy prison sentences or death to anyone who acts "against the independence or territorial integrity of the state." In April 2003, he was sentenced to 27 years in prison.

Rodríguez Saludes was transferred a number of times before he was placed in the Toledo Prison in Havana, where he shared a cell with several men, his wife, Ileana Marrero Joa, told CPJ.

Mijaíl Bárzaga Lugo
Agencia Noticiosa Cubana
IMPRISONED: March 19, 2003

A reporter in Havana for the independent news agency Agencia Noticiosa Cubana, Bárzaga Lugo was tried in April 2003 under Law 88 for the Protection of Cuba's National Independence and Economy. He was sentenced to 15 years in prison that month.

Bárzaga Lugo was jailed at the maximum security Agüica Prison in the western Matanzas province. In October, he met with Laura Pollán, the wife of fellow imprisoned journalist Héctor Maseda Gutiérrez, and told her that he was in good health.

Adolfo Fernández Saínz, Patria
IMPRISONED: March 19, 2003

Fernández Saínz, a Havana journalist for the independent news agency Patria, was convicted under Law 88 for the Protection of Cuba's National Independence and Economy in April 2003. He was sentenced to 15 years in prison.

Fernández Saínz has been transferred among several prisons and has waged a number of hunger strikes to protest prison conditions, CPJ research shows. He was being held in 2006 at Canaleta Prison in central Ciego de Ávila province, a seven-hour bus ride away from his family's home in Havana, his wife, Julia Núñez Pacheco, told CPJ.

The journalist shared a barracks-style cell with at least 23 convicts, Núñez Pacheco told CPJ. A 2004 medical checkup revealed he had several ailments, including emphysema, a hernia, high blood pressure, and a small kidney cyst. In 2006, he was also diagnosed with osteoporosis. His wife said she feared that Fernández Saínz was not receiving appropriate medical treatment.

Alfredo Felipe Fuentes, freelance
IMPRISONED: March 19, 2003

Fuentes, an independent freelance journalist in western Havana province, was tried in April 2003 under Article 91 of the Cuban penal code for acting against "the independence or the territorial integrity of the state." He was sentenced to 26 years in prison.

His wife, Loyda Valdés González, told CPJ that he was being jailed in 2006 at Kilo 5 $1/_2$ Prison in western Pinar del Río province, where he sleeps in a barracks-style cell with at least 80 hardened prisoners. Valdés González, who visited her husband every two months, said that he was diagnosed in September with chronic back problems, which were made worse by the poor conditions of his imprisonment.

Normando Hernández González
Colegio de Periodistas
Independientes de Camagüey
IMPRISONED: March 19, 2003

Hernández González, director of the independent news agency Colegio de Periodistas Independientes de Camagüey, was tried in April 2003 under Article 91 of the penal code, which imposes lengthy prison sentences for those who act against "the independence or the territorial integrity of the state." He was given a 25-year prison sentence.

Hernández González was jailed at the Boniato Prison in eastern Santiago de Cuba province. In August 2003, he joined fellow imprisoned dissidents in a one-week hunger strike. As punishment, he was transferred to the Kilo 5 $1/_2$ Prison in Pinar del Río. In May 2004, the journalist staged a second hunger strike to protest his imprisonment with hardened criminals.

On September 12, 2006, Hernández González was transferred to the maximum security Kilo 7 Prison in his native province of Camagüey. In an interview with CPJ, his wife, Yaraí Reyes Marín, said that he was housed in a barracks with at least 100 other inmates, including hardened criminals. Reyes Marín said prison authorities did not allow her husband to handle his own medicine or keep personal belongings. Hernández González suffered from severe intestinal problems, high blood pressure, headaches, and dizzy spells, according to Reyes Marín.

Juan Carlos Herrera Acosta
Agencia Prensa Libre Oriental
IMPRISONED: March 19, 2003

A journalist for the independent news agency Agencia de Prensa Libre Oriental, Herrera Acosta was tried in April 2003 under Cuba's Law 88 for the Protection of Cuba's National Independence and Economy. He was sentenced to 20 years in prison.

As punishment for having participated with fellow imprisoned journalists in a hunger strike, Herrera Acosta was transferred in August 2003 to the Kilo 8 Prison in central Camagüey province.

According to news reports, he continued to protest the poor conditions of his incarceration throughout 2006 with hunger strikes, self-inflicted wounds, and the use of anti-Castro slogans. The journalist's reactions prompted violent reprimands from prison guards, who beat him severely in March and August, confiscated his personal belongings, took away telephone privileges, and threatened him with solitary confinement.

Herrera Acosta suffered from various ailments since he was jailed. In an interview with CPJ, his wife, Ileana Danger Hardy, said that his health continued to worsen. He lost weight and was weak, but he continued to protest for his rights, she said.

Héctor Maseda Gutiérrez
Grupo de Trabajo Decoro
IMPRISONED: March 19, 2003

Maseda Gutiérrez, a journalist with the independent news agency Grupo de Trabajo Decoro, received a 20-year prison term in April 2003 after he was tried under Article 91 of the Penal Code for acting "against the independence or the territorial integrity of the state," and Law 88 for the Protection of Cuba's National Independence and Economy.

According to news reports, Maseda Gutiérrez was transferred on December 19, 2005, to the maximum security Agüica Prison in the western Matanzas province.

The journalist shared a prison barracks with 70 other inmates, his wife, Laura Pollán, told CPJ. She said the barracks was poorly ventilated and had no bathroom.

Pollán said that her husband suffered from high blood pressure. On April 14, Maseda Gutiérrez requested medical treatment but was instead kept for two hours in a small, dark hallway with at least 12 other handcuffed inmates, Pollán told CPJ. Pollán said the journalist filed a complaint with the attorney general's office.

In 2004, Pollán appealed to Cuban authorities to grant her husband amnesty, but government officials did not respond. In January 2005, she was summoned by the State Security Department and told to keep quiet about her husband's situation. Since then, a security check post has been placed near her home, forcing most of her visitors to be searched and sometimes threatened, Pollán said.

Pablo Pacheco Ávila, Cooperativa Avileña de Periodistas Independientes
IMPRISONED: March 19, 2003

Pacheco Ávila, a journalist with the independent news agency Cooperativa Avileña de Periodistas Independientes, was tried in April 2003 under Law 88 for the Protection of Cuba's National Independence and Economy. He was sentenced to 20 years in prison.

The journalist began serving his jail sentence at Agüica Prison in western Matanzas province, hundreds of miles from his home. In August 2004, he was moved to Morón Prison in Ciego de Ávila, his native province.

In March 2005, his wife, Oleivys García

Echemendía, told CPJ that Pacheco Ávila suffered from high blood pressure, severe headaches, acute gastritis, and inflammation in both knees, which made it difficult for him to walk.

In March 2006, the 36-year-old journalist was transferred to Provincial Hospital Antonio Luaces Iraola after doctors diagnosed kidney problems, García Echemendía told reporters.

Fabio Prieto Llorente, freelance
IMPRISONED: March 19, 2003

A freelance journalist in the western Isla de la Juventud special municipality, Prieto Llorente was tried in April 2003 under Law 88 for the Protection of Cuba's National Independence and Economy. He was sentenced to 20 years in prison.

In January 2006, Prieto Llorente was transferred from Kilo 8 Prison in central Camagüey province to El Guayabo Prison in his native province.

His sister, Clara Lourdes Prieto Llorente, told CPJ that the journalist was moved to solitary confinement beginning August 2, after expressing support for political change in the wake of President Fidel Castro's illness. She said other prisoners told her that the cell measured just six square feet, had no windows, and was poorly ventilated.

The journalist suffered from depression, high blood pressure, back pain, and emphysema, family members told CPJ. Since his transfer, his sister said, his family feared that he was not receiving proper medical attention.

Omar Ruiz Hernández
Grupo de Trabajo Decoro
IMPRISONED: March 19, 2003

Ruiz Hernández, a journalist for the independent news agency Grupo de Trabajo Decoro in the central Villa Clara province, was sentenced to 18 years in prison after he was tried under Article 91 of the penal code, which punishes with prison or death anyone who acts "against the independence or the territorial integrity of the state."

Ruiz Hernández was transferred twice before being sent to Nieves Morejón Prison in the central Sancti Spíritus province in November 2005. His wife, Bárbara Maritza Rojo Arias, told CPJ that her husband shared a cell with more than 10 prisoners.

Ruiz Hernández was diagnosed with high blood pressure in 2004. His wife, who visited him every two months, said she brought blood pressure medication, but her husband was not being treated for dizzy spells and an undiagnosed skin condition. On October 6, 2006, prison guards broke a brace that the journalist needed to ease backaches.

José Ubaldo Izquierdo, Grupo de
Trabajo Decoro
IMPRISONED: March 19, 2003

A journalist for the independent news agency Grupo de Trabajo Decoro in western Havana province, Ubaldo Izquierdo was tried in April 2003 under Article 91 of the penal code for acting against "the independence or the territorial integrity of the state," and handed a 16-year prison sentence.

Ubaldo Izquierdo was being held at the Guanajay Prison in Havana province, said Laura Pollán, wife of fellow imprisoned journalist Héctor Maseda Gutiérrez. Pollán told CPJ that Izquierdo's family visited him every 45 days. His wife, Yamilka Morejón Morfa, was quoted in news reports as saying that prison authorities harassed her and her children during a visit in March.

According to news reports, Ubaldo Izquierdo was diagnosed in February 2006 with a gastrointestinal ailment. Doctors recommended a strict diet, but prison authorities said they could not provide it, the reports said. The journalist was hospitalized in April with abdominal pain.

Armando Betancourt Reina
Nueva Prensa Cubana
IMPRISONED: May 23, 2006

Betancourt Reina, a reporter for the independent news agency Nueva Prensa Cubana, was arrested while covering the eviction of families from homes in the central city of Camagüey, members of his family told CPJ.

Local police told the journalist's family that he was arrested for participating in a protest against the eviction, although several CPJ sources said the claim was untrue. According to his wife, Mercedes Boudet Silva, authorities told her lawyer that her husband would be charged with aggravated public disorder, punishable by at least three years in prison. No charges were publicly filed by November 30.

Betancourt Reina was held at the Cerámica Roja Prison in Camagüey, where he shared a dormitory-style cell with 12 other prisoners. The journalist told his wife during a visit in October that he was in good health, but that he had been denied access to a priest.

Guillermo Espinosa Rodríguez
Agencia de Prensa Libre Oriental
IMPRISONED: October 26, 2006

Espinosa Rodríguez, a reporter for the independent agency Agencia de Prensa Libre Oriental (APLO), was detained by agents of the Cuban State Security on October 26 and held for 12 days at agency headquarters in the eastern city of Santiago de Cuba. After a 45-minute trial on November 6, he was sentenced to two years of home confinement on charges of "social dangerousness."

The vague, preemptory charge of "social dangerousness," punishable by up to four years in prison, is used by Cuban authorities to silence critics. Under Article 72 of the Cuban Penal Code, "any person shall be deemed dangerous if he or she has shown proclivity to commit crimes demonstrated by conduct that is in manifest contradiction with the norms of socialist morality."

Espinosa Rodríguez is allowed to leave his home to go to work, but is barred from attending public gatherings or leaving Santiago de Cuba, his cousin, Diosmel Rodríguez, told CPJ. Espinosa Rodríguez is also forbidden from practicing journalism and has been ordered to work at a state-controlled office, APLO reported on the Miami-based news Web site *CubaNet*. If he does not comply with these terms, authorities told Espinosa Rodríguez that he would be forced to serve his term in prison, his cousin said.

Espinosa Rodríguez had been covering an outbreak of dengue fever in Santiago de Cuba since July. Authorities suppressed news of the outbreak, which was not reported in the official press. He had been detained at least three times in three months and told that he would go to jail for the long-term if he did not stop writing "lies," his cousin told CPJ.

DEMOCRATIC REPUBLIC OF CONGO: 1

Mbaka Bosange, *Mambenga*
IMPRISONED: November 21, 2006

Bosange, a reporter for the private weekly *Mambenga*, was arrested while reporting on clashes between the police and angry demonstrators outside the Supreme Court in the capital, Kinshasa, according to the local press freedom group Journaliste en Danger (JED) and local journalists.

CPJ could not establish why Bosange was arrested. He was held incommunicado and without charge at the Police General Directorate for Special Services, known as "Kin Mazière," according to CPJ sources.

ERITREA: 23

Zemenfes Haile, *Tsigenay*
IMPRISONED: January 1999

Haile, founder and manager of the private weekly *Tsigenay*, was arrested for allegedly failing to complete his national service. CPJ

sources said he was released from prison in 2002 but was sent to the army to perform extended military service. The sources believe that Haile's continued deprivation of liberty is part of the government's general crackdown on the press, which began in September 2001.

Ghebrehiwet Keleta, *Tsigenay*
IMPRISONED: July 2000

Keleta, a reporter for the private weekly *Tsigenay*, was seized by security agents on his way to work sometime in July 2000 and has not been seen since. CPJ sources believe that his continued detention is connected to the government's overall crackdown on the press.

Said Abdelkader, *Admas*
Yusuf Mohamed Ali, *Tsigenay*
Amanuel Asrat, *Zemen*
Temesken Ghebreyesus, *Keste Debena*
Mattewos Habteab, *Meqaleh*
Dawit Habtemichael, *Meqaleh*
Medhanie Haile, *Keste Debena*
Dawit Isaac, *Setit*
Seyoum Tsehaye, freelance
Fesshaye "Joshua" Yohannes, *Setit*
IMPRISONED: September 2001

Eritrean security forces arrested these 10 local journalists in the days following September 18, 2001. The arrests came less than a week after authorities abruptly closed all privately owned newspapers, allegedly to safeguard national unity in the face of growing political turmoil in this Horn of Africa nation.

Authorities have variously accused the

journalists of avoiding the military draft, threatening national security, and failing to observe licensing requirements. But CPJ research indicates that the crackdown was part of a government drive to crush political dissent in advance of elections scheduled for December 2001, which were subsequently cancelled. The fledgling private press covered a split in the ruling party at that time and provided a forum for debate on President Isaias Afewerki's autocratic rule. An open letter in *Setit* published on September 9, 2001, for example, told the government that "people can tolerate hunger and other problems for a long time, but they can't tolerate the absence of good administration and justice."

In a 2006 CPJ interview, presidential spokesman Yemane Gebremeskel denied that the journalists were imprisoned because of what they wrote, saying only that they "were involved in acts against the national interest of the state." He said "the substance of the case is clear to everybody" but declined to detail any supporting evidence.

The journalists were initially held incommunicado at a police station in the capital, where they began a hunger strike on March 31, 2002. In a message smuggled from their jail, the journalists said they would refuse food until they were released or charged and given due process. Instead, they were transferred to secret locations, and no official information has been available since. The government has refused to divulge their whereabouts, their health, or even whether they are still alive.

The government's monopoly on domestic media, the fear of reprisal among prisoners' families, and recently tightened restrictions on the movement of all foreigners have made it extremely difficult to verify unofficial information. An unbylined report circulated on several Web sites in August and deemed by CPJ sources to be generally credible, claimed that journalists and opposition leaders arrested in the crackdown were moved in 2003 to a secretly built desert prison, accessible only on foot and two hours from the nearest populated place. CPJ sources said they believed that the description of the place was credible but some of the details were inaccurate.

The report does not attribute the source of its details, but CPJ sources believe they may have come from at least one prison guard who fled into exile. Its content is detailed and it contains a section on the conditions of the prison and directives for the prison guards. The report was first posted on *Aigaforum*, a Web site considered close to the government of Ethiopia. Ethiopia is a bitter rival of its neighboring country. The report was later posted on Eritrean diaspora sites such as *Awate* and *Asmarino*, which said they believed some of its content to be correct.

CPJ sources could not verify the report's claim that at least three journalists had died in custody. The report named the three as "Mr. Yusuf," believed by CPJ sources to refer to Yusuf Mohamed Ali of *Tsigenay*; "Mr. Medhane Tewelde," believed to refer to Medhanie Haile of *Keste Debena*; and "Mr Said," believed to refer to Said Abdelkader of *Admas*.

In a letter hand delivered to the Eritrean embassy in Washington on November 2, CPJ sought information about all of the jailed Eritrean journalists. In particular, the letter to Ambassador Girma Asmerom sought to determine whether the three journalists cited in the online report were alive. Eritrean officials did not respond.

In 2006, exiled Eritrean journalists organized a group to report on their colleagues' plight and to keep the international spotlight from fading. The Association of Eritrean Journalists in Exile launched a Web site at www.aeje.org.

Swedish diplomats have long sought to gain the release of Isaac, reporter and co-owner of *Setit*, who has dual Eritrean and Swedish nationality. Isaac was released for a medical checkup on November 19, 2005, and allowed to phone his family and a friend in Sweden. Despite hopes that he would be freed, Isaac was returned to jail two days later with no explanation, according to CPJ sources.

The jailed journalists include Yohannes, publisher and founding editor of *Setit*, who in the 1990s was considered a pioneer in Eritrea's fledgling independent press. Yohannes was awarded a CPJ International Press Freedom Award in 2002.

Selamyinghes Beyene, *Meqaleh*
IMPRISONED: Fall 2001

Beyene, a reporter for the independent weekly *Meqaleh*, was arrested in the fall of 2001. CPJ sources believed that his detention was part of the government's general crackdown on the press, which began in September 2001. In 2002 he was taken to do military service, and was still performing his national service requirement, according to CPJ sources.

Saleh Aljezeeri, Eritrean State Radio
Hamid Mohammed Said, Eritrean State Television
IMPRISONED: February 15, 2002

During a July 2002 fact-finding mission to the capital, Asmara, CPJ delegates confirmed that on or around February 15, Eritrean authorities arrested Said, a journalist for the state-run Eritrean State Television (ETV); Aljezeeri, a journalist for Eritrean State Radio; and Saadia Ahmed, a journalist with the Arabic-language service of ETV. Ahmed was released some time around early 2005, according to CPJ sources.

The reasons for their arrests were unclear, but CPJ sources said they believed their detentions were related to the government's general crackdown on the press, which began in September 2001.

Temesghen Abay, Eritrean State Radio (Tigrigna service)
Yemane Haile, Eritrean News Agency
Amer Ibrahim, Eritrean State Television (Arabic service)
Ahmed Idris, Eritrean State Television (Arabic service)
Fethiya Khaled, Eritrean State Television (Arabic service)
Paulos Kidane, Eritrean State Television and Radio (Amharic service)
Daniel Mussie, Eritrean State Television and Radio (Oromo service)
Senait Tesfay, Eritrean State Television (Tigrigna service)
IMPRISONED: November 2006

Security forces arrested at least nine state

media journalists beginning on or around November 12, and they continued to hold at least eight as of December 1, according to several CPJ sources. The reason for the crackdown was not immediately known, but sources said they believed it was intended to intimidate state media workers after several colleagues had fled the country.

Those sources said the government was known to detain and question state media journalists, but the scale and duration of these detentions was unusual. The journalists were initially taken to a police detention center in central Asmara known as Agip, but CPJ sources could not confirm whether they remained there or had been taken elsewhere.

Questioned by Agence France-Presse in the capital, Asmara, Information Minister Ali Abdu claimed that the journalists had been freed. "It was a routine matter and they have been released," AFP quoted him as saying in a November 23 report. But CPJ sources said one week later that only one had been freed and that the eight listed journalists remained in custody.

Eritrean presidential spokesman Yemane Ghebremeskel told The Associated Press on November 23 that he was unaware of the arrests. Eritrea's embassy in the United States did not respond to CPJ's requests for information.

ETHIOPIA: 18

Dawit Kebede, *Hadar*
Feleke Tibebu, *Hadar*
IMPRISONED: November 2, 2005

Andualem Ayle, *Ethiop*
Wosonseged Gebrekidan, *Addis Zena*
Dereje Habtewolde, *Netsanet*
Nardos Meaza, *Satanaw*
Mesfin Tesfaye, *Abay*
Zekarias Tesfaye, *Netsanet*
Fassil Yenealem, *Addis Zena*
Wenakseged Zeleke, *Asqual*
IMPRISONED: November 9-14, 2005

Serkalem Fassil
Iskinder Nega
Menilik, Asqual, and *Satanaw*
IMPRISONED: November 27, 2005

Sisay Agena, *Ethiop* and Ethiopian Free Press Journalists Association
IMPRISONED: November 29, 2005

Dawit Fassil, *Satanaw*
IMPRISONED: November or December 2005

These editors and publishers of Amharic-language newspapers were arrested in a massive crackdown on the private press and opposition that followed antigovernment protests in the capital, Addis Ababa, in November 2005. They were charged in December 2005 along with dozens of opposition leaders with conspiring to overthrow the government. The charges could bring death sentences upon conviction. All of the defendants were denied bail.

The joint trial of these journalists and opposition leaders began in February, with most observers expecting it to last many months or even years. Charges against the journalists included "outrage against the constitution and the constitutional order," "impairment of the defensive power of the state," and "attempted genocide." Nega faces additional charges of "obstruction of the exercise of constitutional powers," "inciting, organizing, and leading armed rebellion against the government," and "high treason." He was charged as a leader of the CUD opposition party but has denied the accusation.

The journalists refused to put up a defense, saying the charges were baseless and the proceedings politicized. A CPJ analysis of evidence provided by the prosecution found that the journalists' work was often antigovernment but did not constitute incitement to violence or genocide. In April, CPJ issued a special report, "Poison, Politics, and the Press," outlining its findings.

In March, a CPJ delegation was allowed to visit Kality Prison near Addis Ababa and meet with some of the jailed journalists. The delegation spoke with Nega, Fassil, Agena, and Yenealem, all of whom said they had been doing their jobs as journalists in criticizing the government. Prisoners complained that their conditions were difficult.

When the trial went into recess in August and September, CPJ received reports that Nega and Agena had been moved to the capital's Karchele Prison, known for its harsh conditions. Several sources said these prisoners were abused and that their visiting rights were severely curtailed. The two were not told why they had been moved to another prison, the sources said. After CPJ wrote a letter to Prime Minister Meles Zenawi expressing concern about the prisoners, sources said conditions improved somewhat.

Solomon Aregawi, *Hadar*
IMPRISONED: November
or December 2005

Aregawi, owner of the defunct Amharic-language newspaper *Hadar*, was arrested in a crackdown that followed the civil unrest in November 2005. He was jailed in Kality Prison in Addis Ababa. Aregawi, who inherited *Hadar* from his father, was charged in March along with 32 other defendants with conspiracy and "outrages against the constitution," state prosecutor Shemelis Kemal confirmed to CPJ in July.

He pleaded not guilty and was denied bail. The charge against Aregawi stemmed from articles published in *Hadar* about the disputed elections, Kemal said. The prosecutor could not say if there were further charges against Aregawi.

Aregawi and the 32 charged with him were being tried separately from the dozens of opposition leaders, activists, and journalists who were charged in December 2005 and put on trial for wide-ranging antistate crimes and attempted "genocide." Kemal said the "nature of the crime" was the same. Aregawi is accused of publishing "seditious" articles as part of an alleged opposition plot to overthrow the government, the prosecutor told CPJ, adding that "different people with different capacities have been involved in the same grand design."

Abraham Gebrekidan, *Politika*
IMPRISONED: March 8, 2006

Gebrekidan, former editor of the defunct

Amharic-language weekly *Politika*, was sentenced to one year in prison for publishing "false news" and was immediately jailed, according to several local sources. His conviction was handed down in connection with a 2002 report attributed to the BBC, which claimed that Ethiopia was training rebels in neighboring Eritrea. Gebrekidan is one of several journalists jailed under Ethiopia's repressive 1992 Press Law, often on years-old charges, after the November 2005 crackdown.

Abraham Reta Alemu, *Ruh*
IMPRISONED: April 25, 2006

Reta, editor of the now-defunct Amharic-language weekly *Ruh*, was sentenced to one year in jail on a criminal defamation charge stemming from a 2002 story that accused government officials of misusing World Bank aid, according to CPJ sources. After *Ruh* stopped publishing, Reta freelanced for several Amharic newspapers, the sources said. He was one of several journalists jailed under Ethiopia's repressive 1992 Press Law, often on years-old charges, after the November 2005 crackdown.

Tesehalene Mengesha, *Mebruk*
IMPRISONED: May 2006

Mengesha, an editor at the now-defunct Amharic-language weekly *Mebruk*, was sentenced to 18 months in jail for publishing "false information." He was placed in Kality Prison. The charge stemmed from a 1995 story about an assassination attempt against Egyptian President Hosni Mubarak, according to CPJ research. Oth-

er details about the story and the prosecution's case were not available. Like many Ethiopian editors, Mengesha has had several criminal charges hanging over him for some time. He was one of several journalists jailed under Ethiopia's repressive 1992 Press Law, often on years-old charges, after the November 2005 crackdown.

THE GAMBIA: 1

"Chief" Ebrimah B. Manneh
Daily Observer
IMPRISONED: July 7, 2006

Security agents arrested "Chief" Ebrimah B. Manneh, a reporter for the pro-government *Daily Observer*, at the newspaper's offices, according to sources who did not wish to be identified for fear of retribution from the authorities. He was arrested shortly after an altercation with the newspaper's managing editor, Saja Taal, according to the same sources. Taal disputed the description, saying Manneh was not at work that week.

Manneh's whereabouts, the reason for his detention, his legal status, and his health were all undisclosed.

According to a CPJ source and the Ghana-based Media Foundation for West Africa, the National Intelligence Agency (NIA) was responsible for Manneh's arrest. In an interview with CPJ in July, NIA investigator Lamine Saine denied that the agency was holding Manneh or that it had imprisoned any journalists. CPJ research, however, showed that at least five journalists were imprisoned in NIA detention facilities during the year. Information Minister Neneh Mcdoll-Gaye told CPJ in July that she had no information about Manneh's whereabouts.

IRAN: 1

Arash Sigarchi, freelance
IMPRISONED: January 26, 2006

Sigarchi, a former editor of the daily newspaper *Gilan-e-Emruz* and a Web blogger, was sentenced to three years in prison by an Iranian appellate court on several offenses, including insulting Supreme Guide Ayatollah Ali Khamenei and propagandizing against the Islamic Republic in his blog.

Sigarchi had posted entries and given interviews to Western radio stations that were critical of the government's harassment of fellow bloggers. He was originally given a 14-year sentence by a revolutionary court in Gilan in February 2005.

IRAQ: 1

Bilal Hussein, The Associated Press
IMPRISONED: April 12, 2006

Hussein, a freelance Iraqi photographer who worked for The Associated Press since 2004, was taken into custody by U.S. forces in the Iraqi city of Ramadi for "imperative reasons of security" on April 12 and held without charge or the disclosure of evidence of a crime.

The U.S. military alleged that Hussein had ties to insurgents. "He has close relationships with persons known to be responsible for kidnappings, smuggling, improvised explosive device (IED) attacks, and other attacks on coalition forces," according to a May 7 e-mail from Maj. Gen. John Gardner to AP International Editor John Daniszewski.

According to AP, one of the most specific allegations cited by U.S. officials is that Hussein was involved in the kidnapping of two Arab journalists in Ramadi by Iraqi insurgents.

But an AP investigation found that the two abducted journalists had never implicated Hussein in the kidnapping—instead singling him out for praise for his assistance when they were released. The military's only evidence to support its claim appeared to be photographs of the released journalists found in Hussein's camera, according to AP.

AP President and CEO Thomas Curley called for Hussein to be charged or freed, and CPJ Chairman Paul Steiger urged the Pentagon to provide due process. The Pentagon's Bryan Whitman said Hussein was given the opportunity to provide information in his defense at two military reviews, but an AP lawyer said Hussein received notice of only one such hearing—and that notice came after the hearing took place.

Whitman gave no specifics about the basis for Hussein's detention or whether the military would charge him with an offense.

Hussein shared a 2005 Pulitzer Prize with other AP photographers for their work in Iraq.

MALDIVES: 1

Abdullah Saeed (Fahala)
Minivan Daily
IMPRISONED: March 26, 2006

Saeed, known as Fahala, was among several journalists employed by the opposition Minivan news group who were targeted with legal action in 2006. Saeed, a reporter for the newspaper *Minivan Daily*, was initially sentenced to a two-month term for refusing to take a urine test after he was detained in October 2005.

In April 2006, he was sentenced to life imprisonment on charges that he intended to sell drugs. His colleagues believe the charges were fabricated and that he was targeted to silence coverage that was critical of the government.

In the trial against Saeed, his lawyer argued that police planted drugs in the journalist's clothing after calling him to the station for unspecified reasons. The lawyer said that police found no drugs during an initial search of the journalist's pockets—while the lawyer was present—only to discover 1.1 grams of heroin after isolating Saeed and removing his clothes from view.

Minivan Daily, affiliated with the Maldivian Democracy Party, was established in July 2005 as the first daily newspaper not aligned with the government of Maldivian President Maumoon Gayoom, who has ruled since 1978. Minivan means "independence" in Dhivehi.

In a meeting at CPJ's office in May, Maldivian Foreign Minister Ahmed Shaheed suggested that Saeed could be held under house arrest pending his appeal. Instead, he has stayed behind bars at high-security Maafushi Prison, where he has been held intermittently in solitary confinement.

MEXICO: 1

Ángel Mario Ksheratto, *Cuarto Poder*
IMPRISONED: November 9, 2006

Chiapas state police detained Ksheratto, columnist for the daily *Cuarto Poder*, outside his home in the southern city of Tuxtla Gutiérrez for allegedly violating a condition of bail by failing to make a weekly court appearance, according to news reports and a CPJ source. Ksheratto was taken to a maximum security prison in the town of Cintalapa, where he was being held when CPJ conducted its annual census on December 1. Ksheratto denied violating the condition.

The case stemmed from a 2003 criminal defamation complaint. While that charge was pending, the columnist was required to appear in court every week to sign documentation before a judge in Cintalapa, 65 miles (120 kilometers) from his home, the daily *La Jornada* reported. Ksheratto had been detained on February 4 and held for 18 days on a similar bail violation allegation.

The underlying case against Ksheratto stems from two August 2002 articles on alleged irregularities in a state-run agency responsible for school construction. The columnist alleged that a public official had used state money to build a house. Ksheratto was arrested on January 9, 2003, after the official filed a complaint; he was released on bail the next day.

Unlike many other places in Latin America, the state of Chiapas has moved to stiffen criminal defamation laws. In February 2004, the Chiapas state congress unanimously approved amendments to Articles 164, 169, and 173 of the state's penal code, drastically increasing penalties for defamation. Articles 164 and 169 raised minimum penalties for defamation and libel from two to three years and maximum penalties from five to nine years.

RUSSIA: 2

Boris Stomakhin, *Radikalnaya Politika*
IMPRISONED: March 22, 2006

Stomakhin, editor of the low-circulation monthly newspaper *Radikalnaya Politika* (Radical Politics), was jailed on charges of inciting ethnic hatred and making public appeals for extremist activity. In November, the Butyrsky District Court in Moscow sentenced him to five years in prison. He and his family said authorities were punishing him for his harsh criticism of Kremlin policy in Chechnya.

In its written ruling, the court cited a number of passages. In one, the court quoted Stomakhin as writing: "Let tens of new Chechen snipers take their positions in the mountain ridges and the city ruins and let hundreds, thousands of aggressors fall under righteous bullets! No mercy! Death to the Russian occupiers!" In another article cited by the court, Stomakhin said a Moscow subway bombing was "justified, natural and legal. ... The Chechens have the full

moral right to bomb everything they want in Russia."

Stomakhin, who had pleaded not guilty, said he was "tried for his views and not for any real crime. ... In the articles, I expressed my opinion, with which people were free to agree or disagree," the news agency RIA-Novosti reported. He said an opinion was not a "call to action."

The charges stemmed from a December 2003 complaint filed by two Communist Party members who said *Radikalnaya Politika* was run by "Chechen bandits," the human rights news agency Prima reported. Police raided Stomakhin's apartment in April 2004, confiscating his computer, copies of *Radikalnaya Politika*, computer disks, books, leaflets, and other editorial material. Stomakhin fled for a time to Ukraine where he unsuccessfully sought political asylum.

He was arrested in March 2006, a day after he fell from the window of his fourth-floor Moscow apartment while trying to elude police, according to local press reports. Stomakhin suffered a broken ankle and back injuries.

Vladimir Korolyov
Permsky Obozrevatel
IMPRISONED: September 11, 2006

Police in the western city of Perm arrested Korolyov, a photographer for the independent weekly *Permsky Obozrevatel*, on a charge of disclosing unspecified state secrets under Article 283 of Russia's criminal code, his lawyer and colleagues told CPJ. Korolyov had just been released from the hospital after undergoing treatment for a heart condition, the U.S. government-funded Radio

Free Europe/Radio Liberty reported.

Authorities subjected journalists at *Permsky Obozrevatel*, the city's only independent newspaper, to months of legal harassment, according to CPJ research. The weekly features critical coverage of the local administration and analytical articles on corruption, privatization, and the redistribution of municipal property.

Police raided the paper twice in 2006, in May and again in August, confiscating servers, computers, disks, flash cards, staff records, and photographs. Investigators also searched Korolyov's home, seizing video and audiotapes, his wife's architectural drawings, and other personal belongings.

In August, authorities formally opened criminal investigations into all eight of the newspaper's staffers on charges of "insult," "violating the right to private life," and "disclosing state secrets."

Korolyov was being held in a Perm pretrial detention center. Karen Nersisian, a Moscow lawyer helping to defend Korolyov, said his client had been pressured to make statements against the newspaper and its founder, Igor Grinberg.

SRI LANKA: 1

Parameswaree Maunasámi
Mawbima
IMPRISONED: November 24, 2006

Maunasámi, a freelance reporter who wrote about the conflict between the Sri Lankan government and the separatist rebel group Liberation Tigers of Tamil Eelam for the Sinhala-language weekly *Mawbima*, was detained at her residence at a boarding house in Wellawatta, south of the capital, Colombo, according to the Colombo-based media advocacy group Free Media Movement. Police detained Maunasámi, who is an ethnic Tamil, along with another Tamil woman living at the boarding house and transferred them to the Terrorist Investigation Division, police told FMM.

Sri Lankan authorities have not given a reason for the journalist's detention. She was held under antiterrorist legislation that allows prolonged detention without charge or trial. Local Sinhala-language newspaper reports linked her arrest to the confiscation of ammunition, but police said that no ammunition was recovered by any police station, according to FMM.

Mawbima has distinguished itself among Sinhala-language newspapers for an editorial line that is critical of both Sri Lankan military and LTTE actions, said FMM spokesperson Sunanda Deshapriya. Maunasámi's colleagues at *Mawbima* expressed concern about her detention and believe she may have been targeted

TUNISIA: 1

Mohamed Abbou, freelance
IMPRISONED: March 1, 2005

Abbou, a human rights lawyer, was arrested by Tunisian secret police on March 1, 2005, and handed a three-and-a-half-year prison sentence the next month. The verdict was based on an Internet article that "defamed the judicial process" and was "likely to disturb public order," but the government provided no details as to when the material appeared or what it said.

Abbou wrote for a banned Tunisian news Web site, *TunisNews*, comparing torture in Tunisia's prisons to that of Iraq's infamous Abu Ghraib. An appeals court upheld the verdict on June 10, 2005.

TURKEY: 1

Memik Horuz, *Ozgur Gelecek*
and *Isci Koylu*
IMPRISONED: June 18, 2001

Horuz, editor of the leftist publications *Ozgur Gelecek* and *Isci Koylu*, was arrested and later charged with "membership in an illegal organization," a crime under Article 168/2 of the penal code. Prosecutors based the case against Horuz on interviews he had allegedly conducted with leftist guerrillas, which *Ozgur Gelecek* published in 2000 and 2001.

The state also based its case on the testimony of an alleged former militant who claimed that the journalist belonged to the outlawed Marxist-Leninist Communist Party. Horuz was convicted on June 18, 2002, and sentenced to 12 years and six months in prison.

UNITED STATES: 1

Joshua Wolf, freelance
IMPRISONED: September 22, 2006

Wolf, a freelance blogger and videographer, was jailed in San Francisco for refusing to turn over to a federal grand jury a videotape of a 2005 protest.

The case pending in a federal appellate court hinges on whether Wolf has a First Amendment or common law right not to turn over his videotape. On August 1, a federal judge ordered him to jail for refusing to turn over the tape. He was incarcerated for 30 days before a two-judge panel of the 9th Circuit Court of Appeals ordered him free on bail while his appeal was pending. On September 11, a three-judge panel for the same appellate court revoked Wolf's bail at the prosecution's request. He returned to jail on September 22 even as his appeal was pending.

Wolf taped clashes between demonstrators and San Francisco police during a June 2005 protest by anarchists against a Group of Eight economic conference. Wolf sold footage of the protest to San Francisco television stations and posted it on his Web site. Investigators are seeking Wolf's testimony and portions of his videotape that were not broadcast. A federal grand jury is investigating possible criminal activity, including an alleged attempt by protesters to burn a police vehicle.

U.S. NAVAL BASE GUANTÁNAMO BAY: 1

Sami Muhyideen al-Haj, Al-Jazeera
IMPRISONED: December 15, 2001

Al-Haj, a Sudanese national and assistant cameraman for Al-Jazeera, was detained by Pakistani forces after he and an Al-Jazeera reporter attempted to re-enter southern

Afghanistan at the Chaman border crossing in Pakistan. About a month later he was handed over to U.S. forces and eventually sent to the U.S. Naval Base at Guantánamo Bay, Cuba, in June 2002.

According to recently declassified military documents, the U.S. military alleged that he worked as a financial courier for Chechen rebels and that he assisted al-Qaeda and extremist figures. But al-Haj was not convicted or charged with a crime, and he was being held on the basis of secret evidence.

Al-Haj's London-based lawyer, Clive Stafford Smith, maintained that his client's continued detention was political. He said that the main focus of U.S. interrogators has not been al-Haj's alleged terrorist activities but obtaining intelligence on Al-Jazeera and its staff. Virtually all of the roughly 130 interrogations al-Haj was subjected to focused on Al-Jazeera, Stafford Smith said. At one point, U.S. military interrogators allegedly told al-Haj that he would be released if he agreed to inform U.S. intelligence authorities about the satellite news network's activities, Stafford Smith said. Al-Haj refused.

CPJ outlined the al-Haj case in an October special report titled "The Enemy?" The report urged the U.S. government to provide fair and transparent due process.

UZBEKISTAN: 5

Muhammad Bekjanov
Yusuf Ruzimuradov
Erk
IMPRISONED: March 15, 1999

A court in the capital, Tashkent, sentenced Bekjanov, editor of the opposition newspaper *Erk*, to 14 years in prison and Ruzimuradov, an employee of the paper, to 15 years. They were convicted of publishing and distributing a banned newspaper that criticized President Islam Karimov, participating in a banned political protest, and attempting to overthrow the regime.

Both men were tortured during their pretrial detention in Tashkent City Prison, which left them with serious injuries, Tashkent-based human right activists told CPJ. On November 15, 1999, Bekjanov was transferred to "strict regime" Penal Colony 64/46 in the city of Navoi. Ruzimuradov was transferred to "strict regime" Penal Colony 64/33 in the village of Shakhali near the southern city of Karshi.

The wives and children of both men fled to the United States in 1999 after their arrests, Erk Party Secretary-General Aranazar Arifov told CPJ.

In 2003, reporters with the London-based Institute for War and Peace Reporting (IWPR) and The Associated Press interviewed Bekjanov in the Tashkent Prison Hospital while he was being treated for tuberculosis contracted in prison. Bekjanov described torture and beatings that resulted in a broken leg and hearing loss in his right ear, IWPR reported.

In 2006, Bekjanov was jailed in the southwestern city of Kasan, according to the independent news Web site *Uznews*. His wife, Nina Bekjanova, who was allowed to visit him in October 2006, said he told her that he was still subjected to beatings and torture that, among other things, caused him to lose most of his teeth, *Uznews* reported.

Exiled journalists, human rights workers, and other CPJ sources said they did not know Ruzimuradov's whereabouts, his conditions, or his health in 2006.

Gayrat Mehliboyev, freelance
IMPRISONED: July 24, 2002

Police arrested Mehliboyev at a bazaar in Tashkent for allegedly participating in a rally protesting the imprisonment of members of the banned Islamist opposition party Hizb ut-Tahrir. After his arrest, police searched his bed in a local hostel and claimed they found banned religious literature that prosecutors later characterized as extremist in nature, according to international press reports.

Mehliboyev was held in pretrial detention for more than six months before his trial began on February 5, 2003. Prosecutors presented as evidence of Mehliboyev's alleged religious extremism a political commentary he had written for the April 11, 2001, edition of *Hurriyat*.

The article questioned whether Western democracy should be a model for Uzbekistan and said that religion was the true path to achieving social justice. Prosecutors claimed that the article contained ideas from Hizb ut-Tahrir.

A Tashkent-based representative of Human Rights Watch monitored the trial and told CPJ that several times during the proceedings Mehliboyev said he was beaten in custody, but the court ignored his comments. Mehliboyev's brother, Shavkat, said the defendant was forced to confess to having connections to Hizb ut-Tahrir.

The Shaikhantaur Regional Court sentenced Mehliboyev to seven years in prison on February 18, 2003, after convicting him of anticonstitutional activities, participating in extremist religious organizations, and inciting religious hatred, according to local and international press reports. The sentence was later reduced on appeal to six and a half years in prison.

Ortikali Namazov, *Pop Tongi* and *Kishlok Khayoti*
IMPRISONED: August 11, 2004

Authorities in the northeastern Namangan region charged Namazov, editor of the state newspaper *Pop Tongi* and correspondent for the state newspaper *Kishlok Khayoti*, with embezzlement after he wrote a series of articles about alleged abuses in local tax inspections and collective-farm management.

Shortly after his trial began on August 4, 2004, Namazov complained that the judge was biased and did not allow him to defend himself. On August 11, 2004, before the verdict was reached, authorities took him into custody. Five days later, the Turakurgan District Criminal Court convicted Namazov and sentenced him to five and a half years in prison.

Human rights activist Mutabar Tadjibaeva, who monitored the 2004 trial, told CPJ that local authorities harassed the journalist's family during the trial, cutting his home telephone line and firing his daughter from her job as a school doctor.

Namazov was serving his sentence at a prison in eastern Namangan, the Tashkent-based Ozod Ovoz press freedom group reported.

Dzhamshid Karimov, freelance
IMPRISONED: September 12, 2006

Karimov, nephew of President Islam Karimov, was involuntarily placed in a psychiatric hospital in Samarkand on September 12. Karimov had worked for the London-based Institute for War and Peace Reporting until 2005, when the news agency was forced out of the country.

Karimov later contributed to a number of independent newspapers and online publications, including the Almaty-based news Web site *Liter*, CPJ sources said. According to the news Web site *Uznews*, Karimov criticized both local and federal authorities in his coverage of social and economic problems.

The Jizzakh City Court ordered Karimov's psychiatric placement, according to international press reports. Government officials did not release any information about the court proceedings, and they did not permit independent experts to examine Karimov, according to press reports.

VIETNAM: 1

Nguyen Vu Binh, freelance
IMPRISONED: September 25, 2002

Two high-profile journalists imprisoned in Vietnam were released in 2006 amid sustained international pressure; only Binh remained in jail. A former journalist who worked for almost 10 years at the official publication *Tap Chi Cong San* (Journal of Communism), Binh was arrested after security officials searched his home in Hanoi.

Binh was held for more than 15 months in Hoa Lo Prison before his trial on espionage charges on December 31, 2003. The Hanoi People's Court sentenced him to seven years in prison, followed by three years of house arrest upon release. His wife was the only family member allowed in the courtroom; foreign diplomats and journalists were barred from his trial.

According to state media reports, Binh was sentenced because he had "written and exchanged, with various opportunist elements in the country, information and materials that distorted the party and state policies." He was also accused of communicating with "reactionary" organizations abroad.

In an open letter to Vietnamese leaders in September 2006, Binh's wife wrote that the charges against him were based on his petitions to form an opposition party and his essay, "Vietnam and the Road to Resurrection," which "expressed my husband's vision of a prosperous, democratic Vietnam with true human rights on par with other neighboring nations."

CPJ sources believe that his arrest was also linked to his August 2002 essay, "Some Thoughts on the China-Vietnam Border Agreement." His detention came during a government crackdown on critics of land and sea border agreements signed by China and Vietnam as part of a rapprochement following the 1979 conflict between the two countries.

Binh's wife said that he was hospitalized several times for food poisoning since his imprisonment. When she visited him in early September 2006, his health appeared to have suffered a decline, and he was on medication for a chronic stomach ailment.

CPJ INTERNATIONAL PRESS FREEDOM AWARDS

Since 1991, CPJ has honored journalists from around the world with its annual International Press Freedom Awards. Recipients have shown extraordinary courage in the face of great risks, standing up to tyrants and documenting events in dark corners of the world. Here are the 2006 awardees:

Jamal Amer, YEMEN

Amer is the courageous editor of one of Yemen's most independent weeklies, *Al-Wasat*. His reporting on corruption, religious militancy, and sensitive political issues has triggered a number of frightening threats and attacks.

In August 2005, he was seized by four men believed to be security agents and held for six hours. The assailants beat him, accused him of being paid by the U.S. and Kuwaiti governments, and warned him about defaming "officials." The men drove a blindfolded Amer to the top of a mountain, where they threatened to kill him. His abduction shocked Yemeni journalists, who took it as an explicit warning against the sort of enterprising journalism that had been a mark of *Al-Wasat*. It was the only Yemeni newspaper to interview a rebel cleric who had waged a long insurgency, and it regularly published reports by human rights and international organizations critical of the government. Just days before Amer's kidnapping, the paper ran a daring story alleging that several government officials were exploiting state scholarships to send their own children to study abroad.

Courtesy of Jamal Amer

Before establishing *Al-Wasat* as an independent watchdog in 2004, Amer worked as a journalist for the opposition weekly *Al-Wahdawi*, where his reporting drew frequent legal attacks from authorities. He has been convicted of harming the public interest, offending King Fahd of Saudi Arabia, and damaging relations between Saudi Arabia and Yemen. A court once banned Amer from working as a journalist altogether.

The harassment continued in 2006. Pro-government newspapers accused Amer of being an agent of the West, and he and his family were subjected to government surveillance.

Atwar Bahjat, IRAQ (1976 – 2006)

Bahjat, correspondent for Al-Arabiya and former reporter for Al-Jazeera, was murdered in Iraq in February along with her freelance cameraman, Khaled Mahmoud al-Falahi, and engineer, Adnan Khairallah. Her bullet-riddled body was found near Samarra a day after the station lost contact with the crew. At the time of her death, Bahjat was on the outskirts of Samarra covering the bombing of the Shiite shrine Askariya, known as the Golden Mosque. A witness said her murderers drove up suddenly and sought out the television "presenter" to be killed.

Al-Arabiya

Bahjat, 30, an Iraqi, was one of the best known war reporters in the Arab world. She had previously worked for Iraqi TV under Saddam Hussein. She was known as a dogged street reporter who knew well the hardships endured by Iraqi reporters. In the course of her work, Bahjat received several death threats and survived a roadside bomb that destroyed her car, none of which deterred her from reporting. "She always liked to be a reporter in the field," recalled Al-Jazeera news anchor M'hamed Krichene, who worked with her in Baghdad. Bahjat reported from the scene of looting at the National Museum of Iraq in April 2003, and she covered the intense battles between U.S. and insurgent forces in Najaf in summer 2004.

Bahjat's colleagues laud her commitment to accuracy and objectivity, especially in the context of Iraq's sectarian violence. Bahjat, whose father was Sunni and mother Shiite, was widely known for taking great care to be nonpartisan and accurate.

Madi Ceesay, THE GAMBIA

Ceesay is a veteran independent journalist from the Gambia who has suffered attacks and imprisonment for his work. He is also a leading press freedom activist, serving as president of the Gambia Press Union, which has headed efforts to fight impunity for attacks on the press, including the unsolved December 2004 murder of prominent newspaper editor Deyda Hydara. The tense national climate was laid bare when the Press Union organized an

Courtesy of Madi Ceesay

international conference to mark the first anniversary of Hydara's murder. Police barred journalists from the site of the murder, along a public road, and assaulted a reporter.

In 2006, Ceesay took over as general manager of *The Independent*, a leading private paper that has suffered frequent official harassment and two unsolved arson attacks. In March, security forces sealed off *The Independent's* offices and detained staff after the paper published critical articles about a purported coup attempt. Ceesay and the paper's editor, Musa Saidykhan, were held for three weeks without charge by the National Intelligence Agency.

Before joining *The Independent*, Ceesay worked for 10 years for the respected independent weekly *Gambia News & Report*, first as a reporter and then as its deputy editor. He was jailed before, in 2000, while covering the opposition United Democratic Party. Ceesay's advocacy and leadership have been crucial in the Gambia, where frequent attacks, imprisonments, and other forms of harassment have made the nation one of the worst in Africa for the press.

Courtesy of Jesús Abad Colorado

Jesús Abad Colorado, COLOMBIA

Colorado is a freelance photographer who has witnessed some of the most violent clashes in Colombia's civil war, capturing powerful images of human rights abuses perpetrated by all sides in the conflict. As a provincial journalist, Colorado knows the adversity faced by colleagues in strife-ridden areas outside the capital, where journalists routinely face threats of reprisal from guerrillas, paramilitaries, and local authorities.

Colorado, whose work is widely published in Colombia, has displayed great bravery and determination in reporting from the front lines. He was kidnapped twice by leftist guerrillas; in one case, in October 2000, guerrillas of the National Liberation Army abducted Colorado at a roadblock and held him for two days.

Colorado won acclaim for his work in the aftermath of a massacre in the town of San José de Apartadó in February 2005. His news account and photographs, published in the national daily *El Tiempo*, pointed to military involvement in the massacre and a pattern of close military-paramilitary cooperation in the region. The report prompted the attorney general's human rights unit to further investigate the killings.

Colorado's work has been displayed in more than 30 exhibitions throughout Latin America, Europe, Canada, and the United States. He is co-author of the 1997 book *Accounts and Images, the Forced Displacement*.

INTERNATIONAL PRESS FREEDOM AWARD RECIPIENTS 1991-2005

1991

Byron Barrera, *La Época*, Guatemala
Bill Foley and Cary Vaughan, United States
Tatyana Mitkova, TSN, former Soviet Union
Pius Njawe, *Le Messager*, Cameroon
IMPRISONED: Wang Juntao and Chen Ziming, *Economics Weekly*, China

1992

Muhammad al-Saqr, *Al-Qabas*, Kuwait
Sony Esteus, Radio Tropic FM, Haiti
David Kaplan, ABC News, United States
Gwendolyn Lister, *The Namibian*, Namibia
Thepchai Yong, *The Nation*, Thailand

1993

Omar Belhouchet, *El Watan*, Algeria
Nosa Igiebor, *Tell*, Nigeria
Veran Matic, Radio B92, Yugoslavia
Ricardo Uceda, *Sí*, Peru
IMPRISONED: Doan Viet Hoat, *Freedom Forum*, Vietnam

1994

Iqbal Athas, *The Sunday Leader*, Sri Lanka
Daisy Li Yuet-wah, Hong Kong Journalists Association, Hong Kong
Aziz Nesin, *Aydinlik*, Turkey
In memory of staff journalists, *Navidi Vakhsh*, Tajikistan
IMPRISONED: Yndamiro Restano, freelance, Cuba

1995

Veronica Guerin, *Sunday Independent*, Ireland
Yevgeny Kiselyov, NTV, Russia
Fred M'membe, *The Post*, Zambia
José Rubén Zamora Marroquín, *Siglo Veintiuno*, Guatemala
IMPRISONED: Ahmad Taufik, Alliance of Independent Journalists, Indonesia

1996

J. Jesús Blancornelas, *Zeta*, Mexico
Yusuf Jameel, *Asian Age*, India
Daoud Kuttab, Internews Middle East, Palestinian Authority Territories
IMPRISONED: Ocak Isik Yurtcu, *Ozgur Gundem*, Turkey

1997

Ying Chan, *Yazhou Zhoukan*, United States
Shieh Chung-liang, *Yazhou Zhoukan*, Taiwan
Victor Ivancic, *Feral Tribune*, Croatia
Yelena Masyuk, NTV, Russia
Freedom Neruda, *La Voie*, Ivory Coast
IMPRISONED: Christine Anyanwu, *The Sunday Magazine*, Nigeria

1998
Grémah Boucar, Radio Anfani, Niger
Gustavo Gorriti, *La Prensa*, Panama
Goenawan Mohamad, *Tempo*, Indonesia
Pavel Sheremet, ORT, *Belorusskaya Delovaya Gazeta*, Belarus
IMPRISONED: Ruth Simon, Agence France-Presse, Eritrea

1999
María Cristina Caballero, *Semana*, Colombia
Baton Haxhiu, *Koha Ditore*, Kosovo
Jugnu Mohsin and Najam Sethi, *The Friday Times*, Pakistan
IMPRISONED: Jesús Joel Díaz Hernández, Cooperativa Avileña de Periodistas Independientes, Cuba

2000
Steven Gan, *Malaysiakini*, Malaysia
Zeljko Kopanja, *Nezavine Novine*, Bosnia-Herzegovina
Modeste Mutinga, *Le Potentiel*, Democratic Republic of Congo
IMPRISONED: Mashallah Shamsolvaezin, *Asr-e-Azadegan* and *Neshat*, Iran

2001
Mazen Dana, Reuters, West Bank
Geoff Nyarota, *The Daily News*, Zimbabwe
Horacio Verbitsky, freelance, Argentina
IMPRISONED: Jiang Weiping, *Qianshao*, China

2002
Ignacio Gómez, "Noticias Uno," Colombia
Irina Petrushova, *Respublika*, Kazakhstan
Tipu Sultan, freelance, Bangladesh
IMPRISONED: Fesshaye Yohannes, *Setit*, Eritrea

2003
Abdul Samay Hamed, Afghanistan
Aboubakr Jamai, *Le Journal Hebdomadaire* and *Assahifa al-Ousbouiya*, Morocco
Musa Muradov, *Groznensky Rabochy*, Russia
IMPRISONED: Manuel Vázquez Portal, Grupo de Trabajo Decoro, Cuba

2004
Alexis Sinduhije, Radio Publique Africaine, Burundi
Svetlana Kalinkina, *Belorusskaya Delovaya Gazeta*, Belarus
In memory of Paul Klebnikov, *Forbes Russia*, Russia
IMPRISONED: Aung Pwint and Thaung Tun, freelance, Burma

2005
Galima Bukharbaeva, Institute for War and Peace Reporting, Uzbekistan
Beatrice Mtetwa, media and human rights lawyer, Zimbabwe
Lúcio Flávio Pinto, *Jornal Pessoal*, Brazil
IMPRISONED: Shi Tao, freelance, China

CPJ BURTON BENJAMIN MEMORIAL AWARD

Since 1991, CPJ has given the Burton Benjamin Memorial Award to an individual in recognition of a lifetime of distinguished achievement in service of press freedom. The award honors Burton Benjamin, the CBS News senior producer and former CPJ chairman who died in 1988. In 2006, CPJ honored Hodding Carter III.

2006

Hodding Carter III

As newspaper editor, television journalist, foundation executive, and teacher, Carter has had a distinguished and diverse career spanning more than four decades. Carter started working at his family's newspaper, the *Delta Democrat-Times* of Greenville, Miss., in 1959 and went on to spend almost 18 years as a reporter, award-winning editorial writer, editor, and associate publisher for the paper. His father, Hodding Carter Jr., founded the paper in 1936 and won a Pulitzer Prize in 1946 for editorials on racial and religious tolerance.

AP/Susan Walsh

A Nieman Fellow at Harvard University in 1955-56, Carter worked on the presidential campaigns of Lyndon Johnson and Jimmy Carter. He served as spokesman for the State Department and as assistant secretary of state for public affairs in the Carter administration from 1977 to 1980. He went on to a successful television career as reporter, anchor, and panelist for public affairs television programs, including "This Week with David Brinkley."

Carter was named Knight professor of public affairs journalism at the University of Maryland in 1994, leaving four years later to become president and chief executive officer of the Knight Foundation. His dynamic tenure at the Knight Foundation included vital support for local journalists in developing countries and for journalists at risk. Carter stepped down in 2005 and joined the faculty at the University of North Carolina at Chapel Hill, where he was university professor of leadership and public policy.

BURTON BENJAMIN MEMORIAL AWARD RECIPIENTS 1991-2005

1991
Walter Cronkite
CBS News

1992
Katharine Graham
The Washington Post Company

1993
Ted Turner
CNN

1994
George Soros
Open Society Institute

1995
Benjamin C. Bradlee
The Washington Post

1996
Arthur Ochs Sulzberger
The New York Times

1997
Ted Koppel
ABC News

1998
Brian Lamb
C-SPAN

1999
Don Hewitt
CBS News

2000
Otis Chandler
Times Mirror Company

2001
Joseph Lelyveld
The New York Times

2002
Daniel Pearl
The Wall Street Journal

2003
John F. Burns
The New York Times

2004
John S. Carroll
Los Angeles Times

2005
Peter Jennings
ABC News

CONTRIBUTORS

The Committee to Protect Journalists is extremely grateful to the foundations, corporations, and individuals whose generosity made our press freedom work possible in 2006:

ABC News
ABC Television Network Sales
Advance Publications / Star-Ledger
Daniel Akpovwa
Marcia and Franz Allina
Altria Group Inc.
American Express
David Andelman
Andrews McMeel Publishing
Argus Media Inc. / Petroleum Argus
Irwin Arieff
Around Foundation
Carol Ash and Josh Friedman
The Associated Press
Harriet Barlow
Alex Belida and Patricia Reber
Lucy Wilson Benson
Alan and Susan Berlow
Tobias and Eva Bermant
Adam Berry
Tom Bettag
Mary Billard and Barry Cooper
Molly Bingham
Barry Bingham
Susan Blaustein and Alan Berlow
Bloomberg
Malcom Borg
Michele Braithwaite
Liane Beebe Brent
Bridgewater Fieldwater Foundation
Meredith and Tom Brokaw
Jerry and Linda Bruckheimer
Brunswick Group LLC
BusinessWeek / McGraw-Hill
Ed Caldwell
Steve Capus
José Carreno

John and Lee Carroll
Virginia Carter
CBS News
Chicago Tribune Foundation
Cisco Systems
Citigroup Inc.
CNBC Inc.
CNN
David and Rosemary Coffin
Community Counseling Service Co.
Condé Nast Portfolio
Condé Nast Publications Inc.
Condé Nast Traveler
Continental Airlines Inc.
Ann Cooper
Copley Newspapers
Cox Newspapers Inc.
Walter Cronkite
Crowell & Moring LLP
Ann Curry
Debevoise & Plimpton LLP
Jan and George Dillehay
Disney Worldwide
Dow Jones Company
Dow Jones Foundation
Drue Heinz Trust
Jerelyn Eddings
Renee Edelman
Stanley Eisenberg
El Dia Inc.
Richard and Gail Elden
Stuart Epstein and Randi Hutter
Ernst & Young LLP
Elizabeth Farnsworth
Jeremy Feigelson
Augustino Fontevecchia
Forbes Media

The Ford Foundation
Ford Motor Company
Fox News
The Freedom Forum / Newseum
Gannett Foundation
Anne Garrels
GE Energy Financial Services
Stephen Geimann
General Electric
Robert and Nancy Giles
Brooke Gladstone and Fred Kaplan
Goldman Sachs & Co.
James C. and Toni K. Goodale
Google
Cheryl Gould
The Iara Lee and George Gund III
   Foundation
Edwin Guthman
The Mark Haas Foundation
William F. Harnish Foundation
HBO
Hearst Corporation / Hearst Newspapers
Sharon Held and Ian Hague
Cherie Henderson
The Herb Block Foundation
Peter Heydon
Amy Hubbard
Kathleen E. Hunt and Bernard Estrade
Charlayne Hunter-Gault
Alberto Ibargüen
Gwen Ifill
Steven L. Isenberg
R. Larry Jinks
Carol and Richard Johns
Alex Jones
Eason Jordan
Judd Kahn
Kahn Charitable Foundation
Marvin Kalb
Fred Kaplan
George and Adelaide Keller
Donald and Gay Kimelman
Kevin Klose
John S. and James L. Knight Foundation

Jane Kramer
Brooke Kroeger and Alexander Goren
Andrea Joyce Kuslits
Landmark Communications Inc.
Thomas and Carolyn Langfitt Family
   Foundation
Esther and David Laventhol
Carolyn Lee
Lehman Brothers Inc.
Frankie Leung
The Leon Levy Foundation
Anthony Lewis
Judith Leynse
Marshall Loeb
Los Angeles Times
John MacArthur
Robert MacNeil
Madigan Family Foundation
Madison Jewish Community Council
Magna Global
Amy and Dave Marash
William Marimow
Kati Marton
Eric Matthies
The McClatchy Company
Robert R. McCormick Tribune Foundation
MediaNews Group Inc.
John Meehan
Merrill Lynch & Co. Inc.
Merrill Lynch & Co. Foundation Inc.
Geraldine Fabrikant Metz
   and Robert T. Metz
Donald Miceli
T. Christian Miller
MSNBC
MSNBC.com
N.S. Bienstock Inc.
Anne and Victor Navasky
NBC Universal
The New York Times Company
The New York Times Company Foundation
New York University
The New Yorker
The New Yorker Festival

Samuel I. Newhouse Foundation Inc.
Newhouse Newspapers
Newmark Knight Frank
Newsday Inc. / Tribune
The Nicholas B. Ottaway Foundation
The Nieman Foundation for Journalism
New York Daily News /
  U.S. News & World Report
Open Society Institute
William Orme and Deborah Sontag
Susan and Peter Osnos
The Nicholas B. Ottaway Foundation
Ottaway Newspapers Inc.
The Overbrook Foundation
Charles Overby
Clarence Page
Mark Palermo
PARADE Publications
Jane Pauley and Garry Trudeau
Frank Pensiero
Barry Petersen
Jane C. Pfeiffer
Erwin Potts
Prudential Financial
Joyce Purnick and Max Frankel
Sir William Purves
Lisa Ramaci
Dan Rather
Reuters Group PLC
Susan and Gene Roberts
David and Laura Ross
Diane Sawyer and Mike Nichols
David and Rachel Schlesinger
Irene Schneider
Scripps Howard Foundation
Scripps-Howard Inc.
The Seattle Foundation
Abhay Singh
Skadden, Arps, Slate, Meagher & Flom LLP
Slate Magazine
Slaughter and May
Kathleen Sloane
Harry Smith
Susan Snyder

Sony Corporation of America
St. Petersburg Times
Paul E. Steiger
Bradlee Steitz
Ian Strachan
Super Nova
Taco Bell Corp.
Paul Tash
Telefonica Data USA Inc.
TIBCO Software Inc.
Time Inc.
Time Magazine
Javier Timerman
Elizabeth Tisel
The Tomorrow Foundation
Seymour and Audrey Topping
Jeff Trimble
UBS
University of Wisconsin Madison
Verizon Communications
Wachtell, Lipton, Rosen & Katz LLP
The Wall Street Journal
Ed Wallace and Pamela Falk
The Washington Post Company
Weil, Gotshal & Manges
Davis Weinstock
John D. Weis
Where in the World LLC
Brian Williams
Williams F1 Team
Steve Wirts
Dinah and Lawrence Witchel
Judy Woodruff
William D. Zabel
Anonymous (3)

We also extend our gratitude to the many contributors who supported the Committee to Protect Journalists with gifts under $500, not listed here due to space limitations.

MEMORIAL AND HONORARY CONTRIBUTIONS

The Committee to Protect Journalists is grateful to the friends and family of the following people, in whose name generous contributions were made:

In memory of George Crile: The Tomorrow Foundation
In memory of Marie B. Dooley: The Alexia Foundation
In memory of Phyllis E. "Terry" Hill: TAROW
In memory of Larry LeSueur: Amy LeSueur and Microsoft Matching Gifts Program
In memory of Paul Klebnikov: David Coffin
In memory of Gordon Manning: William Brown, Walter Cronkite, Toby Crystal, Sarah Hegeman, Edward Pratt, Thomas Vlodek, and Amy Ward
In memory of Lars-Erik Nelson: Brian Moss and Mary Santarcangelo
In memory of Anna Politkovskaya: Zachary Brooks

In honor of Sasha Aslanian: Elizabeth Tisel
In honor of Caroline Baum: University of Wisconsin Madison
In honor of Tom Brokaw: The Associated Press
In honor of Jill Carroll: Barry Bingham
In honor of Becky Diamond and Timothy Golden: Neil Hirschfield
In honor of Anna Gordon: National Council of Jewish Women
In honor of Conduce Jones Hammond: Pierce Hammond
In honor of Daniel Hertzberg: Martin Benjamin
In honor of Dave Kahn, Lisa Parlee, and Sammy: Philip Kahn
In honor of June Massell: Yvonne and Michael Silverman
In honor of Andres Oppenheimer: Telefonica Data USA Inc.
In honor of Abi Wright: Where in the World LLC

IN-KIND CONTRIBUTIONS

Some of the vital resources that help make our work possible are in-kind services and contributions. CPJ thanks the following for their support in 2006:

The Associated Press, CNN, Debevoise & Plimpton LLP, Factiva, NBC Universal, Reuters Group PLC, and UBS

Continental Airlines Continental Airlines is the preferred carrier of the Committee to Protect Journalists.

CPJ AT A GLANCE

How did CPJ get started? A group of U.S. journalists created CPJ in response to the often brutal treatment of their foreign colleagues by authoritarian governments and other enemies of independent journalism.

Who runs CPJ? CPJ has a full-time staff of 23 at its New York headquarters, including area specialists for each major world region. CPJ has a Washington representative and consultants stationed around the world. A board of prominent journalists directs CPJ's activities.

How is CPJ funded? CPJ is funded solely by contributions from individuals, corporations, and foundations. CPJ does not accept government funding.

Why is press freedom important? Without a free press, few other human rights are attainable. A strong press freedom environment encourages the growth of a robust society, which leads to stable, sustainable democracies and healthy social, political, and economic development. CPJ works in more than 120 countries, many of which suffer under repressive regimes, debilitating civil war, or other problems that harm press freedom and democracy.

How does CPJ protect journalists? By publicly revealing abuses against the press and by acting on behalf of imprisoned and threatened journalists, CPJ effectively warns journalists and news organizations where attacks on press freedom are occurring. CPJ organizes vigorous public protests and works through diplomatic channels to effect change. CPJ publishes articles and news releases; special reports; a magazine, *Dangerous Assignments*; and *Attacks on the Press*, the most comprehensive annual survey of press freedom around the world.

Where does CPJ get its information? CPJ has full-time program coordinators monitoring the press in Africa, the Americas, Asia, Europe and Central Asia, and the Middle East and North Africa. They track developments through their own independent research, fact-finding missions, and firsthand contacts in the field, including reports from other journalists. CPJ shares information on breaking cases with other press freedom organizations through the International Freedom of Expression Exchange, a global e-mail network.

When would a journalist call upon CPJ? *In an emergency*: Using local and foreign contacts, CPJ intervenes whenever local and foreign correspondents are in trouble. CPJ notifies news organizations, government officials, and human rights organizations immediately of press freedom violations. *When traveling on assignment*: CPJ advises journalists covering dangerous assignments. *When covering the news*: Attacks against the press are news, and they often serve as the first signal of a crackdown on all freedoms. CPJ is uniquely situated to provide journalists with information and insight into press conditions around the world.

HOW TO REPORT AN ATTACK ON THE PRESS

CPJ needs accurate, detailed information in order to document abuses of press freedom and help journalists in trouble. CPJ corroborates the information and takes action on behalf of the journalists and news organizations involved. Anyone with information about an attack on the press should contact CPJ. Call collect if necessary. Our number is (212) 465-1004. Sources may also e-mail to the addresses below, or send a fax to (212) 465-9568.

What to report:

Journalists who are:
- Arrested
- Censored
- Harassed
- Killed
- Threatened
- Wrongfully expelled

- Assaulted
- Denied credentials
- Kidnapped
- Missing
- Wounded
- Wrongfully sued for libel or defamation

News organizations that are:
- Attacked, raided, or illegally searched
- Closed by force
- Materials confiscated or damaged

- Censored
- Transmissions jammed
- Wrongfully sued for libel or defamation

CPJ needs accurate, detailed information that includes:

- Background, including the journalists and news organizations involved.
- Date and circumstances.

Contact information for regional programs:

Africa: (212) 465-9344, x112   E-mail: africa@cpj.org
Americas: (212) 465-9344, x120 E-mail: americas@cpj.org
Asia: (212) 465-9344, x140 E-mail: asia@cpj.org
Europe and Central Asia: (212) 465-9344, x101 E-mail: europe@cpj.org
Middle East and North Africa: (212) 465-9344, x104 E-mail: mideast@cpj.org

What happens next:

Depending on the case, CPJ will:
- Investigate and confirm the report, sending a fact-finding mission if necessary.
- Pressure authorities to respond.
- Notify human rights groups and press organizations around the world, including IFEX, Article 19, Amnesty International, Reporters Sans Frontières, PEN, International Federation of Journalists, and Human Rights Watch.
- Increase public awareness through the press.
- Publish advisories to warn other journalists about potential dangers.

CPJ STAFF

Executive Director Joel Simon
Editorial Director Bill Sweeney
Director of Development and Outreach John Weis
Director of Finance and Administration Lade Kadejo
Communications Director Abi Wright
Senior Editor Robert Mahoney
Journalist Assistance Coordinator Elisabeth Witchel
Washington Representative Frank Smyth
Webmaster and Systems Administrator Mick Stern
Associate Director of Development Alexandra Hay
Executive Assistant and Board Liaison Maya Taal
Receptionist and Office Manager Janet Mason

REGIONAL PROGRAMS

AFRICA
Program Coordinator Julia Crawford
Research Associate Mohamed Keita
Program Consultant Tidiane Sy

THE AMERICAS
Program Coordinator Carlos Lauría
Research Associate María Salazar
Program Consultant Sauro González Rodríguez

ASIA
Program Coordinator Bob Dietz
Senior Research Associate Kristin Jones
Program Consultant Shawn W. Crispin

EUROPE AND CENTRAL ASIA
Program Coordinator Nina Ognianova
Research Associate Tara Ornstein
Program Consultant Masha Yulikova

MIDDLE EAST AND NORTH AFRICA
Senior Program Coordinator Joel Campagna
Research Associate Ivan Karakashian
Program Consultant Kamel Eddine Labidi

INDEX BY COUNTRY

THE COMMITTEE TO PROTECT JOURNALISTS
330 Seventh Avenue, 11th Fl., New York, NY 10001
t: (212) 465-1004   f: (212) 465-9568   info@cpj.org
visit us online for more information: **www.cpj.org**